"That D----d Brownlow,"

Being a *Saucy* & *Malicious* Description

of Fighting Parson

WILLIAM GANNAWAY BROWNLOW,

Knoxville Editor and *Stalwart* Unionist,

Who Rose from a Confederate Jail to become

One of the Most *Famous* Personages in the Nation,

Denounced by his Enemies as *Vicious* and *Harsh*,

Praised by his Friends as *Compassionate* and *Gentle*,

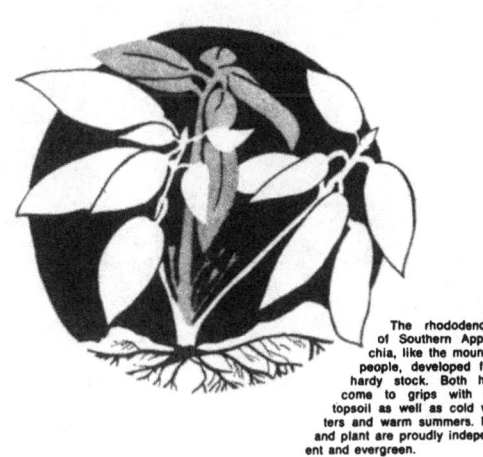

The rhododendron of Southern Appalachia, like the mountain people, developed from hardy stock. Both have come to grips with thin topsoil as well as cold winters and warm summers. Man and plant are proudly independent and evergreen.

William Gannaway Brownlow (1805-1877) photographed circa 1862 by the famous Civil War photographer Matthew Brady. [The collection of the Library of Congress.]

"That D----d Brownlow,"

Being a *Saucy* & *Malicious* Description

of Fighting Parson

WILLIAM GANNAWAY BROWNLOW,

Knoxville Editor and *Stalwart* Unionist,

Who Rose from a Confederate Jail to become

One of the Most *Famous* Personages in the Nation,

Denounced by his Enemies as *Vicious* and *Harsh*,

Praised by his Friends as *Compassionate* and *Gentle*,

Herewith Revived by STEVE HUMPHREY,

a 20th Century Newpaperman and

Former Associate Editor of

the *KNOXVILLE JOURNAL*,

Descendant of the *WHIG*.

APPALACHIAN CONSORTIUM PRESS

Boone, North Carolina 28607

The Appalachian Consortium was a non-profit educational organization composed of institutions and agencies located in Southern Appalachia. From 1973 to 2004, its members published pioneering works in Appalachian studies documenting the history and cultural heritage of the region. The Appalachian Consortium Press was the first publisher devoted solely to the region and many of the works it published remain seminal in the field to this day.

With funding from the Andrew W. Mellon Foundation and the National Endowment for the Humanities through the Humanities Open Book Program, Appalachian State University has published new paperback and open access digital editions of works from the Appalachian Consortium Press.

www.collections.library.appstate.edu/appconsortiumbooks

Original copyright © 1978 by the Appalachian Consortium Press.

ISBN (pbk.: alk. Paper): 978-1-4696-3822-5
ISBN (ebook): 978-1-4696-3824-9

Distributed by the University of North Carolina Press
www.uncpress.org

This volume is dedicated to
two editors of the *Knoxville Journal*,
noted for their forthrightness and courage,
William Rule and Guy Lincoln Smith.

CONTENTS

EDITORIAL NOTE

While it is possible to differentiate writers of the Appalachian character in a number of ways, Dr. Richard Drake, Julian Van-Dusen Professor of History at Berea College, has noted in a collection of essays documenting the history of Appalachian America:

Perhaps the first treatment of the Appalachian as a significant and separate type was presented by a native Appalachian—"Parson" William G. Brownlow, a Methodist minister, Whig politician and journalist, war-time polemist. *Parson Brownlow's Book* was a Civil War best-seller, a bitter anti-Confederate tract which told of the trials and tribulations of the loyal mountaineers of east Tennessee who held to the Union even in the face of a tyrannical Confederate occupation. Brownlow's call was to the North to liberate the freedom-loving folk of the mountains, a call that was finally answered in late 1863. This first 1860 image of the Southern mountaineer, then, was a hard-pressed lover of freedom who held strongly to the Union.

Such distinctions, whether they be of author or subject, of past or present, continue to be used today. Let it be noted that Steve Humphrey, like the Parson Brownlow, is a newspaperman, not a journalist. Humphrey emphatically says of himself:

I am a newspaperman. Among the curmudgeons in the newspaper business with which I consider myself, a journalist is a creature who wears a belted-back corduroy coat, high, laced leather boots, carries a rattan cane, and addresses other human beings as "My dear fellow." It is also true that today newsgathering and disseminating people of all kinds—radio, television, newspapers and magazines—are called journalists. But to be precise, as well as sniffy, people who work for newspapers are newspapermen. I am, of course, in a minority.

To preserve Parson Brownlow's style and flavor, little editing has taken place in the quotations which Steve Humphrey chose for his manuscript; however, it was necessary, for the sake of quick comprehension in reading the quotations, to slightly alter the punctuation at times. Too, although footnoting by Mr. Humphrey may not meet the approval of all critics, they are left in the form which he chose to employ, and only minor mechanical changes have been made. The scope of the manuscript covered by the individual footnotes is usually very sweeping, but so Mr. Humphrey consciously designed them.

The Appalachian Consortium presents this book not because of its agreement or disagreement with the author's or Mr. Brownlow's philosophy and/or prejudices, but because of the saltiness, vitality, humor (both intentional and unintentional), and the significance of a wealth of first-hand information from a man who LIVED during and reported on a critical period of the United States of America.

January 6, 1978   The Publications Committee
                                       Appalachian Consortium Press

FOREWORD

This is a narrative of the *Whig*, a weekly newspaper edited and published for almost thirty years by William Gannaway (Parson) Brownlow. It was the first in a line of newspapers now represented by the *Knoxville Journal*.

Because the *Whig* was Brownlow and Brownlow was the *Whig* the story of one is the story of both. This book in no way is the traditional examination of Brownlow as a historical figure. Historians who have gone over his record as Reconstruction governor of Tennessee and United States senator for six years have given him some very bad marks. Some thawing has appeared in this Arctic front. The man Brownlow and his skill as a circulation builder have been overlooked. He was vituperative, abusive, coarse, relentless with his enemies, and generous with his friends. This has been accepted but not explored. In some ways and at some times he may have been the meanest man who ever walked the streets of Knoxville. But he also was compassionate, gentle, hospitable, courteous, and faithful in his domestic relations. He was such a sure target for those in financial trouble that during his lifetime he paid thousands of dollars to meet notes he had endorsed and which the principals had failed to pay.

His writing was warmed by his remarkable understanding of human nature. It also sparkled with his wit. He was an artist with the skinning knife, sometimes quite crude, but his approach to and treatment of people and events was so unusual that readers looked forward to his newspaper with zest. They knew he would infuriate them or dissolve them in laughter. His pen alone made him a successful circulation builder and his newspaper a splendid advertising medium.

It is true that his defense of the institution of slavery built circulation in the South, and his fierce loyalty to the Union brought him his readers in the North, bringing his newspaper to its largest readership in the pre-Civil War years. But he had done very well before that period.

In the spring of 1969 I was given the task of telling the story of the *Knoxville Journal* and its ancestry. This was an unfamiliar field. However, because Parson Brownlow's fascinating human character and his unusual success as an editor had not been presented before, I soon knew I must tell his story in a book.

A succeeding work will take the story of the *Journal* and its predecessors to the death of Guy L. Smith in November 1968. Mr. Smith was for thirty-one years editor of the *Journal*. He had urged the preparation of the newspaper's history and had taken preliminary steps in this direction. This account will begin with the career of William Rule, who learned newspapering under the Parson and who founded the *Journal* under its present name on February 26, 1885.

In 1898 E. J. Sanford, a wealthy and influential Knoxvillian, bought both the *Journal* and the *Tribune*, and merged them into one morning newspaper. The *Tribune* had been Democratic, but the *Journal and Tribune* was Republican. The *Tribune*'s name was dropped in a few years. The purchaser made his son Alfred F. Sanford publisher, and William Rule was appointed editor, a post that he held until a short time before his death in 1928. The newspaper encountered reverses and went into receivership in 1930. Two years later it was bought by Roy N. Lotspeich, Knoxville industrialist. He installed Guy L. Smith of Johnson City as editor.

Since the purchase by Lotspeich the members of his family have controlled and operated the *Journal* as a Republican newspaper. Upon the death of Roy N. Lotspeich, his widow, Mrs. Ethel Moore Lotspeich, became publisher; and her son-in-law, Charles H. Smith, Jr., moved into an important managerial position. When Mrs. Lotspeich died in 1962, Charles H. Smith, Jr., became publisher. He died in 1972, and Charles H. Smith, III succeeded his father. He occupies the chief executive post as of this writing.

Many people and institutions have given the author assistance in the preparation of this book. The McClung Collection of Lawson McGhee Library afforded its rich store of research material, including private papers, rare books, and the extensive files of the *Whig* and other Knoxville newspapers. At the outset of this research Miss Pollyanna Creekmore, then McClung Collection head and now director of documents at East Tennessee State University, provided expert and friendly guidance, and supplied important books for the use of the author. Also most helpful have been the present head of the collec-

tion, Dr. William J. MacArthur, and his gracious staff. Most helpful
also have been John Dobson, head of the University of Tennessee
Special Collections, which contain the voluminous O. P. Temple
Papers, and the staff of the Andrew Johnson Project, also at the
University of Tennessee. Important material was found in the Division of Archives of the Tennessee State Library in Nashville. Members of the Brownlow family in Knoxville have given special help,
including Mrs. John F. [Jack] Brownlow, widow of the Parson's
grandson; Mr. and Mrs. George T. Fritts; and William G. Brownlow,
IV. Mrs. Fritts is the daughter of Mrs. John F. Brownlow. The library
of the Church Street United Methodist Church also was made available.

Sam Young made important contributions to this book and to the
University of Tennessee Special Collections. He furnished a memorandum made by the late W. T. Kennerly, a Knoxville attorney with
a bent for history, of a conversation with John Bell Brownlow on the
killing of General John H. Morgan, the Confederate cavalry leader, at
Greeneville. He also donated a copy of a letter written by John Bell
Brownlow to A. T. Patterson, President Andrew Johnson's grandson,
which throws more light on the killing of Charles A. Douglas early in
the Civil War.

Some special glimpses of Brownlow were made available through
Dr. William Rule, III, who carried out the wishes of his late brother
F. Gunby Rule, by donating to the McClung Collection the papers of
their grandfather, William Rule.

Much is owed to patient readers, to the late Dr. Stanley J. Folmsbee, formerly head of the University of Tennessee's Department of
History and a specialist in the history of the East Tennessee area; to
Mrs. Lisa Carroll; and especially to Mr. F. A. Ketterson, Jr., chairman
of the Publications Committee of the Appalachian Consortium, who
gave the manuscript extended study and criticism.

Researchers will regret that the complete diary of Parson Brownlow, written while he was in jail at Knoxville and later under guard at
his home, has been forever lost. The custodian of the diary, and of
other Brownlow Papers, a most compassionate person, decided that
it contained observations by the Parson that would reflect upon or
distress descendants of families still living in Knoxville. The original
diary was destroyed.

Steve Humphrey

January 2, 1978   Knoxville, Tennessee.

TENNESSEE WHIG.

"UNAWED by power, unbribed by gain, the people shall be heard and their rights vindicated."   Chapter No. 1

THE SIRE OF THE LINE

The basic facts in the early life of William Gannaway Brownlow, Tennessee's most famous editor, seem simple, bare and uncontroversial. This is in striking contrast to the story of his mature years. Then his words and deeds wove complicated situations, threaded with strife, argument and bitterness that were sometimes illuminated with quaint and unexpected bits of humor and warm flickers of tenderness.

Brownlow recorded his birth, boyhood and early manhood sketchily in the *Whig*, his books and his pamphlets. Biographers, historians and students have been able to elaborate little beyond what he afforded them in these sources. The early details remain sparse.

He was born on August 29, 1805, not far from Wytheville, Virginia, the son of Joseph A. and Catherine Gannaway Brownlow. His father fought in the War of 1812 and was a schoolmate of Sam Houston. Five uncles on the Brownlow side saw military service. Joseph Brownlow was a Presbyterian and his wife was a Methodist. The Brownlow family moved to Blountville, Sullivan County, Tennessee, where Joseph Brownlow died when William, the oldest child, was eleven. His death left the care of five young children to the mother. She followed her husband to the grave in three months.[1]

Years later Brownlow wrote: "My father died when I was so young that I could not have been a judge of his characteristics; but it has been a source of consolation to me to hear him spoken of by his old associates and schoolmates [General Sam Houston among them] as a man of good sense, brave independence, and of sterling integrity."[2]

The death of my father was a grievous affliction to my mother.... Being naturally mild and agreeable in her temperament, she was warmly endeared to a large circle of friends and acquaintance[s]. But their consolation was this, that while sinking into the cold embrace of death, she was happy in the religion of Christ.[3]

1

The Brownlow orphans,were farmed out to relatives; William went to live with an uncle near Wytheville, John Gannaway, "who raised me up to hard labor, until I was eighteen years old." Seven years on the farm apparently induced the youth to look for some other way to make a living for he then "removed to Abingdon, in that State [Virginia] and served as a regular apprentice to the trade of a house-carpenter." The carpenter was George Winniford, a paternal uncle.[4]

Two years after Brownlow had started to learn carpentering, his conversion at a Methodist camp meeting at Sulphur Springs, twenty miles east of Abingdon, diverted the course of his life from manual labor. He had a great respect "for professors of religion, and particularly ministers of the gospel," but conversion produced profound emotions:

There is a concentration of feeling—a glow of fancy—I may say of religious affection, connected with the recollection of that circumstance, which I delight to enjoy. It was here I felt the Lord gracious, and was enabled to shout aloud the wonders of redeeming love. All my anxieties were at an end—all my hopes were realized—my happiness was complete. From this time I began to feel an increasing desire for the salvation of sinners; and in order, more effectually, to engage in this work, I returned to Wythe, and spent the ensuing year in going to school to WILLIAM HORNE, an aimable [sic.] young man and a fine scholar.[5]

Spiritual zeal thus thrust him into the pursuit of learning. Whether Brownlow first accumulated enough money from carpentering to devote full time to lessons or he worked and studied at the same time is not revealed. Since his entire life was one of untiring labor in which he mixed other pursuits with editing and publishing, it would have been in character for him to carpenter by day and study under Horne by candlelight. He must have made rapid progress in his effort to gain sufficient education to be a circuit rider. The fall of 1826 found him at the second regular session of the Holston Annual Conference at Abingdon, where Bishop Joshua Soule presided. There Brownlow was "received into the traveling connexion on trial, and appointed to the Black Mountain Circuit, in North Carolina, under Goodson McDaniel."[6]

Brownlow's soul was aflame with the love of his Lord, and he believed intensely in the Methodist Church, but he knew he would face intense hardships as he rode on horseback from one tiny, isolated congregation to another on his assignment on the eastern slope of the Blue Ridge Mountains. The thought of leaving old friends and meeting with strangers also distressed him. As an orphan, separated from his brothers and sisters, he undoubtedly cherished friends more than those who had enjoyed a full family circle. He wrote, "This was a most affecting time and will not soon be forgotten. . . . I entered on the labors of this year with many painful apprehensions."[7]

Had he been able to see the future this emotional disturbance would have been intensified because the work he was entering turned out to be so turbulent that it was an excellent training ground for his blazing career as an editor and controversialist. The denominations of the time were engaged in bitter disputes. The Baptists and Presbyterians were loosely associated to fight the Methodists, viewed as intruders, offering to the independent people of the region the doctrine of free grace, contrasting with the restrictions of predestination and election placed by the Presbyterians on the route to heaven, and less dampening than the Baptist requirement of immersion. The Presbyterians were split into Old School and New School factions, but still vigorous enough to fight among themselves and to wage war upon the Methodists at the same time. Thus, Christians belabored each other with doctrinal blows in which they mingled harsh, vulgar invectives.[8]

The young Parson was moving into a field that would give him the practical experience needed for his career as a writer and an editor. It was a crude but effective school for the strident newspapering of the time, teaching him how to battle extemporaneously with words and wit, to see the vagaries of human nature laid open, and to gather acute lessons in the laws of slander and libel.

His immediate difficulties were physical, but his hardy, six-foot frame of one hundred and seventy-five pounds was adequate in meeting these difficulties. He possessed boundless energy, he worked tirelessly, and when he had moments to spare he sought men who had some learning—doctors, teachers and lawyers—to learn from them whatever they could teach him. The traveling gear of horse and rider was scant: saddle and bridle for the former; saddle bags stuffed with a few extra garments for the rider, homespun jeans, and the long Methodist coat, one capacious tail carrying the Bible and a hymnal, the other a grammar and writing materials. He expected little money; the salary was limited to $100 annually and he may have collected half that much. And perils were frequent.

The day after Christmas in his first year he led his horse across the frozen Cain River, then crossed a ridge, arriving on the other side "so benumbed with the cold, that I was not only perfectly stupid, but extremely sleepy." Time did not lessen the perils. Six years later he swam the swollen Tugaloo River in South Carolina four times, once barely reaching the bank, and frequently after these experiences "preached in open meeting houses, with my clothes froze on me!"[9]

Perhaps these experiences added to his strong distaste for the Baptist practice of immersion, and he may have had them in mind when he observed that they never sent missionaries to the Arctic, the problem of chopping through several feet of ice to find sufficient water for the ordinance being almost insoluble.[10]

The Parson got firsthand experience in the laws of libel and slander in his third year on the circuit. He was sued for slander in Rhea County, Tennessee, by a Presbyterian elder over statements made in a pamphlet. Brownlow did his homework so well, hunting up witnesses and otherwise preparing his defense on a plea of justification, that when the suit came to trial the elder dismissed the action and paid the costs.[11]

Disaster took its turn with the Parson in the libel field three years later on the Franklin Circuit in western North Carolina, when a fire-eating Baptist preacher, the Rev. Humphrey Posey, with a reputation for scourging Methodist ministers, challenged the young circuit rider "the very next day" after arriving at his charge. The Parson returned the fire, writing Posey:

But sir, I am constrained to believe that you are so destitute of feeling, so blind to the beauties of religion, so hacknied [sic.] in crime, and so lost to all sense of honor and shame, that notwithstanding your faculties still enable you to continue your sordid pursuits, they will not permit you to feel any remorse, or acknowledge your errors.

Posey prosecuted, and Brownlow was indicted for libel in Macon County Superior Court at Franklin in October of 1832. The Parson prepared a defense, again relying on justification, only to find that in North Carolina it applied only to slander, not to libel. The prosecution also hooked him on another point that his lawyers apparently had overlooked. It insisted he could not know what was in Posey's heart, and therefore could not prove the Baptist was inwardly what Brownlow had written he was. The Parson's lawyer thereupon threw his client upon the mercy of the court at the spring term of 1833, which fined the defendent $5.00 and taxed him with the costs.

J. R. Siler, a leading citizen and prominent Methodist, paid the fine and Brownlow met the costs. They were small because only two prosecution witnesses testified and few of those who appeared for the defense claimed their fees. But following the trial a number of other prosecution witnesses proved their attendance. This created additional costs for Brownlow. On a Sunday morning a few weeks later a deputy sheriff waited upon the Parson at a church five miles from the courthouse to collect the extra bill. The next day Brownlow turned over to the officer "an elegant dun mare, saddle, bridle, saddlebags and umbrella." These items brought $65.00 at a court sale. The county received $48.83 and the balance probably went to the officer for his fee. Brownlow did not mention any recovery on his part. The story lives that he had learned of the approach of the officer and his purpose, and thrust his Bible and hymnal into the hands of women members of his congregation. Siler provided him with another horse.[12] The Holston Conference found nothing in the affair for which to censure Brownlow.[13]

The conviction plagued Brownlow for years. His political enemies reprinted the record of the court with lurid type embellishments in 1845 when he ran unsuccessfully against Andrew Johnson for Congress.[14] When the *Whig* and the *Register* fought for survival in Knoxville, the latter goaded the Parson with an account of the affair. This led him to carry a full review of the case with this introduction:

We were indicted for libel on a thieving old Baptist preacher in Western [North] Carolina, and although we have published the whole transaction in two editions of a pamphlet, in a bound book of 300 pages, and again in the *Jonesboro Whig*, yet, "a decent regard for the opinions of mankind" induces us to lay the whole affair before the public, as many of the present generation of newspaper readers may not have heard the particulars.

Brownlow closed his review with a report, savoring of satisfaction, on the fates of Posey, court officials and jurors. The Baptist preacher married a widow for her property, yet died a "wretched and raving maniac." The judge's life ended in vagabondage, poverty and drunkenness. The attorney general was disgraced. One juror died drunk in the woods, another went to prison for burglary, and two others fled the state to dodge indictments. "The *remnant* of the Jurors, we have not heard from for several years, but the probability is the Devil has those of them who have departed this life, while the living ones are likely in some State prison!"[15] Divine wrath pursued mortals who crossed the Parson, both on earth and in the hereafter.

It did not take long for the circuit preacher to be recognized in the Holston Conference as a daring controversialist, who responded zestfully to slurs and insults. A "high-toned professor of religion" at Athens named a dog after Brownlow, but the Holston Conference conferred elder's orders on him in the fall of 1830. A year later the conference reproached the Parson for his "style of writing and manner of conducting his opposition to the institutions and proceedings of other denominations," then stamped him with approval by electing him to attend the church's General Conference to be held at Philadelphia in May of 1832. He fought a few battles along the way to the conference as opposition believers challenged him, and he was with a group of clergymen who called on President Andrew Jackson in Washington. Brownlow was impressed by Old Hickory's appearance and courtliness, but he commented, "I have long since learned that it will not do to take men for their looks."

His mischievous bent cropped out after he had preached to the inmates of a penitentiary in Baltimore. Because his foes had predicted he would wind up as the inmate of such an institution, he wrote a friend in East Tennessee that he had been in prison, and the latter, sensing the Parson's purpose, reported the fact without giving the circumstances. The effects were just what the Parson had intended, for among his enemies "Some of them rejoiced, and others mourned lest the report should not be true."

He played no important part in the conference, but the instinct of the reporter welled up in him, and led him to attend the Presbyterian General Assembly, which was meeting in the same city. He seemed more pleased than horrified to find the debates there would "for intemperance of language and wholesale abuse of private character, absolutely disgrace the lowest porter house, or ale cellar, in the lowest place in the lowest town or city in the lowest country in the world."[16] Brownlow was developing his talent for whaling his enemies with intemperate abuse.

As much as Brownlow loved the pulpit, public affairs and writing were tugging at him. He found South Carolina aflame over the issue of nullification when he was assigned to the Tugaloo Circuit near Pickens in 1832. The state legislature passed an act to nullify a national tariff law, and Congress retaliated with authorization for President Jackson to use all necessary force to uphold the federal government. As a strong believer in federal authority, Brownlow was filled with double indignation because he found many Presbyterian and Baptist ministers sermonizing from their pulpits in behalf of nullification. He was pleased to find that most Methodist divines avoided thus mixing the affairs of state with spiritual responsibilities.[17]

Two years later when the Holston Conference met in Knoxville he was the author of a book of 300 pages that castigated the Presbyterian Church and aimed a few volleys at the Baptists. As he stood in Frederick S. Heiskell's print shop he glowed with pride at the culmination of labor that must have taken him hours of research and painstaking pushing of a pen. He praised the printer, finding

that the type for its size is very good, and seems to be well distributed over the page; so that the words are everywhere sufficiently distinct, which is not always the case with books printed in this country. The paper is good—the ink very good, and the typographical execution quite respectable. Of course, I think that the matter is excellent.

Seven years earlier a young storekeeper, a Presbyterian, of course, had found the young circuit rider, attending his first conference probably not far from Heiskell's shop, such a grotesque figure in his long Methodist coat, an old-fashioned hat shading a face that looked as if it had been hewed out of a walnut log, that he had circulated a subscription to defray the expense of having Brownlow's picture taken in order to preserve the features and dress of this curiosity of the human race. Now this strange appearing creature had written a book that assaulted the Presbyterian Church and defended Methodism. The Parson found the Presbyterian preachers feeble in their expositions and deficient in grammar, despite their claim to a highly educated ministry. The church boldly sought temporal power, and its doctrines of predestination and foreordination placed upon the Creator the responsibility for every vile and evil act upon the face of the earth, rape and murder not excluded. The author was a total abstainer, but because the Presbyterians dominated the American Temperance Society the Parson would have none of it. As he contemplated his picture of Presbyterians bent on political control, the members voting for "an habitual drunkard, a liar, a defrauder, and a whore-monger," rather than an honest Methodist, he spat out: "O hypocrisy! thou brat of hell, how I hate thee! You mingle with all society—but you are particularily fond of temperance societies."

Baptists, on the other hand, were so addicted to alcoholic beverages that they will "church Priest or Levite for the sin of joining the temperance society!"

Methodism actually was smarting under Presbyterian attacks upon that church as monarchial because of its highly centralized organization, and Brownlow's book was basically defensive. It also displayed the Parson's well-developed sense of his importance. He devoted thirty-eight pages of it to his own life. He also laid out for himself a course that he followed rather closely in the approaching years of editing and publishing:

And let my occupation in future life be what it may, God forbid that I ever should pursue that timid and vascillating [sic.] course of conduct, which evinces a greater solicitude to please the multitude than to arrive at truth, and to obtain popular applause at the expense of a good conscience!

The book was not an instant financial success. Brownlow wrote Heiskell from Abingdon, on May 10, 1836, "We have not been able to comply with our contract and pay you according to promise. I need not tell you that I regret this failure—deeply regret it." The Parson, however, had found a friend to assume responsibility for the debt. The letter also gives evidence of Brownlow's quickening sense of news. He sent Heiskell, who also was publishing the *Register* at Knoxville, an item about the son of the postmaster at Abingdon being held for larceny of a bank draft amounting to $890.[18] Whether Brownlow paid Heiskell something to start the work or the printer waived all payment until revenue came in from sales was not revealed. Neither is the number printed available. One copy now is worth $52.50.[19] This is possibly more than the author made in a year of preaching.

Preacher and author the Parson was, but at the age of twenty-nine he lacked a wife. During the conference at Knoxville he was struck by the number of fellow ministers who had married. This led him to pen his plaintive soliloquy:

Old bachelor! are you so lost to a sense of the pleasures and enjoyments of a married life that you can remain contented in a state of "single blessedness," while the old and young, the middle aged, and all around you are joining their *hearts* and *hands* in this lawful and scriptural enterprise? But do you excuse yourself on the ground that no one seems willing to have you? This is by no means a plausible excuse; for it is well known that every old widow, maid and girl, in all the country are *candidates* for matrimony.

He had shunned coquetry, he was never engaged and he had never asked a woman to marry him, "yet I have some good desires . . . on this subject; and I think it quite probable, I shall some day or other make some amorous advances toward some one."[20]

He found his object within a few months, while visiting in Tennessee from the Scott Circuit in Virginia. He decided he would marry Miss Eliza O'Brien, and when his sister, Mrs. Nancy Martin, suggested Eliza might not marry him, the Parson replied: "But she shall marry me." Brownlow did not see Eliza for a year, but he maneuvered to get himself placed where he could court her. He asked to be assigned to the Elizabethton Circuit in Carter County, the home of the O'Brien family and the iron works it operated. The conference granted his request and the courtship began. Poor and homely though he was, the preacher had advantages which Mrs. Brownlow described in later years: "I thought he was smart; everybody said he was talented. He was talked about more than any young preacher in the conference, and when he preached at Elizabethton he had more people to hear him than any other preacher. I was influenced by my respect for his talents; and besides he was so earnest, persistent and eloquent in his wooing there was no resisting him."[21] The Parson's powerful voice, his vivid and incisive language and his striking use of hyperbole, moved sixteen-year-old Eliza as she watched him play upon the heartstrings of the congregation. Her heartstrings responded with more than religious fervor. Indeed, she was smitten.

The lovers were married on September 11, 1836, at Turkeytown in Carter County, during a camp meeting. Brownlow performed a marriage ceremony for another couple during the same day.[22] Mrs. James O'Brien vigorously objected to the marriage, but in later years she grew attached to her son-in-law and made her home with the Brownlows. Father O'Brien not only was agreeable to the union, but also found a job for the Parson at the ironworks.[23]

As a husband, the Parson had to make adjustments. The salary of a circuit rider was meager and he would have had to be absent from home for long periods. The Holston Conference "located" Brownlow, a designation that relieved him of any charge but permitted him to preach when the opportunity presented itself.[24] This left him free to take the job at the ironworks, purchased by the three O'Brien brothers—James, Joseph and John; and William Gott, from William B. Carter of Elizabethton in 1824. The O'Brien brothers "owned 9,000 acres of land and operated the furnace, the Valley Forge, 2 bloomeries and a water-driven hammer. With slave labor they produced pig and bar iron until they sold their holdings to Nathaniel G. Taylor in 1861."[25] Brownlow's job was not a sinecure. He described himself as head clerk and general manager for the partnership. His duties sometimes included the river shipping of iron castings, an experience that taught him something of water transportation.[26]

The Parson had mixed newspaper writing with preaching as early as 1834, when some of his articles, chiefly noncontroversial, appeared in the New Market *Telegraph*. After he retired from the circuit others from his pen appeared in newspapers at Jonesboro and Elizabethton. These anonymous articles advocated Whig doctrines of a protective tariff and internal improvements.[27] The pieces attracted the attention of Carter County Whigs. Their new newspaper at Elizabethton, the *Republican and Manufacturers Record*, was floundering, and they were looking for a new editor. Brownlow took the post under the express conditions that he was to have absolute control of the editorial columns and that his responsibilities at the ironworks must come first. The *Tennessee Whig* was the official name set out in the contract drawn by T. A. R. Nelson. The contract called for Mason R. Lyon to be printer and publisher. Mason was also given authority to execute all business arrangements, including printing and delivery. At the end of the year he would pay Brownlow a third of the net proceeds. The new editor was not to be a partner.[28]

Lyon and William Gott had been partners in the publication of the *Republican and Manufacturers Record*, which had existed for a year. This partnership was dissolved.[29] To give Lyon a hand in getting out the *Whig*, the contract specified that "he has been furnished by the owners of the press, who are mutual friends of the parties, with the free use of the press without charge." The "mutual friends" probably were Whig Party members who were interested in keeping the newspaper going. Subscriptions and advertising accounts were to belong to Lyon. Brownlow and Lyon gave each other $1,000 performance bonds.[30]

Elizabethton was a dismal spot to start a newspaper, even though it was a county seat. The village consisted of 200 souls living in fifty houses. Carter County's total population in 1840 was 5,372, of whom 374 were Negroes. The remaining figure of 4,988 included 811 white illiterates.[31] Mail service was wretched. It operated on a weekly basis between Elizabethton and Abingdon, Virginia, and Jonesboro and Blountville, Tennessee.[32] Rural free delivery would not arrive for another fifty-seven years. Telegraphic services did not exist. Syndicates that supplied special features, articles and news pictures had not arrived. News gathering agencies, such as the Associated Press and the United Press International, were unknown. Drawings and illustration were scarce. Communication was by word of mouth, letters and newspapers. The latter were clipped freely by arrangement for information on the outside world. A newspaper plant and a printer were available at Elizabethton, however, and Whig sentiment in the area was strong. Yet the Parson expressed misgivings in the first issue of May 16, 1839:

Finally, no consideration would have induced us, under all the circumstances, to have embarked in this laborious and responsible business, but an unwillingness to see the only Whig paper in the District to go down;—and a love of country;—an innate regard for freedom of thought and action; and a deep rooted opposition to and hatred of the high handed measure of a *corrupt* and *corrupting* administration (*Whig*, May 16, 1839).

Other influences must have entered into the Parson's decision. The O'Briens, along with other ironmasters in the region, were in deep financial trouble;[33] and Brownlow saw that means of livelihood waning. Preaching did not afford sufficient livelihood to support a family, as much as he liked the pulpit. It was time to get a foothold elsewhere. The Parson liked writing and he believed he was good at it. He knew the power of the preacher over the congregation, and he saw that the influence of the printed word was more lasting than the spoken. He knew that what was printed usually was preserved, and the only limit on the number who read the newspaper was the circulation. Half a century later the Parson's son, John Bell Brownlow, wrote that his father had found "nothing so congenial to his taste as journalism. He loved the power it gave him."[34]

The *Tennessee Whig*'s opener was modest. Seven hundred copies of the five-column, four-page paper were printed, but a month later the Parson proudly reported all had been sold (*Whig*, June 13, 1839). The modern reader finds the first *Whig*, especially the front page, very dull, both as to content and typography. The two leading articles, set in redoubtable old-style Caslon, were clipped from other Whig newspapers, one of which reported speeches made in the gubernatorial campaign three weeks earlier. Brownlow preceded these accounts with a caustic comment which reflected his opposition to James K. Polk, the Democratic nominee, and his enthusiasm for the Whig standard-bearer, Governor Newton Cannon.

Headings were one-line titles in boldface type but were no larger than that used in the body of the account. This is in contrast to the crisp, abbreviated sentences and large type used by modern newspapers, which forcefully convey the central point or major significance of an article. "Candidate Polk's Inconsistency" in the first Whig might emerge today as

Polk Turns
Back Flip
On Policy

Another *Whig* story titled "Governor's Race" probably would read

Governor's Race
Gets Up Steam

Nor was any consistent effort made to summarize in the first paragraph, known in newspaper parlance as the "lead," the latest news and most sensational development reflected in the article.

At the top of Column One the front page announced in black type that the newspaper was "Edited by W. G. Brownlow" and "Printed and Published by M. R. Lyon." Beneath were the advertising and subscription rates. Twelve lines or less of advertising cost $1.00 for the first insertion and fifty cents for each subsequent one. Subscribers paid $2.50 a year in advance, $3.00 if they waited until the end of six months, and $3.50 if they paid at the close of the year.

Lyon printed the paper on a hand-operated, flat-bed press and on an imperial sheet that measured 23 by 21 inches. The front and back pages were printed on one side of the sheet, and pages two and three on the other side. This process resulted in the latest news usually being found on the second page. The third page usually carried varying amounts of advertising, depending on the volume of business. The newspaper's name ran on the front page in 60-point Onyx type, which was probably cast in a foundry and hand tooled to create an outline effect. A curiosity was the placing of a period after *Whig*, a practice quickly abandoned by Lyon and no longer used. Inside pages were headed "The Elizabethton *Whig*" in smaller outline type. The page one motto was "Life, Liberty And The Pursuit Of Happiness." It was printed in small capitals beneath the rules separating the name of the newspaper from the line carrying the name of the town, date, volume and number. This motto came down on July 4, 1839. It gave way to Brownlow's famous paraphrase of Isaiah 58:1: "Cry Aloud and Spare Not."[35]

Lyon's shop carried two families of type, Caslon and Onyx, in roman and italic. He used these type faces in advertising and editorial matter alike, contrary to present practice. Brownlow frequently used old-style Caslon italic for emphasis.[36] [Newspapers discontinued the use of Onyx in modern times.]

The launching of the newspaper involved the usual mechanical troubles and the editor acknowledged that it was necessary for him to clip from his exchanges and to write his editorials "by the light of a candle." The customary statement of the purposes and objectives of the newspaper—the term in vogue for such remarks was "address"—appeared in the first issue and gave two chief reasons: 1) to fight the threat of a "national despotism," which the editor feared if Andrew Jackson's choice, Martin Van Buren, should win again in 1840; and 2) to advance the Whig party's interests. To Brownlow this meant to elect Henry Clay as President. He listed the "cardinal doctrines" of the party as

the right of the *People to govern*—the right of *Instruction* [not bush-instruction]—true *State Rights* and *strict construction*—a liberal system of *Internal Improvements*—an increase of the banking capital of the country—and everything else that is morally and politically right— (*Whig*, May 16, 1839).

The editor also cast in a borrowed peroration which from time to time in his career he rephrased to fit other situations:

Proud, happy America! "the land of the free and the home of the brave." Yes, the asylum of the emigrant—"where the citizen of every clime, and the child of every creed, roams free and untrammelled as the wild winds of heaven! Baptised at the fount of liberty in fire and blood,—cold must be the heart that thrills not at the mention of thy name! When the old world, with all its pride, pomp, and circumstances, shall be covered with oblivion—when thrones shall have crumbled, and dynasties shall have been forgotten—then [if the people but now do their duty] will our America, stand amid regal ruin and national desolation, towering sublime, like the last mountain in the deluge—majestic, proud, immutable, and magnificent, amid blight, ruin and decay—the last remnant of earth's beauty—the last resting place of liberty, and the light of heaven.[37]

Such soaring passages were not typical of the Parson. He preferred the incisive, as his advice to a fellow editor on how to deal with an opponent showed: "Lather him with aqua fortis [nitric acid] and shave him with a handsaw" (*Whig*, May 30, 1839).

The campaign of 1839 found the Democrats better organized than the Whigs and with an excellent campaigner in James K. Polk of Maury County.[38] He narrowly defeated Governor Cannon by about 2,500 votes and he cut rather deeply into the Whig strength of East Tennessee by carrying twelve of the twenty-five counties in the division. The Democrats gained control of the General Assembly and elected six of the thirteen United States representatives, a gain of three.[39] Brownlow took some comfort in the reelection of William B. Carter to Congress from the First District over Joseph Powell, Jr., in a campaign of intense bitterness and hostility.[40]

The parson did what he could to cheer the disheartened East Tennessee Whigs. He suggested the Democrats had stuffed the ballot boxes to increase their statewide vote by 19,000 in two years. He argued that the errors the party had made should be remedied in order for the Whig forces to be put in the best possible shape for the forthcoming Presidential race:

> True, the Whigs of Tennessee have met with a temporary defeat in the recent elections of the State; but this, so far from disheartening them, should stimulate them to embark anew, in their holy crusade against power and corruption. We have the numerical strength—our State is still Whig, notwithstanding the election for governor, has resulted favorable to the enemy [*sic*.]. We were without union among ourselves, relying on our superior strength for success. The enemy were united—they had the money—they held the offices—and they lied, electioneered, printed, swore, and travelled for pay—while their bread was given to them, and their pay was for sure (*Whig*, August 22, 1839).

A policy that would enhance the party's prospects, Brownlow firmly suggested, would be to nominate Henry Clay for the Presidency. He posted the Kentuckian's name on the *Whig*'s editorial page, a position it would occupy often in the years ahead as the editor's zeal for "Harry of the West" approached idolatry. The Parson was bitterly disappointed when Clay did not win the nomination. But along with Tennessee Whigs, he accepted the decision with good grace and an assurance that "never did the Whigs engage in any contest, with more cheering prospects," and lined up vigorously behind the Whig nominee for President, William Henry Harrison, of Ohio.[41]

The Whig Party in Tennessee had arisen as a rallying ground for the powerful opposition which had developed against Andrew Jackson during his second term as President. Members of the Democratic Party who had been waiting for an opportunity to knife the "old hero" included former United States Senator John Williams of Knoxville, United States Representative (later governor) Newton Cannon, Davy Crockett and Andrew Erwin, a wealthy Bedford Countian. Later John Bell of Nashville and Hugh Lawson White of Knoxville, two of Tennessee's statesmen, were found in the Whig ranks. Bell was sometimes credited with having created the Whig Party in the state.

The Whigs humiliated Jackson three times by defeating his candidates for governor, William Carroll and Robert Armstrong, with Newton Cannon in 1835 and 1837; and rebuffing "Old Hickory's" choice for President, Martin Van Buren, in 1836. Van Buren was elected, but Tennessee voted for Hugh Lawson White, 35,962 to 26,120 over Van Buren. Even Jackson's Hermitage precinct went for White, 61 to 20.[42]

His party's vigorous support of a system of internal improvements held great appeal for Brownlow. It fell upon receptive ground in East Tennessee where the agriculturally productive valleys, the timbered mountainsides and ore-supplied industries hungered for greater markets. To reach these markets required transportation by hazardous water routes or by slow and expensive wagon trains. There was a great need for the swifter and developing railroads as well as for river improvement. Jackson and Van Buren opposed these policies. Because they were out of line with the Parson's political views he presented them as inferior and evil. Jackson he disposed of in ghoulish fashion when a false report of his death was circulated:

We now allude to it, merely to express our surprise at the little interest it excited, and the few cold remarks it drew from those who even believed its truth. No lamentations over 'the greatest and best'—no expressions of sorrow at the departure of a great man! For our part, when the report first reached us, we could not rid our mind of the exclamation of the poet:—"Show pity Lord. O Lord forgive!" (*Whig*, December 5, 1839).

In Van Buren he found a double deficiency:

Truly Van Buren is a *bastard*—a bastard in a two fold point of view. First, he was shoved into office by Gen. Jackson, upon *illegitimate* principles; and next he is the *illigitimate* [*sic*.] son of Aaron Burr, by whom he was educated for the practice of the law.

Some Van Buren newspapers, grasping similar ammunition, accused

William Henry Harrison of having had three sons by an Indian squaw in Michigan.[43]

Brownlow found Knoxville a lively center of Whig activity in the summer of 1839. He was delighted to learn his newspaper and its vigor were drawing approval, although "the opinion of the people here is that some of us are going to get killed before August. I reply that we will die in a righteous cause." Knoxville Whiggery transported the Parson to acclaim it the finest on earth. He recorded this impression after hearing John Bell and Senator Hugh Lawson White speak at Knoxville in the fall of 1839. Of Bell he wrote, "Never did I listen to a man with more pleasure in all my life."[44]

Political developments moved rapidly in late 1839 and early 1840. The Democratic General Assembly, elected along with Governor Polk in August, squeezed out of office the state's United States senators, White and Ephraim Foster. The assembly instructed them to vote for Van Buren administration proposals. At that time United States senators were elected by the state legislatures and were accustomed to resign when they could not, with political integrity, follow direction from the bodies to which they owed their posts.

The *Whig* ran in full the statements of White and Foster when they resigned, but printed so little of General Assembly activities that some subscribers complained. Brownlow retorted that he held the "majority of brawling Democrats" in the legislature in such contempt that "We, therefore, shall fill our columns with what *we* think is most suitable, and those who have been told we are *one-sided* had better subscribe for some paper that gives both sides."[45]

While in Knoxville for a party convention in February 1840, Brownlow reaped benefits from being hanged in effigy. Before the hanging he had obtained ten subscriptions, and after it twenty-four. The Knoxville *Argus* annoyed him with a report that a Whig delegation had arrived in Knoxville on a Sunday night "*whooping* and halloing [*sic*.] like wild bacchanals," and at the convention engaged in a "public and wanton debauch." The Parson insisted the Whigs were well behaved although they did drink "many bottles of excellent wine." The use of the adjective "excellent" to describe the wine was a substantial concession on the Parson's part, and indicated how far he would go to defend a Whig gathering. Late in the previous summer as he rode the stage to Knoxville he had winced because "still-tubs and still-houses seem to be undergoing thorough repairs! Mean whiskey and new apple brandy, and modern *Democracy*, which all go hand in hand, are to overrun the country from this till next corn-planting time." [46]

Criticism of the Whig delegation's behavior came from the pen of E. G. Eastman, "imported" from the East to edit the newly established *Argus*. Editor and newspaper were signals of the Democratic Party's determination to fight vigorously the East Tennessee Whigs. The Parson previously had described Eastman as a "bloated drunkard" and in a private letter as "all for peace. He is not very sharp." But he must have envied Eastman a new $900 press that arrived for the *Argus* the following week.[47] Eastman quickly began sneering at Knoxville Whigs. When the Nashville *Banner* complimented Colonel W. B. A. Ramsey, brother of the historian James G. M. Ramsey, upon his retirement from editorship of the Knoxville *Register*, the new Democratic editor snapped: "Truth, every word of it; but no part of it is applicable to his successor."

The target of Eastman's shaft was Thomas W. Humes, one of the most cultured men in Knoxville. After attending East Tennessee College Humes had studied at Princeton University to be a Presbyterian minister, then turned to newspapering, and later was rector of St. John's Episcopal Church. From 1865 until 1882 he was president of East Tennessee University, which, by the time he retired, was the University of Tennessee. Brownlow shot back at the *Argus* editor:

> When such drunken, stupid, *pilgrim-jack-asses*, as the nominal Editor of the Argus at Knoxville, a certain bloated down-cast, red-faced *Mr. Eastman*, can use such language as the foregoing, in reference to a gentleman of the raising, education, talents, and acknowledged veracity of Mr. Humes of "The Times," we have certainly fallen upon evil times.

Humes had been editor of the *Times* and continued as editor of the *Register* when the newspapers were merged.[48]

The denunciation of Eastman demonstrated that the Parson was developing mightily in a field where eye gouging, knifing, groin kicking and shooting, literal as well as figurative, were not unusual. So violent had newspapering grown in Tennessee that a British traveler and author, stopping at Jonesboro in 1839, described editors and their publications as

> the most abusive, unjust, and unprincipled that are anywhere to be found; for with a few honorable exceptions only, they appear to me to sacrifice truth, honor, and courtesy, to party-feeling; hesitating at nothing to blacken the char-

acter of a political opponent, though he be of the most pure and spotless reputation; raking up slander of bygone years, to serve a monetary purpose; and sparing neither age nor sex, neither the living nor the dead.

In contrast, the Britisher, who attended several East Tennessee political meetings found them to be in direct contrast to the newspaper instances:

Speaking was sensible, moderate, free from bombast, and much calmer and more argumentative than election-speeches usually are in England. The rival candidates were spoken of with the greatest respect, and not a sentence of declamation [defamation], or a word of vituperation, either of the parties or individuals, took place. . . Audiences were most quiet and orderly that could be imagined, as much so, indeed, as a congregation hearing a sermon.

The witty pen of Samuel L. Clemens found the East Tennessee newspaper field such an appropriate territory for his satire that he wrote a piece about it in which pistols and cowhide whips were flourished as frequently as pens.[49]

The same year that the Britisher set down his observations saw the beginning of a long and envenomed battle of words, brewed as United States Representative William B. Carter, a Whig, won a seat in Congress for the third time by turning back a determined bid by Dr. Joseph Powell, a Democrat. Both men were from prominent East Tennessee families. Carter's ancestors were from Virginia, and an uncle, also named William B. Carter, had been president of the Constitutional Convention of 1834. The congressman had completed studies for the Presbyterian ministry at Princeton University, but gave up preaching because of ill health. Powell was the son of a wealthy doctor of Sullivan County, who also practiced in Carter County. The father died the year of the campaign. The junior Powell had raised a company in Carter County that served in the removal of the Cherokee Indians to Oklahoma, during which he attained the rank of colonel.

Brownlow and young Landon C. Haynes found themselves on opposite sides in the campaign. The two men had known each other as intimates of Thomas A. R. Nelson, Brownlow as a political ally and personal friend, Haynes as a student reading law under the attorney. The student had been "taken up by the Whigs of this county [Carter], while very young, and while he was trying to *write* himself into notice, in the newspapers." But while Haynes was studying under Nelson he married Eleanor Powell, daughter of Robert W. Powell

HON. T, A. R. NELSON.

Hon. T. A. R. Nelson [From T. M. Humes, *The Loyal Mountaineers of Tennessee*, Knoxville, 1888.]

and the granddaughter of Dr. Powell who died in 1839, two months before the *Whig* was started. Haynes then switched parties and became an ardent advocate of Joseph Powell in his race for Congress.

The *Whig* dredged up every charge and slur it could against Powell and drew return fire from Haynes. Brownlow ignored him for months, but they were such natural opposites that a counter blast was inevitable. Landon was the son of David Haynes, a wealthy Carter County farmer, and had made a name for himself as a debater and a rhetorician at Washington College. He was an aristocrat for his time and location, and his speech was florid, flowing and expansive. Brownlow, who was reared in poverty, had labored on the farm and at the bench of the carpenter. His education was meager, so far as the classroom entered into it; his speech was unpolished, although blunt and incisive, and carried something of the flavor of the barnyard and the mechanic's shop. Both men were bold and in their sharply contrasting backgrounds lay the seeds of natural animus.

The Parson decided in January 1840 to notice Haynes. He recalled false statements that the youth had made during earlier months, and he also complained that in a recent political speech Haynes had denounced

this paper as a lying, slanderous production, and its conductor a *"hireling."* . . . He more recently *"poetised"* us in the *Sentinel*, connecting us directly, and by name, with a notorious *prostitute*, and in addition to all this, he has frequently, and still does, in conversation, speak disrespectfully of us.

Therefore, I, William G. Brownlow, of the town of Elizabethton, and of lawful age, pronounce *Landon C. Haines* [*sic.*] , of the county of Carter and State of Tennessee, a *liar, a puppy* and a SCOUNDREL and if he does not call me to an account for it, the first time he comes to this village, I insist he does not possess the courage of a *Spaniel Dog* (*Whig*, March 26, 1840).

The contest of abuse and insults now raged in full fury. When Haynes revived and circulated an account of Brownlow's having been convicted of libel in 1833 in Macon County, North Carolina, the editor ran his side of the story, citing that he had reviewed it himself in a pamphlet and in a book. He accused his young critic, an aspiring orator, of having used the productions of others as his own, including an address of the Rev. Creed Fulton, a Methodist preacher. "And I am told," the Parson related, "that one of the best speeches he ever delivered at the Washington College was the one I wrote for him, *at his urgent solicitations*, while I travelled this circuit. Indeed, I heard his friends applaud the speech so highly that I could scarcely repel the temptation to believe that I was *smart*, in as much as I had written it for him!" Landon's father now entered the brawl and suggested Brownlow was an ingrate for attacking his son, for he had been fed and entertained at the Haynes home while he was riding the circuit. The Parson retorted:

Your next allusion is, to the *chickens*—aye, the several meals of victuals I ate at your house, several years ago. I would call on you to make out your bill, and I would pay it, but for the fact that you had pressed me to call, for the purpose of writing out speeches for your son to deliver at college, to make him a great man!—I studied and wrote faithfully, and I think, it was as little as you could do, to give me my victuals while there—I made no other charge (*Whig*, May 14, 1840).

The war of words had brought violence to the Parson's home during the 1839 campaign, but he did not reveal it until his foes accused him of having taken shelter behind his wife and mother-in-law. He printed the accusation in the *Whig*. He relished publishing charges against himself in the belief that his retorts were more destructive than anything his foes could bring against him. Then he told his side of the story. Joseph Powell, father-in-law of Haynes, had followed Brownlow to the O'Brien works and attacked him. The Parson knocked him down with a club. Joseph retreated, vowed retaliation. Later, Robert Powell and a cousin, Jack Powell, returned to punish the editor. Robert presented a pistol; Brownlow fired at

him once, probably with a pistol and ran for a rifle. "In the meantime . . . my mother-in-law came running out, and taking me by the
hand, reminded me of the then situation of my wife in the house,
who she said, was lying prostrate in the house. I went with her into
the house, and this ended the affray." Eliza had borne her first child,
Susan, and was carrying her second, John Bell. [50]

Another tense episode arose after the *Whig*'s first denunciation of
Haynes on January 30, 1840. It was referred to sketchily in the *Whig*
but was detailed in a confidential letter to T. A. R. Nelson and
carried a directive to "Burn this." Instead, Nelson preserved it, as he
did many letters and papers. The Parson wrote that he had dressed
and shaved to go to a Jonesboro meeting:

but Bob Powell rode out to bring in Landon Haines [*sic.*] and the understanding
was that I was not to live until today. I therefore declined leaving, as I would
have been branded with cowardice. They came in yesterday—and old Dave swore
publicly that they had come for that purpose, and would not leave until they
had done 'something serious.'

I have been twice through the streets today, and in the houses of Lyon,
Singletary and Daily—and they have seen me but nothing has been yet done. . . I
have not seen Landon at all. I understand he is at Jo Powell['s] prepared for the
attack.

It is said this evening that Brewer, Rockhold and others, have visited Landon
and persuaded him not to notice me! I am glad of this, as I do not wish to fight.

Should they not kill me I will leave for the convention on Thursday next. . .

Our town is all commotion. When I am in the street the people get in their
doors to see me killed. . . .

Since I have moved to town, and it is understood the paper goes on, they
have become desperate towards me. Jo Powell is at the bottom of the whole
business.

Brownlow had separated himself from the iron business before
moving into Elizabethton and devoted full time to editing. He was
not fired upon in the streets, but on the night of March 9, 1840,
while the editor was seated by the fire in his home, two bullets
crashed into the room. Both passed close to his breast, one lodging in
the chimney and the other in the ceiling. The Parson fired once at
what he believed to be the form of the marauder. The Brownlow
household was disrupted: "Our wife, otherwise afflicted, and having
a sick child," the editor removed to the home of her parents, while
he boarded at the tavern, slept at home, and continued to walk the

streets "if our life pay the forfeit."

The experience enabled Brownlow to shift his ground without lessening his editorial fire. He notified the younger Haynes:

Sir—As you are strongly suspected for being an *assassin*—of having aided and abetted, in the late cowardly attempt to shoot me after night; & as public opinion has settled down on *you*, as a party concerned, as at least having a perfect knowledge of all the preliminaries connected therewith; and as you, in your late publication, so far from making an effort at *defence* have passed the whole matter by in *silence*, I can have no further controversy with you (*Whig*, March 26, 1840).

Thereupon he took out after Landon's father, but always managed to keep the son in the line of fire. This enabled the Parson to reproach the father, not only for his behavior, but also for having a son whom the editor described as being very badly behaved.

The firing upon the Parson's home followed by four days his publication of an extended defense of his own actions and a scathing attack upon Landon and the Powell family. He taunted Landon for failing to chastise the editor "when you came to this village for that very purpose? . . . You poor, pittiful [*sic.*], contemptible, lying, sneaking up-start, and cowardly rascal! *You* offer personal violence to me! You would sooner stick your head in a forge fire, than to come in contact with me."

Young Haynes came back with two columns of vituperative defense in the *Tennessee Sentinel*. He denied Brownlow's charge that the elder Haynes had requested Brownlow's friends to restrain him from noticing what the son was saying about him because Landon "was set on by the d--d Powell's—that they were a d--d thieving set—and that you done [*sic.*] all you could to prevent his marriage in that family." Landon also had dug up the skeleton of an uncle of the Parson's, Isaac Brownlow, who had died nine years earlier in Lauderdale, Alabama. William G. conceded that Isaac was a bad man, but suggested the noxious disease of which he had died had been prevalent in the Powell family. Since Landon had been married to Eleanor Powell only a year the editor's purpose was to drive a wedge of distrust between the families.

The controversy fell considerably below the gutter. Haynes reflected upon Brownlow's parents, both dead for almost a quarter of a century. The Parson defended the reputation of his parents with opinions from those who had known them and countered with some hints and charges about Landon's activities which again linked him as a conspirator, if not a participant, in the shooting into the Brownlow home. Brownlow told David Haynes:

And as to the *shooting*, Davy, your son's *own relations*, or many of them, both by *father* and *mother's* side, unhesitatingly say they believe he was concerned. His *broad, square toed Boots*, and the *track* thereof, which we measured at Powell's horse rack, compared with the track in my *garden* (*Whig*, March 26, 1840).

The Parson also claimed Landon's hasty departure from Elizabethton the morning following the shooting and conflicting accounts as to where he was at the time the shots were fired pointed to his connection with the affair.

David Haynes and Brownlow, at a chance meeting on horseback in mid-April, discussed terminating the quarrel, but the Parson declined to take back what he had written, and later accused Landon of having reopened the exchange of insults. A circular issued by young Haynes went so far as to accuse a Miss O'Brien of having borne a black baby and the Parson's father of having been a drunkard. Brownlow gritted his teeth and answered. The Miss O'Brien referred to by Haynes, he said, was not related to the iron manufacturers, and while the Parson admitted his father drank liquor it never threw him off his feet. He demanded: "Has ever any man witnessed such fiend-like ravages among the tombs, as are exhibited in this foul circular, the production of these Hayneses and Powells?"

A short and ominous line was in this long blast: "Your slander of my Mother, we will settle at the proper time, and in such a way as may be deemed proper."[51]

CHAPTER I / NOTES

[1] Autobiographical material on Brownlow's early life is found in two of his books, *Helps to the Study of Presbyterianism, or an Unsophisticated Exposition of Calvinism, with Hopkinsianism Modifications of Policy, with a View to a More Easy Interpretation of the Same. To which is Added a Brief Account of Life and Travels of the Author; Interspersed with Anecdotes*, pp. 242-243 (Page 243 is misnumbered 233), (Knoxville, 1834) hereafter cited as *Helps*; and *Sketches of the Rise, Progress and Decline of Secession; with a Narrative of Personal Adventures among the Rebels*, pp.

16-17 (Cincinnati, 1862), hereafter cited under the binder's title of *Parson Brownlow's Book*. Brief references to Brownlow's parents and their background are made in the *Whig* of March 26, May 14, 1840. Brownlow's newspaper, the title of which was varied from time to time, contains a wealth of biographical material on the editor. The titles were *Tennessee Whig*, with some inside pages headed "Elizabethton *Whig*," May 15, 1839, through May 14, 1840; the *Whig*, sometimes with inside pages headed "The Jonesborough Tennessee *Whig*," Jonesboro, May 20, 1840, through May 11, 1842, "The Jonesborough *Whig and Independent Journal*," Jonesboro, May 18, 1842, through April 19, 1849; *Brownlow's Knoxville Whig and Independent Journal*, Knoxville, May 19, 1849, through April 7, 1855, *Brownlow's Knoxville Whig*, Knoxville, April 14, 1855, through July 27, 1861, *Brownlow's Weekly Whig*, August 3, 1861, until suspended, October 26, 1861, the *Tri-Weekly Whig*, Knoxville, January 4, 1859, through August 3, 1861, *Brownlow's Knoxville Whig and Rebel Ventilator*, Knoxville, November 11, 1863, through February 21, 1866, *Brownlow's Knoxville Whig*, February 28, 1866, until Brownlow relinquished complete control of the newspaper, January 1, 1869. A very limited number of the files of the *Tri-Weekly Whig*, published in 1868, exist, and are in miscellaneous Knoxville newspaper files, McClung Collection, Lawson McGhee Library, Knoxville. All other files of the *Whig* and of the *Tri-Weekly Whig* are on microfilm in the McClung Collection. A tart opposition reference says the *Tri-Weekly Whig* was published only four or five months in 1868, daily *Press and Herald*, December 6, 1868. Hereafter all Brownlow's newspapers will be referred to as the *Whig* or as the *Tri-Weekly Whig*.

[2] *Parson Brownlow's Book*, p. 16. The quotation used differs slightly in punctuation and working from that in *Helps*, p. 242. The reference to Houston is only in *Parson Brownlow's Book*.

[3] *Ibid.*, pp. 16-17. The quotation used differs slightly from the account in *Helps*, pp. 242-243. (The latter is misnumbered 233) principally in simplified puncutation. The maiden name of the Parson's mother is spelled Ganaway in *Helps*, but in *Parson Brownlow's Book*, and in the *Whig*, it is consistently spelled with a double n.

[4] The full names of John Gannaway and George Winniford appear in R. N. Price, *Holston Methodism from Its Origin to the Present Times*, (Nashville, 1903-1914), 5 vols., III, p. 315; hereafter cited as *Holston Methodism*, and in E. Merton Coulter, *William G. Brownlow, Fighting Parson of the Southern Highlands* (Knoxville, 1971), p. 4; hereafter cited as Coulter. Brownlow failed to mention the full names in *Helps*, p. 243, and in *Parson Brownlow's Book*, p. 17.

[5] *Helps*, pp. 243-244.

[6] When Brownlow wrote *Helps* he termed his education in the common schools "plain, though regular," but twenty-eight years later he described it as having been "imperfect and irregular," *Helps*, p. 244; *Parson Brownlow's Book*, p. 17.

[7] *Helps*, p. 244.

[8] *Ibid.*, pp. 246-248; William Rule, Ed., *Standard History of Knoxville*, Tennessee (Chicago, 1900), p. 428; hereafter referred to as Rule, *Standard History*; Samuel Mayes Arnell, "The Southern Unionist," unpublished typescript, University of Tennessee Special Collections, pp. 13-14; hereafter referred to as Arnell; Price, *Holston Methodism*, III, p. 338.

[9] O. P. Temple, *Notable Men of Tennessee* (New York, 1912), p. 281; hereafter referred to as Temple, *Notable Men*; *Helps*, pp. 245, 266; Arnell, pp. 13-14.

[10] W. G. Brownlow, *The Great Iron Wheel Examined; or, Its False Spokes Extracted, and an Exhibition of Elder Graves, Its Builder. In a Series of Chapters* (Nashville, 1856), pp. 238-239; hereafter referred to as *The Great Iron Wheel Examined*.

[11] *Helps*, p. 249.

[12] *Ibid.*, pp. 259-260, 269-272; Price, *Holston Methodism*, III, pp. 339-343; John Patton Archer, *Western North Carolina. A History from 1790 to 1913* (Asheville, North Carolina, 1914), pp. 226-227.

[13] *Helps*, p. 275,; *Whig*, July 5, 1851.

[14] Tennessee *Sentinel*, Jonesboro, July 19, 1845.

[15] *Whig*, July 5, 1851. Brownlow also had reviewed the case less elaborately, *ibid.*, February 27, 1840. He called Posey "a thieving old Baptist preacher" because he believed Posey had sold for money or services Bibles that had been sent to him for free distribution.

[16] *Helps*, 256, 253, 262-265; Price, *Holston Methodism*, p. 258.

[17] *Helps*, pp. 266-267, *Parson Brownlow's Book*, pp. 20-23.

[18] *Helps*, pp. 288, 246, 148, 178-182, 211, 103, 106, preface, *pp. v-xiii*; Price, *Holston Methodism*, III, pp. 157-160; W. G. Brownlow to Frederick S. Heiskell, May 10, 1836; Mrs. J. T. Howard Papers, Sherrod Library, East Tennessee State University, Johnson City, Tennessee. Mrs. Howard, of Bristol, Tennessee, is the granddaughter of Heiskell.

[19] Current value of this volume was supplied by John Dobson, Special Collection librarian, the University of Tennessee.

[20] *Helps*, pp. 287-288.

[21] Price, *Holston Methodism*, III, pp. 345-346.

[22] *Ibid.*, III, p. 315; Arnell, p. 43. A compilation of the marriage licenses issued in Carter County, 1797-1850, by Miss Pollyanna Creekmore, director of documents, Sherrod Library, and formerly McClung Collection librarian, shows one issued to Hiram O. Mackin and Sarah K. O'Brien, solemnized on September 11, 1836, by W. G. Brownlow. Sarah was not of Eliza's family. See "Genealogical Tables," by Gaines Strother Pendleton, p. 13, manuscript in University of Tennessee Special Collections.

[23] Price, *Holston Methodism*, III, p. 346; Arnell, p. 44; *Whig*, September 28, 1842, October 20, 1849.

[24] Price, *Holston Methodism*, III, p. 309; Coulter, fn p. 34.

[25] See inscription about O'Brien Furnace on a marker erected half a mile east of Valley Forge on U.S. Highway 19E by the Tennessee Historical Commission, also Tennessee Historical Markers, 5th ed., p. 68.

[26] *Whig*, August 8, 1839; Brownlow to T. A. R. Nelson, March 23, 1850, Nelson Papers, McClung Collection. The contract between Mason R. Lyon and Brownlow for operating the *Whig* at Elizabethton suggests Brownlow

was a partner in the O'Brien operation, Nelson Papers, May 4, 1839. See also *Whig*, October 20, 1849.

[27] *Helps*, p. 279; manuscript sketch of Brownlow by William Rule in files of *The Knoxville Journal*, and newspaper clippings in William Rule Papers, McClung Collection. Thomas Emmerson, first mayor of Knoxville and later publisher of the Washington *Republican and Farmer's Record*, at Jonesboro, is credited with having encouraged Brownlow to write on political subjects, after having published some of his articles. Brownlow also had written articles opposing Andrew Johnson for the Tennessee General Assembly in 1837, which were printed in Emmerson's paper under the signature of "Western Virginia," *Whig*, May 14, 1853; Price, *Holston Methodism*, III, p. 319.

[28] Rule Manuscript; *Whig*, May 16, 1839; Lyon-Brownlow contract, Nelson Papers. For an examination of Brownlow's first years as an editor see also " 'Cry Aloud and Spare Not'; The Formative Years of Brownlow's *Whig*, 1837-1841," University of Tennessee Master's Thesis, by Nancy Marlene Haley, August 1966.

[29] Rule Manuscript, *Whig*, May 16, 1839.

[30] Lyon-Brownlow contract, Nelson Papers.

[31] Coulter, p. 35; Temple, *Notable Men*. p. 273. *Sixth Census, or, Enumeration of the Inhabitants of the United States, as Corrected by the Department of State*, (Washington, 1841) *1840*, pp. 264-265; hereafter referred to as U.S. Sixth Census.

[32] *Whig*, May 16, December 16, 1839; January 30, 1840. The *Whig*'s first issue carried a notice asking for bids to carry the mail to Abingdon and return, weekly.

[33] *Ibid.*, March 26, 1840; Arnell, pp. 44-45.

[34] John Bell Brownlow to O. P. Temple, June 21, 1892. Temple Papers, University of Tennessee Special Collections.

[35] The complete verse reads: "Cry aloud, spare not, lift up thy voice like a trumpet, and show my people their transgressions, and the house of Jacob their sins." King James Version of the Bible.

[36] Type identification and characteristics were furnished by Walter Amann, who has been compositor, proof reader, copy reader, makeup editor and managing editor of the Knoxville *Journal*.

[37] *Whig*, May 16, 1839. Brownlow used quotation marks around the major portion of this passage but failed to give the source. He rephrased it for his inaugural address as governor, in his debate with Abram Pryne on slavery, and in his largest selling book. *Ibid.*, April 12, 1865; *Ought American Slavery to be Perpetuated? A Debate between The Rev. W. G. Brownlow and the Rev. A. Pryne* (Philadelphia, 1858), pp. 272-273; *Parson Brownlow's Book*, pp. 26-27.

[38] Stanley J. Folmsbee, Robert E. Corlew, and Enoch L. Mitchell, *Tennessee: A Short History* (Knoxville, 1969), pp. 198-199; hereafter referred to as Folmsbee *et al.*, *Short History*; Robert H. White, *Messages of the Governors* (Nashville, 1952—), 7 vols. to date, p. 274, gives Polk 54,012, and Cannon 51,396, on the basis of official returns from every County but

Shelby, in which instance figures are taken from the *Republican Banner* of Nashville, and which *give* Polk 54,639, Cannon 52,177.

[39] Eric Russel Lacy, *Vanquished Volunteers; East Tennessee Sectionalism from Statehood to Secession* (Johnson City, 1965), pp. 112-113; hereafter cited as *Vanquished Volunteers*; *Whig*, August 18, 1841; Folmsbee *et al.*, *Short History*, p. 199.

[40] *Whig*, June 27, July 11, 25, 30, August 15, 1939.

[41] *Ibid.*, September 5, August 22, 1839.

[42] Folmsbee *et al.*, *Short History*, pp. 178-179.

[43] *Whig*, January 30, 1840. The charge of illegitimacy was hinted at in the memoirs of John Quincy Adams, Herbert S. Parmet and Marie B. Hecht, *Aaron Burr, Portrait of an Ambitious Man* (New York, 1967), p. 335. The bastard charge is unsubstantiated.

[44] *Whig*, November 14, 1839; Brownlow to Nelson, July 8, 1839. Nelson Papers.

[45] Folmsbee *et al.*, *Short History*, pp. 199-201; *Whig*, December 12, 1839, January 16, February 13, 1840.

[46] *Ibid.*, February 20, March 5, 1840, August 15, 1839.

[47] Jesse Burt, ed., "Editor Eastman Writes James K. Polk," East Tennessee Historical Society *Publications*, No. 39, pp. 103-104; Burt, ed., "Tennessee Democrats Employ Editor E. G. Eastman, 1846-1849," East Tennessee Historical Society *Publications*, No. 38, pp. 83-85; *Whig*, December 26, 1839; Brownlow to Nelson, June 8, 1839. Nelson Papers.

[48] *Whig*, February 13, 1840; March U. Rothrock, ed., *The French Broad-Holston Country* (Knoxville, 1940) pp. 431-432; hereafter cited as Rothrock, ed., French Broad-Holston; Rule, ed., *Standard History*, p. 318.

[49] James Silk Buckingham, *The Slave States of America* (London, 1842), 2 vols., II, pp. 246-248, 257-261; Samuel Clemens (Mark Twain), "Journalism in Tennessee," in *Editorial Wild Oats*, pp. 11-29.

[50] Temple, *Notable Men*, pp. 88-89; James W. Bellamy, "The Political Career of Landon Carter Haynes," ETHS *PUBL.*, No. 28, pp. 102-104; Landon C. Haynes to Nelson, March 12, 1839, Nelson Papers. *Whig*, January 30, February 27, March 5, 26, May 7, 14, 1840. Susan was born July 3, 1838, at Kingsport, and John Bell in Carter County, October 19, 1839, Pendleton, "Genealogical Tables," p. 13.

[51] *Whig*, March 5, 1840; Brownlow to Nelson, February 2, 1840. Nelson Papers. *Whig*, February 13, March 12, 26, 5, 26, May 5, 26, May 14, 7, 1840.

A BULLET IN THE THIGH

In eight months William G. Brownlow proved he was a successful editor. His predecessor had a circulation of 300 papers. He started the *Whig* with 700 papers and during the first year the number of subscribers reached to between 900 and 1,100. Not only did the provocative Parson's cutting, colorful prose and his severe treatment of his foes see him hanged in effigy at Knoxville, but also the Democratic postmaster there, so Brownlow said, became so sensitive to the heat the *Whig* generated that he resorted to handing it out "with a pair of tongs." His original agreement to edit the *Whig* had been limited and tentative. He could do it only by candlelight because he would not abandon his generous father-in-law who had provided him with a job, and he wasn't sure he could make it as an editor. Now, the collapsing iron industry could spare him, and he had learned that newspaper editing suited and delighted his controversial nature. He moved himself and his family the four miles into Elizabethton to devote full time to editing and to receive a fixed salary, a basis more satisfactory than a share of the profits. The newcomer displayed other unmistakable signs of progress. Lyon took on another printer, Valentine Garland, new print shop materials were bought, and the typographical appearance of the paper was improved.[1]

The delighted Whigs looked for a broader field in which to pit their new champion against the Democrats and hit upon Jonesboro, the county seat of adjoining Washington County. This county had a population of 11,744, double that of Carter.[2] Because the Parson drew so much attention from a tiny point like Elizabethton his blasts could be expected to carry further and wider if released from the larger Jonesboro with its more central location and better mail facilities. Tom Nelson had led the way in the summer of 1839. He married Anne Elizabeth Stuart and moved with his bride to Jonesboro.[3]

Late in the same year Brownlow had decided to cut loose from Lyon when their contract expired and the decision to move to Jonesboro was made. Lyon was a part-time Baptist preacher; he drank heavily, and he was behind on payments to the Parson. As a result Nelson wrote a contract for Brownlow, Garland and Lyon on March 7, 1840. Under this contract Lyon sold the type, cases and his interest in the subscription list of the *Whig* to Brownlow and Garland for $550.00, but agreed to collect outstanding accounts for the first year and to pay the Parson for his services as editor for the year. Lyon wished the two new partners well, in print, and pleaded ill health for not continuing as publisher. However, Garland had written Nelson months earlier that the Parson would not edit the *Whig* beyond the first year with Lyon as publisher. He wrote that Lyon was so bitter he would do anything to crush the Jonesboro project.[4]

At the close of Brownlow's first year as editor it was obvious that he liked what he was doing and the way he was doing it, as he reviewed what he had accomplished, and concluded:

Such have been our convictions, all along that, in every material respect we were right, we were willing to loose [*sic*.] our life in defense of our principles and party. . . .

A review of a complete file of the *Whig*, will perhaps conduct any candid and dispassionate mind, to the conclusion, that in point of severity, and wholesale abuse of individuals, our paper is without a parallel in the history of the American Press. The existence of this truth, in connexion [*sic*.] with this bold confession, however, finds an apology, in the fact, that it has been peculiarly our misfortune to have to encounter a most disciplined corps of the most obdurate sinners and unprincipled scoundrels that ever annoyed any community (*Whig*, May 14, 1840).

Scoundrels also infested Washington, D.C., for there President Martin Van Buren and his party trampled upon the laws and the Constitution, and were corrupt. The Parson turned from the fate that awaited the wicked upon death to

the man, who is alive to the importance of an eternal state of being, and makes it the subject of his hopes and fears, as well as of his future enquiries. But, with the upright man, how calm is the *evening* of life! With what tranquillity does he lean his head upon his dying pillow, while the lamp of life gradually dies away in its socket!

.   .   .

To our numerous patrons, who have so nobly sustained us, and our cause, we have one word to say, and we are done. That your journey through life may be as sweet as it is short; that poverty and want may always be a day's march behind you; that you may be happy and your enemies know it; that while you travel through life you may live well on the road; and that while you do live you may live under the guidance of the four greatest and best of Generals—General *Providence*, General *Peace*, General *Plenty*, and General *Satisfaction* (*Ibid.*).

Brownlow's first year, with its shouting controversies and its rich harvest of subscribers, left him eagerly anticipating the move to Jonesboro, where he would be "at the very door of the lying *Sentinel*, to correct its slanders while yet smoking" (*Whig*, March 19, 1840). He knew that his entry at the Washington County seat was the equivalent of bursting into a den of angry, spitting wildcats. Lawson Gifford, the *Tennessee Sentinel* publisher, was politically allied with the Haynes and Powell families, and he had social relationships with the former. On September 28, 1842, he married Miss Mary Taylor Haynes, the daughter of David Haynes.[5]

Gifford seemed bent on stirring up the *Whig* editor in every way he could, as though being a Democratic publisher and in the Haynes-Powell corner was not sufficient provocation. Just before the *Whig* moved to Jonesboro he hired as editor Thomas A. Anderson, son of a former United States senator, Joseph Anderson, and brother of the current United States senator, Alexander Outlaw Anderson. Thomas A. opened up on the Parson in his first issue of the *Tennessee Sentinel*. Brownlow said he himself was at a loss to understand why his competitor had flown into such a quick rage; all the Parson had done was to run a defense printed by another Whig editor, a Mr. Wales who had been denounced by the Knoxville *Argus*. It happened that in making his defense Mr. Wales had found it important to prove that Anderson once "was so *beastly drunk*, at a certain still-house near Rogersville that he could not get on his horse without assistance." Just how this incident was a part of Mr. Wales' defense was not explained, nor was it clear which galled Anderson the most, his reported drunken state or his inability to mount his horse. Anderson had been a Presbyterian minister, and he had practiced medicine before taking up the pen. Brownlow said Anderson still doted on being called "doctor." The Parson, however, who had touched him up in *Helps to the Study of Presbyterianism*, recalled that he was sometimes known as "*Lord Hackberry*." Now, Brownlow dubbed Anderson as "the *profane swearer, apostate Presbyterian Preacher, and drunken blackguard* who now edits the *Jonesborough Sentinel!*"

Gifford also touched the Parson in a most sensitive spot, ridiculing him before the guests in a New Market tavern by reading the Haynes circular he had printed and apparently throwing in his own comment. A man who heard the reading was infuriated at the way "your mother's [the Parson's mother's] name has been dragged into this filthy piece, and spoken of in the most disgraceful terms. I was acquainted with her personally: or partially so at least, from my infancy almost, and I have yet to hear the first person of respectability say one word against her character."[6]

The *Whig* editor lost no time in taking an intimate examination of Gifford:

Point us to a female on the pavements of our streets, arm in arm with *Lawson Gifford*, and we will show you a female of suspicious character—or one whose family is under the weather, because of some thefts or frauds committed by the heads thereof. . . . We are not anxious to acquire the reputation of a bully;—but if this scoundrel will publish one slanderous sentence in his paper relative to either of our parents, who have now been dead upwards of twenty years, we will, upon sight, thereafter give him such evidence of our *cowardice*, as will amount to a *practical demonstration* of the utter falsehood of the charge. In relation to us, and every living relative we have, he can and may, publish with impunity (*Whig*, May 14, 1840).

The *Whig* in which Brownlow took after both publisher and editor of the *Tennessee Sentinel* was the last he put out under an Elizabethton dateline. On May 6, 1840, he published at Elizabethton, but under a Jonesboro dateline, a specimen of the new volume. In it he said that the newspaper in the new location would appear thereafter on Wednesday instead of Saturday.[7] When the second number appeared in Jonesboro it carried one of the biggest stories in the life of the editor.

On May 14, 1840, Brownlow was seated with a group of men in front of a store. He rose from his chair, without a word of explanation, and walked down the street. Haynes was walking from the other direction. The Parson drew his pistol. Haynes stopped, holding his right hand behind him, a position he had maintained from the moment the two men were seen approaching each other. Brownlow three times demanded to know if Haynes was armed. Haynes replied that he was not, but kept his right hand behind him. Brownlow kept advancing, Haynes retreating, until they were at close quarters, the Parson's advance being more rapid than Haynes' backward steps. Brownlow demanded that Haynes retract what he had said about Brownlow's mother. Haynes either refused to retract or failed to do so. Brownlow shifted his pistol to his left hand and moved a sword cane to his right, with which he began striking Haynes. The latter then brought out a pistol and fired it. Witnesses differed as to whether the cane blow by Brownlow and the shot by Haynes were simultaneous. Three said they were simultaneous, one that Haynes fired first.

The ball from Haynes' pistol entered the center of the Parson's thigh, three or four inches below the groin. The men grappled. Though wounded, the Parson struck Haynes again with the aforesaid cane, fought off the younger man's attempt to take his pistol, and beat his head with the weapon, holding Haynes with his left hand as he did so. After the men had been separated witnesses saw blood dripping from Brownlow's leg. He was helped across the street to a store and placed on a bed.

One witness reported that when Haynes came out of a store and before walking up the street, one hand, and perhaps both, were in his coattails. It was his statement and the impression that the weapon fired by Haynes was a "pocket rifle," requiring both hands to cock it, that led to the conclusion by some that Haynes had started his march up the street prepared to discharge it without delay. Brownlow acknowledged himself the instigator, explaining: [8]

Our motive for approaching Haynes in the way we did was to induce him either to take back an insinuation against our mother or to render personal satisfaction for it. Knowing our mother to have been a correct woman in every respect—to have died a Christian—and to have been in her grave twenty-four years—no man *can* or *shall* assail her character, or disturb her ashes with impunity (*Whig*, May 20, 1840).

A completely objective determination of what took place is impossible, as only the accounts given by the *Whig* remain. Files of the *Tennessee Sentinel* reporting the fight do not exist, and so far as is known Haynes left no statement for posterity. The unsworn accounts of the fight published by the *Whig* were made by four men, the most extensive being made by Thomas B. Emmerson, son of the lawyer and publisher, Thomas Emmerson, who had once urged Brownlow to engage in the newspaper business.

The bullet wound was severe, Brownlow acknowledged, but five days after the "recountre" he reported he was able "to set [*sic*.] at our table and write." He read his exchanges and talked politics with his friends. Word circulated that he was making threats, but he wrote that he only awaited events and then would "act just as our inclination may lead us to do." The *Whig* did not miss an issue.[9]

Brownlow suffered a misery of the flesh, but he also reported that his enemies gloated, and that a "lady—no, *a woman*, the wife of a distinguished Democrat, said to a Whig lady, 'I wish it had gone through his heart instead of his leg.' " With only a few exceptions

there positively was greater rejoicings, in all the Locofoco ranks of East Tennessee, at the prospect of our death that there could have been in the Church of God on earth, in Europe and America, upon hearing of the death and burial of his Satanic Majesty, the Devil! (*Whig*, May 27, 1840).

The former circuit rider demonstrated what he had said that he carried weapons but would use them only in his defense, although in this instance it was for the defense of the reputation of his long dead mother.[10] The vilification he received, the boisterous glee of his foes at his wound, and the regrets of some that the bullet was not fatal, enlarged him in the public eye. That publicity probably repaid him for the physical pain he endured. The "recountre" also was a splendid curtain raiser for his vigorous campaign in behalf of the Whig Party nominees for the nation's highest offices, General Taylor and John Tyler of Virginia. The stories of his boldness and of the arms he carried may have been the reason that later in the summer he was able to outthreaten "drunken bullies" at the courthouse door in Madisonville.[11]

The Parson's pen grew bolder. When Editor Anderson belittled attendance at a big Whig rally at Cumberland Gap, Tennessee, Brownlow impaled him with an audacious shaft. Anderson's estimate of the crowd was that "to count them over three times there *was* 3,000 including boys, negroes [*sic.*] and PROSTITUTES—WHO NUMBERED AT LEAST FIVE HUNDRED!!!!" Brownlow quoted the *Tennessee Sentinel*'s report, then wrote that all the women at the meeting did not exceed 500, so that the Democratic newspaper had branded all those there as females of pleasure. He took an even more daring step, printing the names of many of the wives and daughters of prominent and respected Whigs who were present, inferring that Anderson had classed these women as prostitutes. Aware that repercussions would follow, for newspapers at that time rarely published names of good women, the Parson asserted that all the females at the rally were "ladies, for such we know them to be, and their friends will please pardon us for thus using their names" (*Whig*, October 7, 1840). He could always say, if criticized, that he had done what he did to protect their names.

When Harrison and Tyler were elected the Parson went wild with joy. He turned out his newspaper on November 25 and 28, each issue displaying a front page that was garish, outlandish and vulgar, by modern standards. He disposed of Anderson, after having written his name as Thomas Ass Anderson for months, with a brief note that the *Tennessee Sentinel* "has not done our case any injury—but it has made fearful havoc in the ranks of Democracy—it has slain its own party as efficiently as Sampson did the Philistines and with the same weapon—the jawbone of an ass." During the campaign the *Whig* had run in three issues a five-column account of Anderson's life, and had proposed to have it printed in book form, embellished with additional details about other Van Buren leaders, including a "minute account of their stealing of money, pocket-books, negroes [*sic*] and goods, burning of barns, using false weights and measures—their church trials &¢, &¢." But Anderson left town and the Parson saw no reason to publish the book.[12]

Editors of Democratic newspapers were certain targets of Brownlow's pen, but the Parson had found Anderson most detestable. This was not only for the reasons previously given but that he was the brother of Senator Anderson who was elected when Hugh Lawson White of Knoxville, the revered man, was forced to resign by a Democratic legislature in early 1840. White died a few months later, and Brownlow in his obituary notice brought up a very bitter point with Whigs; as White returned from Washington the Rogersville Democrats were prepared to treat him ignominiously. Rather than risk the main street where gibes and insults awaited him, White took a circuitous route through the outskirts of the town. In time Democrat leaders realized their treatment of White had hurt them, and that it gave the Whigs effective political ammunition.[13]

With the departure of Anderson, Brownlow offered a cautious truce: "Let us alone and we will let you alone," he told the *Tennessee Sentinel*, but if the Democratic newspaper started a fight the *Whig* would carry on "a war of extermination" (*Whig*, November 18, 1840). He may have been too busy exulting over the victory of Harrison and Tyler to concentrate much fire on his enemies. He changed his page one motto from "Unawed by power, unbribed by gain, the people shall be heard, and their rights vindicated," to "WE HAVE MET THE ENEMY AND THEY ARE OURS—Commodore Perry," the victor's famous report on the outcome of the Battle of Lake Erie. Brownlow had discarded "Cry aloud and spare not," on moving to Jonesboro, and while he did not gamble he was Whig enough to chuckle at his fellow partisans having won at least $5,000 in election bets in the area.[14]

Landon Haynes took some part in the 1840 campaign; the Parson gave him a few light touches, but sometime after Anderson resigned Haynes became editor of the *Tennessee Sentinel*.[15]

The *Whig* editor began to display skill as a roving reporter when he spoke for his party's candidates throughout lower East Tennessee during the 1840 campaign (*Whig*, September 23, 1840). He was ripening into a keen observer of the human scene, bringing to his readers with style, color, verve and tickling satire what he saw. This skill, as well as his ingenuity, sharpness and force in the delivery of invective and abuse, made him a great circulation builder. The first talent has been overshadowed to the point of neglect as writers have dwelt heavily on his ability and disposition to club, knife and throttle his foes with words. Another characteristic was an aid to his career; he was a born rover. After a decade as a Methodist circuit rider he refused, as an editor, to be pinned to a desk. He used every means of locomotion: horseback, buggy, stage, watercraft, railroads, and his own sturdy legs. Wherever he went he wrote of it.

An early development of this skill appears when Brownlow was present in Knoxville at the hanging of a Sevier Countian, George Long, who had murdered his wife. As a minister Brownlow labored with the doomed man to the last. In the agonizing moment "Just before he was hanged, and while sitting on his coffin, in the waggon, with the rope tied around his neck, we stepped up to him and asked if he still alleged his innocence—he said he did." The Parson watched Long bid farewell to his father and "assisted the poor old man in getting out of the waggon, and in leaving the crowd; after which we turned our eyes toward Long—saw him rise up off his coffin, and walk up to the gallows, with an indifference which astonished us beyond description." A crowd of from 5,000 to 8,000 witnessed the hanging. The editor placed himself on record against public executions and added the hope that "for the honor of their sex, if for no other reason, we shall never again see as many *females* assembled together on such an occasion" (*Whig*, August 22, 1839).

The inauguration of Harrison as President gave Brownlow an opportunity to travel and to mix at the nation's highest political level as the Whigs exulted in victory, and Washington was undergoing the spasm of a change in administration. He found great improvement in traveling after he reached Raleigh, North Carolina, from Jonesboro, a stagecoach trip that took two weeks. From Raleigh to Washington he enjoyed his first ride on a railroad, and after reaching the capital marveled:

Only think of traveling 360 miles in 36 hours! If I had never seen or heard of a train of Railroad Cars, propelled by a steam Engine, and were conscious of having so conducted myself as to warrant the Devil's title to my person, upon meeting the Engine, I should peacefully surrender!

The Parson was proud to be the guest in the House of Representatives of his friend John Bell, who was to be appointed secretary of war in a few days, but he was not overawed. The members in session "reminded me of a Methodist camp meeting, at night, when the Negroes had taken possession of the altar!"

The editor's first letters dealt chiefly with developments in the change of administrations, but he did not neglect church going. Although he praised a sermon he heard given by a presiding elder, he regretted that the "pompous manner, affectation, and seeming vanity of the speaker, destroyed its good effect upon the congregation." His Protestant soul was horrified when it was discovered that he and a friend had taken lodgings in a "*Roman Catholic* house, and were put in a room, where there was a *little puter* [pewter] god." The Parson was restrained from smashing it, and he at once found other quarters.

He listened to John Quincy Adams argue a case before the United States Supreme Court, and he met both the outgoing and incoming Presidents. He reported Harrison was in excellent health, an error on the Parson's part, for Harrison died in a few weeks. Van Buren he found displaying a "kingly-courtlike politeness," and an "everlasting, artificial smile." Yet he credited him with bearing his defeat "like a Stoic." A fellow boarder of the Parson's was John Tyler of Virginia, the Vice-President-elect, a "gentleman—easy in his manners—and full of life and conversation."

A couple of observations must have brought gasps from the *Whig*'s readers. Brownlow examined the White House minutely and found, "Some of the rooms, on the second floor, are more filthy, upon my word, than any Negro kitchen I ever noticed in East Tennessee!" And on the night of the inaugural ball, "I noticed a number of ladies, passing out of their doors, into their carriages, and to the scene of action, and many of them are so very 'hardfavored,' that if I had to dance with them, I should insist upon dancing with our backs fronting each other!"

Invited to attend a dinner of Whig editors he declined, "first, because it savoured of *Jacksonism*; next, because it intended to suggest to each editor the propriety of keeping *secret* what everybody ought to know; and last, though not least, because I dont [*sic*] intend to be dictated to, without reserve, or committed in favor of *measures* til [*sic.*] I know what they are to be." This forecast a policy he often would follow. He was a Whig, but he reserved to himself the right to decide what was correct Whiggery. He bound himself to Whig principles, as he saw them, but not to every Whig nominated by the party if he felt the nominee was out of line with party doctrine.

Before leaving Washington for Baltimore, Philadelphia and New York, the Parson peeped over a sofa to watch as Senator William King of Alabama sat writing a challenge to mortal combat which Senator Henry Clay accepted. The dispute was adjusted without benefit of firearms. [16]

From New York City he sent letters that mixed political observations with comment on the great city and its people, along with accounts of perplexing situations in which the countryman found himself. He was forced to ring for a servant when he was unable to find his way down from the fifth floor of the Howard Hotel, but he enjoyed the food, described the extensive menu, and detailed:

The way for a back-woodsman to manage on occasions of this kind, is to throw himself back in his chair and *look* grave—and to *seem* to be perfectly at himself—aye, just in his element! When a servant dashes by me and enquires, "what will you have, sir"—I look at my "bill of fare" and pronounce the name of what I want, with such a grace, that I am certain, I am *almost* taken for a member of the Diplomatic Corps at Washington! True, I have no idea *what* I ask for, and whether the servant brings what I call for, or something altogether *different*, I have no means of determining! This is another matter. My business is to eat what is brought, and to be ready for the next call!

He toured Wall Street, a newspaper office, viewed the city from the top of a six-story building, walked the length of Broadway, stared at the "dense forest of masts and rigging" in the harbor, stopped at the Methodist Book Concern and looked upon that center of political infamy, Tammany Hall. New Yorkers, he decided, suffer from

all sorts of *diseases*, mental and corporeal. Among these maladies which I have noticed most the prevalent, and the most injurious in their effects, are dizzyness, restlessness *at night*, obstinate coughs, pains in the joints, bleeding at the nose, sore eyes, inclination to *steal*, headache, disposition to lie, vertigo, torpor, disturbed dreams, sleep broken by rioting convulsions occasioned by defeat in politics, thirst for liquor, palid [*sic.*] hue, bad taste in the mouth, down looks, guilty conscience, offensive breath, itching of the head, occasioned by the crawling of *legtreasurers*, griping of the bowels, swelling of the stomach, nausea, squesmishness [*sic.*], leanness, meanness, dejection of films and mums—and in short, a total want of all that is required to constitute the man.[17]

The Parson loved to exaggerate, and here he let himself go for the benefit of his readers, who could laugh and imagine themselves as better off than those city people, with all their conveniences. He gave them a picture of life in the great city that not only filled them with delight and wonder, but also left them with the impression that they were just a little bit more fortunate than their city cousins. This he could do because he had a gift for which an enemy who hated him intensely would give him full credit two decades later—he understood human nature as few men do.[18]

CHAPTER II NOTES

[1] Brownlow gave two sets of figures for this circulation, *Whig*, November 10, 1841, February 28, 1840, January 30, 23, February 13, 20, 1840.
[2] *United States Sixth Census*, pp. 264-265.
[3] Thomas B. Alexander, *Thomas A. R. Nelson of East Tennessee* (Nashville, 1956), p. 16; hereafter referred to as Alexander, *Thomas A. R. Nelson.*
[4] Valentine Garland to Nelson, December 24, 1839, Nelson Papers. *Whig*, November 12, 1841; Frank Merritt, *Early History of Carter County, 1760-1861* (Knoxville, 1950), p. 94; Lyon-Garland-Brownlow contract, March 7, 1840. Nelson Papers.
[5] *Whig*, October 5, 1842; Bellamy, "The Political Career of Landon Carter Haynes," p. 104.
[6] *Whig*, May 14, 1840; Rothrock, ed., *French Broad-Holston*, pp. 413-414; Faye E. McMillen, "A Biographical Sketch of Joseph Anderson (1757-1837)," ETHS *PUBL*. No. 2, pp. 84-87.
[7] *Whig*, May 7, 1840. Also dated May 6, 1840.
[8] *Ibid.*, May 20, 1840.
[9] *Ibid.*
[10] *Ibid.*, May 27, 1840, December 5, 1839, April 9, 1840.
[11] Folmsbee *et al.*, *Short History*, p. 201; *Whig*, September 23, 1840.
[12] *Ibid.*, November 25, 28, November 18, 1840. The three issues on Anderson's life were *ibid.*, August 12, 19, 26, 1840.
[13] *Ibid.*, April 16, 1840; Folmsbee *et al.*, *Short History*, p. 200.

[14] *Whig*, November 25, 28, 1840.

[15] The first record of Haynes as editor of the *Tennessee Sentinel* is *ibid.*, May 8, 1841, in a loose file of this newspaper, not on microfilm. McClung Collection. See also *Whig*, July 21, 1840.

[16] *Ibid.*, March 10, 31, 24, 1841.

[17] *Ibid.*, March 24, 31, April 7, 1841. The meaning of *legtreasurers*, films and mums has been lost.

[18] An editorial in the *Knoxville Register* in early 1862 described Brownlow as "the best judge of human nature within the bounds of the Southern Confederacy." The *Register* editor, J. Austin Sperry, was one of the Parson's bitterest foes. *Register* files are limited, but it is found in Parson Brownlow's Book, pp. 342-345; Temple, *Notable Men*, p. 351; and in *The War of the Rebellion: A Compilation of the Official Records of the Union and Confederate Armies*, 130 vols., Series 2, Vol. I, pp. 925-926; hereafter cited as *O.R.*

SUCCESS THROUGH UPROAR

Three months after William G. Brownlow moved the *Whig* to Jonesboro, he emerged as both publisher and editor, a remarkable step for a man who had entered the business field when he did, uncertain of his ability to succeed in this entirely new work. The O'Briens and the iron industry had gone down as the Parson and the *Whig* made substantial progress. The holdings of the O'Briens were sold at sheriff's sales or to satisfy judgments, and the *Whig*'s circulation reached 1,600. The Brownlow-Garland partnership was dissolved by "mutual consent," and on August 12, 1840, page one of the *Whig* displayed in the first column the legend, "William G. Brownlow, Editor and Publisher." Valentine Garland may have found the fury of political campaigns and his position in the line of fire between the Parson and his enemies too hot for comfort (he claimed to have been attacked by Landon C. Haynes and a confederate), or he may have been aggravated by Brownlow's frequent trips to rallies and conventions. He also resorted to the bottle too frequently to suit the bone-dry editor, as this *Whig* item a few years later showed:

We are much gratified to find in the Boonsville (Mo.) Register . . . a lengthy article in defense of the temperance cause from the pen of V. GARLAND, late of "these diggins." Having left here on board of a flat boat, screaming like a wildcat, and with about six inches [of] "plum liquor" in him, we were not prepared to hear of him warring against *baldface*! [1]

The page one makeup of the *Whig* changed with the Jonesboro opening. The name of the newspaper as given at the top of the page was shortened to *The Whig* in solid black, 60 point Onyx, the title printed in four columns rather than in six, with columns one and six brought to the top of the page; thus the heading was islanded on three sides with body type. The date line also appeared in heavier black type: "Jonesborough, Tenn." The name *Tennessee Whig* was carried in column one underneath the name of the editor and publisher and just above the subscription and advertising rate. The name of the newspaper was carried infrequently on the inside pages. Such inside identification lacked importance since the entire newspaper was printed on one sheet that was folded to make four pages.[2]

More significant than the changes in the management and makeup were developments in news policy and reporting. The Parson's dispatches from the many points where he visited and spoke were heavily political, but they were vivid, entertaining and streaked with humor—at least for the Whigs. At the great Whig convention of 1840 at Nashville, where Brownlow's idol, Henry Clay, spoke so thrillingly that it left the editor wordless, he condemned Democratic rowdies:

> During the speaking last night, on the Square, a gang of these same *vermine* [*sic.*] were passing to and fro, and yelling like savages to attract attention, while another set, supposed to be their *partners*, were stealing pocket-books by the dozen, as they clandestinly [*sic.*] passed [through] the crowd.[3]

More items lacking political flavor began to appear, for example, a complaint that some "popular literary" works were frivolous. The editor could see not benefits flowing from reading "such legends and romances as the following—*Blue Beard—Jack The Giant Killer—Tom Thumb—Robin Hood—Goody Two-Shoes—Puss in Boots—Sinbad the Sailor—Fairy Tales—Robinson Crusaw* [*sic.*]—*The Novels of Waverly—*." The Parson did not carry his disapproval to the point where he shut off the merchandising opportunity available through the paid agency of the newspaper because a few months later the *Whig* carried full, two-column advertisements of the novels of Sir Walter Scott, including the Waverly series, inserted by a Philadelphia publishing house.[4]

Sabbath violations were outrageous, the *Whig* complained on February 10, 1841, because while the devout worshipped at the churches, "the streets are surrendered to the Slaves, and the Free Negro [*sic.*] and boys." The civic conscience was quickening, however, in view of a city ordinance passed regulating the use of horses and other draft animals, forbidding milking on the sidewalk and the flying of kites. Shooting was confined to the killing of hogs or beef. A special duty was laid upon the constable: he was to preserve morals.

The Parson's piquant dispatches from Washington, Philadelphia, Baltimore and New York, now often ranging far afield from politics, must have brought a gratifying response, for he kept them up as long as he had strength to write them. He showed little hesitation in leaving to foremen the mechanical task of getting out the newspaper. He wrote a friend years later that he could manage editing almost as well when absent as present.[5]

Quarrels on the Jonesboro scene, however, which Brownlow must have counted upon to build circulation, proceeded more lustily if he was at home, as he was in the summer of 1841, when seats in the Tennessee General Assembly were at stake. R. W. Powell, with whom the Parson had had physical and political brushes, was running as a Democrat for a Senate seat against Elijah Embree, a Whig and the son of Elihu Embree, iron manufacturer and formerly editor of emancipation newspapers published at Jonesboro. The Parson accused Powell of having written in earlier years articles hotly criticizing Andrew Jackson and the Democratic Party, which were published in the Elizabethton *Republican*. Brownlow relied upon a statement given to him by William Gott, who along with Mason R. Lyon had operated the *Republican*. Gott told Brownlow they could be found in the *Republican*'s files. The *Whig* editor sent an emissary to Lyon, who returned with copies of the newspaper marked in pencil. The Parson charged Powell with being the author. But Lyon, possibly still smarting because he had not been included in the move to Jonesboro, cast doubt by stating that he had not positively identified the pieces marked as being from the pen of Powell, only that they might have been. Brownlow, already infuriated, was further angered because Landon Haynes, now editor of the *Tennessee Sentinel*, had opened the column of his newspaper to Lyon's retorts to Brownlow. The Parson retaliated with certificates supporting his side of the argument, and continued to abuse Lyon until late in the fall. He took a final slap at Lyon when the latter recieved only 13 out of 900 votes cast in the 1842 race for County Court Clerk of Carter County.[6]

The Brownlow-Lyon dispute fed the acrimony between the two editors, now confined to words. The Parson pointed out in the following quotation that the dispute had been blown up during the 1840 presidential campaign:

The public mind ... was deeply absorbed in the politics of the country, so much so that ... a hearing for the more spiritual truths of the Gospel, could hardly be had. The people had no ears to hear ought beside the harangues of their partizan [*sic.*] orators, and the reports of their newspapers. And such was the active and whole hog part I took in the contest, that I deemed it for the best to attend only to my paper and the interests of my party. I acted conscientiously, as did others. I believed that the fate of the country was at stake, on the issue of the late political contest. And that the warfare of that contest did beget a habit of universal distrust, and mutual abuse of character, no man will deny, as no good man and lover of his country does not lament the fact. But whose fault is it? Certainly not mine. I acted well my part—I claim to have been as bad as the worst—but I was not alone in this crusade. Others acted badly—they *bid* better than I did, and denied with an effrontery that I am incapable of—this is the difference (*Whig*, September 1, 1841).

The Parson made this assessment in August 1841 as he appeared before a quarterly conference of the Jonesboro Circuit of the Methodist Church. He expected to be faced with accusations, among others, that he had neglected his duties as a preacher. He announced his presence with: "And sir, I *am here*, but where are my accusers? . . . I desire to meet them here, and face to face compare notes with them, but it seems I am not to enjoy that privilege." Brownlow rarely was caught at a loss when there was a prospect for debate; consequently, he supplied the charges he said his enemies would have made had they been present. He acknowledged in the following words that he had abused people:

Yes, and others abuse me—I am calumniated—vilified—denounced in season and out of season . . . But I use a severity that they do not resort to. No, they do not use as many severe epithets as I do, but it is because they cannot just think of them at the time. They do their best. And I take the *will* for the deed. But I deny that I slander my opponents. To slander an individual, or a party, one must utter in relation to that individual, or party, charges which have no foundation in truth. I call for the specifications—give me chapter and verse, and I will plead to them. I ask for something more than *rumor*. Madam rumor, I am aware, has long since pronounced me the prince of evil-doers. Who is it that she has not condemned?

The Parson had brought partisan affairs into his speech because the Democrats of Jonesboro had sought to destroy him through the Methodist Church. They had accused him of outrageous abuse of people, yet the Democratic *Tennessee Sentinel* "has been slandering the ministers and members of the Methodist, and of every other church, who have dared to think differently from itself." Yet, "these pious brethren, who object to the severity of my paper, patronize the *Sentinel*—enjoy its abuse of their brethren—and read its contents with pleasure." The *Whig* editor had no intention of moderating his blows, as his enemies demanded. Instead he intended to increase them because the growing circulation of his newspaper, among subscribers of "respectability, and high moral and intellectual standing," comparable to those "of any newspaper in Tennessee or elsewhere" constituted approval of the way he was running it.

Ruthless enemies, who would spare him from attack only when they knew he was armed, forced him to

carry *Pistols*, aye, deadly weapons. Yes, I do, and I intend to do it. I have Pistols of a superior quality, and I always have them about me. I daily move in the midst of an unprincipled band of assasins [*sic.*], bloodhounds, and murderers, who seek my life, and nothing but my arms, and a belief on their part that I will use them, prevents them from attacking me. My weapons will hurt no man unless I am assailed, then, and in that case, I will use them. Last fall, it was gravely proposed, by a portion of the Democracy of Jonesborough, in a political caucus, to employ some two or more irresponsible characters to beat the life out of me, or forsooth, to tar and feather me! Others are carrying and have carried large *Republican Democratic Hickory Clubs*, for my benefit, and nothing but a fear of the consequences has prevented an attack. Under these circumstances I have been induced to go armed at all times, and I intend to continue this state of preparation. I am a poor man—all I have consists in and of a Printing Establishment—I have a wife and two small children to support—and to defend my life against the midnight assults of Locofocosim is a duty I owe to myself and the Whig Party (*Ibid.*).

Brownlow held that "the most contemptible trickery of which Locofocoism has been guilty" was the proposal of certain Presbyterians, and some who were members of no church, to join Methodism, "if I can be got out of it." He finished his defense with a tribute to the church, laced with some politics: "Infidelity must fall, sound principles must triumph, modern Democracy must go down, *Isreal* [*sic.*] must prevail." On the vote to aquit or censure, the Parson won, as he knew he would, 20 to 3 (*Ibid.*).

The mingling of religion and politics furnished a dramatic scene at a camp meeting in the summer of 1842, at a place and exact time not specified. It was early in 1843 before Brownlow wrote that on the occasion "We opened the door . . . as we were directed to do for the reception of members into the Church—making an argument of some length in favor of persons attaching themselves to the Church—and some thirty persons were added therein. . . ." Among them was one who reached out his hand for the Parson's, who turned from the supplicant and "left him to the agencies of those whose faith in his conversion was stronger than ours."[11] The penitent whose hand the Parson rejected was Landon C. Haynes. Brownlow's rigid unforgiveness at the altar must have brought sharp criticism, for the editor went to some pains on several occasions to justify his rejection of Haynes' hand. The younger man also made repeated offers of friendship, but Brownlow spurned them, stating:

His friendship for us is like Sampson's sleep; it is intended solely to deprive us of our locks. It is friendship of the nature of opium—intended to produce a loss of feeling—to put one off his guard—a presage of death.

Haynes got religion, the Parson observed, in much less time than most men:

He was thought to be some twelve or fifteen minutes only, in seeking and finding his Lord. Indeed we thought he had scarcely got upon his knees as a mourner, till [sic.] he was up, shouting, screaming, and cutting up some of the tallest shines we had ever seen (Ibid.).

Brownlow professed to have been astounded when Haynes threw his arms about the neck of W. B. Carter, who he had fought bitterly in the congressional campaign of 1839, "and confessed to him in the hearing of an hundred of us, that when he was opposing and abusing him he was *insincere*, that he had always liked him, though he was publicly and privately pretending otherwise" (*Ibid.*). Haynes originally was a Presbyterian. Brownlow called him "a Presbyterian imposter, as he himself confesses," and reproached his foe for revealing "confidential conversations" exchanged with Presbyterian ministers.[7] The Parson kept hammering away with his belief that Haynes' conversion was synthetic, citing that when the young convert did receive grace "it was obtained in about five or ten minutes. We were standing by, and such screams, such raising [sic.] up and down, and such a blowing of a long nose, we never witnessed" (*Whig*, February 1, 1843). The *Whig* was reviewing with unbelief Haynes' conversion until early in 1844 (*Whig*, February 14, 1844).

After Haynes had joined the Methodist Church, he lost little time getting into the ministry. He delighted in oratory; he probably saw that if he obtained a place in the Methodist organization above the rank of layman he would be better prepared to fight the Parson, now that all prospects for friendship were removed. This was not lost on the *Whig* editor, who grumbled:

He has been in the Methodist Church *five months* and in the Ministry five *weeks*; and he now looks to be put up on Sunday, at all popular meetings, and is really disappointed and displeased if he is not. Should he *"grow in grace,"* for the next five months as he has done for the five that are past, by next fall, he will attempt to supplant our Bishops, and preside at our Annual Conferences!

A shooting brought the controversy to a head in the Methodist Church. In the selection of arbitrators to settle a dispute over a load of tin, James H. Jones objected to William H. Crouch because the latter was *"a thick-headed man, and has not sense enough to do his own business."* Crouch did not like this accusation. They got into a fight, and Crouch was wounded. Brownlow's account of the affair infuriated Crouch's friends. As citizens lined up on either side, the dispute took on almost classic characteristics. Jones was a Whig and a Methodist; Crouch was a Democrat and he and his family "were enemies of the Methodist Church" (*Whig*, January 4, 1843). Haynes pushed into the battle, his partisanship putting him on Crouch's side, which enabled Brownlow to accuse Haynes of opposing Methodism. Two Methodist preachers reproached Haynes for getting into the dispute, telling him, "You had no business" to enter it, that it involved only Brownlow and the participants in the shooting. The preachers reported that Haynes said:

"I DID NOT WANT TO COMMENCE OR ENGAGE IN THIS CONTROVERSY BUT MY PARTY AND FRIENDS HERE WOULD GIVE ME NO PEACE TILL I AGREED TO DO IT—THEY SAID I MUST DO IT: AND AS I HAVE BEGUN I WILL HAVE TO GO THROUGH!!!"

The printing of this lame justification in his adversary's newspaper gored Haynes deeply. He insisted that he had said only that "friends" had persuaded him into this step and denied that he had mentioned pressure by Democrats. He faced the Rev. C. W. Harris, the Methodist preacher who had told the story to Brownlow, and accused Harris of lying. The quarrel now became a sustained uproar. The *Whig* devoted almost three pages of its issue of February 1, 1843, to Haynes and quoted him as having published this advice to the Parson:

But I cannot close this letter without admonitions to repentance. I have no other desires than those for the salvation of your sinblackened and sinpoluted [*sic.*] soul as I cannot but believe it to be. I ask you then to repent and turn from your thousand sins.

For though you may live in the follies of wickedness, you cannot, you will not, die a fool.[8]

The Jonesboro Circuit held its quarterly conference at Earnest's Chapel on Saturday, February 11, 1843. It unanimously cleared Harris of the accusation of falsehood brought by Haynes, and then charged the *Tennessee Sentinel* editor with falsehood and slander. Because Haynes pleaded he was not prepared, the trial was delayed. But while awaiting this hearing he pursued a course of violent hostility toward members of the conference who had voted against him. He even printed a defiance that stated, "We would like to see any Conference turn us out of the Methodist Church and leave William G. Brownlow in! They cannot do it—were it done IT WOULD SHAKE THE CHURCH INTO ATOMS!" Haynes was convicted by the quarterly conference at Bethesda on April 29, 1843, and silenced from preaching, but he found a new issue. The conference had voted to find Haynes guilty of falsehood and slander, 14 to 10, but on the question of silencing the members stood 12 to 12 until the presiding elder, Samuel Patton broke the tie, voting against the *Tennessee Sentinel* editor. The silenced minister charged one of the twelve votes cast against him was illegal, which would not have required Patton to decide the issue, and which would have left Haynes with his license. Patton held the vote was legal, and there the matter stood except for a mass of denunciations and vituperations erupting from both newspapers. Brownlow lost on one point. He claimed the conference had ejected Haynes from the church. Patton held it did not.[9]

So conflicting were the reports of the two contending newspapers and their partisans that Methodists from Blountville and Knoxville called upon the quarterly conference of the Jonesboro Circuit to provide a clarifying statement from the minutes. The statement supported the Brownlow-Patton position.[10]

Fifteen years later, in a strange aftermath, the same conference, on learning that Haynes still wanted to preach, voted to restore his license. He never claimed it. Brownlow was in Knoxville then, the pre-Civil War issues were raging and both men probably were too occupied otherwise to give the revival of an old grudge their attention.[11]

A side effect of the controversy was a rehash of the Jonesboro street fight of May 14, 1840, and the attempted assassination of the *Whig* editor at Elizabethton on March 2, 1840. Haynes tossed this taunt to Brownlow over the Jonesboro fight:

LIBEL!

"Superior Court of Law, Minute docket
April Term 1833.

"State,
vs.
"William G. Brownlow,

"Charged and plead not guilty. The following Jury sworn and Charged: (to wit:)
Daniel Rogers,   M. Wikly,
Samuel Wikly,   Jas Whitaker, Jr.
John Wyke,   Spencer Shearer,
George Penland+F. Poindexter,
Hartley Wilson, J. Pendigrass,
John Davis,   Grey Crow,

"Who find the defendant,

W. G. BROWNLOW
GUILTY

of the Libel as charged in the bill of indictment. Whereof the Court adjudged that the defendant pay a fine of five dollars. The parties having become mutually reconciled, defendant

Acknowledged

open Court, he was mistaken in the facts which he supposed were true when

WRITING THE
Libel!

"I, Silas M. Daniel, Clerk of the Superior Court of law for Macon county, do hereby certify that the above is a true copy of the proceedings held in this Court, in the case of the State against William G. Brownlow for a libel, as appears on the Minute docket for the April term, 1833. In testimony of which I hereunto subscribe my name and affix my seal of office, at office this 10th day May 1834

S. M. DANIEL, Clerk."

CERTIFIED.

"Capt. N. S. Jarret, Wm. Rinzy, Thos. Shepherd, Esq. T. Johnson, John More. Esq. Joseph A. Johnson, John M'Clure, Esq. T. A. Tanner, Nathaniel Hagan, Elijah Williamson, Nathan D. Ammons, Thos. Mc Clure, Thos. Kinsey, Capt, J. W. Killia

"I hereby certify, that after the difficulty between Col. Haynes and my brother Wm. G. Brownlow, in which the latter was wounded by the former, my esther

PRIVATELY

proposed to me that I should, by lying in wait at the forks of the road, 1½ miles East of Jonesboro', in the barrens, beyond widow Stuart's plantation, commit

MURDER!

by the assassination of Landon C. Haynes.
"A. S. BROWNLOW."

Known to be be monstrously corrupt, desperately wicked, a pest to society, a common tattler, a shameless blackguard, an unblushing hypocrite, a deliberate calumniator, a convicted libeller, we have determined that the above libel, and certificate of his brother shall be an eternal answer to any perseualities against us or others by Wm. G. Brownlow.

L. C. HAYNES.

CRIMINAL STATISTICS!

LANDON C. HAYNES !

The "ROORBACK" editor of the Jonesborough Sentinel, while a Whig, published articles in the "Elizabethton Republican," over his own proper signature, denouncing Dr. Chester of this town, as a CORRUPT man—Mr. Van Buren as a corrupt and black-hearted man, and GENERAL JACKSON (!) as having neither CIVIL or MILITARY TALENTS!!! When the late Presidential canvass opened between him and Mr. Nelson in this town, the latter quoted him against these great leaders, and the former plead the

INFANT ACT!!

alledging that he was a BOY at the time! Mr. Nelson procured the proof of his having been TWENTY-TWO YEARS OLD at the time, and tried afterwards to get him out again, but he kept dark about his age!

CASWELL TAYLOR, a very respectable gentleman, testifies that this Haynes once

Boasted

to him of having cheated his father's poor tenants out of their RENT CORN! in a settlement with them, which all know is as bad as

STEALING
CORN!

Col. AVERY, of North Carolina, testifies, that this
YOUTHFUL CRIMINAL
sat out in life, by palming upon him a

Diseased Hog!

that he afterwards pursued him—overtook him—and made him give up the money he had paid him!

Excerpts from one of the more odious exchanges between Wm. G. Brownlow and Landon C. Haynes. The original accusation was made by Brownlow in the *Whig* on July 16, 1845 and was repeated again and again. Haynes' reply appeared in the *Tennessee Sentinel* on July 19, 1845.

You will recollect, Minister of the Gospel, as you were, and perhaps, with your license in your pocket, you *sneaked* upon me, and with the *same hand* which had often held up the Bible in the pulpit, while you tried to preach, you drew upon me a five or six barrelled pistol, for the purpose of *murdering me*.

This terse account is at variance with those of the four witnesses whose statements were published by the *Whig* in 1840 and reprinted in it in 1843, with this comment:

On the occasion alluded to, we offered Haynes an honorable fight—we met him in open day, face to face, on the main street, and in the most business part of our touwn [*sic*]. We had previously notified him through our paper, that we would call him to an account, and we expected him to be prepared. We knew him not to be possessed of one honorable principle—we believed him to have been guilty of attempting to assassinate us, by being with or aiding and abetting those who fired on us through a window after night. Notwithstanding all this, we say we offered him an honorable fight—we met him openly and boldly—asked him *three times* if he were not armed, and he as often lied, saying he was not—when we shifted our pistol out of our right hand into our left, grasping it around the barrel, and taking the cane we were walking with, into our right hand. So soon as we did this, and incapacitated ourself to shoot, if we had been so disposed, this base, truckling, tool of tools, with that cowardice which has characterised his short, vascilating [*sic*] and infamous career, *stoled* [*sic*] out from behind him a pistol he had *cocked*, and which he had not only not *exhibited* but *three successive times* denied having, and fired on us.

The reopened dispute over the shooting at Elizabethton preceded an account that spread over five columns of the *Whig* of February 8, 1843. It produced the first—and only—existing defense against the accusations of Brownlow in the affair. Rather curiously, the *Whig* reprinted it from the Murfreesboro *Times* of August 29, 1840, over the signature of Haynes. This defense offered two points: that Brownlow had staged the shooting and that Haynes had an alibi, furnished in a statement by H. L. Dulaney, that he was with the young law student in Brewer's Hotel at the time the shots were fired. The *Whig* countered this with statements that Haynes was not at the hotel when the firings were heard but appeared very soon afterward and was "much agitated" (*Whig*, February 8, 1843).

The pistol that Brownlow fired that night when he ran out of his house and took aim at a fleeing form may have found a mark. A relative of the Powell family was confined to his bed for several weeks immediately after the shooting. The reason given for his being bedridden was that during a drunken frolic he had been pitched out a window and injured. The *Whig*, however, charged that this relative had confessed, in a drunken moment, that Brownlow's ball had wounded him. The Parson reported that upon the death of the relative "gentlemen of standing" examined the corpse and saw a round scar upon its thigh. He maintained that whoever may have shot at him, Haynes knew of the plot, even "if he did not *directly aid and abet* in the nefarious work." The Parson added this sentence in his continuing effort to justify his rejection of Haynes' hand at the camp meeting altar: "And for these and other reasons, we have no confidence in him, and cannot, and will not, whether in or out of the Church, repose confidence in him, or extend to him the hand of fellowship."[12]

The uproar led Brownlow to disclose in the *Whig* details of his arsenal. He owned two pistols, a single-shot, which he carried and for which he had paid $35.00, and a five-shot, costing $10.00, which he kept in a drawer at his office. It was patented by N. J. Colt. The editor had brandished a six-barrel pistol at a hearing in Sullivan County in the summer of 1842 (*Whig*, August 31, 1842). This gave rise to the impression he owned such a weapon, but he denied ownership, and revealed that the one he kept in his office had one barrel, "yet in the *breech part* of the instrument, *five loads* are deposited, and hence it is called a *five-shot* pistol."[13]

Brownlow's single-shot pocket pistol failed to fire at a critical moment that summer, and probably spared him from killing a fellow man in self defense. In reporting on a barbecue for James K. Polk as the Democrat made his second race for governor, the *Whig* accused Fayette McMullens, a state senator from Virginia who spoke at the Rogersville rally, of having stolen corn. A few days later as Sabbath preaching was under way at the Reedy Creek Campground, McMullens and some allies waylaid Brownlow and two companions as, arm-in-arm, they walked out at the gate. The *Whig* editor took nine blows from fists or clubs:

CORN-STEALING FAYETTE, rushed upon us with a stick—struck us in the back, and again on the back of the head in quick succession—which pitched us forward on our hands and knees—we instantly sprang to our feet—turned upon him, and presented at his bosom as good a single barreled Pistol as ever was fired, well loaded and primed, the cap only exploding! A friend afterwards took the same pistol, and without doing anything but to put on a new cap, burried [*sic*.] the ball in a log, the pistol firing as clear as a rifle. It is now owing to the veriest accident on earth, that the vile thief, blackguard, and debauched demagogue is not in eternity.

Principals on both sides were hustled off to a quick trial before a Sullivan County magistrate, where they were directed to leave their arms outside. A friend managed to slip Brownlow a weapon, and when McMullens drew a pistol halfway out of his bosom, the editor "eased a six barrel pistol out of our pocket, and politely bowed to him." The Parson was "barely acquitted," and a McMullens, not otherwise identified, was fined $5.00. Reporting the trial gave Brownlow an opportunity to probe more deeply into the background of McMullens, where he found, in addition to larceny, infidelity, and gambling, that McMullens had cheated on mileage collected as a state senator [*Ibid.*] .

Nature took a hand in the violence of the summer. A lethal bolt of lightning struck into a group of worshipers at Nelson's Campgrounds, near the present site of Johnson City, on the night of August 7, 1842. It killed two people and injured possibly a score. The bolt fell at 10 o'clock on a shelter where five or six hundred worshipers

most of whom were engaged in the exercises . . . had taken shelter from the rain. Nearly this entire assembly felt sensible the shock and so very much so indeed, that no sooner had the report of the thunderstroke died away in the distance, than one long, loud, continued scream, was heard in every direction (*Whig*, August 10, 1842).

The dead were Miss Mary Taylor, member of a prominent family of Carter County, and John Miller of North Carolina. The tragedy changed the course of Nathaniel G. Taylor's life, so stricken was he at the death of his sister. He had begun the practice of law, but in the tide of religious emotion that followed the deaths he delivered a "surpassingly fervid, impassioned and thrilling religious exhortation." Soon after this he became a Methodist minister.[14]

The catastrophe bred speculation, both pious and irreverent. The latter view carried a political tinge. The *Whig* saw the bolt *"as emphatically a work of Providence,"* designed to lead those who were present to set in order their spiritual houses; it found the benefits of the religious fire spread by the calamity most impressive:

SIXTY FOUR PERSONS were added to the Church, beside many obtaining a knowledge of sins forgiven. But only a fiend, and a political one at that, could account for the bolt as showing Divine disfavor because the campground had

been the scene of a Whig convention two years earlier. An individual who engaged in such speculation "deserves to have his fate chained to the wheels of
damnation, and the car of iniquity, and drawn by two mad bulls through brier
thickets, frog ponds, and log fires" (*Whig*, August 17, 1842).

The *Whig* kept a few other balls in the air in the controversies of
the early forties. Brownlow found the Mormons quite dangerous,[15] and the Baptists aggravated him into writing a book dis-
puting their doctrines, particularly that immersion is required for
Christian baptism. It was *Baptism Examined; Or the True State of
the Case. To which is prefixed a Review of the Assaults of the
Baptist and Pioneer. To which is also Added an Appendix.* It was
published at Jonesboro in 1842.[16]

Politically he wrangled with Thomas D. Arnold, a Whig whom he
and Thomas A. R. Nelson fought unsuccessfully as Arnold obtained
the First District congressional seat in 1841.[17] He broke with
President Tyler, who became chief executive upon Harrison's death a
month after inauguration. The *Whig*, embittered by Tyler's veto of
the National Bank Bill and by his failure to fire Democratic office-
holders and reward Whigs, called him a "*Long-eared Virginia Ass.*"
The cabinet, including the Parson's favorite, John Bell, but with the
exception of Secretary of State Daniel Webster, resigned when Congress adjourned in the fall of 1841.[18] Perhaps as a memorial to
Harrison the editor carried for a long time on page one, between *The*
and *Whig*, an illustration of a log cabin with a coonskin flung upon
the roof and a coon on each side of the structure. The log cabin and
the coon theme had played quite a part in Harrison's presidential
campaign, along with free barbecue and whiskey. The new page-one
device restored the five-column heading.[19]

If the Parson lacked human foes there were other animals, and in
the *Whig* of July 21, 1841, he served notice, "This is emphatically
Dog Town, a town litterally [*sic*.] overrun with dogs! There cannot
be less than 150 surplus dogs in this place," prowling through
gardens, backyards, smokehouses and kitchens. His expensive pocket
pistol proved inadequate to cope with the animals. Therefore he
loaded a double-barreled shotgun and "in two nights, we were enabled to shoot six." He looked forward to moonlit nights and "then,
no preventing cause, we will make them squat." This was a war he
carried on for years (*Whig*, July 21, 1841).

In the midst of these varied and extensive wars the Rev. William G.
Brownlow appeared in an almost unbelievable role, the champion of

young lovers. He was ready to unite eloping couples even at the risk of incurring parental displeasure for performing the ceremonies. In the *Whig* of March 9, 1842, as spring was beginning to stir, he laid out this policy:

> We have recently married several pair [*sic.*] of youngsters, who have either come to us, or sent for us, to perform the ceremony; but in no single instance have we, [*or will we*] since we have resided in the county, aided or abetted, directly or indirectly, by our advice or otherwise, either in carrying on a courtship, or in assisting the parties to get off. When individuals of respectability call on us to marry them, we do so, and will continue the practice.

As a general policy he disapproved of runaway marriages, as he did disobedience of parents by children; but exceptions should be made. Children of infidels, forbidden to attend church, should disobey. In the long run parents have better judgment than their young. "Nor shall we deny the right of parents to even kick up a dust, when a man of bad habits and morals is like to runaway [*sic.*] with a daughter." Yet, all runaway matches should not be condemned, for "in nine cases out of every ten that occur, the party stealing is at least equal to the plunder stolen, and one-half of all that have fallen under our notice, we believe to have been their *superior*" (*Whig*, March 9, 1842). Now, enchanted with the role of counselor, the Parson narrowed his advice:

> to young ladies, substantial young ladies—not the heartless and false doll of dress . . . never to take a husband for his carriage and his house—for his land and negroes, or to enter matrimony for the liberty it allows them. In other words, never marry an ASS—a stupid, beef-headed clown, because his father is wealthy, or because, forsooth, his industrious habits may have caught the attention of your parents. . .—Sooner "cut dirt" with a substantial young man—a man of sharply defined feelings, the beaming glances of whose liquid eye, promise something in future, though he may not now have the second shirt to his back.

The advice was extended, but accounts of weddings were terse. They appeared under one column headings of "Hymenial" or "Married" and usually gave only the date, the place, the names of the principals, and the officiating minister. Sometimes he listed the father of the bride, but never the mother unless she was a widow. When the bridegroom was a printer the *Whig* often identified him as such. Perhaps the compositor saw to this as a tribute to the craft.[20]

Compassionate as the *Whig* editor was toward young couples

yearning to be wed, he did not extend it to young men who treated lightly or took advantage of pledged young women. In a column adjoining his advice to the love lorn on March 9, 1842, he bore down wrathfully upon a defendant found to have seduced a girl and then violated his promise to marry her. The judgment of $2,225 Brownlow found inadequate: "A young man who will gain the affections of a respectable young woman, promise her marriage, and upon the faith of that promise seduce her, and abandon her, deserves to be kicked out of every decent company he falls into. Nay, more, he deserves to have his body chopped into pieces, and given to the dogs, and his soul sent to hell." The *Whig* not only printed the names of the litigants but also went a step further to present a fact of some significance, at least to the editor: "The parties . . . are all Democrats" (*Whig*, March 9, 1842).

Chapter III Notes

[1] *Whig*, August 12, 19, May 20, November 25, 1840, August 6, June 1, 1842. *Baldface* was a term for whiskey, used as a noun and as an adjective.
[2] For example, *ibid.*, September 23, 1840. The name of the town was spelled *Jonesborough* until some time after the Civil War.
[3] *Ibid.*, August 26, September 2, 1840.
[4] *Ibid.*, January 20, December 22, 1841, and thereafter.
[5] *Ibid.*, February 10, 1841; Brownlow to Temple, September 6, 12, 1859. Temple Papers.
[6] *Whig*, July 21, 21, August 6, 1841; Folmsbee *et al.*, *Short History*, p. 223; *Whig*, November 10, 1841, March 6, 1842.
[7] *Ibid.*, January 18, 25, 1843.
[8] *Ibid.*, February 1, 1843.
[9] *Ibid.*, February 15, 22, May 10, 1843.
[10] *Ibid.*, February 13, 1844.
[11] *Ibid.*, *Tri-Weekly Whig*, July 5, 12, 23, 30, 1859.
[12] *Whig*, July 5, 1851, February 8, 1843.
[13] *Ibid.*, January 4, February 15, 22, 1843.
[14] *Ibid.*, August 10, 1842; Temple, *Notable Men*, pp. 198-199; Folmsbee *et al.*, *Short History*, pp. 494-396. Nathaniel G. Taylor was the father of two Tennesseeans who served their state as governor, Robert L. Taylor and Alfred A. Taylor, Democrat and Republican, respectively, who campaigned against each other in what was known as "The War of the Roses." A grandson of Nathaniel G. Taylor is United States District Judge Robert L. Taylor of Knoxville, the son of Alfred A. Taylor. Judge Taylor followed the political course of his uncle, the Democrat.

[15] For examples see *Whig*, January 12, August 17, 1842.

[16] *Ibid.*, May 25, July 20, 1842. The *Baptist Banner and Western Pioneer* was published at Louisville, Kentucky, *ibid.*, February 15, 1842. James W. Patton, author of *Unionism and Reconstruction in Tennessee, 1860-1869*, wrote this author that the only copy of the book of which he has any knowledge is at Duke University.

[17] *Whig*, May 5, June 30, 1841, September 21, 1842; Temple, *Notable Men*, p. 61.

[18] *Ibid.*, August 25, November 24, September 15, 22, 1841.

[19] The altered page appeared in *ibid.*, May 28, 1841. See also Folmsbee *et al.*, *Short History*, p. 201.

[20] For examples see *ibid.*, October 14, 1840: "In Knoxville on the 8th inst. by Rev. Isaac Lewis, Sterling G. Murphey, *printer*, of this place, to Miss Susan E. Atkin, daughter of Widow Emily H. Atkin"; *ibid.*, May 1, 1867: "Married at the residence of the bride's father, Monday, the 27th of April, by Rev. Thomas H. Pearne, D.D., Esq., to Miss Mary, daughter of Gov. w.g. [*sic.*] Brownlow"; and with a political touch, *ibid.*, September 30, 1840: "In Kingsport, Sullivan County, on Tuesday the 22nd inst. by the Rev. James McLin, Mr. James Armstrong, of this place, to Miss Margaret W. Netherland, of Kingsport. All for Harrison, Tyler and reform."

THREE BRAWLERS OF DESTINY

William G. Brownlow entered the 1844 Presidential campaign exhilirated because the Whigs nominated his political idol, Senator Henry Clay of Kentucky, for President. He had raised Clay's standard on the editorial page of the *Whig* in the fall of 1841, soon after he broke furiously with President Tyler. For months thereafter as he flogged Tyler he exalted Clay. The Democrats nominated the Tennessee favorite son for President, James K. Polk, whom Brownlow had fought unsuccessfully in his first year as editor, 1839. But in 1841 and 1843 the Whigs defeated Polk with James G. (Lean Jimmy) Jones, a rail-like creature with only a moderate knowledge of public affairs but who possessed an uncanny ability to attract the rural electorate. When Polk ran against Jones the second time the former was burdened by the obstructionist record of "The Immortal Thirteen," a group of Democratic senators who blocked the election of two United States senators. This action left Tennessee unrepresented for two years rather than let Whigs serve there. They also rejected important items of Governor Jones' program. Public opinion set in against the Democrats, a trend the talented Polk could not reverse.[1]

But in 1844 Polk's political fortunes boomed nationally as he won the Democratic nomination for President. The *Whig* now had a quiver full of reasons to exalt Clay and to oppose Polk, along with its record of supporting one and opposing the other. Brownlow produced early in 1844 a book to promote the interests of Clay, the Whig Party and, of course, the author himself. It was entitled *A Political Register, Setting Forth the Principles of the Whig and Locofoco Parties in the United States, with the Life and Public Service of Henry Clay. Also an Appendix Personal to the Author; and a General Index.* The book contained 350 pages and apparently sold on a modest scale, for just before the Civil War the *Whig* shop offered it for the original price of $1.00 postage paid. Brownlow dedicated the book to Governor Jones.[2] The Parson campaigned in every direction. He filled the *Whig* with Clay songs; he was a delegate to the Baltimore convention where the Whigs nominated Clay. On his way to Baltimore he made several speeches, including one at Raleigh where the *Register* was delighted with "the way he did curry the Locofocos," and the *Standard* found his talk "smutty, ultra, insulting and blasphemous." When Brownlow heard Clay speak at Raleigh on April 13, 1844, it was as if the stars had clasped hands in ecstasy and danced across applauding heavens. The Kentuckian spoke for two hours and fifteen minutes, then "closed his able—aye—his omnipotent Address."[3]

The Parson was in a state of exhiliration, for in addition to his zest in campaigning for Clay he could boast that the circulation of his newspaper had reached between 2,000 and 3,000, the largest weekly circulation in the state. He defied his Jonesboro critics to do anything about his policies: "We edit and publish a newspaper for the benefit of our subscribers, and not for the town of Jonesborough. The two thousand subscribers to whom we send our paper, beyond the limits of the county, expect us to give them the news, and in doing so, to give them the *truth*, without consulting the wishes of a few selfish persons in this town." His exuberance led him to announce that when he moved the *Whig* into quarters formerly occupied by the *Tennessee Sentinel* the office was cleansed by fresh air, the application of lime to the walls and the singing of Clay songs by the Clay Club.[4] His conviction that his policy of piling invective and colorful abuse on as many adversaries as he could find was the road to success and grew so strong that in closing his fifth volume he flung out this tart observation:

We never can consent to conduct a paper that won't say *any thing* on *any subject* calculated to offend *any body*, provided truth warrant it, and the public interest require it. Such a tame, quiet and contemptible print is a curse to any community, an injury to any party, and can never be conducted by the Editor of this paper (*Whig*, May 1, 1844).

He boasted of his accuracy as a reporter, and attributed some of the rapid growth of the *Whig* to "the confidence the public repose in our statement of facts." He then proceeded to ice the slice of cake that he had cut for himself with the statement that in the five years in which he had been battling political foes, "never, in all that time have we been found to deviate from the truth," a statement to which his enemies surely took exception. And "severity" having proved such a boon to circulation, he promised more of it.[5]

The Tennessee Whigs fought so vigorously that they beat Polk in his home state by 113 votes, but the rest of the nation provided him with sufficient ballots to defeat Clay by an electoral vote of 170 to 105. Brownlow was crushed, but in the midst of catastrophe his unquenchable sense of humor flashed out this advice to his fellows who came to him to learn the outcome:

We reply, once for all, that you are beat, badly beat, and no mistake. And for those of you who took an active part in the contest, we are really sorry, for judging from your looks you must feel bad. You had better be *neutral* in politics, as *we* are, and when your party meets with defeat, you can bear it as we do, with good grace.

To be serious, however, we are not of those, who, after meeting with a Waterloo defeat, turn about and say we *expected* to be beaten, and had no hope of success. We have never been worse deceived in our lives. We had no idea of defeat, but, up to the melancholy hour of hearing from New York, we had every confidence in the success of our favorite candidate. We now confess, to all the world, that we have been the worst deceived man who ever gave an opinion relative to a coming event. We are now so perfectly astounded at the result that we know not what to say, or where to begin our remarks.[6]

Brownlow drew some comfort from the Whig vote in Tennessee, in which the electorate rejected the efforts of Polk and his mentor, Andrew Jackson, both men of political stature. The fight was bitter and harsh, for "in every town almost in Tennessee, has Mr. Clay been hung and burnt in effigy... Verily, the victory here is greater than any ever achieved in the civilized world; and the people, in voting as they have have passed a verdict upon the 10,000 lies perpetrated by the Locofocos upon the fair name of Mr. Clay." Defeat for Brownlow had been routine. He philosophized: "In five Presidential contests, we have never been on the successful side but once. And in twenty years, we have never lived but *one month* under an Administration of our choice."[7]

So sure was Brownlow that Clay would win that early in the year he had offered his *Whig* to Democrats on a seven-month basis, the subscriber to pay the money when, not if, Clay was elected, Two hundred people accepted this proposal and won. The editor woefully announced: "They will receive this week, their last number on that score, along with this, our receipt in full, for their payments, which have been made through the *ballot-box* with interest." The Parson, who never gambled, then was indicted for betting on an election. He accused Haynes of being behind the true bill. The State Supreme Court, sitting at Knoxville, advised judges and lawyers that this did not constitute a law violation, and the charge was wiped out by a directed verdict.[8]

The pangs of the 1844 defeat seemed to feed the Parson's resolution to carry the Whig banner, no matter how desperate the cause, for by midsummer of the following year he was the nominee for Congress. His opponent was the crafty and indomitable Andrew Johnson who was seeking re-election after serving his first term in the United States House of Representatives from the First Congressional District. Johnson was a member of the Tennessee Senate in 1842, when the General Assembly passed a redistricting bill that changed the political complexion of the First from Whig to Democrat, shifting the balance in his favor. Johnson was accused of having contrived to give the district a Democratic majority,[9] although his record shows that he voted against the bill that became law. During this session he also was one of "The Immortal Thirteen," a point which Brownlow utilized in his statement of principles at the campaign opening.[10]

Johnson had demonstrated his skill as a politician in 1843 when he stood off the aristocratic wing of the party in his district, which had recoiled at the thought of sending a tailor to Congress, and won the nomination.[11] The Whigs, disheartened at what gerrymandering had done to their prospects, failed to nominate. Brownlow, faced with the prospect of supporting a Democrat or no one, because Johnson's only adversary was John A. Aiken of Johnson's own party, engaged in political buffoonery. Much earlier the Parson had predicted Democrats would carry the district, and expressed the hope that they would choose Johnson, because he "is mean, corrupt, selfish, and notoriously reckless," and added, "The leaders of his party in this district, all hate him, because he is in their way. This is the true secret of their hate, and for this reason alone, we hope he will be the nominee." Three weeks later he offered another backhanded reason for supporting Johnson: "Aiken is a much more genteel man than Johnson, but we want the Locos to have the next Congress, and to go the whole dog against the interests of the country. Aiken would not do this, while Johnson would, which explains our preference." Next, Brownlow wrote of Johnson: "We are sorry that we stand committed to his support [*sic*.], he is such a notorious demagogue. But what better can we do. Colonel Aiken is also a Democrat!" The *Whig* switched to Aiken when Johnson denied Brownlow's charge, an unsubstantiated one, that a cousin of his, Madison Johnson, had been hanged at Raleigh, North Carolina, for murder and robbery. He decided to abandon Johnson, saying, "It is bad enough to have mean kin, but it is much worse to deny them."[12]

The Parson's clowning ended with Johnson's election as he exploded: "God of compassion! What could the people have been thinking of when they elected this huge mass of corruption to Congress!—this beast in human form, whose violence and rule of passion, vicious life and unprovided death, alone qualify him to serve as one of the body guards of Belzebub! [*sic*.]" (*Whig*, December 13, 1843).

The reason for Brownlow's race against Johnson two years later remains obscure. When the Whigs nominated the Parson he published an extra (*Whig*, June 25, 1845), containing a statement that was part clowning, part self-ridicule, but an acceptance, along with an admission that he had said he would never declare for public office:

> But the sovereign people having met in their primary assemblies, without my knowledge or consent, and having declared me to be *their* candidate, and avowed their determination to vote for me at all hazards, I am too much of a *patriot*, too warmly attached to the interest of my country, to decline serving them, to the best of my abilities, if elected, as I in all probability will be! (*Whig*, June 25, 1845, Extra).

He had expected some such honor for years, "And although I have never complained, yet I will not disguise the fact that I considered public opinion a *little slow* in its movements toward me." Election would add nothing to his character and fame, but "I, will greatly adorne [*sic*.] the office of a representative in the American Congress! The truth is, [think me not egotistic] I am well and favorably known, from the lakes of Canada, to the Gulf of Mexico, and to upper Missouri." He might even be nominated for President in 1848 (*Ibid*.).

Perhaps Brownlow wrote as he did to get attention; perhaps it was a shaft against the scores of affected, trite, stuffy and pompous acceptances he had read or heard in his career. He must have sent laughter rolling across the district, and furthered his reputation—and circulation—for doing the unpredictable. But his tone was deadly serious when he issued a statement of his principles ten days later. It was set in wide measure, some of it in 12-point type, much of it in blackface. It occupied the front page of the *Whig* of July 16, 1845, and spilled over to the next page. He condensed his Whig principles in a first paragraph, opened up on Johnson's record in Congress, then touched upon one of the most heated aspects of the campaign, Brownlow's editorial upon the death of Andrew Jackson, printed shortly after the editor's nomination (*Whig*, July 16, 1845]. It opened thus:

> After a life of eighty long years, spent in the indulgence of the most bitter and vindictive passions, which disgrace human nature, and distract the human mind, the existence of Andrew Jackson terminated, at his residence near Nashville, on Sabbath the 8th inst., at 6 o'clock P.M. We were not prepared to hear of his death, because for every few weeks in the year, for the last five years, we have noticed a letter in the paper, from him to "Dear Blair" or some one else, in which, he would speak at length of his failing health . . . each letter seeming to be the last (*Whig*, June 16, 1845).

During Jackson's last days he had permitted himself to be surrounded by associates who employed themselves in "stirring the embers of his dying resentments and depraved vindictiveness which made his heart, through a long career in life, a volcano of furious and ungovernable passions!" The Parson considered the elevation of Jackson to the Presidency as "the greatest curse that ever befell this nation," and laid to his administration all the evils besetting the country. He closed with this prediction on the destination of the "mock Hero's" soul:

> But he is "gone to a land of deepest shades," and we are willing to take our leave of him. He has passed out of our hands, into the hands of a just God, who will deal with him and by him "according to his works." We would not, if even we could, turn aside the veil of the future, to show his deluded followers, and blind admirers, what awaits him! (*Ibid.*).

The Parson's announcement for Congress noted:

> The mourning and sighing of Mr. Johnson over an obituary notice of Gen. Jackson in my paper of the 17th of June, as he reads it to the people, is equalled only by the lamentations of *Jeremiah*, on a much more important occasion!—I take back nothing I said in that article, and I said nothing that I did not most conscientiously believe. I felt nothing on the occasion of hearing that Gen.

Jackson was dead: neither regret nor satisfaction—neither pleasure nor pain. Had I said that I regretted his death, or venerated the man, I would have played the hypocrite; I am too honest and too candid to display the outward badge of a mourning which is not felt in my heart (*Whig*, July 16, 1845).

Typographically the *Whig* gave Jackson the printer's salute and final tribute—the turned rules, dividing the columns of type with heavy black lines, compared with the standard thin lines (*Whig*, June 16, 1845). Brownlow's obituary editorial was a singular prelude to a campaign by a Whig in a Democratic district. If Brownlow designed it to attract the votes of the many anti-Jackson Democrats, it may have had the opposite effect, for even in these days of atrocious personal slurs it must have repelled some Jackson haters. It was probably born of pure vindictiveness on the Parson's part, for it displayed no softening of his hatred. Aware of this, he reminded his readers that Johnson, on the floor of the Tennessee General Assembly, had denounced Hugh Lawson White, a Whig Party saint, " 'for a traitor,' a 'Federalist,' a 'viper and snake, who went out of this world, striking at honest men and patriots!' " (*Whig*, July 16, 1845).

The Parson also found time and space to touch up Landon C. Haynes, who was running for the state House of Representatives and who had joined Johnson in condemning Brownlow for this editorial on Jackson. He described the two as "This pair of villains . . . shedding tears over our obituary notice of Gen. Jackson," and he worked in another reminder of Haynes' youthful anti-Jackson articles. The ugly tone of the campaign was further reflected in the reason Brownlow gave for not meeting Johnson on the stump, that on the first time they faced each other the result would be a "personal difficulty." The Parson also directed at Haynes a lurid broadside in the *Whig*, set up like an advertisement and run in a column adjoining space purchased by merchants and tradesmen. It led off with "Criminal Statistics! Landon C. Haynes," and artfully listed in large black type these subheadings: "Stealing Corn," "Diseased Hog," "Campmeeting Confession," "Drunken Locofoco," "Expelled," and "Flasehood and Slander." The Parson had some damaging facts in his presentation, and the dress he gave it was masterfully vile.[13] Haynes snapped back with a similar typographical gem, not as long but which led off with Brownlow's conviction for libel in North Carolina. He struck one blow that must have had a shattering effect on Brownlow. It was a statement from his brother, A. S. Brownlow, which read:

I hereby certify, that after the difficulty between Col. Haynes and my brother, Wm. G. Brownlow, in which the latter was wounded by the former, my rother [sic.]

PRIVATELY

proposed to me that I should, by lying in wait at the forks of the road, 1/2 mile East of Jonesboro, in the barrens, beyond widow Stuart's plantation, commit

MURDER

by the assassination of Landon C. Haynes.

A. S. BROWNLOW

Haynes added this brief oration over what he may have regarded as the Parson's political and newspaper coffin:

Known to be monstrously corrupt, desperately wicked, a pest to society, a common tattler, a shameless blackguard, an unblushing hypocrite, a deliberate caluminator, a convicted libeller, we determined that the above libel, and certificate of his brother shall be an eternal answer to any personalities against us or others by Wm. G. Brownlow.

L. C. HAYNES[14]

The *Whig* failed to collapse. The editor came back with an extra, the lead article headed "A CALM ADDRESS, To the candid of all parties." It was anything but calming in detailing the trail of circumstances that led to the signing of the certificate by the Parson's brother. Alexander drank heavily and under the influence of alcohol became quite dangerous. In one of these moments he had cruelly assaulted R. M. Bishop, a *Whig* employee. T. A. R. Nelson, the attorney general, called for stiff punishment and the execution by the defendant of a peace bond. Upon Alexander's promise to behave he was fined $50.00 and directed to make a $500 bond. Alexander failed to behave, made threats, was jailed. An arrangement was worked out under which two men went his bond, not that they were interested in Alexander but that they saw in him an instrument with which to torpedo the Parson.[15] The *Whig*'s version was:

Democrats of this village taking advantage of the relations existing between Alexander Brownlow and myself, and his unfortunate propensity to indulge in the use of ardent spirits, first procured him to publish a false certificate againt [sic.] me, and then kept him in pay to bully me, urging him to shoot me, and furnishing him with a shot gun for the purpose, as he solemnly swears under oath, in the hope that by falsehoods and misrepresentations, they might finally urge him on to imbure [sic.] his hands in a brother's blood, while they would

stand off, and with a fiendish delight and savage maliginity, enjoy the scene!—
(*Whig*, August 2, 1845, Extra).

Brownlow produced documents to support his story and came up
with one that was a reporting exploit, a bond behind a bond. This
hitherto secret instrument, signed by fifty-six men, indemnified the
two bondsmen of record for Alexander against having to put up the
$500 if he violated the bond. In this secret list of indemnifiers were
two men who made top pledges of $30.00 each if Alexander failed to
keep the terms. They were Landon C. Haynes and A. Johnson.[16]
The Parson then unloaded this fresh blast against his adversary:

ANDREW JOHNSON is my opponent for Congress, and on Monday of the late
Circuit Court, called for me when he had spoken, to come and defend myself,
and had my brother there intoxicated, to assault me with weapons, so soon as I
had appeared! . . .

I may be murdered in my house in the dead hour of the night—my blood may
be most villainously shed, by those who watch my path by night, or lay in
weight [*sic*.] at noon day, but with my latest breath, I will expose these corrup-
tions—I will act upon my motto which is *"cry aloud—spare not."* And if attacked in day light by many or few, in an open and manly war I promise to fall,
if fall I must, with my feet and face to my foes! And for the support of a poor
and helpless family, I will trust to a kind Providence, and the magnanimity of a
party with whom I have acted long, and for whom I have labored hard.

Alexander made an affidavit that the certificate he had given Haynes
was false, signed when "I was kept continually in liquor and in a
situation to do anything I was called on to do."[17]

Johnson went back to Congress and Haynes was elected a state
representative. Brownlow sought consolation in the reflection he had
been beaten by 1,200 votes after a redistricting designed to give the
Democrats a district majority of 2,800. He had announced late, had
never left home, and "had no right to look for anything but defeat."
When the campaign was ended, Johnson gave Brownlow credit for
having made a dent in the often repeated charge that he was an
infidel. Because the believer accepts the existence of Satan along
with God, Johnson vowed he had demonstrated belief in the devil,
for he had actually campaigned against him. The Parson sought consolation in a different direction. He took himself and his family to
the Brush Creek Campground, where he found that out of nineteen preachers, only five were Locofocos.[18]

Three men and two newspapers that summer had fought a battle of vilification, a field in which all were eminently skilled. Yet out of this verbal clawing and flinging of sewage emerged no litigation, civil or criminal. They asked the courts for no redress, no prosecution for assault, slander or libel. The people were their courts and in this forum they fought for years.

An attempt to "moderate the *Presses* of this town [Jonesboro], and to confine them within certain bounds!" was made in May of 1844, the presidential campaign year. A Vigilance Committee was organized after the killing of a young saddle maker. The vigilantes immediately drew Brownlow's fire: "We are advocates of law and order, and have been waring [*sic.*] against the bad conduct of citizens ever since we lived here. But we are for suppressing riots in a lawful way." He accused the committee of favoring the wealthy and the influential while terrorizing the poor and unimportant. His indignation flowed more furiously when he heard the vigilantes had developed a plan to gag both newspapers, a scheme in which he said Haynes had acquiesced. Friends of the *Whig* immediately got word to Brownlow that the real reason for such an arrangement was not to restore peace and order but to silence his newspaper. The editor moved swiftly:

We issued an *Extra* this morning after this high handed measure of dictation was put on foot—informed the public generally, and our friends in particular, that this was a villainous Locofoco movement—that their own Press was down, had fought itself out of subscribers, character and influence, and that, now, its party were [*sic.*] willing to send it to a "lower deep," if they could but send ours with it.

Brownlow had also planned to give a further exposure of the plot from a goods box on the public square, but when he was informed that the movement had died after his revelation of it he cancelled his appearance. In a letter to T. A. R. Nelson he revealed more details than he did in the *Whig*. He told how the true purpose of the scheme was conveyed to him and how threats of physical violence were made to him as he sat in a store after publication of the extra by a lawyer who "had with him six or eight Loco, cutting sticks with open knives."[19]

Another effort to destroy the *Whig* followed the searing campaign of 1845. Brownlow charged that the Democrats had discussed removing his printing equipment and tarring and feathering the editor and possibly setting fire to him in this condition. The *Whig* delivered a sermon on the evils of mob law, the low morals of Jonesboro, the attempt to restrict the freedom of the press, and the increase of crime, developments for which the Parson held the Democrats were responsible. The Democrats were distressed because in winning they had lost their best voices on the local scene. Johnson was going back to Washington, as they had expected, but the fiery Haynes was leaving his post as editor of the *Tennessee Sentinel* to go to the legislature. He made his farewell in five and one-half columns of type which Brownlow described as "consisting mostly of abuse of us."[20] The faltering Democratic newspaper lasted into June 1846. The lusty *Whig* survived.[21]

As December 1845 arrived the Parson felt the sharp teeth of a foe so powerful that he wrote of it with awe, without a trace of railing:

Truly, the last month of Autumn is gone, and stern old Winter is here! It is a monster without a head, and cannot think; it has no heart and cannot feel; it moves but in wrath; it pauses to exult over its work of destruction;—and if for a moment it stops in its flight, it is to whet its frozen beak on some cold mountainside, for more sanguinary destruction! (*Whig*, December 10, 1845).

The summer had been hot, campaigners spit hatred against each other while the sun joined to broil their bodies. But now congealing cold had settled upon the earth and encompassed all human creatures with its icy claws, except when they could flee to the warmth of a fireplace, or sink deep into the softness of a feather bed. However much the Parson's body may have been chilled as he sat writing in the drafty print shop, in his heart burned a gentle, worshipful glow, and the pen that had all but scorched the paper as he consigned his enemies to hell, scratched out a reverent Christmas editorial, the nearest to a sermon which has been preserved among his writings:

Tomorrow is Christmas Day. Tomorrow, churches will be crowded, altars illuminated—and bells will sound joyfully.—Throngs of worshipers in the Greek, Syrian, Armenian, Roman and English churches will march up to their altars to-morrow, and, according to the forms of their respective churches, worship the God in whom they profess to believe, and to whom they expect to give an account for the deeds done in the body—at least such of them as believe in rewards and punishments, after death. Meanwhile, another and a still more numerous class of human beings, will on to-morrow, be engaged in serving the Devil at a rate and after a fashion, that will make Heaven weep, all good men sorrowful and Hell shout for joy!

Eighteen hundred years ago, and upwards, a poor *Babe* was born in a *Stable*, in the vicinity of Jerusalem, and a few lonely Sheperds [*sic.*] heard heavenly voices, warbling over the moonlit hills so softly, proclaiming *"peace on earth, and good will towards men."* Earth—cold hearted earth, made no response to the chorus; either from the want of proper feeling, or because it delighted in the entertainment of angels *unawares*. The former, we should say, because when the HOLY ONE came among the inhabitants of the earth, they mocked and crucified him. But now, the stars in their midnight course listen to millions of human voices and deep organ tones soaring upwards, vainly striving to express the hopes and aspirations, which that advent concentrated from the past, and prophesied for the future. From East to West, from Nor [*sic*] to South, men of every age and station chant hymns of praise to the despised and crucified *Nazarine* [*sic*] and kneel and worship in honor of his cross. How beautiful is this universal homage to the Prince of Peace! Now, however little delight a corrupt and darkened world may take in the mercy of Christ's divine perfections, how small soever the enjoyment it yields them, to contemplate the untainted glory of Christ; how insipid the things of salvation may be to an earthly understanding; however this great theme of redemption may fall upon the heavy ears of a listless world without making any impression; the Bible tells us that the sinless spirits that surround Christ's throne, who are transported with all the ecstasy of an overwhelming affection, and lend themselves in rapturous adoration at the shrine of infinite and unspotted purity; and behold with heavenly fascination that moral beauty, which throws a softening lustre over the awful grandeur of a crucified and risen Saviour! Well may adoring millions—aye, myriads, gaze upon this Redeemer—stretching all their faculties, and bending their eyes toward the throne, which has the firm pillars of immutability to rest upon, linked with the fulfillment of Christ's glorious promise to man! This is the divine idea which distinguishes ours from all other religions. See the wonder working Saviour, who has strewed the field of immensity with so many worlds, and spread the shelter of his omnipotence over them—see the everlasting Son, moving from his dwellingplace in heaven, to carry forward this scheme of redemption; through all the difficulties by which it is encompassed! O Christ! Thou are great in counsel! Thou art the wonderful counseller! [*sic.*]

Centuries have passed, and through infinite conflict have "ushered in our brief tomorrow;"—and is there peace and good will among men? Sincere faith in the words of Christ would soon fulfil [*sic.*] the prophecy which the angels sung. But the world persists in its sinful course—the same course which bound the Saviour [*sic.*] down to the burthen of this mysterious antonement . . . .

Those who dare to trust the principles of Christianity have always found them perfectly safe. They can never prove otherwise. If all nations could but attain to such high wisdom and faith, they would abjure war and proclaim peace and good will towards all men . . . The world has been deluged with arguments about war, slavery, democracy, commerce &*c*., and the wisest product of them all, is simply an enlightened application of the principles of Christ. His doctrines are not beautiful abstractions, but living vital truths . . . Like the algebraic *x* they stand for the unknown quantity, and if rightly consulted always give the true answer (*Whig*, December 24, 1845).

The Parson was a man of many moods.

CHAPTER IV NOTES

[1] Folmsbee *et al.*, *Short History*, p. 207; *Whig*, September 6, 1841; Folmsbee *et al.*, *Short History*, pp. 202-205; *Whig*, February 9, November 16, 1842, July 3, June 12, May 15, 1844.

[2] *Ibid.*, January 17, 1844, March 3, 1860. Copies of the book now bring from $50.00 to $80.00. Prices were furnished by John Dobson, Special Collections librarian, University of Tennessee.

[3] *Whig*, April 3, 24, May 1, 8, April 24, 1844.

[4] *Ibid.*, May 22, 29, September 4, 1844.

[5] *Ibid.*, May 1, 8, 1844.

[6] Folmsbee *et al.*, *Short History*, p. 208; *Whig*, November 20, 1844. Early in the spring Brownlow was convinced that Clay would win, writing, "I never saw Clay look better than at present. He is better calculated to make votes before a crowd than any man I ever saw try it," and "The Locofoco Party are [sic.] perfectly disbanded and they [sic.] acknowledge it. They [sic.] are a gone party and intend to tell all they [sic.] know on each other, and that is not a little!" Brownlow to Nelson, April 20, May 13, 1844. Nelson Papers.

[7] *Whig*, November 20, 1844.

[8] *Ibid.*, February 14, November 20, 1844, October 1, 29, 1845.

[9] *Ibid.*, July 16 extra, June 25, 1845; Temple, *Notable Men*, pp. 62, 216-217; *Acts of Tennessee, 1852, Special Session*, Chapter VII, p. 22.

[10] *Senate Journal, 1842, Special Session*, pp. 181-182. The 1842 act re-apportioning the congressional districts did not entirely suit the Whigs, but they accepted it rather than let the state go unredistricted. The Parson acknowledged that the measure would give the Democrats a 700 majority in the First District, but his outcry was not strident. *Whig*, November 23, 1842. Johnson was responsible for the legislation, but no reason is offered as to why he voted against it. LeRoy P. Graf and Ralph Haskins, eds., *The Papers of Andrew Johnson*, 4 vols. to date, I, xxvi. A contemporary of Johnson's, who also ran against him, described him as having maneuvered the redistricting, but does not mention the opposition vote. *Notable Men*, pp. 62, 216-217. See also *Whig*, July 16, 1845; Folmsbee *et al.*, *Short History*, p. 204.

[11] Temple, *Notable Men*, p. 62; Robert W. Winton, *Plebian and Patriot* (New

York, 1928), p. 42; *Whig*, April 5, December 18, 1843.

[12] *Ibid.*, April 5, 26, May 3, 10, 1843.

[13] *Ibid.*, July 16, and thereafter through October 1, 1845.

[14] *Tennessee Sentinel*, July 19, 1845. Newspaper miscellany on microfilm, McClung Collection. See also newspaper miscellany, not on microfilm, McClung Collection.

[15] *Whig*, August 2, 1845, extra.

[16] *Ibid.*

[17] *Ibid.*, July 5, 1851.

[18] *Ibid.*, August 20, 27, 1845. Temple estimated the First District gerry-mandering gave the Democrats a majority of 1500. Temple, *Notable Men*, p. 378.

[19] *Whig*, May 29, 1845; Brownlow to Nelson, May 29, 1845, hand delivered to Nelson at Rogersville. Nelson Papers.

[20] *Whig*, September 10, 17, October 10, 1845.

[21] Lawson and Francis Gifford announced that after "ten years of vigilance and struggle," the *Tennessee Sentinel* would be discontinued. *Old Hickory*, Jonesboro, June 1, 1846. The Giffords sold their interest to William H. Smith who operated the newspaper under the name of *Old Hickory* and *Hickory State Herald* before abandoning the field to the *Whig*. Paul M. Fink, "The Early Press of Jonesboro," ETHS *PUBL*. No. 10, November 1938, p. 65.

THE WHIG.

| "Cry aloud—Spare not; show my people their transgressions, and the house of Jacob their sins."—Scripture | Chapter No. 5 |

THE JONESBORO YEARS

Parson Brownlow was licking the wounds inflicted by Andrew Johnson in their congressional race when he came upon an exciting new controversy, this time in the denominational field. He heard a debate in Sullivan County between the Rev. Frederick A. Ross, Presbyterian, and the Rev. William H. Rogers, Methodist, upon the argument of Ross that *"The doctrine of the Direct Witness of the Spirit, as taught by the Rev. John Wesley, was false, unscriptural, fanatical, and of evil or mischievous tendency."* The preachers volleyed at each other from 10:00 a.m. until sundown, and the discussion must have been stimulating for 2,000 heard the speakers out, and a friend of Ross' asked Brownlow the cost of having 2,500 copies of the debate printed (*Whig*, August 20, 1845).

The Presbyterian Church, alarmed at the growth of Methodism, had undertaken to counter its spiritual rival by reviving the *Calvinistic Magazine*, formerly published at Rogersville, Tennessee, but now issued at Abingdon, Virginia. In Ross they found a competent spokesman for their cause in pulpit and in print. He was a wealthy and philanthropic landowner and manufacturer, with a fine education. Ross, along with James King, James McChain, and Isaac Anderson, founder of the seminary at Maryville, were editors, but Ross carried the burden of the fight against the Methodists. The Presbyterian campaign was a general one, approved by the Tennessee Synod and justified:

For the previous twelve years, the Methodists had been allowed a clear field to abuse and misrepresent Presbyterians . . . almost nothing had been done, during this period, to refute these slanders and disabuse the public mind of these representations . . . Methodists were still pursuing this course of abuse, misrepresentation and proselytism and were spreading through this region of the country a vast amount of fanaticism and false religion.[1]

Methodist preachers, their guns already hot, replied at once from the pulpit, and the church established at Knoxville its own organ, the *Methodist Episcopalian*. It was edited by the Rev. Samuel Patton, Brownlow's friend.[2] The *Whig* editor could not resist such an inviting controversy, although for his forum he relied solely on the pulpit. He used his newspaper to announce a list of six appointments at which he would reply to Ross in a speech of three hours. But, with the exception of an outline of his position, he promised to keep the controversy out of the *Whig* (*Whig*, December 9, 1846), and made this uncharacteristic condition:

> To the idle statements of certain personal enemies of mine, relative to my *abuse* of Mr. Ross and the Presbyterians, I shall pay no sort of attention. *Abuse* of Mr. Ross or of the Presbyterian Church is no *answer* to his grave charges against the Methodist Church. Beside, I show that *Rossism* is one thing, and *Presbyterianism* another.—I shall introduce my addresses on these several occasions, as I did in September, by stating that Mr. Ross is a gentleman in private life—an obliging neighbor—a scholar—and a Minister of the first order of talents in the Church to which he belongs (*Ibid.*).

The contest grew more heated, a development to be expected with Brownlow on one side. Neither did Ross contribute to a calm, dispassionate discussion, for while he did not single out individuals for scurrility, his indictments of the Methodists were harsh and insulting. He charged them with having copied some of the practices of the Roman Catholic Church, described the intimate class meetings as "the swap of sins," and likened them to the confessional. Protestant Methodists were infuriated at being likened to Roman Catholics, but Ross went a step further. He hinted at something beneath delicacy as women at these meetings examined each other of their fleshly temptations.[3] His language was colorful, as shown in this passage as he sized up Roman Catholicism, the Church of England, and the Methodists:

> *Old Romanism* is too gross as yet for this land, and our people are aroused to abhor and watch it. *High Church Episcopacy* is a thing of exclusiveness, and has no affinities for the people, and will hurt none but the select few, who may rely upon sacrements [*sic.*] and genuflections. But this *Young Romanism* has not the geegaws, and paint, we see upon the drunken *grandmother*. Nor has she the old-fashioned headgear, the smirking fan, the stays, the hoops, the satin-spangled train, and the high-heeled shoes of the Puseyite *mother* of England.[4]

A dozen years earlier in *Helps to the Study of Presbyterianism* Brownlow had accused this denomination of grasping for temporal power. Ross now accused the Methodists of moving in that direction:

Animated by two great controlling principles—the *fanatical* and the *political* . . . the fanatical Methodist acts supremely for Methodism. He is honest; he would die for Methodism heartily, if the *convenient* doctrine of *falling from grace* did not teach him the *folly* of *dying* for his *religion*. The political Methodist, may be free from fanaticism. Then he goes just for himself. He may not care a straw for Methodism. He may be a Methodist to sell a yard of calico, or to buy votes to make him constable, clerk, sheriff, member of Assembly or Congress. Another may, however, be very much a Methodist as well as a politician. He will, of course, be swayed by the one or the other impulse according to *expediency*. *Now* you may see him all for the camp-meeting altar, the groan and the shout. *Now* all for the ballot-box, while hugging a voter round the neck at the Whiskey barrel. [5]

The Parson tried to keep the controversy out of the *Whig*. He extended his speech to more than four hours and resorted to a separate publication devoted to Ross, the *Jonesborough Quarterly Review*. In a few months he shifted it to the *Jonesborough Monthly Review*, with a promise it would be "less *smutty* than our Quarterly has been."[6] The Parson reflected Methodist resentment of Ross' slur on the sexually exciting nature of the questions posed in the class meetings of women. He stormed that Ross "represents '*every married woman and single girl*' in the Methodist Church, who attends these meetings, as liable to be *seduced* by Methodist Preachers—Class and Band Leaders."[7]

The injection of a political issue intensified the fight. At Athens in October 1846 the Synod of the New School Presbyterian Church officially approved Ross' course and his writings. It also took a further step that raised hackles on Methodists. It called on the bench and bar to "unite with the opposition to Methodism to put it down, and to do it away *now*, because it is '*dangerous to civil and religious liberties*,' and '*death to all the institutions for which Washington bled and freemen died*.' " The Methodist response was sharp. The quarterly conference of the Jonesboro Circuit, with Brownlow officiating as secretary, passed resolutions that defended the church, called on all Methodists to abstain from communion at the hands of any preacher who had taken part in the synod's action at Athens, and demanded the names of lawyers who made donations to "what is called the secret fund for putting down Methodism." Thirty-seven preachers and laymen, who met at the Stone Dam Campground of the Rheatown Circuit on September 21, 1847, went on record "that in future we cannot and will not support men for offices of honor and profit who endorses [sic] Mr. Ross' slanders, or who agree with him, that the Civil authorities of the country should interpose their power and influence to put us down." The quarterly conference of the Greenville Circuit adopted similar resolutions. [8]

Because the quarrel was now on the political level the Parson flung the *Whig* into the controversy. He protested that the Methodists had not followed religious affiliations in their political choices.

But how are matters and things, in those quarters, whence come all these complaints? Who have charge of all the public Colleges, Academies, and Schools in the Country? Who *force* upon these institutions their Presidents and Professors? Who have monopolized all the Common School funds in the Country?— Who fill all the Clerkships in the several counties? Who are the Sheriffs? Who are the Registers and Trustees of the Counties? Generally speaking they are our Presbyterian friends, placed there with the aid of Methodist votes; when, as all know, their own friends and brethren were just as capable. If the county is Whig, Presbyterian Whigs fill the offices. If the county be Democratic Presbyterian Democrats fill the offices. In either, and every case, it is a *Presbyterian* triumph! And now that the Methodists, who are greatly in the majority, propose to *divide* the spoils with them, a great hue and cry is raised against them (*Whig*, November 10, 1847).

By midsummer of 1848 Brownlow had returned to a more normal role and trained upon Ross this diatribe:

We tell all whom it may concern that he is deficient in all that constitutes a man, except it be in talents alone, and his are certainly respectable. But what is he in *principle*? He is a vituperative and envenomed slanderer. He is a hypocrite in religion. He is a heartless and dishonest knave, who can now, only be regarded with feelings of the deepest detestation. A *spendthrift*, he had brought his family to the verge of poverty and want. A *blackguard*, he has become hateful in the eyes of those who once regarded him as trying to conduct himself prudently. An adulterer, he has polluted the marriage bed with the refuse of the common stew. A liar, a coward and a *common slanderer*, known and recognized as such, here in Tennessee where he resides [sic] it will soon be esteemed a disgrace to be thought of as his friend (*Whig*, June 21, 1848).

The brawling wore wearily to an end. Brownlow published his last

Review in April 1849 and moved on to new controversies in Knoxville. The *Calvinistic Magazine* made its last appearance in December 1850. Ross was ruined financially. He had lost his large fortune in unsuccessful manufacturing ventures and was reduced to preaching for a living. Out of his own funds he had built a brick church at Kingsport and preached there for thirty years without salary. After leaving Kingsport he preached for a number of years at Huntsville, Alabama.[9]

The *Whig* editor's quarrel with Ross brought a temporary coolness between Brownlow and his old friend, Thomas A. R. Nelson, who was an elder in Ross' church. The difference arose over a contribution by Nelson to help finance Ross' pamphlet on the direct witness of the spirit. It was aired in letters published in the *Whig*, rather stiff, but moderate for the times, and Brownlow later revealed that Nelson had written Ross a letter in which he objected to his reflections on Methodist women and girls and his wholesale condemnation of Methodists.[10]

The denominational war had fallen short of being lethal, but on the battlefields of Mexico, Americans were suffering wounds and death. The *Whig* laid the responsibility for the conflict on President Polk and his pledge to annex Texas. Annexation took place in March 1846 and war began in May. Brownlow charged that Polk had brought on the war by sending General Zachary Taylor with troops into disputed territory. Yet he called for unstinted support of military action, once fighting began, because "whether it is a just or an unjust war, it is the duty of all good citizens, and patriots, to engage heartily in the defense of their country." The Parson travelled the countryside urging men to volunteer, but his Protestant soul recoiled when Roman Catholics were appointed chaplains for some military units. When a company was raised by Hezekiah Bayless as captain and William G. Brownlow as first lieutenant, it bore the name of "Protestant Invincibles." It was tendered to the state with the stipulation it must have no Roman Catholics as its chaplains. This condition barred acceptance of the unit, but the "Invincibles" continued to function at home. Lieutenant Brownlow made a speech at a drill muster, and the company paraded in uniform at Jonesboro on July 4, 1846. The editor placed such importance on war news that he permitted it to crowd out advertisements which he carried in an extra the following day.[11]

Brownlow did not make it to the war front, but a bullet whistled near his head in Knoxville as he helped quell a brawl among soldiers from his area who were waiting for boats to transport them on the Tennessee River. During the struggle a pistol was fired and the bullet missed the Parson's head from one to three inches. He accompanied the two companies to New Orleans and sent back correspondence. The East Tennesseeans set foot on Mexican soil after the peace treaty was signed on February 2, 1848.[12]

The Parson had declared himself "ready to sustain our Government in any and every crisis which concerns the integrity of our *Soil*, or the honor of our *Flag*,—no matter who may preside over the Nation, or however wicked and corrupt may be our rules." But he let his readers know he believed the war had cost too much in dollars and in lives. The Whig nominee for governor in 1847, Neill S. (Lean) Brown attacked Polk's conduct of the war. He defeated the incumbent, Aaron V. (Fat) Brown, who defended the national administration's course. Whigs also gained control of the legislature.

Brownlow chastised the General Assembly, Whig though it was, for delaying for more than six weeks in the election of a United States senator and in other business: "I am sorry to say that little else than drunkeness, profane swearing, lewdness, logrollings and downright *corruption* has been attended to by a majority of both political parties." He relented some when John Bell, who had been United States representative, was elected to the senate. But upon the assembly's adjournment he found the members had been "reckless, profligate, and unworthy," and had failed to do anything to establish "an efficient system of common schools, so much needed and so ardently desired by all the wise and good."[14]

The 1848 presidential campaign saw Brownlow in one of the most unusual political positions of his career. Late in the spring of 1847 he again had posted Henry Clay's name at the top of his editorial page as his choice for President, and with a bow to the Mexican war hero he put up General Zachary Taylor's name for Vice-President. It was not in Brownlow to desert Clay, although he recognized Taylor's vote appeal, for a month earlier he had written: "The war was provoked with a view to make a Democratic President, in 1848; but let it terminate as it may, it has made a Whig President of old Zach Taylor!" The general had just won the battle of Buena Vista. Brownlow saw a basic objection to Taylor in the general's statement: "I cannot in any case permit myself to be brought before the people exclusively by any one of the political parties that now so unfortunately divide our country, as their candidate for office." When Taylor later defined his position as that of a Whig, Brownlow retorted: "He avows himself a Whig, but he still does not suit us. He says he is not an ultra but a moderate Whig. We are *ultras,, and we want ultra for our candidate.*" He dropped Taylor's name from his masthead in the fall of 1847,[15] and on the eve of the Whig National Convention he served notice:

Should GEN. TAYLOR be the standard bearer of the party, we will not support him, because we have no confidence in the man. Meanwhile, we cannot and will not favor the election of GENERAL CASS for in doing so, we should lend our support to principles ruinous to our country, and against which we have fought all our days ... We shall continue *Whig* however, and publish a *newspaper*, in which we will advocate what we believe to be right, and oppose what we believe to be wrong (*Whig*, June 7, 1848).

The Democrats nominated Senator Lewis Cass of Michigan. When the Whigs nominated Taylor with Millard Fillmore as his running mate, Brownlow set out one condition under which he would go along: If we had any assurance that Taylor would die as soon as he is elected, and Mr. Fillmore would take his place, we would be willing to support the ticket. As it is we will not. Yet he forecast Taylor's election.[16]

Brownlow had seen death take a hand in the disposition of political affairs. When his favorite, William Henry Harrison, died soon after taking office as President, he was succeeded by John Tyler, whom Brownlow detested. When the Parson offered this macabre condition for the support of the Whig ticket in 1848, he surely had no premonition that Taylor would die in a little more than a year after his inauguration and Fillmore would become chief executive. Yet it turned out that way.

The role Brownlow had assumed brought a flood of letters. He printed two out of the hundred and one he had received by August, then set out his position in detail:

We will not array ourselves directly against Gen. Taylor, because he is the nominee of the party of which we are a humble member, and with which we have so long acted; because the leaders of that party believe he can be induced to administer the government on true Whig principles; and because there is associated with him, on the same ticket, one of the very first men in this nation, of his age and experience, to wit, MILLARD FILLMORE, of New York. We will not vote for Gen. Taylor, or any set of Electors who will cast their votes for him—because he has refused to identify himself with the party to which we belong; because he has refused to endorse the principles of the party with which we act—a party, we believe, holding the most orthodox principles of any party in existence, because we will not be *bullied* into the support of a candidate who has attempted to run rough shod over all parties, and last, but not least, because we will not sanction the trampling under the *heel of a military boot*, a long and tried statesman, a patriot, and the champion of our party, who was the choice of the *Whig people*, though not of the *Whig leaders*. We are not in an awkward position, as some suppose, having committed ourselves in a moment of excitement, by hasty writing. What we have said and done, we have said and done *deliberately (Whig*, August 2, 1848).

His decision may not have been hasty but it was undoubtedly caused by his emotional loyalty to Henry Clay, for he launched into praise of the Kentuckian, extended and lavish. It was not in Brownlow's soul to forgive any man for standing in the way of Clay's progress to higher political station. On the same page of the *Whig* of August 2, 1848, in which he had set out his determined opposition to supporting Taylor, but in a separate letter, he mourned Clay's loss of the nomination to Taylor: "But now I give up HENRY CLAY. I dismiss from my mind the idea of his ever being President of these United States, and it is like taking my life!" (*Ibid*.)

Campaign heat melted some of Brownlow's resolution and he praised his friend T. A. R. Nelson for the speeches he was making as Whig elector. Brownlow even put in a good word for Andy Johnson when the former met Nelson at Washington College. There the two filled "six dreadful hours" with speechmaking. The *Whig* not only described Johnson as "eloquent and able . . . "but made this further flattering estimate: "We regard him as the Napoleon of his party, in East Tennessee, having no equal upon the stump in the Democratic ranks." He complimented the speakers for a discussion that "was courteous and manly, free from anecdotes, and everything light and trifling, creditable to both the gentlemen, and one that the most refined ladies and gentlemen could have listened to with pleasure and interest." By the end of the summer he was expressing the hope that Taylor and Fillmore would be elected and on the eve of the election he was clamoring for the Whigs to vote for the party ticket even though "We will not do it." Technically he clung to his commitment not to vote for Taylor, but he promised to get two Democrats to vote for Taylor to make up for his disability. He made his usual contribution of extras and Whig tickets. He was in no wise unhappy when Taylor and Fillmore were elected. Taylor carried Tennessee with 64,700 votes to Cass' 58,616, and East Tennessee 20,163 to 13,980.[17]

A lesser political development had given the *Whig* minor but extended ruffling. Lewis Reneau, a Whig seeking the Second District congressional seat, obtained indictments for libel in Jefferson and Blount counties against Brownlow and the editor's Methodist friend, the Rev. James Cumming; Brownlow had supported Reneau's opposition and had printed an article by Cumming opposing Reneau. When the trial was held at Dandridge in August 1846, the Circuit Court set aside the indictment. Reneau appealed to the State Supreme Court. Brownlow's lawyers, T. A. R. Nelson and Robert J. McKinney, got a quick hearing before this court, sitting at Knoxville, and the circuit judge was sustained.

Brownlow expressed bafflement at Reneau's bitterness, which extended over two congressional campaigns: "We supposed we had a right to prefer one man over another and done so [*sic.*]." The Parson praised the three members of the high court for

a most righteous decision, and shows that the Judges, who all agreed, are men of high legal attainments, have a just sense of propriety, and correct views of equity. The opinion was delivered by JUDGE TURLEY, and was an able one— such an one as will show well upon the pages of the court in after ages.—Judge Turley is an intellectual man and, an impartial judge. This is saying a good deal, coming as it does from the editor of this paper: but it is true . . . His God intended him to be a Whig, and we hope to hear of his leaving the party with which he is now associated (*Whig*, September 30, 1846).

The Parson's lavish praise of Judge William B. Turley represented a spectacular reversal of opinion on his part. Eighteen months earlier, in an item headed "A Judicial Beast," he had applauded a Davidson County Circuit Court clerk for severely clubbing the judge because the latter had insulted a female relative of the clerk. Brownlow was doubly furious because an effort had been made to suppress the story in Nashville. For his part he vowed to "pour hot shot into all such rascals, irrespective of their stations or politics. True, Turley is a Locofoco, and this disgraceful act of his is a Democratic measure, but if he were a Whig we should take him off just the same (*Whig*, January 24, 1844).

Because dismissal of the indictment in Blount County was something of a formality after the Supreme Court ruling, Brownlow did not remain in the courtroom. W. H. Sneed of Knoxville represented him, and the Parson went ahead on another of his trips to the Southeast, this time beginning at Asheville. Sneed had agreed, at Nelson's request, to represent Brownlow at Maryville. But Sneed was under some apprehension about it, since as the editor probably knew, Mr. Sneed had stopped the *Whig* from being delivered at his home in the name of his wife. The lawyer [Sneed] wrote Nelson that he was Brownlow's friend, that the editor was entitled to publish the kind of newspaper his judgment directed, but "The paper is not such a one as in my opinion a lady ought to be a subscriber to." Although the *Whig* had been sent to Mrs. Sneed by Dr. William Hunt of Jonesboro, the Parson's brother-in-law, the "personal strife . . . blended with politics," in the upper East Tennessee area, repelled Sneed. So he asked Hunt to cancel the subscription as diplomatically as possible to avoid angering the Parson.[19] If Brownlow knew of Sneed's aversion to his newspaper, he did not mention it.

Outspoken and defiant as Brownlow was, he sometimes yielded to the request of friends to use restraint. He honored a request by Temple that the former not stir up the Democrats when that young Whig from Greeneville ran against Andrew Johnson for Congress in 1847. Temple sought to capitalize on the dislike many Democrats in the First District felt for Johnson by conducting a campaign that would leave the Democrats lulled. Temple wrote Brownlow, "If they [the Democrats] become alarmed or excited they will rally to the support of Johnson. If, on the contrary, they think there is no danger they will suffer him to fight for himself and won't care much whether he is elected or not." The Whig complied and Johnson won by only 314 votes.[20]

Brownlow gained sufficient newspaper maturity to offer at the close of the seventh volumn (*Whig*, May 6, 1846) this evaluation of the *Whig*: "We do not suppose, for one moment, that we have discharged in seven long years of angry and protracted political excitement the delicate, difficult and important duties that devolve upon the conductor of a public journal," a failure for which he accepted half of the responsibility became of human frailties. The balance of the blame he laid "Upon the heads of an ALLIED ARMY of personal and political enemies, who, in vain, sought to out-quarrel and out-abuse us," for "our failure to come up to the true moral standard of editorial duty." This position he held throughout his career, always claiming that he was opposed by vile, wicked enemies who tried, but failed, to overpower him in the exchange of vituperation. And he gave a further hint of satisfaction with himself as he added: "Although this article is the winding up of a career of *personal warfare*, of seven years duration, that career will long stand out in Upper East Tennessee, dispite [*sic*] its imperfections, as one of the most remarkable in the history of Tennessee politics." Historians and researchers, grubbing through the records, will not be disposed to challenge that statement.

Events of 1847 and 1848 sucked some of the enthusiasm out of the Parson, and bitterness replaced bounce. In addition to his political struggles with the powerful Democratic group in Jonesboro and libel sections against him, he also engaged in the furious church battle with Ross. This involved the labor of producing a second publication, as well as extended speaking tours.[21] He was indeed gloomy as he wrote on June 7, 1848, for the beginning of his tenth volume:

We have no disposition to boast, and if we had, we have nothing to boast of—beside, few of our readers will feel interested in our individual affairs. Still, we beg leave to observe, that in the outset, our support was not extravagant—our entire Press and fixtures were purchased on a credit, and at an extravagant rate—our paper was laid in upon the "credit system"—and our hands were hired at extravagant prices. Our share of job work and advertising was valueless, the county officers in the District being opposed to us, and giving their patronage to the opposition press. We never had any printing from either the State or General Government, no one ever contributed a dollar to aid us, except in the way of subscriptions for a paper. Yet, in the midst of all this, we have struggled on, paying every year some *security* debts, and now, tho' hard pressed still, we thank Providence that we are what we are, and where we are . . .

We have done a great deal of printing for our party in this District in the way of tickets, hand-bills, notices of political meetings, circulars, extras, &¢, without fee or reward. We have never missed being present at each Whig district and county convention, attending Mass Meetings in other States, and National Conventions, invariably at our own expense. We have never failed to contribute our share of all the funds raised in our district, for political and party purposes. Nor have we ever failed to attend the polls, where there was a National, State, or county contest, and vote with an open ticket. There are few editors in the country who can say all this (*Whig*, June , 1848).

Three weeks later he turned bitterly upon the Whigs of upper East Tennessee, asserting, "Had the party . . . had for an editor a man of less energy and perseverance, that [*sic.*] the editor of this paper, they would have been in a 'state of orphanage' years ago." Excluding Nelson and a few others he found:

The Whig leaders of this district are a mean, niggardly selfish pack, who will oppress an editor for *security debts*, and even *pay their yearly subscriptions in old claims on insolvent men*.

We have printed their notices, tickets, extras, and circulars for ten years, without fee or reward, and we now intend to do it no longer, *on the same terms!* (*Whig*, June 28, 1848).

The year saw Brownlow's greatest summer and fall of discouragement in that decade. His idol Clay had failed to get the nomination, he had exhausted himself in the fight against Ross, he had lost subscribers because of the controversy (*Whig*, June 7, 1848), and for the first time in his warm friendship with Nelson a coolness had arisen. His vow to endorse no notes probably was broken upon the first application for this favor from a friend. As for his refusal to vote for Taylor he probably regretted it, for he finally was caught up in the fervor of the campaign and pitched in to help his party in every way he could, printing bills, circulars and extras, although he stuck by his word that he would not cast his ballot for Taylor. After all, no matter how repugnant the party's standard bearer might be, there was something to be said for beating the Democrats.

On the eve of the presidential election that fall it was not surprising that Brownlow asked himself how he had ever got into newpapering and into the paradoxical situation into which his pen had led him; yet out of his sense of weariness, exasperation and exaggeration came this touching bit of inward turning humor:

Young man, if this brief epistle meets your eye, do not become the Editor of a newspaper, if you have not chosen a profession. Rather than do so, beg—clean out stables, work in gardens—keep ledgers—attend a saw-mill—take in washing—take up a country school—sell rags—black boots about a decent tavern—carry a horse mail from one village to another—set up a rope walk—do anything rather than become the Editor of a newspaper (*Whig*, November 1, 1848).

CHAPTER V NOTES

[1] C. C. Ross, comp., *The Story of Rotherwood, from the Autobiography of Rev. Frederick A. Ross, D.D.* (Knoxville, 1923), pp. 34-35, 30-32, 5; *Calvinistic Magazine*, new series (Abingdon, 1846), I, No. 7, pp. 146-157, *ibid.*, I, No. 11, p. 292, *ibid.*, No. 1, p. 1.

[2] Price, *Holston Methodism*, III, pp. 158-159, 162.

[3] *Calvinistic Magazine*, new series, I, No. 4, p. 116.

[4] *Ibid.*, III, No. 10, p. 314.

[5] *Ibid.*, IV, No. 1, p. 42.

[6] *Whig*, January 27, March 24, June 9, 1847. The first issue of the *Jonesborough Monthly Review*, new series, was for December 1847, II, No. 1, see p. 1.

[7] *Ibid.*, I, No. 1, December 1847, p. 22, *ibid.*, II, No. 2, January 1848, p. 103.

[8] *Whig*, September 29, November 10, October 20, 1847.

[9] *Jonesborough Monthly Review*, new series, II, No. 12, p. 380; *Calvinistic Magazine*, new series, V, No. 1, p. 384; Ross, *The Story of Rotherwood*, pp. 19-20, 32-33.

[10] Alexander, *T. A. R. Nelson*, p. 34; Temple, *Notable Men*, p. 179; *Whig*, October 6, 1847, September 13, 1848.

[11] Folmsbee *et al.*, *Short History*, pp. 211-214; *Whig*, May 27, June 3, 10, July 15, June 10, 17, July 8, June 3, 1846.

[12] *Ibid.*, March 29 (also dated March 22), April 5, 12, May 24, June 7, 1849; *Folmsbee et al.*, *Short History*, p. 214. Marginal notes by John Bell Brownlow state that parents of the young soldiers asked the Parson to go with the troops as far as New Orleans. *Whig*, March 29, April 5, 1848.

[13] *Ibid.*, June 17, 1846, June 9, July 7, 1847; Folmsbee *et al.*, *Short History*, p. 213; *Whig*, August 11, 18, September 1, 1847.

[14] November 10, December 1, 1847; Folmsbee *et al.*, *Short History*, p. 210; *Whig*, February 23, 1848.

[15] *Ibid.*, May 26, April 21, 1847, March 1, May 10, 1848, November 24, 1847.

[16] *Ibid.*, June 28, 21, August 2, 1848.

[17] *Ibid.*, August 2, September 6, 27, August 16, November 1, October 25, November 1, 22, 1848.

[18] *Ibid.*, August 26, September 30, August 26, 1846.

[19] *Ibid.*, October 14, 21, 1846; W. H. Sneed to Nelson, April 24, 1846. Nelson Papers.

[20] Temple to Brownlow, July 18, 1847. Temple Papers. Temple, *Notable Men*, pp. 229-230.

[21] Brownlow spoke against Ross at thirty places to an estimated 21,000 persons. *Whig*, October 6, 1847.

"Cry aloud—Spare not; show my people their transgressions,   Chapter No. 6
and the house of Jacob their sins." Willing to Praise;
But not afraid to blame.

A NATURAL EDITOR

The Parson's first decade as a newspaper editor and publisher showed he had an aptitude for, and a delight in, bold and blistering quarrels and controversies. It is on this characteristic that most of his fame, or infamy, rests because it is the side of him that has been portrayed most thoroughly by writers. But Brownlow was much more. He was cutting, but he witty; he exaggerated, but he was not solely gross when he drove a nail into an enemy; he threw in sparkles of humor that certainly pleased his friends and perhaps entertained his foes, with frustration as well as anger. The Parson was read for amusement as well as for his fury, and thereby he got what every newsman wants to achieve: circulation, the element that gives the writer influence with the reader, and which enlists the interest of the advertiser because of the scope of the readership.

Brownlow's political speeches in the summer and fall of 1840 brought the Democrats down on him, and he replied with such ferocity that the Chattanooga *Gazette* observed: "The everlasting Brownlow of the *Tennessee Whig* is still using the *tilt-hammer* on the heads of all unfortunate wights who cross his path." The Parson dismissed such comment with: "It so happens that wherever I go I give offence to every *thief, mail robber, land pirate and counterfeiter*, with whom I meet." Early in the next year he had attracted attention as far away as New England as the *Bay State Democrat* fumed: "There is a huge mass of self-conceit, somewhere out in Tennessee, by the name of Brown*low*—that is to say, bread unbaked, who edits a British Federal newspaper, and who annoys society very much. He is said to be a great drunkard—a savage looking monster near seven feet high—and he has been a vile Federalist for the last fifty years." The *Whig* editor, in a long answer, supplied corrections, for he was six feet tall, aged 34, and had never been accused of drinking even by his enemies. [1]

It delighted him to announce, later in the same year, underneath the title "Our Greatness—how it increases": "In one week, we have received as many as seven newspapers, an average of one each day—in which we were *praised* and *denounced*." This led him to the thought, "We think it not unlikely that we may yet run for the Presidency." The Parson was poking a little fun at himself, as he did when he published an issue of the *Whig* short on news and long on editorial comment, and explained, "We act upon the principle that it will never do for an editor to say nothing, even when he has nothing to say." A few years later, as he watched a locomotive pull a train over a newly built line into Dalton, Georgia, he chuckled, "When it first came puffing away over this Rail Road, it was a greater *curiosity* here than I am."[2]

Again out of New England, from the pages of the *Olive Branch*, published by a Methodist splinter group at Boston, came this enormous lie:

The fighting clergyman of Tennessee was at one time settled near Vicksburg, in Mississippi. He kept the Bible open on the pulpit by laying a *bowie knife* across the leaves, and on the Sabbath, before he pronounced the benediction, he would read the *programme for the horse races on the ensuing week*, and inform the congregation that he was ready to *back his favorite horse against whatever* bets they would make! (*Whig*, September 13, 1843).

The Parson had never been in Mississippi, and he never gambled, but such accounts, blatantly untrue, showed that his enemies feared him enough to manufacture about him the worst habits of which they could think. Some stories, however, paid tributes to his surgical skill upon his opponents without reflecting on his morals. A Georgia newspaper offered this recipe for making indelible ink: "Read the *Jonesborough Whig*, with gloves on, taking care not to touch it with the naked hands—then wash the gloves in a tub of water. The water may be bottled for immediate use."[3]

It was characteristic of the Parson to predict success for his newspaper, but he also wove into these promotion pieces the mischievous distortions in which he delighted and the humor that bubbled from his depths. When President Harrison, whom he liked, died soon after taking office and Tyler, whom he grew to hate, succeeded, Brownlow came up with this forecast:

To our kind patrons, we can only say that by constant reading, hard study, and a great deal of writing, we intend this journal—this establishment—to be-

come the centre and soul of a mighty intellectual, moral, political, financial and
religious revolution! For what we may lack in *actually accomplishing*, it is our
settled purpose to make up in boasting. Therefore, success, with us, is inevitable.
We intend to make Victoria tremble on her throne, Louis Phillippe burst with
grief, John Tyler squat like a fawn in a thicket, and Santa Anna jump like a dog
in high rye! Heaven save the Republic—God prosper the Church—let the people
revere the memory of Harrison—may our Job Work and Advertising custom
increase—and may Satan, with all of his Locofoco coadjutors, speedily take to
their hottest quarters—Amen! (*Whig*, January 12, 1842).

Brownlow's humor was broad; subtlety would have been wasted
on many of his readers. Even the Democrats must have let out roars
of laughter when he made this defense of a Whig convicted of larceny: "the act of stealing is *Democratic*. In other words, the Man is
Whig, but the Measure is Democratic (*Whig*, June 15, 1842).

The editor delighted to make news, especially when he could drive
home a point. As he rode through Washington on his way to Baltimore and Philadelphia in the spring of 1845, following the election
of Polk as President, he seized an opportunity to needle the Democratic office seekers lining the sidewalks:

Being on top of the Omnibus . . . I determined to relieve the minds of these
cormorants, and accordingly make proclamation, to this effect: "Gentlemen,
give yourselves no uneasiness about us—we are not after offices—we are a different breed of dogs—and we are going on to Baltimore, having no sort of
business here." To this some fellow on the sidewalk responded—"That is that
d—d Brownlow."—"Yes," said I, "and for one, I shall keep my nose and eyes
closed, till I get through this filthy crowd, that I may neither see nor *smell* the
stench of Locofocoism (*Whig*, April 16, 1845).

Brownlow was on the longest trip he had made, both in time and
in distance, and it marked the true beginning of his career as a roving
reporter. In charge of a band of forty horses, he left Jonesboro in
March. They were to be sold in southeastern centers but the outcome
was not profitable because the market for these animals was depressed. He wrote from Morganton and Charlotte, North Carolina,
Cheraw and Sumterville, South Carolina, then cut back through
Lumberton and Raleigh, North Carolina, where he caught a train. He
went through Petersburg and Richmond, Virginia, Baltimore, Philadelphia and New York, and pushed into New England, where he
visited Providence, Rhode Island, and Boston. He was gone three
months. [4]

Few of Brownlow's readers had the time or the means to travel extensively. Probably none had his gift for conveying to them what he saw and heard, vividly, humorously and quaintly, as seen through the eyes of a native Appalachian. He brought the outside world to the fertile and frequently travelled valleys and to the more inaccessible ridges and hollows of his land, quite often managing to convey to his readers that they were better off than the city populations.

A distaste for South Carolinians, implanted when he watched that state's effort at nullification, probably colored the estimate of her citizens made on the long 1845 trip:

The real South Carolinian assumes to be a man of much importance—he crosses streets at an angle no matter how many crosswalks there may be, and in his *Buggy* or *Sulky*—a mode of travelling very much in vogue here—he throws himself back like an English Lord . . . he always has his whip in his hand, a cigar in his mouth, and upon his countenance, an air of great self-importance (*Whig*, March 6, 1845).

Months later he was more compassionate as he wrote from Camden, "They have great need of prayers and religion here; for it is a low, flat, sickly region and they die off in great numbers" (*Ibid.*, November 11, 1846).

Brownlow was a valiant trencherman. He boasted as he wrote from a New York hotel where the "meats really melt on one's tongue," that "I can eat anything that comes on the table, and I can eat a *good deal* of it!" He put on a false front of dignity in ordering from the French menu, pretending to be familiar with that language (*Whig*, April 30, 1845).

Traveling afforded some unpleasant experiences, such as one he encountered in a town "Somewhere in Southwestern Virginia":

Sleepy and tired, retiring to a fine room well furnished, with a magnificent bed, a Turkey carpet, looking-glass, wash stand, pitcher and clean towel, hair-brush, &c., &c.; and lo! upon blowing out the candle, and laying our carcass down to rest, we were instantly covered with *bed-bugs*, varying in size from something less than a grain of corn, to a mustard seed (*Whig*, May 5, 1847).

The incident so upset the Parson that he wrote an editorial about it instead of including it in his correspondence. And in an unusually delicate treatment for him he did not locate the town or identify the hotel. Sympathy, as well as laughter must have greeted his account of having torn his pants on a fence at Camden, South Carolina, and having to remain in bed until repairs were made.[5] Many of the Parson's readers, like the Parson himself, had only one pair of trousers fit for a traveling outfit.

Brownlow's tour of New England produced a singular observation from him, advocate of slavery and foe of abolition that he was. As he looked at the thriving industries of the region, all operated by free labor, he concluded that "slavery as it exists in the South and West is a curse instead of a blessing (*Whig*, April 30, 1845).

A year later as he paused in wonder at the Harbor of Charleston, South Carolina, he described the masts of the sailing ships there as resembling a forest, he collected $600 for friends at home, he boasted that he was so widely known that he could prove his identity anywhere in the United States, and he marvelled at the sight of droves of hogs being driven to market, 6,000 alone from Jefferson County in East Tennessee.[6]

Back in Jonesboro after his long trip, the Parson offered single men some pointed suggestions in selecting a wife: "Lay hold of the girl with her sleeves rolled up—the one with her ears laid back—her eyes wide open with a broom in her hand, or standing half bent over a washing tub—and not the one with a novel in her hand and a box of snuff, turning up her nose at her betters" (*Whig*). Months later he found, "The young ladies have a strange walk nowadays to what they used to have. Each one flirts as if a flea were biting her on each hip." The Parson must have aimed this rebuke at certain maidens. He was too observant not to have noticed this characteristic earlier. He mellowed on dancing; he found it more foolish than sinful. When church officers in Jonesboro discussed bearing down on members who indulged in the pastime, he offered the realistic opinion: "Tho' we believe it is wrong in members of the Church—we are against that, simply on the ground that there will not be enough left to constitute the Scriptural requisition of 'two or three' gathered together in the name of the Lord."[7]

The editor's indignation at the public mistreatment of a wife by a husband is understandable, but the interposition of his caustic comment below an advertisement terminating support would be most startling today. Perhaps it was a bold step when Brownlow printed this:

NOTICE

I hereby forwarn [*sic*] all persons from trading with my wife, Charlotte Bacon, or giving her credit on my account. She has left my bed and board, without any just or reasonable cause, and I am determined not to pay any debt, or debts, she may contract.

I have a good house for her, and plenty to live upon, and she has no reason to absent herself, as she has done, for some three or four months, maliciously and voluntairy [sic] , and without just or sufficient cause,

JONATHAN BACON

Note by the Editor!—We publish the foregoing for Mr. Bacon, as an advertisement and for his money, who came with it to our office three different times. We are not to be understood as endorsing it, or approving it. The friends of his wife will not trouble him with supporting her, and she will not attempt to run him in debt, as he very well knows, and as far as *malice* is concerned, we have seen none, except in this advertisemen[t] (*Whig*, November 29, 1848).

Some personal knowledge of the Bacon domestic issues must have entered into the Parson's objections to the advertisement, as the editor's note indicated. A year earlier he had run, without comment, a notice by a husband refusing to pay the debts of his wife "by reason of her having had a child six weeks and four days after our marriage, which she says is not mine."

An outrage against a beast and against its owner, a Baptist preacher, brought down forked lightning from the *Whig* upon miscreants who broke into a stable and shaved the tail of the minister's horse. Brownlow's judgment was, "If hell were raked with a fine tooth comb it is exceedingly doubtful whether any such material could be found there as inhabit this village; and should the devil seek a substitute for hell Jonesboro would qualify."[8]

Yet when a slave convicted of murder was hanged in Jonesboro, he did not appear to be revolted in reporting a macabre battle over the cadaver. The Parson did not go to the hanging, although 3,000 to 5,000 persons did. He stood in his front yard and watched as the doomed man was taken from the jail. The prisoner wore a long, white shroud and sat upon his coffin as he was taken to the place of execution. An armed guard of 200 men surrounded him. Witnesses told the Parson that the prisoner "often smiled and was careful to wipe the mud off his shroud, that might chance to light upon it, and gracefully gather the folds of it around his knees!" The battle over the body did not strike him as grisly, judging from his account:

After hanging some thirty minutes, his body was cut down—placed in a coffin for burial, and interred on the spot. As soon as the Clergy who had officiated on the ground, and the greater part of the crowd had left, a regular *scramble* came off, among the Physicians from different towns and their representatives, as to who should have his body. Several fights ensued, and among the rest, a party of Negroes who were there, his relatives and others, tried their hands. The *Jonesborough* boys, as usual, triumphed, and now have the body of Dave in a Dissecting Room, and are working on it scientifically![9]

Life in the little county seat was by present standards primitive and brutal. When a Whig convention was held near Jonesboro in the fall of 1840, a public-spirited citizen leased a ten-acre field and offered it to those who wanted a place to sleep. No other facilities were mentioned. They could have the ground. When Brownlow came home from a seven-week trip that included his attendance as a delegate at the Whig convention in Baltimore he was alarmed to find five of the ten members of his household ill. A few days later he predicted much illness for the summer of 1844, if "the notorious Ponds, at the upper and lower ends of town, are not drained off, as they should be; and if the dead hogs and other filth are not taken out of the Creek, and the back streets and stables."[10] The winter scene described by the Parson was even more depressing:

Our town is located on a *sink hole*, surrounded by hills, making our location admirably adapted to the collection of all the *filth* pouring in from the surrounding hills, and nothing is wanted for our complete *inundation with nastiness*, but the closing up of the gap below the town where the spring branch breaks through the hills! Until recently, we have exhibited more mud and filth in our streets, than any other little town could boast of in this end of the State—wintering our cows under our porches, and emptying our *slop buckets* into our front streets! At one time in December, there were but about 3 fords, or crossing places, on main street; but our citizens have nobly commenced the work of cleaning our streets, and upon a scale worthy of their just importance. They have much of the filth in piles on main street, which seem destined to *stand* as a lasting ornament to the place—a blessing to the community, and a monument of liberality and enlightened views of the town authorities! (*Whig*, February 7, 1844).

Jonesboro authorities later required Brownlow to move a stable and manure pen he had maintained on a back street. He acknowledged the officials were acting properly, but he questioned whether the regulation would be enforced as to others. He also reported a high mortality among his cows; four had been poisoned, one recovered, during a five-year period (*Whig*, February 2, 1846). Many families kept a cow for milk.

Brownlow tried several business ventures while at Jonesboro. All were unprofitable, and finally he announced his withdrawal from all outside projects to give his entire attention to his newspaper and the Whig Party. A friend wrote later that these ventures ended "always with disaster. Incompetent or dishonest associates or agents got the better of him every time. The truth is, he was too liberal, too unsuspecting, too negligent of details for a successful business man."[11]

The *Whig*, however, thrived. Advertising volume reached almost fifty per cent of the newspaper's space. And late in 1845 Brownlow trumpeted that the *Whig* was "the only newspaper published in Tennessee east of Knoxville," again at the beginning of the year 1847 that the "circulation of this paper is now so great and its readers so numerous—not only in Tennessee but in other states—that it has become the interest of many to get their advertisements into these columns," and again a few months later that the *Whig* had such a circulation "in point of numbers and intelligence, that has not been enjoyed by any country paper of the same age, situated in so remote and mountainous region of the country."[12]

This was promotion, which is assumed to contain boasts, and the Parson always kept his talent for exaggeration in good order. The Audit Bureau of Circulation had not been created; hence there was no professional check on his claims, but he had proved he was a successful newspaper editor, and sometimes publisher.

The Parson was no stranger to the difficulties involved in newspaper publication. Collections and deliveries presented constant annoyances. The *Whig* management offered incentives for cash or early payments by setting the subscription price at $2.50 annually if paid in advance, $3.00 if paid at the end of three months, and $3.50 if paid at the close of the year. The subscription rate was cut to $2.00 annually when the *Whig* and the job shop were combined early in 1845, with Byers taking over business management. Byers sold his interest to the Parson early in 1847, but the subscription price remained the same for years.[13] Brownlow chastised delinquents by printing their names under the heading "Black Knights." Payment was taken in almost any form. When the *Whig* sent a wagon into Carter and Johnson counties in 1847 it offered to take iron castings and food for man and beast, "*whiskey* and *brandy* always excepted!"[14]

Collection of legal advertising accounts, which made up a considerable amount of the revenue, grew quite difficult. Publishers through-out the state adopted a rule not to accept it unless paid in advance or complete responsibility for payment given. Brownlow had so many outstanding accounts of this kind in 1841 that he announced that if all were met he could pay every debt and buy a good house and office on the main street of Jonesboro.[15]

Most of the *Whig*'s subscribers must have received their copies by mail. If only a few of the Parson's many complaints were justified the postal system must have been wretched. He carried an ingrained prejudice against postmasters because they were more often appoint-ed by Democratic administrations than by Whigs. Since Brownlow was the political foe of these postmasters, some of them may have felt it appropriate to look after the *Whig* with less zeal than in handling Democratic newspapers. Mail deliveries were vital to pub-lications, and Brownlow's constant hammering on the point is under-standable. He complained not only of failures, late deliveries and mutilated papers in the summer of 1840 but also reported that "some of our correspondents say that the *Sentinel* reaches their offices regularly but the *Whig* does not." When Newbern, Virginia, subscrib-ers reported irregular deliveries, the Parson recommended that they "talk firce [*sic*] to the Post Master . . . with fists drawn and they will soon perceive a change." He also charged that the Post Office Depart-ment had notified the mail contractors operating between Jonesboro and Blountville not to carry the *Whig*. A possible explanation for this was that the mail bags would not hold the more numerous *Whig*s, while they would those of the fewer *Sentinel*s. The next spring, in a notice to postmasters at Blountville and Knoxville, Brownlow charged that the bags would not hold his newspaper and as a result delivery was delayed at least a week, while the *Sentinel*s were carried to their destinations on time. The nettled *Whig* editor pointed out that he was paying $800 annually for newspaper and letter postage.[16] The rates for newspaper postage were lowered in 1845, and revised up-ward slightly in 1847.[17] Complaints of inferior service continued. The mail to Russellville was left in a stream overnight and the news-papers ruined, the *Whig* complained in the summer of 1847, and also that the mail was transported in uncovered carts. Early in 1848 the Parson announced that in his nine years as an editor he had never known "more corruption to exist among the post-masters and mail carriers than at present." *Whig*s were thrown out of the mails, destroyed, or delivered late, and it took from two to four weeks for the newspaper to be delivered at Parrottsville, forty-five miles distant, although a horse mail went directly to the town from Jonesboro.[18]

Brownlow restlessly changed the page one makeup. He shifted from six columns to five on his third volume; a year later he inserted beneath *The Jonesborough Whig*, but in smaller type, *An Independent Journal*. As he launched his eighth volume, the Mexican War was raging, creating a greater demand for news, and he promised better newsprint and type. Transportation of paper brought problems. Early in 1848 he missed an issue while a wagon waited in Knoxville to load newsprint, and at the close of the year he suspended the Christmas issue because he didn't have the paper, observing that the hands would enjoy the long holiday. Newsprint costs, amounting to $1,100 during his first year at Jonesboro, were a substantial expense.[19]

Aside from the editor's worries over the business operation and his political foes, he encountered a segment of the human race that waits upon almost every publication, versifiers and poets. They left him worn and angry, but not frustrated. He not only proclaimed he was "sick and tired of their worthless effusions," but that if in saying so he had given offense "we have accomplished our object, provided we get rid of all such, in all time to come." His wrath was fuelled by the submission of a poem as an original work that turned out to have been written by Lord Byron, the famous English poet. He was equally firm, if not as brittle, in a declaration of policy on the publication of death notices, pronounced early in the Jonesboro era with the lament: "When the death of an individual is published, unless he is *written* up into the third heavens, and declared to have been sinless and undefiled in life, loud complaints are made." He therefore announced that if the friends of the deceased would write out, or otherwise furnish details, "We will give the desired blast," but "to sit down and *write* a man to heaven when we have every reason to believe he is in hell, just to please his friends, is rather a tedious business."[20]

Editors often feel the same way today, but they do not so express themselves. No Parson Brownlows are editing newspapers now.

These were the usual problems of any newspaper, but Brownlow did not follow the normal course of an editor; therefore, it was not surprising that what befell him next, which arose from the boiling religious and political controversies of the day, should breeed the most critical physical violence he would meet. In his struggle with Ross, the Parson had gone to pains to demonstrate that Presbyterians, rather than Methodists, as Ross had argued, were bent on political domination. After he surveyed the national scene he narrowed his point to Washington County, where he lit upon John Ryland, calling him

a Presbyterian Democrat, who had made a little fortune out of the public offices, and who had solemnly pledged himself, at the last election for Circuit Court clerk, that he never would trouble the people again, if they would elect him; he is again a candidate for that office (*Whig*, November 10, 1847).

Running against Ryland were a Methodist Whig and a Methodist Democrat. Ryland was humiliated for he came out third. Bitterness on the Ryland side was compounded when the *Whig* identified John Ryland, son of the former county official, as a deserter from a Washington County company at Jalappa, Mexico. Brownlow based this on a letter from Captain John T. O'Brien. Ryland's unhappiness was intensified when the report of his desertion reached the postmaster at Knoxville, thus preventing his drawing wages. Young Ryland thereupon vented his wrath upon the Parson noisily. In the fall of 1848, armed and shouting, he posted himself at the fence in front of the Brownlow residence between ten and eleven o'clock at night. He invited the editor to come out and fight. He bawled accusations against Brownlow. He cursed him for having helped in the defeat of his father for the clerkship, for having "slandered the most pure and evangelical minister of the gospel the world ever knew," and for having meddled in his courtship. Brownlow printed two columns in the *Whig* about the disturbance. On the subject of Ryland's courtship the editor wrote, "We believed any young lady that wanted him, *with a knowledge of his character*, and brilliant exploits, ought to be encouraged to marry him--and that whoever got him, would get a liar, a scoundrel, a coward, and a Deserter from the United States Army!" Ryland made three shouting appearances before the Brownlow home on the public square of Jonesboro that night. The last trip brought the Parson out of bed, who took down a "double barreled gun, well loaded with buck shot, cocked it, and went at him when he swiftly retreated." The editor's last paragraph in the account sounded his usual warning: "He never can, and never shall, with impunity, make another attack upon us, in public or private, by day or by night, in word or in deed, when we are present." [21] Brownlow was wrong, if the identification of his next assailant was correct.

The blow fell on a Sunday night, April 2, 1849, as Brownlow in company with two Methodist presiding elders, walked home from church. A form slipped out of an alley between two stables and struck the Parson on the head. The preachers, T. K. Catlett and C. D. Smith, gave a statement that they did not know the assailant, but that they saw him fleeing with a stick or club in his hand and that a Negro identified him as John Ryland, Jr. Brownlow's account, published in the *Whig* on April 19, 1849, acknowledged that Ryland had denied making the assault, but he also reported that two white boys had identified Ryland as the assailant. Brownlow saw no one and was left unconscious. He was unaware of what had happened or how he reached his home, one hundred and fifty yards distant. The editor was confined to his home for fifteen days before he was able to write his story of the attack, and then did so "without the knowledge or consent of my physician." However much his head may have ached, he remembered that he was a newspaperman. The story was entitled to more than routine display. He broke away from the usual one-line head with this screamer:

ATTEMPTED MURDER BY AN AS
SASSIN, A SCOUNDREL, AND A
COWARD, IN THE PERSON OF
JOHN RYLAND, JR.

He further dramatized the story by leading it with a few lines from Shakespeare. The Parson attributed his being alive to a strong beaver hat he was wearing—one which broke the force of the blow. He told the *Whig*'s readers that he would resort to neither the courts nor violence, that he was competent to look after his own affairs, and that as soon as he recovered he would move himself, his family and his hands to Knoxville, where he had previously announced he was taking the *Whig* (*Whig*, April 19, 1849). This was his message:

I can assure him that I shall institute no suit against him. I have seen too much of the "glorious uncertainty of the Law," and of the acts and doings of corrupt Jurors to trouble them with the settlement of my personal difficulties.

Some reports have gone out touching messages I should have sent to this candidate for the honors of the gallows. I have sent him no message—I have none to send. I have made no threats—I have none to make. I have advised with no man—I shall not consult any man. I am of age—I am in my right mind—I am competent to attend to my own business. [22]

William Rule, who in later years was long associated with Brown-low in the newspaper business, recalled that when he first saw the editor in early 1850 the latter observed, in commenting on reported threats by Ryland to kill him, "I would rather run some risk of losing my own life than to take that of a fellow being however vile he might be or however justifiable I might be, under the law, in so doing."[23]

Whether Ryland was guilty or not, he failed to bring any action for libel, despite the punishment that the *Whig* gave him. When Ryland died in Dallas, Texas, in 1852, the Parson disposed of him crisply: "Thus sinks to a grave of ignominy the *dastard*, who it is believed to have crept upon us from a dark alley, in the darkness of the night, and inflicted a blow, upon the back of our head, from the effects of which we have suffered for several years." A decade later, in reviewing some of his difficulties, Brownlow expressed the conviction that Ryland had gone to hell, "and there I propose to leave him for the present." The Parson reserved to himself, however, the right to designate the course Ryland's soul took after death, because when John Bell Brownlow, junior editor of the *Whig*, found occasion in 1867, to repeat that Ryland had gone to perdition, the Parson reproached his son. The junior editor, in reporting the death of Elder Catlett, who was walking with Brownlow the night of the assault, also wrote that the Parson had announced Ryland had gone to hell.[24]

The effects of the clubbing have been given wide interpretation. R. N. Price, Methodist historian and a friend of Brownlow's, believed the fracture had seriously affected the Parson's health "to the day of his death," and "doubtless shortened his life." He did not mention, however, mental incapacity. O. P. Temple, who knew Brownlow more intimately than anyone who wrote about him, neglected the Jonesboro assault in his extended sketch of his friend, with the exception of this general statement: "Although stealthily waylaid and assailed by would-be assassins in the dark, or from behind, four or five times with deadly intent, and more than once with nearly fatal effect, he never attempted to punish the miserable cowards, much less retaliate on them." He maintained that when Brownlow served a six-year term in the United States Senate that although "His body was enfeebled . . . his intellect still glowed with all the fire and energy of 1861." Temple's opinion was "By his confinement in the crowded and loathsome prison [the Knoxville jail where he was held by the Confederacy] and his exposure in his wanderings, his wonderful constitution was broken down, his nervous system was destroyed and he became prematurely old and an invalid for the rest of his life." The Knoxville *Register*, in a moment of fury while battling for its life with the *Whig*, snarled at a Methodist publication which had condemned ministers for active participation in politics: "You should be careful how you throw brickbats. Don't you know that a slight lick on the head of one whose brain has been 'addled' will throw him into fits." E. Merton Coulter, in his biography of Brownlow, took the position that the blow impaired the Parson's mental and physical health. He concluded, "Certainly as time went on, he became more reckless as his power increased; perhaps it was not due entirely to his natural bent—his assailant's club left permanent marks and impressions on his skull." A year after the attack Rule found that Brownlow still suffered from the effects. Much later—the Parson had a habit of revealing more and more details as time passed—he acknowledged that he was "Under the care of a physician for more than one month, and a portion of that time I did not know my friends and neighbors." He also revealed that the blow cracked his skull from the point of impact to his forehead. His recovery was slow, for he was "Sorely afflicted the entire summer, and were [*sic.*] not half a man, in point of physical strength."

Certainly Brownlow's power increased. The pages of the *Whig* reveal many long, furious fights in which he employed to the fullest his talent for castigating without mercy those who crossed or opposed him. The pre-Civil War times and events were traumatic for Brownlow because of his emotional devotion to the Union and to his newspaper. The first split and the second he abandoned through fear and economic necessity.

If Brownlow's mental machinery went awry, two of his newspaper contemporaries failed to see it that way. J. Austin Sperry, editor of the Knoxville *Register*, astounded and dismayed when Brownlow was released by Confederate authorities in 1862, paid him an extraordinary compliment for his keen understanding of human nature, his skill in maneuvering and his diplomacy. When Brownlow was governor, George Prentice, editor of the Louisville *Journal*, sometimes his friend but at that time his foe, considered the Brownlow administration in Tennessee so evil that he clamored: " 'Tis a pity for him that he isn't insane, for it would be the only excuse, utter mental imbecility excepted, for the disgrace he is inflicting upon the

State in which he dwells."[25] Both editorials contained exaggerations, but evil as the writers saw Brownlow, they did not suggest any lack of competency; if anything, he had too much to suit them.

CHAPTER VI NOTES

[1] *Whig*, September 9, 1840, January 6, 1841.
[2] *Ibid.*, September 17, 1841, November 23, 1842, January 5, 1848.
[3] *Ibid.*, April 19, 1843.
[4] *Ibid.*, February 2, 26, March 5, 12, 26, April 2, 9, 16, 23, 30, 1845.
[5] *Ibid.*, May 5, 1847, November 11, 1846.
[6] *Ibid.*, November 11, 25, 1846.
[7] *Ibid.*, May 21, 1845, June 16, January 6, 1847.
[8] *Ibid.*, November 3, 1847, September 3, 1845.
[9] *Ibid.*, November 29, 1848. See also *ibid.*, November 22, 1848.
[10] *Ibid.*, October 7, 1840, November 3, 1847, June 12, 1844.
[11] Brown and his friend, the Rev. C. W. C. Harris operated the Wool Hat store in Jonesboro, *ibid.*, June 19, 1844; the former had a vague connection with Clem, Harris, Hunt and Company, another mercantile house which ran the first full page advertisement in the *Whig*, March 5, 1845; Temple, *Notable Men*, p. 274.
[12] The *Tennessee Sentinel* was discontinued and other newspapers appeared intermittently in Jonesboro. *Whig*, December 10, 1845; Fink, "The Early Press of Jonesboro," ETHS *PUBL.* No. 10, p. 68; *Whig*, December 10, 1845, January 20, May 12, 1847.
[13] Subscription and advertising rates were carried on page one. Brownlow cut the original $2.50 annual rate, if paid in advance, to $2.00, *ibid.*, February 5, 1845, February 24, 1847.
[14] *Ibid.*, January 19, 1842, January 6, 1847.
[15] *Ibid.*, July 1, 1846, December 8, 1841.
[16] *Ibid.*, June 24, July 29, September 23, 1840, May 19, 1841.
[17] *Ibid.*, March 26, 1846, April 28, 1847.
[18] *Ibid.*, July 28, 1847, January 19, 1848.
[19] *Ibid.*, May 28, 1841, May 18, 1842, May 13, 1846, March 15, December 13, 1848, May 28, 1841.
[20] *Ibid.*, December 24, 1845, December 1, 1841.
[21] *Ibid.*, March 8, June 7, 1848, October 4, 1848.
[22] *Ibid.*, Arpil 19, 1849. Alex Williams to "Dear Sir," April 14, 1839. Nelson Papers.
[23] Memorandum on Rule's first look at Brownlow. Rule Papers.
[24] *Whig*, October 2, 1852, October 27, 1862. John Bell Brownlow marginal note, *ibid.*, March 13, 1867.
[25] Price, *Holston Methodism*, III, p. 239; Temple, *Notable Men*, pp. 280, 341, 314; *Register*, March 20, 1851; Coulter, p. 43; *Whig*, October 27, 1860, July 5, 1851; *Register*, quoted in *Parson Brownlow's Book*, pp. 342-345; Temple, *Notable Men*, p. 351, O.R. Series 2, I, pp. 925-926; *White*, Messages, V, p. 661, quoting Louisville *Journal*, May 14, 1868.

Very Respectfully, &c,

W. G. Brownlow

This much more sophisticated portrait of the Parson came from the frontispiece of *Parson Brownlow's Book*. [*Journal* Staff Photograph by Hugh Lunsford.]

THE WHIG.

"Truth is omnipotent, and public justice certain."   Chapter No. 7

THE CRIPPLED INVADER

William G. Brownlow arrived on the Knoxville newspaper scene as an invader, and crippled though he was, he was received with all the power that could be raised against his invasion. He was warned that he faced a fight for survival with the *Register*, but with characteristic boldness he had retorted that his publication would triumph. Brownlow knew Knoxville well. He had seen it when he was a young and gawky preacher, he had made boat trips to it down the Holston River for the O'Briens, and as an editor and party leader he had been drawn to it because it was a vigorous center for Whiggery. He liked Knoxville for its bustle as a transportation hub and for its business advantages.[1] He anticipated a tough fight, but he had thrived on frequent and deadly struggles. At Jonesboro he had reached the top by surmounting one uproar after another, and the only way he could climb higher would be to scale a bigger mountain. Knoxville was that mountain.

The *Whig* had been successful as a newspaper. But its editor had taken severe financial losses because of his inability to turn down applicants for his signature as a note endorser. Before he left Jonesboro he had paid thousands of dollars for borrowers whose paper he had endorsed, but who had failed to pay and left him to make up the loss.[2] Perhaps he wanted to leave the scene where he had, in a most painful way, found that some members of the human race cannot be trusted to carry out their financial pledges. Primarily, though, the inviting vistas of Knoxville must have drawn him more than the disappointments of Jonesboro pushed him. He set out the advantages in a prospectus published in the *Whig* at Jonesboro.

The undersigned goes to Knoxville, because that is an eligible position, affording the necessary mail facilities, and because he believes that he can be more useful to his party, and to the country at large; and last, though not least, because he thinks he can advance his own pecuniary interests, now at the bottom of the wheel of fortune (*Whig*, February 5, 1849).

As Brownlow penned this piece on his removal to Knoxville he must have felt assurance that he had laid his plans well. He had sold his printing press, type and fixtures and taken notes in exchange. In Washington he had arranged with Senator John Bell and United States Representative Meredith Gentry to go security on his own note. This note, with the two members of Congress as endorsers, and the paper he had taken in the sale of his Jonesboro plant he gave in Philadelphia for the purchase of the printing equipment. He arranged for the shipment of these goods and materials to Knoxville by way of Charleston and Chattanooga. When they reached Knoxville they were to be stored until the Parson arrived to start his newspaper. The shipments were in the names of Bell and Gentry.[3]

When Brownlow came back through Washington in March 1849, after arranging the purchases in Philadelphia, he fell into an almost fatal blunder, a mistake that grew out of his tendency to place complete confidence in men he believed to be his friends. He not only unfolded his plans to retiring United States Representative John H. Crozier, but also entrusted to him some of the arrangements to be made when the shipment arrived in Knoxville. He gave Crozier the bills for the goods and authorized him to see that they were stored in the commission house of the congressman's brothers-in-law, James and Walter Williams.[4] According to the Parson, Crozier duped him outrageously. In time it turned out that the retiring congressman and the Williams brothers were part of a combine which set about to fight the *Whig* with their money, their influence and a consolidated newspaper. Crozier was able to give the group the details of Brownlow's plans.

The Parson's announcement that he was moving to Knoxville, supplemented by the information Crozier had, brought significant developments. The *Register*, the most venerable weekly in East Tennessee and staunchly Whig, had lost ground. Competition had arisen in a second Whig newspaper, the *Tribune*, edited by James C. Walker and John Miller McKee, who had started it in the spring of 1846. The Moses brothers, James C. and John L., sold the *Register* to McKee, who consolidated it with the *Tribune*, but retained the *Register*'s name alone, probably because of its age and reputation. Five outstanding and powerful Whigs gave the *Register* financial muscle. They secured a $6,000 loan for McKee. Among the five was John H. Crozier. The others were William G. Swan, a prominent lawyer;

Thomas W. Humes, once President of the University of Tennessee.

James W. Campbell, clerk of the State Supreme Court and of the United States District Court; W. H. Sneed, another outstanding lawyer; and Thomas W. Humes, a former *Register* editor and rector of St. John's Episcopal Church.[5] Thus, while Brownlow lay in bed at Jonesboro, semiconscious from the blow on his skull, his Knoxville enemies took advantage of Crozier's information and the Jonesboro assailant's blow. Years later, while reviewing the events that took place after he had trusted Crozier to look after his shipment to Knoxville, the Parson gave this summary of the obstacles thrown in his way:

I stated all this to Crozier [the arrangement], and informed him that I had written the same by him to his relatives. He promised to see to it, professed great friendship; and it was not until after he had returned and the goods arrived that I learned he was insincere, a vile hypocrite, and a dirty, mean, deceitful and hateful little scoundrel! He came home—went to work against me—arrayed his two brothers-in-law against me, and sought by the most disreputable means to defeat me in every respect (*Whig*, October 27, 1860).

The Parson then, returned to Jonesboro, was struck on the head and left half-conscious:

While I lay in this condition, my goods arrived in Knoxville—the Williams [*sic*.] acting in concert with and under the influence of this deceitful, malicious, and utterly unprincipled scoundrel, refused them house-room, and they were thrown out upon the bank. They advised the Captain of the Steamboat to return them again to Chattanooga, and to sell them there for double freight. While, however, the Captain was preparing to sell them here, a friend of mine from Carter County, James W. Nelson, whose remains rest in a grave in this vicinity, chanced to be here on business, and stepped forward and paid the charges, amounting in all, to some *Seventy Dollars*—Nelson and other friends procured an office for me on Gay Street where Rawlins now has a Hardware Store, and there deposited my goods. [6]

Brownlow reached Knoxville on May 1, 1849. Eighteen days later, on May 19, 1849, he produced his first number of *Brownlow's Knoxville Whig*. He was proud of that issue, not only because he had surmounted his physical illness and the obstacles placed in the way of getting the mechanical plant going, but also because it was an excellent product. Even the *Register*, eyeing the newcomer with hostility, complimented it as to size and typography. But it viewed the *Whig*'s content disdainfully: "We had intended, upon the perusal of its columns, to reply to some of the things which they contain, but after some reflection, have concluded not to do so, as *everybody knows Brownlow*." [7]

The *Whig* editor, in characteristic fashion, had opened fire immediately. His awareness of Crozier's duplicity and other steps taken to oppose him steamed up his combative disposition. When McKee boasted that the reorganized *Register* had a circulation of 3,000, Brownlow needled back that this figure was melting because many subscribers were dropping the *Register* and taking the *Whig*. He put it thus:

Nor have we sought, directly or indirectly, to induce any man to quit the *Register* and take our paper. They come voluntarily and declare that they have been "sold to the Dutch"—handed over, soul and body, to the "tender mercies" of an organized *Company of Capitalists*, who have purchased the *Register*, and placed at its head, the *anti-railroad patriots* of the late *Tribune*! (*Whig*, May 19, 1849).

The *Tribune* had achieved a reputation of outright opposition to the construction of the East Tennessee and Georgia Railroad from Dalton, Georgia, to Knoxville, and while its name had disappeared the editor now was at the helm of the *Register*.

Defiance was a characteristic of the Parson, and it burst out with this notice in his first Knoxville issue:

To such as have generously informed us, *second handed*, that we will not be permitted to do here, as we did in Jonesborough, and that for any abuse of them or their friends, we will be shot down in the street, we have only to say let them abuse us, either through the city papers, or in the private circle, and we will teach them, in terms not to be misunderstood, that they have mistaken their man. We may not satisfy them that we are a man of richly stored intellect—of vigorous eloquence—of earnest devotion to truth—and of superiority to all selfish views—but we will convince them of our *incapability of fear* (*Ibid.*).

Before leaving Jonesboro Brownlow had charted a course designed to gain the support of rank and file readers, especially the rural ones. In a statement in the *Whig*, accompanying the prospectus of his forthcoming newspaper in Knoxville he asserted:

We have no right to expect the patronage of Knoxville, as the different wings of the Whig party there and of the religious factions have their papers and are committed to them respectively. These papers, moreover, can be managed by them, as they long have *been*—while our press will utterly refuse to wear the color of any clique. We shall rely upon the *real People*, in all the counties of East Tennessee—not on the *leaders* of parties and cliques in the towns and villages for our support (*Whig*, February 5, 1849).

He caught up this theme in his first issue at Knoxville, pointing out the benefits of competition:

We shall go for all kinds of business being thrown open to free and full competition, and for all classes and conditions of men having restored to them those equal rights which a certain system of favoritism has been the means of filching from them. For strenuously asserting such views and maintaining such principles, those whose *selfishness* will likely suffer may regard us as laboring under mental derangement. But if this be lunacy, it is at all events such lunacy as will be passed for sound and excellent sense in the judgment of the patriotic and intelligent masses of both parties (*Whig*, May 19, 1849).

Two months later he wrote more bluntly:

The People are against all monopolies—so are we. The people are for Railroads and a liberal system of Internal Improvements generally—so are we, for the latter because needed so much, and for the former, because they are demanded by the masses and are their dues . . . .

A House-Carpenter, by trade, and a poor man by birth and by raising, our

Above: the home of William G. Brownlow on East Cumberland Avenue in Knoxville (right in the picture) was taken with the camera facing west, stationed at a point about 400 feet west of the Coliseum-Auditorium. [McClung Collection, Lawson McGhee Library, University of Tennessee.]

At top right: this photograph of the west side of Brownlow's home looking east on East Cumberland was taken in 1923 by the late Russell Harrison, an artist with the Capper Engraving Co. [McClung Collection, Lawson McGhee Library, Knoxville.]

At bottom right: Parson Brownlow's massive walnut bed was used for many years, certainly during the Civil War when he was a prisoner under guard at his home. A top piece about 18 inches high and containing another carving has been lost. The bed, thought to resemble the Lincoln bed in the White House, is now in the home of Mrs. John F. Brownlow, widow of the Parson's grandson. [*Journal* Staff Photograph by Hugh Lunsford.]

sympathies are with the Mechanics, Farmers and laboring classes. We neither wish to pull down the rich, nor bolster them up by partial laws, beneficial to them alone, and injurious to all besides. All we desire is . . . that the *property* of the rich may be placed on the same footing with the labors of the poor.—The *scrub* aristocracy of Knoxville, whose pride we have rather wounded of late, have recently held us up through the columns of the *Register* as a man making fun of *poor* men and as the enemy of *Mechanics*! An orphan boy, in the adjoining State of Virginia—raised and schooled by a charitable Uncle—serving a regular apprenticeship to the Carpenter's trade—having always been poor—and being still poor—it is highly becoming in us to make sport of poor folks and mechanics! The idea is so absurd that it needs no contradiction (*Whig*, July 28, 1849).

The *Register* maintained only briefly its policy of ignoring Brownlow. By midsummer it described the *Whig* as "a vile and licentious newspaper," and called the Parson the "black mail editor." It accused him of trying to threaten merchants and a bank with reprisals for failure to advertise, and of writing some of the letters he attributed to correspondents. [8]

The controversy edged over into the religious field as Brownlow charged McKee and the *Register* with hostility toward the Methodist Church. This was not a surprising development because upon coming to Knoxville the *Whig* editor had obtained the contract to print the *Methodist Episcopalian*, edited by his old friend, Sam Patton. Brownlow and Patton stated that the *Whig* shop had obtained the contract by underbidding the previous printer. An unidentified contributor viciously attacked Patton in the *Register*. Patton demanded the contributor's name from McKee. The *Register* editor refused to divulge it and snatched up for a target this statement by Patton in replying to a charge that Brownlow exercised a large hand in the *Episcopalian*'s policy: "W. G. Brownlow has never written one line for the paper we edit, since it came to his office, and probably he never will—we have never taken one article from the columns of the *Whig*, and probably we never will." [9] McKee, with considerable imagination and some gleeful, malicious humor, presented this as "Brownlow Condemned by His Church," with this elaboration:

But it is a religious phenomenon when one minister of the Gospel considers it due to his own reputation, and the moral and religious sentiments of his subscribers and the community, to ostracize from his paper the writings of another minister of the Gospel of his own church of twenty years standing, and who professes to possess more piety and honesty than any of his companions . . . .

The judgment pronounced upon him from the bosom of his own Church, will meet with a hearty response . . . . A wholesale and retail dealer in falsehood and slander, his vanity and love of notoriety has [*sic.*] spurred him on to hunt up his victims with the keen scent, and to pursue them with the ferocity and cruelty of the bloodhound. *Always* the assailant, *never* the first assailed, in order to minister to the morbid and vicious appetites of those who do not consider the evils he inflicts upon society, or some of them would turn from him in disgust, he has plunged his poisonous fangs into numberless females, and with the most insatiable cruelty, held them up to the glaring gaze of the world, until some of them have fled from his presence broken-hearted—bereft of reason, and lain themselves down to die the most pitiable objects of anguish and despair!

The same issue of the *Register* that construed Patton's statement as a condemnation by his church also blazoned "The Black Mail Editor Presented By A Grand Jury!" in reporting that the *Whig* editor had been indicted for conducting a lottery.[10] Brownlow had printed an advertisement of a lottery by an eastern firm, but apparently he had no interest in the outcome, and the charge against him was dismissed in Anderson County Circuit Court. Before the charge was dismissed Brownlow had accused the *Register* of having carried similar advertisements and reported that two of its financial backers, Humes and Campbell, each had bought $5.00 tickets in a lottery.[11] He soared into print with this offer:

We propose to Mr. Humes that he can have his *church organ* taken in [to jail], and we will carry with us a Methodist Hymn Book, and the best pair of lungs in Knoxville; and like Paul and Silas, we will make the Prison walls resound with criminal melody at the hour of midnight! Nay, more, if we don't *sing* and *play* the prison doors open, why then let us serve out our lawful time! (*Whig*, December 1, 1849).

This shaft, tinged with Brownlow's sarcastic humor, was the first he had sent against Humes. Earlier in the war with the *Register* and its backers he had written that he did not associate Humes and Sneed with the hot fire the older newspaper was concentrating upon the newcomer. The Parson seemed to be a little unsure where Campbell stood and directed most of his wrath against Crozier and McKee, with a portion for Swan. Perhaps Brownlow's deference to Humes lay in the fact that he owed the rector for a note of undesignated amount that the Parson probably contracted before the move to Knoxville. Humes had sent the note to T. A. R. Nelson at Jonesboro for collection and in the fall of 1849 asked for its return in order to make arrangements for payment or additional security.[12] The Parson appears nowhere to have mentioned the obligation.

The controversy took on a sinister cast shortly before the close of 1849. Brownlow accused his enemies of a bold plot to seize by force his office "and to destroy our presses, type and fixtures." Weapons had been collected and stored in a law office on Gay Street, and the assault was planned for a time when the Parson was away from the plant. The plot was leaked, however. Several of Brownlow's friends, heavily armed, stationed themselves in front of the *Whig* office. Upon the editor's return he and a guard of friends remained in the office for several days and nights to repel the attack. It never came. The *Register* brushed off the story as something concocted by Brownlow to enlist sympathy. The Parson threatened to lay evidence of the plot before the grand jury and invited Swan to sue over the accusations made in the *Whig*, but no legal action of any sort followed. In later years Brownlow accused Crozier of having stirred up the lottery indictment and the plot to destroy the newspaper plant. Crozier's law office was the place used as a depository for the collected arms, Brownlow claimed. At the time Brownlow reported the plot he did not identify Crozier by name.[13]

It became obvious early in 1850 that after months of ruthless, furious and envenomed newspaper warfare with words, influence, trickery and probably an attempted destruction of Brownlow's newspaper plant, the *Whig* was firmly established in Knoxville. Perhaps a formal announcement by the *Register* that it intended to ignore Brownlow because he was "UNWORTHY OF NOTICE" constituted such an admission. The Parson so construed it in these triumphant passages:

Not wishing to be outdone by them [the *Register* owners and editors] in *courtesy*, however, we take our leave of them, one and all, in this our *New Year's Address*. We take leave of them because they have retired from the field in disgust, and not because we have discovered *they are unworthy of notice*. We deem the "Joint Stock" party altogether worthy of our notice, and pledge ourselves to the public, that whenever they meddle in our affairs, either publicly or privately, we will notice them again, as we have been doing, regardless of consequence (*Whig*, January 12, 1850).

The *Whig* editor boasted that his subscription list had gone up as the *Register*'s had gone down, in spite of the fact that the "vanity, aristocracy, *fictitious* capital, and *pretended* decency of Knoxville is

against us, and we desire them to continue their opposition." He
thanked

the PEOPLE of EAST TENNESSEE, for our success, and for a subscription list
superior to any in this division of our State. The People have sympathized with
us in our struggle against Merchants, Banks, Universities, Cliques, and corrupt
money-holders—and it is the People that have written out our subscription list
(*Ibid.*).

Whig policies that had worked at Jonesboro also proved successful
at Knoxville. The Parson opposed the rich and powerful, championed
the farmer and workman, and strove for mass circulation. This forced
the advertisers to recognize the value of his wide readership, and
thereby, he escaped local domination. His fearlessness let him select
any target, and his confidence that he was among the best in fighting
and writing, as it seemed to be required of most editors, led him to
believe he could command readership. It did. He achieved this strong
position a year and a half after entering Knoxville uninvited. Temple
told of his having held a "consultation on the advisability of moving
with his paper to this larger town," in Knoxville in the spring of
1849, but does not suggest he was urged to do so. He was, as mentioned before, warned to stay away. The Parson acted upon his own
conviction and counted himself as the *Whig*'s major resource. The
blow on the head at Jonesboro failed to stop him, although it left
him close to being an invalid for months. He acknowledged this two
years later. He conceded, "We were sorely afflicted the entire
summer and were not half a man in point of physical strength—
although we said nothing about it and claimed nothing from that
consideration."[14]

As Brownlow opened his second volume in Knoxville, he must
have been in high spirits as he published this summation of the
Register and its backers:

We know *whom* we have to meet, and we know *how to meet them*. Restrained by
no principle, moral or religious, by no feelings of humanity, by no mercy for an
intended victim—and destitute of everything like manly courage—the vile men
who are most active in their opposition to us here would consumate [*sic.*] their
wicked design with the torch of an incendiary, or under the more [*sic.*] black
and disgraceful flag of the midnight assassin. In the hollow concaves [*sic.*] of
secret malice, these wanton and fiendish instruments of the Prince of Darkness
regularly convene for our benefit; and the infinitely infernal council held at
Pandemonium, where all the devils meet in 'committee of the whole' to plot

treason against the God of the Universe, afford a more perfect exhibition of the malice of hell, than is displayed by these miscreants (*Whig*, May 25, 1850).

The *Register* fought back with everything upon which it could lay its hand. It reversed its old position of not noticing Brownlow. It revived the old story that Brownlow had been whipped for stealing jewelry in Nashville, reveled in reporting that the Parson submitted to the libel charge in North Carolina brought by Humphrey Posey, and republished the story of the *Whig*'s war with Landon C. Haynes and the *Tennessee Sentinel*, in which the editor's drunken brother, A. S. Brownlow, had accused him of trying to get him to assassinate Haynes. As already mentioned, A. S. Brownlow repudiated this statement as having been made when drunk. The Parson had been through these charges before and he reprinted his answers, with numerous certificates and thundering accusations. The *Whig* boldly pronounced McKee to have been caught as a thief years earlier in upper East Tennessee. It even relied on its old foe, Haynes, to support the charge. Brownlow also shifted his fire against the opposition, concentrating on Swan and Campbell rather than on Crozier. He also identified Campbell as the author of articles published by the *Register* attacking Sam Patton; and he hinted he might alter his mild treatment of Humes.[15]

The controversy reached such a pitch late in 1849 that a town meeting was called to reduce the fury. It failed. Materially the *Whig* prospered, in both circulation and advertising volume. The Parson's confidence that he was on top was reflected in his resumption of his travels and editorial correspondence that he had neglected during the early stages of the Knoxville newspaper war.[16]

Late in 1854, a few months after a devastating cholera epidemic, the *Register* collapsed. McKee assigned his interest to W. C. Kain, member of a prominent Knoxville family, who attempted to keep the publication going and to sell it as an operating business. This failed, and the *Register* was sold at public auction on January 1, 1855. The assets brought $2,000, which the Parson graciously estimated was about their value. He rubbed a final application of salt into the five underwriters by holding that McKee had outsmarted them by pocketing a political slush fund, running up large and unpaid bills at the stores, and meeting the wages of his help in personal notes. He complimented McKee because he not only made money, but he "pocketed it and left his friends and creditors to pay for the roast." McKee, however, lost his house and moved to Nashville.[17]

The fallout from the struggle and the collapse of the *Register* was extensive. The original backers of the investment lost heavily. James W. Campbell, clerk of the State Supreme Court and of the United States District Court, had been directed to quit writing for the *Register* and was fired from the other clerkship by United States District Judge West Humphreys. Judge Humphreys replaced Campbell with a Colonel Cummings, but whether the judge's action was taken because of Campbell's attacks upon Patton and Brownlow was not apparent. The *Register* bitterly resented Campbell's discharge (*Whig*, May 14, 1853).

CHAPTER VII NOTES

[1] Marginal note by John Bell Brownlow, *Whig*, May 19, 1849. In 1847 Knox County voted 2,126 for the Whig nominee for governor, 573 for the Democratic nominee; in 1848 it cast 2,140 votes for General Zachary Taylor, the Whig nominee for President, and 439 for Senator Lewis Cass, the Democratic nominee. *Ibid.*, November 22, 1848. See also *ibid.*, October 18, May 20, 1840.

[2] Marginal note by John Bell Brownlow, *ibid.*, May 19, 1849; Arnell, p. 128; *Whig*, October 27, 1860.

[3] *Ibid.*, Brownlow to Nelson, March 19, 1849. Nelson Papers.

[4] Temple, *Notable Men*, pp. 274, 335; *Whig*, October 27, 1860. It is unfortunate that no records are available giving Crozier's response to Brownlow's charges. He was too bold and too skillful a lawyer not to have offered a strong defense.

[5] Rule, ed., *Standard History*, pp. 318, 316, 328; *Whig*, August 25, 1849. Sketches of four of the trust deed signers appear in Rothrock, ed., *French Broad-Holston*, Crozier, pp. 404-405, Swan, pp. 493-495, Sneed, pp. 487, 488, Humes, pp. 431-432. Detail on Campbell is in the *Whig*, August 23, 1851, February 12, June 11, 1853.

[6] *Ibid.*, October 27, 1860; receipt given to James W. Nelson, in Knoxville, April 17, 1849, by H. A. M. White, cashier of the Union Bank. James W. Nelson was in the Brownlow home at Elizabethton the night the editor was fired upon. John Bell Brownlow marginal note, *Whig*, February 8, 1843.

[7] *Ibid.*, October 27, 1860; *Register*, May 30, 1849.

[8] *Ibid.*, July 25, 1849; *Whig*, September 8, 1849.

[9] *Ibid.*, August 25, June 2, November 10, 24, 1849.

[10] *Register*, December 1, 1849.

[11] *Whig*, March 16, 23, 1850, December 1, 1849.

[12] For example, *ibid.*, August 25, 1849; Thomas W. Humes to Nelson, November 17, 1849. Nelson Papers.

[13] *Whig*, December 15, 1849, printed on one sheet of paper, four columns to each side; *ibid.*, December 19, 1849, quoting *Register*, December 22, 1849, *Whig*, December 15, 29, 1849, March 6, 1858, October 27, 1860.

[14] *Ibid.*, January 12, 1850. Temple, *Notable Men*, pp. 274, 346.

[15] *Whig*, July 5, August 23, July 5, August 23, June 21, July 5, August 23, 1851.

[16] *Ibid.*, December 22, 1849, March 9, 1850; for editorial correspondence see October 18, 25, November 1, 8, 15, 22, 29, December 6, 20, 27, 1851, January 10, 17, 31, February 7, 1852, March 19, 26, April 2, October 15, 29, November 5, 1853.

[17] *Register*, September 1, 1854, November 25, 1854, February 21, 1855; Rothrock, ed., *French Broad-Holston*, p. 348; *Whig*, January 6, 1855; Rule, ed., *Standard History*, p. 316.

THE WHIG.

"Independent in all Things—Neutral in Nothing."   Chapter No. 8

AHEAD OF THE TIMES

Parson Brownlow could deliver smashing blows, but he also knew how to select vulnerable targets. Upon his arrival in Knoxville he assailed the *Register*, as lukewarm, if not actually opposed to the building of the railroad line from Dalton, Georgia, to Knoxville. The Parson had always warmly embraced the Whig Party doctrine calling for a system of internal improvements, and now he riddled his opposition as taking a stand that went against its own party. As mentioned before, McKee had been an editor of the *Tribune* when that newspaper had fought railroads. The *Register* adopted the line that its critical, or lukewarm, stand on the Dalton line was for the benefit of the public and helpful to the project because it pointed out mistakes that could be corrected.[1]

The Parson, however, charged the *Register* with repudiating fundamental Whig Party policy and with opposing the public's demand for better transportation facilities. He made the *Whig* stand out by carrying far more railroad news than did the *Register*. In the course of this policy Brownlow conveyed the impression that McKee was a figurehead and was forced to publish as his own articles written by his financial backers. The nettled McKee retorted that he was solely responsible for the *Register*'s editorial position. With considerable sarcasm and exaggeration Brownlow construed McKee's reply as a challenge to a duel which he said he could not accept because McKee had so many masters he would have to fight six men, not one.[2]

These policies, added to the *Whig*'s defiance of the powerful and the wealthy and its espousal of the interests of the farmer and the laborer, brought what Brownlow wanted, mass circulation. The first *Whig* published in Knoxville claimed a circulation of 2,000, a calculated and gross exaggeration designed to meet the *Register*'s boast of 3,000. For at the close of the first volume on May 18, 1850, Brownlow admitted that the *Whig* had something more than 1,000 at the

outset, and increased it to more than 2,000 only during the year. At
that time he proudly wrote, "The circulation has penetrated into
every state in the Union and has reached almost every class of readers, being taken by all parties, political and religious."[3]

The *Whig*'s first quarters in Knoxville were crowded and inadequate but his mechanical equipment was new and up-to-date. He
bought two Washington presses, one at least of the cylinder type
rather than the flatbed utilized at Elizabethton and Jonesboro type
and other print shop equipment. Into the "one-story frame building
on Gay Street, 45 by 18 feet, one square north of the business part
of the city, standing 'solitary and alone' without the advantage of a
lot," which Nelson had obtained for him when he rescued the equipment, Brownlow crowded his two presses, stands, cases and ten
hands.

The original rental was $50.00 a year, but early in 1850 it was
doubled. The Parson offered his note for $100, but additional
security was demanded. Brownlow rounded up fourteen cosigners.
The note, dated January 25, 1850, was given to Barkley McGhee,
"guardian of the minor heirs of A. R. Humes, deceased." This Humes
was a brother of Rector Humes, one of the *Register*'s underwriters
who only a few months earlier had been pressing for the collection of
a note signed by Brownlow. The Parson absolved McGhee of any
spitefulness. He said the pressure came from "a certain unholy alliance in *Knoxville* and is but another link in the great chain of
opposition to us."[4] The editor solved his rent problem by con-
structing his own building on the lot where his residence stood on
East Cumberland Avenue. In less than a year he had moved his plant
and office into it, thereby escaping from "a miserable old rat harbor
and shelter for dead pigs," as well as excessive rent.[5] The new
location also freed him from

all obligations to a hateful scrub aristocracy who govern the city under the name
of the "corporate authorities" of this place. We are without the limits of the
corporation—we are residing in that part of the city—ancient and venerable—
known as "hardscrabble" upon premises where we cannot be disturbed and
where no pious pretenders, no religious fraud or priestly cunning can double the
price of rent on us (*Whig*, December 14, 1850).

The Parson got around to gouging his spurs into Rector Humes. The
identification was clear, if not by name. He must have taken care of
the note Humes held.

The ten hands, headed by Brownlow's experienced foreman John W. O'Brien from Jonesboro, made Brownlow's partner upon the Knoxville move, found the work of composition increasing. By early 1850 the *Whig* was carrying eleven columns of advertising out of the newspaper's twenty-four. A year later, with more than two pages of advertising, Brownlow estimated one issue contained more than $200 of revenue from that source. The Whigs won a smashing victory in Tennessee in August 1851. They elected William Campbell governor and won majorities in both houses of the General Assembly. Sweet as this news was the Parson weighed political victory against the advantages of advertising revenue and came up with this conclusion: "Owing to a large supply of new advertisements this week, which must be inserted, we can publish but little of election news."[6]

The Parson's sole selling point for advertising was circulation. He followed a policy that would drive modern newspapers with their large sales and promotion staffs frantic; he permitted no solicitation of advertising. The advertiser had to feel the pull of the *Whig*'s circulation, and Brownlow warned them to see that their own copy was properly prepared; his staff could not undertake this chore. Once an advertiser walked into the *Whig* office, however, he was warmly treated, and sometimes favored with puffs. This policy appeared to get out of hand and the Parson avowed on Christmas Day 1852 that he would run no more of them for free. This rule probably wilted as did his repeated pledges to sign no more notes, for the puffs reappeared.[7]

Brownlow produced his first Knoxville *Whig* with six columns; before long he shifted to seven, then to eight. He introduced a much smaller body type which he announced would permit the newspaper to carry more advertising and news in the same space as previously. Despite these steps, advertisements soon began to encroach upon the editorial page space, usually on page two. The Parson also adopted a tougher subscription policy, one he described as the "Pay-Down System." He had required that out-of-state subscriptions be accompanied by the $2.00 annual charge. He now extended it to all subscribers. Even advertisers felt this rule: cash was required with the advertisements to be inserted, exceptions being made for Knoxville merchants and those placing legal notices.[8]

Brownlow and his original Knoxville partner, John W. O'Brien, parted company late in 1852. O'Brien went to Loudon to publish the

Free Press. The Parson announced in a few days that "having disposed of my office two weeks ago to a good printer who pays me in services, I shall now give my whole attention to the editorial management," but he mentioned no names, and on the front page the usual legend of ownership and management read "William G. Brownlow, Editor and Proprietor." Just before the close of 1853 the editor announced that "W. G. O'Brien, who has acted as foreman in our office for some time," was being sent out to collect delinquent accounts.[9]

The details of management are obscure for eight months because the files of the *Whig* from January 28 to October 7, 1854, are missing. The resumed files show W. G. O'Brien and H. K. Lathim as publishers and proprietors, and as the *Register* expired significant changes were forecast. The publishers and Brownlow announced the *Whig* would be printed "on a new power press, with new type and an entire dress of new materials." Brownlow would remain as editor, but "a new and competent gentleman, who comes into the concern, will take charge of the local and advertising columns, and the entire business department.[10]

The announcements that followed suggested that the changes to be made required financing and experience more extensive than was possessed by O'Brien and Lathim. Three Kinsloe brothers—W. A. and E. P. B. of Philadelphia, and J. B. G.—the last already in the printing business in Knoxville, joined forces and began publication of the *Whig*, the *Register*, the *Presbyterian Witness* and the *Southern Journal of Medical and Physical Sciences*, along with which business was a bindery. J. B. G. became the *Register* publisher with Hardin P. Shannon as editor. E. P. B. purchased the subscription list, advertising custom and good will or the *Whig*, and retained "its old, fearless, independent and successful editor, Dr. Brownlow," who had "exclusive control of the editorial columns."

Brownlow's contract was with William Augustus Kinsloe, who agreed to pay the Parson $2,000 for the newspaper's good will, patronage, subscription and advertising properties. Payment was to be made in installments: $500 on April 1, 1855, $500 on or before October 1, 1855, and $1,000 on or before April 1, 1856. The sale did not "include any portion of the materials now belonging to said *Whig* office, nor any debts due said office for advertising or job work," up to the contract date of February 5, 1855.

The Kinsloes obviously continued to use the *Whig* plant in East

Knoxville until their new equipment was installed in a Gay Street building.[11] Brownlow made his headquarters in his "sanctum in East Knoxville," and advertised his old equipment for sale.

He was glad to shed the burden of publishing and devote himself to the happier task of writing. He had gone through a long and arduous struggle with the *Register*; he had beat off an attempt to unionize his workmen, which was started in 1851 and collapsed early in 1852, and which he claimed was instigated by McKee and the *Register*; and he had remained in Knoxville during the cholera epidemic in 1854, helping as he could the few hundred people remaining after thousands fled.[12] He permitted himself this congratulation:

This is an arrangement I have long desired to complete, so as to secure for the paper its publication after a style, alike creditable to its Proprietors, and becoming the growing interest of our City; and next, so as to give my entire time to its editorial management, that I may make it, as I believe I can and will do, second to no Journal in the South and West.

I will remain the sole editor of the paper—the judge of what goes into its columns—the owner of its exchange list, and, as should be the case under the circumstances, I will be alone responsible for what appears in its columns of an offensive character. I am not insensible to the responsibility of this position, but I have assumed it of choice, and without any hesitancy (*Whig*, February 10, 1855).

The Kinsloes cleaned up the front page of the *Whig*, which Brownlow had cluttered with rules, two mottoes and the double title of the newspaper. *Brownlow's Knoxville Whig*, in reduced but clean sharp 72-point, letter spaced type, was all that remained at the top of the page, even the words *An Independent Journal* being swept aside. The new body type was Old Style Caslon 471, condensed so that it gave 7.2 more characters to the line than that previously used. This represented a substantial gain in wordage when applied to a 32-column newspaper. Also introduced was a column rule with a slightly wider base so that more white space appeared between the columns of body type. The *Whig*'s appearance was more professional, and the additional space available for news and advertising was considerable. The Parson estimated that the new dress "requires about *three times* the amount of copy" previously needed. It also was the first time that the word "copy," now in general use in print shops, newspapers and other places preparing materials for reproduction, was used by Brownlow.[13]

The arrangement for a separate, or joint, company to assume

responsibility for the mechanical, advertising, business and circulation operations of two competing newspapers, while each publication retained its editorial identity, was far in advance of its time. In recent years such developments have taken place in many major cities, as dailies, faced with crushing costs, resorted to such organizations to stave off financial ruin. The competing newspapers engaging in such arrangements today often represent opposite political views, and have different hours of publication, as morning and afternoon. The *Whig* and the *Register*, although distinctively flavored by the writing of the respective editors, Brownlow and John M. Fleming, were both based on Whiggery. They supported the American or Knox-Nothing Party, something of a refuge for many former Whigs as that party disintegrated. The only major difference was that the *Register* came out on Thursday, the *Whig* on Saturday. While in Nashville Brownlow sent Fleming an item for publication in the *Register* that he believed would be harmful to the candidacy of Democrat Andrew Johnson, who was running for a second term as governor. The Parson had weighed against the rule that one newspaper never helps another get news the importance of getting the story to injure Johnson in the first newspaper published. He was willing to sacrifice an item for the *Whig* in order to damage Johnson at the earliest moment. The *Whig* also republished from the *Register* an article seeking to justify the use of smaller type in advertisements, a point in which they had a common interest.[14]

The Kinsloes also picked up type from both newspapers to fill the columns of the *American Campaigner*, an American Party propaganda sheet which reached a circulation of 12,000, and in the fall of 1856 prior to the national election the *Whig* reported 6,000 subscribers. Late in 1854 the Parson reported it required two men hand operating the press to run off 2,500 *Whigs*. The partnership solved its much larger circulation by installing a steam engine that had been manufactured in Knoxville.[15]

Brownlow found another outlet for his energies in the Sons of Temperance, a secret organization founded in 1842 and chartered in Tennessee in 1848. The Parson was a confirmed foe of alcoholic beverages, and the order also offered him opportunities to travel and to speak. The Sons sported fancy and colorful regalia; white, red and blue collars to distinguish the divisions; with "rosettes of blue, white and red ribbons." The *Whig* gave extensive coverage to the organization's activities.[16]

Opposition to the order sometimes arose in church circles. Brownlow debated the question with a Baptist preacher from Dandridge who "avowed that he *made* liquor, that he *drank* it, and that he loved it," at the Sulphur Spring Campground in Jefferson County. Brownlow routed the Baptist, according to the *Whig*'s account. The Sons were present in force and in regalia, and after six hours of debate the members of the order, led by a band, "marched around the encampment." The audience was so large the Parson described it as "a sea of heads, spread out before us."[17] Regardless of who made the greatest impression as a debater [and Brownlow was most adept at this kind of encounter], the editor-preacher had dramatized his appearance and built his name and that of his newspaper more firmly into the minds of hundreds.

CHAPTER VIII NOTES

[1] *Whig*, May 19, June 2, 1849; *Register*, May 30, July 25, 1849. Green was not a success in this project. Rothrock, ed., *French Broad-Holston*, p. 106.
[2] *Whig*, June 2, 16, July 7, 1849. For examples of railroad coverage see *ibid.*, May 19, June 2, 16 and thereafter; *ibid.*, July 28, 1849.
[3] *Ibid.*, May 19, 1849, May 18, 1850.
[4] *Ibid.*, October 27, 1860, February 2, 1850; Rothrock, ed., *French Broad-Holston*, p. 471; *Whig*, February 2, 1850.
[5] *Ibid.*, November 30, December 14, 1850.
[6] *Ibid.*, February 2, May 19, February 5, March 9, 1850; February 15, August 23, 1851; Folmsbee *et al.*, *Short History*, p. 230; *Whig*, August 23, 1851.
[7] *Ibid.*, May 19, 1849, December 25, 1852, February 26, April 2, 1853.
[8] *Ibid.*, May 19, November 24, 1849, October 1, 1853, January 1, 1854.
[9] *Ibid.*, September 11, October 2, 1852, June 2, December 24, 1853.
[10] One issue for the period of the missing files appears in a microfilm miscellany, *ibid.*, September 30, 1854. McClung Collection. O'Brien and Lathim appear as partners after the lapse of files, *ibid.*, September 7, December 30, 1854.
[11] *Ibid.*, March 14, 1855; *Register*, February 21, 1855; *Whig*, February 10, 1855; Ben Harris McClary, Ed., "The Sale of Brownlow's *Knoxville Whig*; An 'Article of Agreement between William Augustus Kinsloe and William G. Brownlow,' " ETHS *PUBL.* No. 35, pp. 96-99; hereafter cited as McClary.
[12] *Whig*, April 7, March 18, 1855, July 26, August 9, 16, September 6, 1851, January 10, 1852, October 11, November 4, September 30 (this issue is in newspaper miscellany, not on microfilm. McClung Collection) 1854.

[13] For examples of old and new front pages see *ibid*., March 24, May 5, 1855, for the Parson's estimate of copy required, May 5, 1855.

[14] *Register*, June 21, 1855; *Whig*, April 21, 1855, April 12, 1856.

[15] *Ibid*., April 12, 1856, October 4, 1856, December 23, 30, 1854, June 9, 1855.

[16] *Ibid*., September 14, October 12, November 23, 30, 1850, January 11, 1851, and thereafter for years, September 27, 1851.

[17] *Ibid*., June 14, 21, 1851.

The Whig

"Put None on Guard but Americans."   Chapter No. 9

THE BUSY PEN

The voice was William G. Brownlow's first instrument for reaching and influencing people. He directed it principally at Methodist and camp meeting congregations. But soon he saw that the printed word was both more lasting and carried further in the controversies into which he naturally gravitated. Today no written record of his sermons remains. But the printed accounts of his struggles on political and religious issues, written by his hand, were contained in nine books, eight of which may be found, several pamphlets, a publication in his quarrel with the Rev. Frederick Ross, first quarterly and then monthly, and the files of the *Whig*, for which he wrote for more than twenty-eight years. He was, however, proud of his powerful voice and he used it unsparingly[1] until it failed him just when he had relied upon it to serve him in a forum of national importance on one of the great issues of the day. He abjectly wrote to his opponent in the debate to be held in Philadelphia, in September 1858, on "Ought American Slavery to be Perpetuated?" that his voice had failed him, and he asked for a postponement. The Rev. Abram Pryne, prepared to take the negative side, declined, and the Parson was forced to hear his arguments spoken by a reader.[2] Brownlow's pen never failed him. It scratched on for years.

The young preacher dashed off his first pamphlet, entitled "Address to the Hiwasseans, on the Subject of Sabbath Schools," in 1830, and two years later two more. He opposed the South Carolina nullification movement in the first, and defended himself for the libel conviction which Humphrey Posey obtained against him in the second.[3] His first book, *Helps to the Study of Presbyterianism*, already mentioned, took some licks at the Baptists, and in 1842 he gave this denomination the benefit of a full scale work of 229 pages. Brownlow started it as a series of articles in the *Whig*, incorporating them into a book.[4]

The Parson's first full length book on national affairs was a campaign document designed to help the candidacy of Henry Clay for President. He published it at Jonesboro.[5] A banner year was 1856, in terms of quantity production. The Parson turned out two volumes. One arose from another controversy between Methodists and Baptists, and the second was a mixture of political and religious issues. The arrangement with the Kinsloes freed him from business management of the *Whig* and gave him greater opportunity to write. The Parson produced *The Great Iron Wheel Examined: or its False Spokes Extracted, and an Exhibition of Elder Graves, its Builder, in a Series of Chapters.*[6] The Rev. J. R. Graves, pastor of a large Baptist church in Nashville and editor of the *Tennessee Baptist*, published in that city, had written *The Great Iron Wheel; or Republicanism Backwards and Christianity Reversed* [Nashville, 1856]. The book was a collection of letters that first appeared in the *Tennessee Baptist*. Graves addressed them to Methodist Bishop Joshua Soule, who lived in the Nashville area. The Baptist clergyman portrayed the Methodist church organization as monarchial, with its leaders resembling the outer edge of a great iron wheel, while turning inside it were thousands of small wheels representing lesser pastors and members. The Methodists themselves used the illustration to describe favorably their church organization. Graves called attention to the lack of freedom which the inner wheels enjoyed, in contrast to the Baptist principle of self-government by the individual churches. Graves also described Methodism as "the popery of Protestantism," and told the church: "According to your own frank admissions, your Mother is the Episcopal Church, and this church is called by Christ a *harlot* and an *abomination*, and your Grandmother is the Church of Rome—the great whore and mother of harlots. . . ."[7]

Bishop Soule, who had preached since he was seventeen and had now reached his seventy-fourth year, ignored the letters, but other Methodists felt an answer was necessary. Among them was the Parson. In later years he revealed that he wrote the reply to Graves at the solicitation of agents for the Methodist Publishing House in Nashville.[8] It was such a splendid opportunity to engage in a church controversy on a broad scale that the Parson probably relished it. Some sentiment may have entered into his decision, for it was at a Holston Conference at Abingdon, Virginia, in 1826, presided over by Bishop Soule, that Brownlow received his first appointment to a Methodist Circuit.

Harsh as Graves had been in his diatribe against the Methodist Church, he had not resorted to insulting personalities. The Parson maintained no such delicacy. He ridiculed and castigated in characteristic fashion. At one point he accused Graves of telling twenty-five falsehoods in twelve pages. The book was a commercial success for in 1862, when a new edition was published, it was reported that 100,000 copies of the first had been sold. Brownlow disclaimed having made any profit out of the book, although it had paid the agents, Stevenson & Evans, reasonably. He was mortified when a South Carolinian inquired by letter if he and Graves had conspired to create the controversy in order to stimulate the sale of the book. The Parson denied having entered into such a dastardly deal, and also vindicated Graves from any such "infamy."[9]

Close upon the heels of this book, Brownlow brought out *Americanism Contrasted with Foreignism, Romanism and Bogus Democracy, in the Light of Reason, History and Scripture; in which Certain Demagogues, in Tennessee and elsewhere, Are Shown Up in their True Colors* [Nashville, 1856], hereafter referred to as *Americanism Contrasted*. In announcing that it was ready for sale, the author correctly described it as "Our Book for the Campaign." The major portion of its 200 pages consisted of a polemic against the Roman Catholic Church and the Democratic Party and accused them of a political alliance. Brownlow expanded the work with a number of editorials from the *Whig* and a bitter speech he made against Andrew Johnson in Nashville after the latter's reelection as governor in 1855. The Parson, having cast his lot with the American Party, supported Millard Fillmore in his forlorn 1856 race against Democrat James Buchanan and Republican John C. Fremont. Buchanan won, and the Democrats carried Tennessee by a majority of almost 7,500.[10]

Graves had been preparing another blast against the Methodists even as he wrote the first book. It was *The Little Iron Wheel, a Declaration of Christian Rights and Articles, Showing the Despotism of Episcopal Methodism* [Nashville 1856], by H. D. Bascomb, D.D. Bascomb, formerly a Methodist bishop, had written a critical piece on the tight control at the top of the Methodist organization and sympathized with fellow preachers who had called for more republicanism. Graves picked up Bascomb's work and applied it to his own "Notes of Application and Illustration." He also found room to include the well-frayed story of Brownlow's submission on a charge of

libel in the Humphrey-Posey case, and of A. S. Brownlow's repudiated affidavit that the Parson had tried to get him to murder Landon
Haynes. Graves did not mention the repudiation.[11]

Brownlow got out a final book in the controversy, The "Little
Iron Wheel" Enlarged; or Elder Graves, its Builder, Daguerreotyped,
by way of an Appendix. To which are Added Some Personal Explanations [Nashville, 1857]. Much of the book was given over to
villification of Graves, but the Parson also included his defense in the
Posey and A. S. Brownlow affairs, and tacked on a "sermon" on
slavery he had delivered at the opening of the Southern Commercial
Convention at Knoxville the same year as the book was published.
Thus padded, the book contained 137 pages, but as in Graves' second
work they were sized much smaller than the first two works by the
combatting authors.[12] Brownlow must not have viewed this work
with much satisfaction, for he neglected to mention it in the files
that are available, much less to promote it, in the Whig.

All traces of a book on temperance and a defense of the Sons of
Temperance which Brownlow wrote in 1850 seem to have disappeared. It consisted of 112 pages in twenty-six chapters, but the author
did not print its title and copies of it are not available.[13] Two
more books lay in the Parson's future. One he would co-author with
his opponent, the Rev. Abram Pryne. It would be an account of the
debate on salvery in Philadelphia. The other would be his most famous, his story of the events leading up to the Civil War, his closing
of the Whig, his imprisonment, release and triumphant and profitable
tour of the North. But they belong to the later era when the crisis
intensified and exploded into conflict.

The prevailing historical view of the Parson presents him as a
whirling dervish of hatred, dedicated to the evil art of denouncing,
and constantly on the search for new and more lurid controversies.
His books and a first look at his newspaper support this impression.
His friend O. P. Temple wrote of the Jonesboro Whig under the
Parson's direction: "There was not in the United States such another
volcano as this paper became, constantly muttering, seething and
boiling. Woe to the man on whom this storm bursts."[14]

But the Parson had a talent, somewhat lost to history, that of a
roving reporter. He displayed it first in depth as he attended the
inauguration of William Henry Harrison in 1841, and later went on
to the great cities of the East. As he roved the Southeast and East in
the years that followed, he satirized and caricatured his fellow man.

His moods ranged from the amused to the somber, his eye falling at one moment on foodstuff, then on whiskey, and from it to church edifices and their congregations. The Parson compressed great variety into his dispatches. He wrote from Chattanooga in the spring of 1851 of bustling business, new manufacturing plants, the price of bacon, corn and flour, and wound up with two criticisms. The Parson thought that townspeople were getting too much whiskey to drink, judging from the barrels at the landing, and while the Methodists had "a large and commodious house of worship," the Presbyterians, "who have means and influence, worship God in an old rat harbor and dirt pen of which they individually ought to be ashamed. They live in fine houses—they sell goods in comfortable houses, but they worship God in the verriest [sic.] hog pen in the place."[15] The Parson hoped that his criticism would stir the Presbyterians to do something about their church structure. He also was distressed on his first visit to Augusta, Georgia, to find there Tennessee bacon "badly cured and badly smoked" and Tennessee butter so carelessly packed it was soiled with dirt.[16] He sent home information for farmers and shippers, and in Savannah he spoke on the development of trade relations between Knoxville and the coastal city. When he spoke he competed with a singer and the British author, William Makepeace Thackeray, then lecturing in the United States.[17]

The sessions of the Tennessee General Assembly attracted Brownlow to Nashville, but the news he sent home extended beyond legislative and political affairs. A speech he made on temperance "took tolerably well," but he was bored with a Methodist preacher who spoke at McKendree Church and

complained of being unwell, which was fortunate for the congregation, judging from the length of his sermon. Had he been *well*, he might have been preaching until now! In this truth-filled universe, where all the important principles in nature and in morals are at the fingers end of any hearer, there is no reasonable excuse for a preacher to obtrude a long discourse upon a congregation—especially a city congregation, accustomed to hear two and three sermons each Sabbath. Preachers ought to have pity upon their hearers, and not *persecute* them until they are forced to stay at home! (*Whig*, November 22, 1851).

The Parson gave considerably more space—and surprising respect—to a discourse by a Roman Catholic priest delivered the same afternoon. He toured the Cumberland River wharf to report on cargoes and prices. The weather was cold, the mercury hovering a few degrees above zero,[18] but tempers were steaming as

F. K. Zollicoffer and John L. Marling, editors of the *Banner* and *Union*, each
with two or more friends, were on the Square, loaded down to the guards, with
implements—not of *husbandry*, but of uncivil warfare, when the city authorities
arrested both parties, and bound them over to the peace, in bonds of $5,000
each. The cause was crimination and recrimination, in their editorials. The
parties are understood to be game (*Whig*, January 31, 1852).

Among the doctors, also, denunciations were being offered in the
newspapers and in handbills, and challenges were being written. No
one was killed but hostility was strong. The Parson assured his readers, "I take no part in these contests but look quietly on (*Ibid.*).

On the train to Memphis in the spring of 1857 he exchanged
frothy chaff with Isham G. Harris, who was running for governor on
the Democratic ticket. In Somerville, where he visited a relative, he
denounced the Agricultural Bank of Brownsville as a wildcat operation, then turned full circle on the human race and praised "*Jim
Findlay*, the polite and accomplished Barber, a gentleman of color,
alike opposed to Sagnichtism and Black Republicanism . . . in waiting
on me at my room."[19]

The Parson rated himself as a trencherman of the highest order,
and in 1851 when Dr. Jeptha Fowlkes, his friend and fellow editor,
entertained him in Memphis, he marvelled at the menu offered by
the U.S. Hotel:

only think of soup, roast beef, boiled mutton with sauce, good sallad [*sic.*],
ham, and vegetables, green peas, buffalo-tongue, rice blance mange [*sic.*], jelly,
and custards, nice puddings, nuts of every kind, strawberries and cream, and ice
water to cool off on! Had it not been that these are cholera times, I should have
gone it stronger than I did (*Whig*, May 31, 1851).

Brownlow was in Memphis to deliver an address on the evils of
intemperance—in alcoholic beverages. A few days later at Holly
Springs, Mississippi, he encountered a breakfast so revolting he
moaned:

But what had we? A plate of rancid butter, beautifully mixed with *dirt*, to make
it palatable—some crude and indigestible fat meat—some eggs so old as to be all
of a color inside, the *White* having turned *yellow*—some coffee, supposed to have
been made of *rye* or *chestnuts*—some bread with *streaks* of *dirt* running diagonal-
ly through pones, the *latter* resembling in *form* and *scent*, the dirty negro wench
at the head of the table, dishing out the coffee! With the most penitent humility,

I closed my eyes upon all terrestial objects, and *forced* a little of this matter into my unoffending stomach (*Whig*, June 7, 1851).

Sometimes the Parson gorged himself. At Huntsville, Alabama, in 1857, he "partook of the finest dinner I have sat down to in twelve months. I have not fully recovered from the effect of the founder yet."[20] Six years earlier, while staying at a Nashville boarding house, he remained indoors one Sunday because he was "absolutely unwell, *from eating too much*." The Parson and five boarders, all sleeping in one room with three beds, stretched themselves out and bellowed this praise of the landlord's fare:

> Oh, carve me another slice,
> Oh! help me to more gravy still,
> There's nought so sure as something nice
> To conquer care, or grief to kill.
> "I always loved a bit of beef,
> When youth and bliss, and hope were mine,
> And now it gives my heart relief,
> In sorrow's darksome hour to dine"
> (*Whig*, December 13, 1851).

Pretty women, as well as food, caught the Parson's fancy. When Miss Julia Dean appeared at the Adelphi Theater in *Romeo and Juliet* and *The Duke's Wages*, he proclaimed her "one among the prettiest women in America," and as she crossed a muddy street in Nashville, "The grace with which she raised her *petticoat*, and the manner in which its ample folds did undulate, would have charmed John Randolph, a woman hater."[21]

Brownlow found New Orleans so large that he could see but little of it in a week. This he learned when he went there early in 1858 to open a lecture series sponsored by the Mercantile Library Association, a fund-raising operation. He described its churches, hotels, markets, theaters, cemeteries, harbor and rail facilities, but strangely for a city renowned as a gastronomic center, he did not mention his experiences at table (*Whig*, January 30, 1858). The darling of the Parson's eye among Southern cities was Memphis, and in her attractions, especially her feminine ones, he revelled, as he stopped on the first leg of a tour in the spring of 1858. Even some of the Memphis disadvantages attracted his attention:

The *streets* of Memphis are in a worse condition than any streets I ever beheld. The *mud* is deeper, softer, filthier, meaner, and more universally diffused over the city, than any mud, in any civilized town on this continent. . . . They have no paved streets here, and no materials with which to pave streets. . . .

The Irish, known as "the chain gang," are profitably employed in opening out crossing places for each square, on the principal streets. These fill up during the day and night, and are to reopen every morning. It has changed my opinions in part, as to the necessity of a *foreign population* here. They are useful here, and seem to be answering the end of their creation. They commit offenses—are cast into the City Prison—and then made to work out their fines and costs at 50 cents per day; [*sic.*] in shoveling up mud in the streets. Now, if they could be kept in this kind of employment, and not allowed to control the elections of the country, I am not opposed to an increase of our foreign population!

Yesterday was a beautiful day over head, and despite the mud, the ladies were out, in crowds, with fascinating symmetry of form, rustling silks, ruddy cheeks, flowing tresses, and *expanded hoops*!—Hoops are not adapted to mud, or the mud is not adapted to hoops. They sweep over too wide a space and drag too much mud after them. I stood still on the side walks and gazed in profound astonishment at the pit-a-pat glide of the damsels in slippers, as bewitching as the skip of a fawn, holding up hoops and all in front, to the knees, exhibiting well turned ancles [*sic.*], while all in the rear was dragging heavily in the mud! Slippers, like crepe shawls, should yield to the season, and the ladies, *to a man*, especially in Memphis, should wear boots. . . .The rough tramp of boots, on the pavement, concealing legs and ancles [*sic.*], would atone for the *bounding swell in crinoline*! (*Whig*, March 20, 1858).

The Parson left this entrancing subject, probably with great reluctance, to report on markets and finances. He mentioned that flour ground in Knoxville was being used in Memphis and giving great satisfaction (*Ibid.*). But he soon turned to the luxurious appointments of the recently opened Gayoso House, where he was staying. His dispatch dripped with praise of it. He described it as "the finest hotel South of the Potomac." He reported that the building, halls and rooms were exceptional in size and

its furniture is magnificent, and its carpeting rich and costly, The bedsteads are all of mahogany and rosewood; the matrasses [*sic.*] are of superior quality, with springs, and the bed clothes and linen corresponding. The chairs are of mahogany, with spring bottoms. The washstands and bureaus are adorned with Italian marble tops! while damask curtains, guilded [*sic.*] cornices, and silken tassels adorn the windows. . . . The house is lighted up with gas, from gas works in the back yard, belonging exclusively to the house. In each room is a beautiful chandelier, with from three to six burners, according to the size of the room; and each hall, or large passage, is lighted up by a half dozen of these chandeliers. The dining room is richly ornamented and furnished, and is much the largest I have ever seen—it is even *fifteen feet longer* than that of the St. Nicholas in New York. No less than *eight* large chandeliers, lighted with gas, throw a flood of golden light upon the *six* tables of vast length, loaded with shining silver plate[s] , dazzling cut glass, superb white dishes. . . *(Ibid.)*.

While the Parson was staying at the Gayoso a festival and ball were held to celebrate the opening. Apparently this event fell on Thursday night, prayer meeting night perhaps, for the editor attended a religious service. When he returned to the hotel at 10:00 p.m. he found the flower and chivalry of five states—Tennessee, Alabama, Mississippi, Arkansas and Kentucky—dancing with gay and glittering abandon, a thousand strong. The scene captivated Brownlow's eyes and pen, and he wrote this ecstatic review:

I entered the ball room, and occupied the music stand for two hours, where I could scrutinize all that was passing, learn something of human nature, and gaze upon the fair daughters of the South, robed in costly attire, with *forms* and *faces*, making even a married man forget that he had a family, and so fascinating him as to make him "wish I were a boy again."—They were all ladies of the first class, whose splendid dresses, ease and grace of manners, made them "the observed of all observers." The style of dress is new, indicating a pure and cultivated taste, greatly admired, and producing a bewitching effect upon gentlemen!

Full and flowing robes are the *go* now—dazzling colors, such as pink, pure white, velvet jets, blue and dove-colored satins, striped and plaid silks, with numerous heavy flowers, each supporting a figured lace flounce, with Scotch plaid velvet, or ribbon bows in the back and front; and up the sides of some, velvet and ribbon lozenges rose in pyramids, while the sleeves were ornamented with puffs, frills and fringes! costly and beautiful necklaces, bracelets, earrings, breast pins; and wreathes upon the brow, and other descriptions of ornaments, turned all eyes to the ladies.!

Now I wish to say that I believe in *hoops*, and for two hours, from the most favorable standpoint, in this unequaled ball room, I tested their beauty and advantages, with the aid of eight brilliant chandeliers. Observe, ladies. I say *hoops*, using the plural number. Shame on your clumsy, single hoop, made of a hickory pole, or an oak split, which many of our ladies in our small towns use, wearing them about opposite the knee, showing its entire and rough shape through a flimsy skirt, dragging the dress down by its weight to the shape of a *cone*, while the twelve or fourteen inches of the dress below the hoop, tucks under, and flaps in and out, as the weight of mud, or the force of the wind may require!

The *hoops* used on this great occasion are the hoops for me. They are made of rattan, whalebone, and brass, extending from the waist to the feet, only two or three inches apart, gradually increasing in size, as they fall downward, with that graceful swell that gives to the dress the airy *contour* of the handsomely inflated balloon, preserving the lovely mien touching *circumference* that never fails to captivate a gentleman of modesty and good taste, such as I claim to be! These hoops make a skirt look uniformly graceful, as I can bear witness, and when the outer dress is raised a few inches by the lady, as she glides around in the dance, the flounces, needlework, and lace on the petticoat show to great advantage. . . .

I am no advocate of *dancing*, and never tried the exercise in my life, but I could not resist the temptation to look on at this scene, for largely upwards of one hour. My "vulgar curiosity" was satisfied, however, in seeing fifty fellows with long beards, goatees, and huge whiskers, playing the waltz or polka, with as many charming ladies. "He quadrilles—she polkas," was the exclamation! One feature of the waltzing got me. It was to see a young fellow dressed and perfumed within an inch of his life, *squeezing* a lady tight around the waist, with one arm, and with the other, as they mingled with, and cross[ed] each other in pairs, in the dance, *gently lifting her dress*, and she occasionally *raising it higher*, all, however, to keep it off the floor, and the lady leaning up to him like a sick kitten to a hot brick-bat! In those *squeezing* quadrilles, I noticed the hoops were rather in the way! (*Ibid.*).

The Parson retired at midnight, but he was told the dancing continued until daylight. The conduct of the crowd drew from him this compliment: "Though one thousand ladies and gentlemen were present, none were drunk, none were rude—all was order, and gentlemanly propriety. It was, out and out, a display of brilliant enjoyment, the like of which is seen only in a lifetime!" The gawky, ill-garmented young preacher, so grotesque that he had once been made sport of on the streets of Knoxville, had come a long way.

Before Brownlow left Memphis he attended the funeral of the Rev. William C. Ross, the presiding elder of the Memphis District. Mingled with the Parson's somber observations on the death of his fellow preacher was more of his philosophy that life is to be enjoyed: "He was one of my sort of men. He put on no long face—he exhibited no sour godliness—he was cheerful, possessing a fine flow of spirits, and yet dignified and religious."[22]

The editor's coverage of the Memphis ball must have set tongues wagging up every hollow in East Tennessee. It probably generated some whoops from the compositors in the *Whig* shop as they set his copy. He had found much to condemn and little to commend in the East Tennessee social scene, where the planter aristocracy existed only on a small scale. Six years before he wrote the Memphis letters, he had loosed indignation against men who spat tobacco juice and women who dipped snuff during church services. He had taken off on the men first, then turned to the other sex with:

Dipping! Ladies dipping! Oh! ecstatic bliss, to have the pleasure of sitting for hours with a snuff bottle in one's lap, enervating the system, destroying the constitution by a practice alike profitless and disgusting. We conceive the practice of using the snuff box and brush, in Church by ladies as rediculous [*sic*.] as that of chewing tobacco by gentlemen (*Whig*, June 19, 1852).

The Parson gave a spicy, racy touch to a report on the opening of the General Conference of the Methodist Church, South, at Nashville in May 1858. He covered the religious and historical aspect of the gathering, paid a high tribute to the presiding bishop, Joshua Soule, found him in excellent health for one who had been ministering since 1799, reviewed the legislative and spiritual affairs of the conference (*Whig*, May 15, 1858), and then produced an account which must have raised eyebrows and brought gasps across the South. He heard the Rev. P. P. Neely of the Alabama Conference preach a sermon at famous McKendree Church that for "beauty, rhetoric and eloquence was fully equal to my highest expectations." The church was filled to capacity and Brownlow admitted he had gone out of "*sheer curiosity*" because Neely, in 1819, had brought scandal on his head by being found by police

on Water Street, in the yard of one of the houses of ill fame, at a late hour of the night, in conversation with the inmates of the dwelling. He had gone among them, as he said, in company with a Local Preacher, in disguise, with a view to see something of human nature in that line of business. He was then tried in Church and acquitted and was not believed to have had any criminal intentions. I do not believe he intended anything wicked, but it certainly was the most imprudent act I ever know a Minister guilty of, who had a decent wife, as he had. It has crippled him from that day to this, and he will never survive it. . . .

The most remarkable feature of the case was the crowd of ladies in attendance, both young and old. I was there the previous night, and heard an eloquent sermon by a Georgian, but there were not half as many ladies present. The *curiosity* of women is far greater than that of men. The ladies were of the first respectability, and perfectly familiar with the outlines of the case; they were attracted to the spot by a desire to see and hear the man who had been arrested on the notorious *Water Street* under the circumstances detailed (*Whig*, May 15, 1858).

This form of curiosity, the Parson observed, was not unusual, for in Washington women frequently asked to have pointed out a Mormon in the House of Representatives who had twelve wives, "supposing him to present some extra appearance over and above the man who seems to be content with living with one woman!" Should Brigham Young have an appointment in Nashville, Brownlow predicted, the public square could not "contain the ladies who would attend, and ladies of respectability at that." Brownlow, having scolded the women for their strong curiosity in unusual domestic affairs, then showered them with compliments on their physical charms:

I have never seen so many beautiful, elegant and lovely women together on any occasion. I have gazed upon them as they have gracefully glided by me on the pavements—as they have ascended and descended the several flights in the steps in the capitol—as they have been seated in the galleries and at church, and still the wonder grew that so much *silk* and so many *hoops* could encircle the angelic forms of so many lovely and beautiful women! All I regret is that skirtdom is still expanding, and the fashions in vogue are still increasing the *distance* between man and woman! At one moment I feel like exclaiming, "Oh, that I were a boy again!" The next moment I feel indignant at hoops and feel willing to join a regiment of good men in a vigorous assault upon the ratine, whalebone, cords, brass and steel that have put asunder what God hath said ought to be joined together! Only think of the display on our streets, in the State capitol, at church, and in the parlor, of the grand, *graceful and undulating skirts*, looming up all around one, fascinating, charming, and swinging to and fro, like so many things of life! Talk about the grandeur of a first class steamer or a train of cars propelled by steam! Give me a *train of hooped skirts*, under the folds of which are so many *living, breathing locomotives*, standing five feet ten inches in slippers, fired up by the blood of warm hearts, and puffing and blowing with love, kind words and winning smiles, and I will show you a sight that would run a young man crazy, raise a dead bachelor to life, and make an old widow commit suicide!

I cannot trust myself upon this glorious theme; I must desist or go crazy (*Whig*, May 15, 1858).

The Parson had picked up much about writing since he had woodenly soliloquized a quarter of a century earlier in *Helps to the Study of Presbyterianism* that he yearned for a wife, and had "some good desires"—he also had caught on to some biological facts.

The *Whig*'s readers were accustomed to find the editor bitter and raging in one column, and compassionate and gentle in the next, but when the 1854 cholera epidemic was subsiding he underwent an experience—and told about it in print—that revealed a complexity uncommon to most members of the human race. Brownlow stayed and published "slips" that reported deaths for the few hundreds remaining in Knoxville. The *Whig* reported sixty-six deaths but possibly a hundred died, among them Colonel John McClellan, a brother of General George B. McClellan, who at that time was supervising work on the Tennessee River at the foot of Gay Street.[25] One undertaker filled orders for seventy-two coffins in six weeks. Some died in scenes of squalor and filth.[23] So great was the need for medical care that James H. Sawyers, who was studying medicine, turned doctor overnight and plunged into practice. He married the Parson's daughter, Susan Brownlow, three years later.[24] Early in September a committee of six doctors announced there was "no further cause for alarm" (*Whig*, September 30, 1854).

Brownlow surely was spent, emotionally and physically, but a new experience faced him. It was an accusation that he had printed a false account of the habits of a barkeeper who died of the cholera. The Parson expected his enemies to call him a liar, but this challenge to his reputation for truth and veracity invoked no denunciation of his accuser. His defense, however, opened the windows of his nature and revealed three sides of this complex man. He wrote his defense in a letter to Miss Sallie Vanmeter, sister of the barkeeper and a resident of Lynchburg, Virginia. Miss Vanmeter had objected to certain statements in the *Whig*'s obituary of her brother (*Whig*, November 4, 1854). The Parson's letter to her, which he published in a prominent position in his newspaper, began

I have been shown a portion of a letter you addressed to Mr. Helms, our post master, in reference to the death of your lamented brother, and especially the brief notice I took of his death through the columns of the "Whig," of which I am the editor. I would address you a private letter, but you request me to *correct*, through the same medium, the erroneous impression I have left on the public mind, as to his habits and morals, and to request the *Lynchburg Virginian* to copy my correction, as that journal had copied my statement. You speak of letters you have received from the Rev. Mr. Humes, Rev. Mr. Park, of Rogersville, and others satisfying you that I was misinformed as to your brother's habits, or words to this effects, as I quote from memory.

The only remark I ever made about your brother was in the Whig-Extra for Sept. 4th, and the same with the other Extras was transferred to our regular issues of the 16th of September. Here they are:

"Mr. Van Meeter, the bar keeper at the Mansion House, was taken on Saturday morning, and died in 10 hours. He was a constant drinker of ardent spirits. We saw and conversed with him the day before, and he was alarmed to a fearful extent, in anticipation of having the disease."

Now, in my hurried reports of the ravages of Cholera in this city, when I was publishing the only slips that appeared, I endeavored *to account for* the deaths of those who had been called off, by briefly, but frankly setting forth their habits of life. I was not actuated by any hostility towards any one person, of the *sixty* whose deaths I reported.—And I may say, without subjecting myself to the charge of egotism, that but few men in the place, during the prevalence of this dreadful scourge, labored more faithfully to relieve the sick, and especially the needy, in every possible way, than I did.

In my peregrinations through this City, during the three weeks the epidemic prevailed, I often met with Mr. Humes, and I testify freely to his faithfulness as a Pastor, as I do to the diligence of the other Pastors of Churches, Presbyterians, Methodist and Baptist. Mr. Humes was especially kind to your brother, in his efforts to pour the consolations of the Gospel into his ears. Mr. Helms, who now has the control of his temporal matters, was one of his intimate friends. Mr. Helms and myself are on opposite sides in politics here, but I know him well, and pronounce him an honest man and a gentleman. He will conduct the affairs of your brother's estate to your entire satisfaction. It is due to him that I state to you, as I now do, that he has no knowledge of my writing this letter, until it meets his eye in print, on the morning of its date.

So far as your brother was concerned I always entertained kind feelings toward him. He was personally respectful, and especially accommodating to me, in matters of stage travelling, and whatever business I might have about the Hotel. I will further add, for your consolation, that he was attentive to his business—he was honest—he was esteemed by all who knew him—he had no enemies here; he gave every necessary evidence of having been well raised—and his untimely death was regretted by our citizens. He was cared for in his sickness, and handsomely buried in our Cemetery, in the family burying ground of Mr. Helms. Here I might close my remarks, and for your sake, and for the sake of your aged and afflicted parents, I would gladly do so, but justice to myself, to you, and to all concerned, requires me to be a little more explicit. If you please and I say it with the most tender emotions, justice to myself, requires that I should now give the dark side of this picutre.

I state, as you will observe, that your brother "WAS A CONSTANT DRINK-ER OF ARDENT SPIRITS." This I am sorry to inform you is *strictly true*, and I cannot admit it to be an error of mine, much less can I attempt its correction, if by correction is ment [*sic.*] *taking it back*. I never intended to convey the idea that your brother was a drunkard, or that he was at any time so influenced by liquor, as to be incapable of business. I intended to say, and I hope my numer-ous readers so understand me, that the deceased was *constantly in the habit of drinking ardent spirits*, as many of the most highminded, honorable and liberal gentlemen of the country are. Your brother drank prudently, and in moderation, but *constantly*, and it was growing [illegible but possibly "on him"] at the time of his death. There was an Orderly Grocery kept in the basement story of the Hotel, and on the same floor on which your brother kept the stage office, with all that variety of liquors usually kept in such establishments. Previous to his going into the Hotel he was a Clerk in a Wholesale Liquor House, owned by a Mr. Campbell (*Ibid.*).

The editor had now made a case for his veracity, but since he also was a Methodist preacher, he had some pointed observations to make to the anguished Miss Vanmeter on the fate of her brother's soul. The harsh and flinty theologian penned these relentless convictions:

Whether or not, your brother attained to a saving knowledge of Gospel truth before his death, about which it is natural you should express such great anxiety, I am unable to inform you. He was a profane swearer, and but seldom, if ever, attended Church. I have heard one man say that he *thinks* he once saw him at the Episcopal Church. Others who knew him well, say that they never saw him at Church. I never did. I am thus frank with you, because I think it is wrong to create false and unfounded hopes of the future happiness of the dead, merely to relieve the anxieties of their living relatives. Mr. Park, of Rogersville, resides 75 miles from here, and if he was here during the prevalence of the Cholera, I have met with no one who saw him. Mr. Humes was here, and acted the part of a faithful Pastor and was kind in his attention to your brother. I called in to your brother's room, just after Mr. Humes had left him and had prayed with and for him, at his request, made previous to that visit. I found him so far gone, as not to be capable of conversation on any subject. Indeed he was dying.

I have but little confidence in a death bed repentance. In other words, I am not one of those who looks upon the hardy tree of Repentance as the sickly growth of a few hours. During the last 25 years, I have read the Bible through 25 times, besides Commentaries, and other Theological works; and if I have any just conceptions of the nature of Gospel repentance, it is a *godly sorrow wrought in the heart of a sinful person, by the word and Spirit of God, whereby, from a sense of his sins, as being offensive to God, murderous to Christ, and defiling to his own soul; and from an apprehension of the mercy of God in Christ, he, with hatred of all known sins—the whole catalogue of the inward and outward iniquities of his past life—turns from them to God, as his only Saviour and Lord!*

However, God for the display of his power and mercy, might instantaneously convict and convert *Paul*; yet this is not his way of working in the nineteenth century. . . . I will venture to say that in ninety-nine cases out of every hundred, justification, or a preparation to meet death, follows a course of reflection, study, repentance and prayer (*Ibid.*).

Yet as the Parson wrote this chilling message, something was thawing in his soul. Perhaps it came home to him forcefully that a minister also has a responsibility to bring to the bereaved all the consolation within his power. Abruptly his manner changed and he wrote these gentle, touching lines:

But while I have given you my views of a death bed repentance:—and while I affirm that it is a very poor dependance, I pretend not to say that your brother did not mournfully and happily find redemption in the blood of the Lamb. I trust such was the case—that he had followed the gilded pleasures of this poor world, long enough to learn the genuine character of their insignificance and that in his dying moments he found an enchanted bower in the paradise of God.

Assure your aged parents from me that I have intended them and their surviving children no injury whatever—and that no gentleman who has addressed them or you a letter on this painful subject would be at more trouble to do them an act of kindness than I would. Say to your parents especially that tho' I am a stranger to them personally, I hope they may live to enjoy many of the comforts of life, and that ultimately, in the grave!—aye, in the grave, themselves and their daughter, whose frank and well written letter I am now replying to, may find a calm and welcome retreat in the cares and vicisitudes [*sic.*] of this life!

> Very Respectfully &c
> W. G. BROWNLOW,
> Editor of the Knoxville *Whig*. [25]

CHAPTER IX NOTES

[1] *Parson Brownlow's Book*, pp. 18, 406; *Whig*, December 3, 1845, July 28, 1860; *Portrait and Biography of Parson Brown, The Tennessee Patriot, Together with His Last Editorial in the Knoxville Whig; also His Recent Speeches, Rehearsing his Experiences with Secession, and His Prison Life,* [Indianapolis, 1862, also published with slight variation in title, Cincinnati, 1862], p. 16; hereafter referred to as Portrait and Biography.

[2] *Ought American Slavery to be Perpetuated? A Debate between Rev. W. G. Brownlow and Rev. A. Pryne, held at Philadelphia, September 1858* [Philadelphia, 1858], pp. 15-16; hereafter referred to as *Ought American Slavery to be Perpetuated?*

[3] *Helps*, p. 257; *Parson Brownlow's Book*, p. 21; *Whig*, July 5, August 23, 1851.

[4] The series ran in the *Whig* from June 1 to July 20, 1842; for examples of chapters and prospectus, *ibid.*, February 9, 16, July 6, 20, August 17, 1842. The book was sold for fifty cents bound, twenty-five cents in pamphlet.

[5] Brownlow began printing the *Political Register* early in 1844. It contained 350 pages and was sold for $1.00. *Whig*, March 15, November 11, 1843.

[6] This book was produced in the middle of March, 1856, on the heels of Graves' work. It contained 331 pages, although the Parson promoted it as having almost 400. *Whig*, May 24, 1856.

[7] Graves, *The Great Iron Wheel*, pp. 169, 33.

[8] Price, *Holston Methodism*, III, pp. 219-220; *Whig*, November 24, 1860.

[9] *The Great Iron Wheel Examined*, p. 243; *Parson Brownlow's Book*, p. 459; *Whig*, May 24, 1856, November 24, 1860.

[10] The book was sold for seventy-five cents. *Ibid.*, July 19, 1856; *Americanism Contrasted*, p. 6; *Whig*, October 27, 1855, February 2, 1856; Folmsbee *et al.*, *Short History*, pp. 237-238; *Whig*, November 15, 1856.

[11] The book contained 321 pages. Graves, *The Little Iron Wheel*, p. 83 and introduction.

[12] The Methodist Publishing House produced these two works, but its name does not appear as publisher. Each carries only "Nashville, Tenn.: published for the author."

[13] *Whig*, December 28, 1850, January 4, February 8, 1851. It sold for twenty-five cents.

[14] Temple, *Notable Men*, p. 274.

[15] *Whig*, March 26, 1845, November 11, 1846.

[16] *Ibid.*, June 7, 1851, April 2, 1853.

[17] *Ibid.*, March 26, April 16, 1853.

[18] *Ibid.*, November 22, 1851, January 10, 31, 1852.

[19] *Ibid.*, May 23, 1857. *Sag nicht*, translated from the German, means "say nothing." It was a nickname for the Democratic Party. John Bell Brownlow marginal note, December 1, 1855. The American Party also was known as the Know-Nothing Party.

[20] *Whig*, December 19, 1857. Brownlow used the verb *founder*, usually meaning *overeating by livestock*, as a noun.

[21] *Ibid.*, December 13, 1851; F. Garvin Davenport, *Cultural Life in Nashville on the Eve of the Civil War* (Chaper Hill, 1941), p. 121.

[22] *Ibid.*, March 20, 1858. Cost of the Gayoso building was put at $300,000, the furnishing at $85,000. *Ibid.*, January 16, 1858.

[23] *Ibid.*, October 28, 1854; Rule, ed., *Standard History*, pp. 526-528; *Register*, September 1, 1854. A slip was a sheet of reduced size. For example, a *Whig* slip published December 15, 1849, consisted of two pages of four columns each, compared with the standard four pages of seven columns each. None of the slips issued during the epidemic are available. See *Whig*, November 4, 1854. Twenty-four burials of cholera victims, three of them blacks, are listed in a record book of Gray Cemetery for 1851-1867. Special Collections, University of Tennessee.

[24] *Whig*, September 5, 1854. This issue is in miscellaneous newspaper files, not on microfilm, McClung Collection, *ibid.*, June 5, 1858; Rule, ed., *Standard History*, pp. 526-528. The marriage was solemnized on October 20, 1857, and was carried in the *Register*, October 22, 1857. The item could not be found in the *Whig*.

[25] *Whig*, November 4, 1854. The barkeeper's name is spelled both Van Meeter and Vanmeter. "Grocery" was a colloquialism for a saloon or liquor shop. Brownlow mentions sixty deaths in the letter, but earlier he had put the deaths at sixty-six. *Ibid.*, September 30, 1854. This *Whig* is on microfilm in a newspaper miscellany. McClung Collection.

𝕿𝖍𝖊 𝖂𝖍𝖎𝖌.

"Put None on Guard but Americans."   Chapter No. 10

SUPREMACY AND SORROW

The Kinsloes were good at the printing craft. They gave the *Whig* and the *Register* attractive new dress and their entries emerged handsomely from the competition held at the State Fair in Nashville in 1855. The *Whig* proudly reported: "This office took the premium of a *Ten Dollar Silver Cup* for the finest specimens of *Fancy Job Printing*. And the *Book Bindery* connected with this office would have taken the premium of two large Books, had not the judged desired, and properly too, to distribute their gifts and encourage other offices likewise."

But W. A. Kinsloe was unable to leave Philadelphia and move to Knoxville, as he had planned. A half interest in the business was offered for sale. The announcement offer listed the investment at $21,000 and suggested that any prospective purchaser should have $5,000. The Kinsloes were printing the *Whig, Register* and *Presbyterian Witness*. The *Southern Journal of Medical and Physical Sciences* had disappeared. Included in the investment were power and hand presses, good will, subscription lists, bank accounts, real estate and a steam engine. The Kinsloe notice put the annual revenues from job work and binding at $6,000, from advertising at $7,000, and listed the subscribers to the three publications at 6,500.[1] It did not itemize the circulation of the three.

Kinsloe & Brother in Knoxville consisted of E. P. B. and J. B. G. Kinsloe. E. P. B. was the *Whig* publisher, J. B. G. occupied the same post at the *Register*.[2] Charles A. Rice bought the half interest offered for sale and the operating partners became Kinsloe & Rice. The partnership name appeared as publisher in both newspapers.[3] It was not made clear if one or both of the Kinsloes were in the end of the partnership bearing their name. After the spring of 1856 when E. P. B. accompanied the Parson on a trip to Washington and Philadelphia, he disappeared (*Whig*, February 23, 1956). Kinsloe &

Rice offered the *Register* for sale (*Whig*, June 25, 1857) and through some unexplained arrangement Rice became *Register* publisher. He fired the dilatory and convivial Fleming as editor.[4] In the meantime J. B. G. Kinsloe had become foreman in the *Register* shop (*Register*, April 15, 1858). The Kinsloe & Rice partnership appeared again. It offered the *Whig* plant for sale (*Whig*, February 14, 1857). Early in 1859 Rice sold the *Register* to a group headed by Postmaster J. F. J. Lewis. They made the *Register* Democratic. Later James W. Newman became editor and C. W. Charlton, Methodist minister and agriculturist, appeared as owner.[5]

Brownlow's prediction that if it came to a lethal struggle between the two Whig newspapers in Knoxville his would survive had been substantiated. He was the sole voice of the party in Knoxville and the most significant and powerful in East Tennessee. He also moved back into complete ownership and operation. The exact date when Rice sold him back the *Whig* is obscured by the lack of the newspaper's files for the last six months of 1858. A light caning attempted against Kinsloe and Rice by W. G. Swan may have contributed to the departure of the two from the publishing field. Swan had been offended by a sharp piece the Parson had written about him.[6] Kinsloe and Rice may have decided that publishing a newspaper edited by Brownlow involved occupational hazards from which they desired to escape.

The Parson celebrated his return to publishing by bringing out the *Tri-Weekly Whig*, the first issue appearing on January 4, 1859. "The Weekly *Whig* is a self sustaining institution, and derives its support from all the States South of the Potomac," he wrote in the salutory of this number. "The *Tri-Weekly* is an experiment, and must rely for its patronage mostly upon this city and those cities interested in the trade and commerce of East Tennessee." He started the new enterprise, he wrote, not because he expected it to pay but to benefit businessmen and to meet the needs of the growing city. The *Tri-Weekly Whig* appeared Tuesday, Thursday and Saturday. He published the final issue of the week concurrently with the older newspaper. Brownlow printed the *Tri-Weekly* on pages of a smaller size, five columns to the page and in larger body type, much of it in 10-point. The annual subscription rate was $5.00, with reductions for clubs of three, five, seven and ten copies. Content of the *Whig* and the *Tri-Weekly* was to be identical. The weekly *Whig* was to be "made up of the reading matter of the three Tri-weeklies, intended for more distant subscribers." Because the weekly paper was being printed in smaller type and of a narrower column width, the work of typesetting had been doubled.

Brownlow appeared in high spirits as he resumed full control. He thrust aside all job work, he exulted in the volume of letters he was getting, the largest of any post office user, and he described the increase of subscribers as the largest he had known in twenty-one years of publishing. On February 1, 1859, he cut off five hundred subscribers who were in arrears and listed $365.06 as the receipts in one week from subscriptions, press work and advertising.

He tartly warned his foes that the *Whig*'s circulation outside Tennessee was sufficient to sustain it without an advertisement or subscriber in the state. And he sent a less than subtle message to merchants with an advisory that he and his hands employed in the plant were spending $10.00 to $20.00 for every dollar received from Knoxville.[7] He was making the solid point with merchants that as a result of his widespread and extensive circulation and the advertising given him from distant customers he was bringing money into Knoxville which was being spent there.

The Parson hired the experienced J. B. G. Kinsloe as his foreman. Apparently Kinsloe had recovered from the indignity of Swan's light caning. He moved his plant into quarters at the rear of O. P. Temple's law office at the southeast corner of Gay Street and Hill Avenue, but continued to do his work at the office he had built adjacent to his home on East Cumberland Avenue. In the spring of 1859 he revealed that because of illness he had not been in the printing office "until this week, since the first of December."[8]

Brownlow took a revolutionary step, concurrently with the publication of the *Tri-Weekly*, by contracting for telegraphic dispatches three times a week. They brought the latest news from New York, Liverpool, Washington, New Orleans, Philadelphia, Baltimore and other points. A week's dispatches filled more than a column in the weekly newspaper.[9]

The editor gave the impression that his spirits were high, but he admitted as the summer of 1859 was closing:

The shattered condition of our health—the enfeebled state of our system—worn down by inordinate attention to business—long residence in town—excessive mental anxiety—we find ourselves to be an exhausted and sighing invalid, attended by an insupportable sense of weariness and lassitude; and as such we go to the mountains of Virignia to seek a *panacea* in the delightful and refreshing baths and other uses of their curative waters. In a word, we are afflicted with a nameless but wide-spread tribe of infirmities, embraced in the general term *debility.* . . . While we desire to live for the benefit of our family, we have no wish to gratify a numerous class of human being, by giving up to die! (*Whig*, August 27, 1859).

If the Parson's health was shattered his pen fingers were agile and his sense of humor and powers of observation were working well, for from the watering places he fired back a volume of scintillating dispatches. It was on this occasion he wrote Temple that he could edit his newspaper almost as well as if he were home.[10]

Brownlow had undertaken some strenuous travels later in 1857 and during the first part of 1858, in addition to his editorial duties. He spoke in Huntsville, Marion, Auburn and Mobile, Alabama; West Point, Mississippi; New Orleans, Louisiana; and at LaGrange, Georgia. At Montgomery he addressed the two houses of the Alabama legislature, and in Memphis he plugged hard for the sale of stock in the proposed Southern Pacific Railroad, even on the heels of the financial panic of 1857.[11] At home he engaged in a nettlesome fight over the election of a Circuit Court judge, and saw his candidate defeated by one backed by the expiring *Register*. Fleming prodded Brownlow, who was also in the midst of one of his frequent wars on dogs, with this item: "The complete returns of the judicial election reached Knoxville on Saturday. We understand that on Saturday night the editor of the *Whig* shot four dogs. We fear our neighbor was in a bad humor."[12]

Litigation piled up. Brownlow was indicted for slander in two counties, was sued for damages involving the same controversy, and brought the first lawsuit in his life in an attempt to collect something for the depositors of a failed Knoxville bank. Politics threaded through all of these court actions. They were involved, long and acrid.

The first encounter arose over the close cooperation between Brownlow and Fleming in supporting the American Party. Martin Patterson, editor of the *Eagle*, a Democratic paper at Kingston, accused Fleming of being Brownlow's tool. The Knoxville editors reacted, each in his own way. Brownlow branded Patterson as a horse thief and a perjurer; Fleming found Patterson in Knoxville and kicked him into the side of a cow that was serenely passing in front of the Coleman Hotel on Gay Street. Patterson must have felt that what Brownlow printed against him was more painful than the boot Fleming gave him, for he confined his court actions to the Parson. Patterson and Brownlow were in and out of the courts of Knox and Roane counties for three years. After two mistrials in Knox the criminal charge against the Parson was dismissed upon motion of the assistant attorney general. In Roane County a jury acquitted him. Mistrials were declared twice in the Knox County civil suit, and apparently there the controversy ended [13] so far as Patterson was concerned.

The second instance of litigation arose over the suspension of the Bank of East Tennessee at Knoxville late in 1856 on the eve of the financial panic. Dr. J. G. M. Ramsey and Major Thomas C. Lyon, directors of the bank, were appointed trustees to handle the affairs of the crippled institution. Swashbuckling William Montgomery Churchwell, president of the bank, conveyed to the trustees not only the assets of the bank but also his personal real estate. "The bank is broke and the loss is no inconsiderable one," the *Whig* soon announced. It also reported that the institution's assets were bringing from fifteen to twenty cents on the dollar. Brownlow received so many inquiries about the bank that he undertook to accept the issues from holders, at their own risk, attempt to recover thirty cents on the dollar, and failing this, to return the bank notes. The Parson grew suspicious that Churchwell had used the bank for his own profit. The failure of the trustees to impart information on what was happening heightened his fears. So he, along with George W. Ross of Athens filed a Chancery Court suit that charged Churchwell with reckless management. The action sought judgment for the holders of the issues and demanded an accounting. The Parson and his co-plaintiff brought this suit against the trustees, Ramsey and Lyon. Holders of the issues poured their paper into Brownlow, and early in 1859 he held $50,000 of them, all entered in the lawsuit. [14]

Brownlow's first role as the instigator of litigation opened up a mad scramble of realignments and intensified old animosities. During the Jonesboro era, the Parson's opinion of Dr. Ramsey had been very low. When commenting on Ramsey's forthcoming history of the state Brownlow had described him as "very vain and equally credulous." But after three years in Knoxville, Brownlow conceded he had been misled. And when Ramsey's famous *Annals of Tennessee to the End of the Eighteenth Century* appeared he described it as "a work of great merit and marked ability" and added that a "copy of it ought to be owned by every family in the State." The *Whig* also listed places where the book could be bought. Now, in 1860, Ramsey again became Brownlow's constant target, in the courts and in the *Whig*'s columns.

His accusations against Churchwell, charging him with having plundered the bank, was another reversal. In 1851 and 1853 he had supported Churchwell in successful races for Congress, even though he was a Democrat. Brownlow had backed him because of his bitterness against the Whig Party in the district. He claimed a Whig faction had stacked a convention at Clinton in 1851 so that it nominated Horace Maynard instead of the editor's friend, O. P. Temple. An animosity that grew hotter, if such were possible, was that between Brownlow and John H. Crozier, who had fought him in the Patterson lawsuits. Crozier now appeared against him as counsel for the bank trustees. The Parson scorned Crozier as a "renegade" because he had switched to the Democratic Party in the Presidential campaign of 1856.[15]

The Crozier quarrel had deep roots that dated back to the former congressman's having duped Brownlow when the Parson moved to Knoxville. Crozier had a talent for infuriating the Parson. During an argument in one of the Patterson libel trials he sank a shaft rather deep in Brownlow. He charged the Parson with having given editorial support to the ruined Bank of East Tennessee. Crozier had facts, if not complete truth on his side, and he was aware that some of the jurors before whom he laid his argument had suffered in the bank's suspension. Brownlow had praised Churchwell's management of the bank in 1853, and wrote that great demand existed for its issues. Whether Crozier, in his speech to the jury, alluded to this approval in the *Whig* or to one appearing in the newspaper in December 1856, which expressed confidence in Trustees Ramsey and Lyon, is not clear. In the latter instance the *Whig* called for "forbearance and charity" on the part of the public. Brownlow chose to accept the meaning as applying to the second incident. This puff had appeared in the *Whig* while the Parson was absent from the city. It came as the result of pressure by bank officials upon the man that Brownlow had left in charge. The Parson quickly corrected it, and assumed a position hostile to the trustees. Brownlow probably flinched at having to admit his newspaper had been hoodwinked into giving help to the floundering bank, but it was the only recourse by which he could disown authorship of the editorial (*Tri-Weekly Whig*, February 8, 1859).

The controversy dragged on for years. The Parson's accusations in his newspaper were far more racy than the bill of particulars drawn by his lawyers. The Parson accused Churchwell of having pocketed $102,000 of the bank's funds and then setting up an office on Wall Street. Obviously, he did not know that Churchwell had established his mistress, Miriam F. Follin, an actress whose stage name was Minnie Montez, in a house he had purchased at 37 Seventh Street, New York.[16] Brownlow was not the man to keep silent about such a development, had he known of it.

He won a decisive victory when Chancellor Seth J. W. Lucky of Knox County held that the complainants, with claims amounting to $100,000. were entitled to recover from the bank and the trustees; that the trustees had no right to prefer creditors in distributing assets from the $125,000 of real estate which Churchwell had deeded to them; that the complainants were bona fide holders of the bank notes and entitled to recovery in full, regardless of the price under which they had last been sold; and that the clerk and master was to sell the remaining assets of the bank. Churchwell's deed of real estate to the trustees had specified that certain creditors were to be preferred in liquidating these assets, and the trustees had sought to carry out this provision. Brownlow had vigorously contested on this point, and it was gratifying to him that the chancellor had held that this preference was invalid. This compensated him somewhat for the court's finding that the trustees had been guilty of neither fraud nor negligence. The defendants appealed (*Whig*, January 28, 1860).

The State Supreme Court affirmed the opinion of the chancellor, with modifications. The ruling left the way open for the Knox County clerk and master to conduct an accounting and to sell the assets of the bank. The high court, in a brief aside, suggested that Churchwell's management of the bank was something more than irregular, for:

The record discloses a vast number of facts; some of which are startling in their character; but most of them refer to the management of the bank prior to the assignments; and therefore have but little to do with the determination of the questions under review in this court.

But since the courts move slowly and because men's minds were aflame with the issues soon to explode in the Civil War, delay followed delay as investors stayed out of the real estate market. The result was that the winding up of the bank's affairs stagnated during the war.[17]

The filing and prosecution of the lawsuit was a sound and legitimate newspaper exploit. It put the *Whig* in the role of successful
advocate for the many victims of the collapse. Brownlow reported
after the Supreme Court opinion that he represented claims of 600
persons holding $50,000 of the bank's issues. He had shown that the
Whig and its editor could fight successfully against powerful interests
in the financial as well as in the religious and political fields. The
Parson credited the bank group with having hired seven attorneys,
and T. A. R. Nelson charged that Churchwell had hired "almost
every prominent lawyer there [Knoxville] of both political parties
(*Whig*, February 4, 1860).

The Parson had a personal stake of $4,000 in the litigation, repre-
sented by issues he had taken for debts, and with these he tried to
purchase some of the real estate held by the trustees. His offers,
made both directly and indirectly, were rejected. If in suing he was
motivated in part by pique, he made no effort to conceal it for after
having won the suit he wrote:

As they [the trustees] would neither redeem these issues with money or sell
property for them to us, while they were selling to others, we thought we would
bring them to terms, and we accordingly instituted this suit. . . .

The Trustees supposed, we imagine, that no one would dare sue them, and no
lawyer would dare take fees against them. If such was their supposition, their
minds have been disabused in this particular! (*Whig*, October 20, 1860).

Brownlow had another cause to be jubilant. His newspaper was
approaching the peak of its pre-Civil War influence and prosperity. In
the mid-summer of 1860 he bought $600 of a new and smaller type,
enabling him to give readers a third more editorial matter, while
condensing advertisements, which had been filling twenty of the
thirty-two columns in the *Whig*. He announced a weekly circulation
of 9,000 that grew at the rate of 350 a week. He was printing more
copies than the combined circulation of the other nine political
newspapers in East Tennessee. Six weeks later he placed the *Whig*'s
circulation at 11,000. Brownlow's annual income from the *Whig* may
have reached $10,000 at this period.[18]

The same year that saw the Parson's triumphs also produced a
family tragedy that must have drained him emotionally. His son,
John Bell Brownlow, a senior at Emory and Henry College, killed a
fellow student, James W. Reese, a Georgian. The killing occurred
after Reese, a much larger youth, had knocked the Knoxvillian to the

muddy ground. Brownlow seized a chestnut stick from a woodpile and struck Reese on the head as other students were attempting to restrain Reese. The assailant, who was helped from the scene, died a few hours later. Young Brownlow went home immediately, then returned to Virginia and surrendered to authorities at Abingdon. At the time of the encounter on February 22, 1860, the Parson was in Nashville attending a convention of the Constitutional Union Party,[19] but on arriving home he published a brief account of the affair. He wound it up with the observation:

As he is not, and never was, a quarrelsome young man, and in morals will compare favorably with the better class of young men at Colleges, I respectfully suggest to newspaper Editors and their correspondents, the great injustice of visiting upon him, the political or personal sins of the father, over whom he has never exercised any control! (*Whig*, March 3, 1860).

The Parson's foes seized upon the killing with ferocious glee and distortions. An example was the Morristown *Intelligencer* whose account provoked the *Whig* into retorting:

This is a religious paper, and is edited by three Methodist Preachers, two of whom are presiding elders, and the other is a professor in a Female College. In the latest issue of the paper there is an editorial upon the *"increase of crime"* in the country, in which the late affray at Emory & Henry College is given of the evidence of this increase—the parties are named, and the case is declared to be a case of *murder*. The writer is a free man, and has a right to take any side in a controversy he may choose, while many will doubt the propriety of an article just in advance of the trial which fixes the character of the "crime" and consequently the punishment (*Ibid.*).

Father Brownlow spared no expense to see that John Bell was well represented by counsel and that coverage was complete and objective when trial was held in Washington County Circuit Court at Abingdon. Young Brownlow had seven Virginia lawyers and one from Tennessee, John S. Brien of Nashville. Five of the lawyers argued the case over a period of nine hours, after three days of testimony in which forty-eight witnesses were heard. The substance of the testimony, taken down by "an able and experienced criminal lawyer," occupied thirteen columns of the *Whig* of April 21, 1860. A jury that was out only a few minutes acquitted John Bell. The jurors obviously decided that the defendant had acted justifiably in self defense (*Whig*, April 21, 1860).

The aftermath was curious. The *Whig* printed two accounts of the trial taken from democratic newspapers, both extremely favorable to Brownlow and son. They had been printed in the Atlanta *Confederacy* and the Knoxville *Register*. George W. Bradfield, a Democrat with whom Brownlow was on friendly, even cordial terms, edited the latter paper. The *Register*'s report of young Brownlow's acquittal found that the news

sent a thrill of joy through our whole community. The course pursued by himself and father, from the beginning to the end of this sad affair, has met with universal approval of our citizens irrespective of parties. They had our sympathy in their day of trial and grief, our warmest admiration in respecting the laws and meeting the responsibility, and we fully share their joy at his triumphant acquittal. . . .

The testimony showed that the deceased was greatly the overmatch of Brownlow in strength, that he had first assailed Brownlow in words, and had afterwards stricken [*sic*.] the first blow in the affray that led to his death, had crushed Brownlow to the earth, and when pulled away, made a second assault upon him; and that Brownlow seized a stick from a woodpile, and with it inflicted a blow on the head of his assailant not regarded as serious by the medical gentlemen called in, but which resulted in his death after 17 hours.

The whole testimony allowed of but one inference as to Brownlow's intent when he struck the blow, and that was to *punish* and *repel the battery upon himself, yet impending and already severe*—and not to *take the life of the assailant* .

It is ironical that out of the Brownlow family which fought furiously in political campaigns for years, the only one who struck a lethal blow over the outcome of an election was young John Bell—and this in the instance of the election of officers of a collegiate literary society.[20]

CHAPTER X NOTES

[1] *Whig* October 20; McClary, p. 97.
[2] *Whig*, March 24, 1855; *Register*, February 21, 1855.
[3] *Whig*, January 12, 1856; *Register*, January 10, 1856.
[4] *Ibid*., June 10, 17, 1858.
[5] *Tri-Weekly Whig*, January 13, 25, July 23, 1859. For Charlton background see Rothrock, ed., *French Broad-Holston*, pp. 394-396.

[6] The gap in the files of the weekly *Whig* extends from July 31, 1858, to August 6, 1859. It is partially filled by numbers of the *Tri-Weekly Whig*, January 4, 1859, until resumption of the weekly files. *Whig*, March 28, April 4, 1857; *Register*, March 26, 1857.

[7] *Tri-Weekly Whig*, January 4, 6, 8, February 10, 1859. The price of the *Tri-Weekly Whig* was cut to $3.00 annually. *Whig*, August 13, 1859. *Tri-Weekly Whig*, January 6, 15, 25, February 10, March 31, 1859.

[8] *Ibid.*, April 7, 1859; *Whig*, February 18, 1860; *Williams Knoxville Directory, City Guide, and Business Mirror for 1859-1860* [Knoxville, 1859], p. 79; *Tri-Weekly Whig*, April 7, 1859.

[9] *Ibid.*, January 4, 1859. The dispatches for the three issues of the *Tri-Weekly Whig* were consolidated in the *Weekly*.

[10] *Whig*, September 3, 10, 17, 24, October 8, 15, 1859.

[11] *Ibid.*, December 19, 1857, January 9, 16, 30, February 13, January 9, 1858.

[12] *Ibid.*, August 8, 22, 29; *Register*, August 27, 1857.

[13] *Whig*, April 26, May 3, 17, 1856; *Register*, April 24, 1856; *Whig*, November 14, 1857, February 20, 27, March 6, June 26, July 3, 10, 1858; *Tri-Weekly Whig*, March 12, 1859.

[14] The history of the bank's suspension and the litigation that followed is spread over the pages of the Parson's newspapers in great detail, *Whig*, December 20, January 3, February 25, 1857, February 13, April 17, 1858, January 7, 28, February 4, October 13, 1860. The suit by Brownlow and Ross was filed August 1858, a period for which files of the *Whig* cannot be found. February 8, 1859. A complete history of the law suit, with the exception of the court findings, and including the petitions of the litigants, and Brownlow's observations and summary in the *Tri-Weekly Whig*, February 8, 10, 12, 15, March 1, 1859.

[15] *Whig*, June 6, 1844, August 18, December 4, 1852, April 2, August 13, 1853, January 7, 28, 1860, August 2, 1856.

[16] *Whig*, January 28, 1860, December 10, 1859; Ruth Osborne Turner, "The Public Career of William Montgomery Churchwell," thesis, University of Tennessee, 1954, pp. 52-59; Madeline B. Stern, *Purple Passage, the Life of Mrs. Frank Leslie* [Norman, Oklahoma, 1953], pp. 1, 23-24, 212n.

[17] The clerk and master advertised the bank property twice, without getting results. *Whig*, November 17, 1860, April 13, 1861.

[18] *Ibid.*, July 14, August 25, 1860.

[19] *Ibid.*, March 3, 31, 1860.

[20] *Ibid.*, May 5, 1860. Testimony of L. S. King, *ibid.*, April 21, 1860.

The Whig.

"Put None on Guard but Americans."   Chapter No. 11

PARTY STRINGS HANG LOOSELY

Parson Brownlow had established himself as a man devoted to freedom of speech and action before he came to Knoxville. But in 1852, with the *Whig* firmly rooted, he issued a manifesto that surpassed all those of the past. It signalled greater independence, politically and economically, than ever. In opening his fourth volume in Knoxville, and his forteenth in all, he recalled:

For the last three years we have lived in Knoxville, and have had to endure the degraded impotence of despised poverty—we have agonized in excessive toil and heart-rending grief, amidst an organized and villainous opposition few men have ever had to encounter in this end of the State—contending with men who have sought to immure our person within the mouldy walls of loathsome county dungeons;—men, who, by letter-writing, and electioneering in person, sought to deprive us of patronage, at home and abroad, and thus force us to grope at noon-day, along the sterile path of starvation;—men who bought claims upon us, and forced their collection, and sought by every possible means to destroy our credit in business;—and in addition to all this, armed themselves with clubs, and deadly weapons, to maim, bruise and destroy our body, and were only prevented from the accomplishment of these hellish purposes, by an *innate cowardice*, alike ridiculous and disgraceful! . . .

With those who sought to break us down, but failed in the attempt, we desire no compromise: we have placed our *mark* upon them; and until their groaning ghosts fill all hell with wailings, and heaven rings jubilee in our behalf, and loud hosannahs on our tongue fill the eternal regions, we intend to hold these men in remembrance! . . . In politics we shall be WHIG, supporting men only, in whom we have confidence. Party strings hang very loosely [*sic*.] upon our shoulders (*Whig*, June 19, 1852).

In truth the Parson laid his pen to party snarls like Alexander the Great whittled the Gordian knot. He served notice that he would not support General Winfield Scott, the Mexican War commander, if the

Whig Party nominated him. He did not believe in elevating military heroes to public offices, he distrusted the Northern leaders supporting Scott, and he feared the general's election "would widen and deepen the gulf between the North and South—which Heaven knows is almost impassible now" (*Whig*, March 20, 1852).

A smoldering bitterness against James G. (Lean Jimmy) Jones, the former governor, had been fanned into extreme heat by Jones' defeat of T. A. R. Nelson for the United States Senate seat a few months earlier. The coveted post was almost within Nelson's grasp in the early balloting, but four members of the East Tennessee delegation forsook him. Their defection brought a stinging reproach from twelve East Tennessee Whigs. Brownlow was hurt to see his friend Nelson lose, but he was infuriated because Jones defeated him. The former governor had become the editor's enemy over a question of Brownlow's veracity. The Parson had bottled his resentment. Now, eight years later, he pulled the cork from the bottle of his bitterness and let it spew forth in a furious issue of the *Whig*.

The issue had arisen when Jones denied having told a story to the effect that Andrew Jackson had insisted upon the expulsion of a widow from the Hermitage Presbyterian Church. The Parson had repeated it, Jackson heard of it, demanded that Jones confirm or deny the story, and Jones said he hadn't told it. Because Whig leaders feared an open row between Brownlow and Jones would hurt party interests, the Parson let the issue rest. Now, Brownlow said, he had "*writhed in spirit* long enough under the insulting taunts of Jones, and his friends, saying "that our long silence had been owing to having no defense to make, and to consciousness of having *lied*," so, "duty to ourself and to our innocent and helpless children requires us to satisfy the world that we are a man of *truth* and that Jones is a *liar*—and we have done it."

The *Whig* issue, which the Parson blazoned on page one as "A paper worth preserving," recounted the entire story, along with a number of statements supporting Brownlow's account of Jones telling the tale on Jackson. This newspaper also carried a long article on the manipulations by Jones and the venality of some Whigs in the election for senator. Brownlow anticipated he would be charged with party disloyalty, but he was "a Whig from *principle*, and not from *interest*." And "like a true man, as we are and ever have been, we will continue the work of unmasking rascals, irrespective of their party association, or of their position in society, and all too regardless of consequences" (*Whig*, March 6, 1852).

Scott was nominated (*Whig*, June 26, 1852) and Jones campaigned across the state for the Whig Presidential nominee. The Parson's raging animosity reached a point very close to violence when the senator filled a speaking appointment at Knoxville on September 11, 1852. Brownlow expected Jones to single him out and repeat his accusations of the editor's falsity. He had prepared himself by selecting "eight friends [four Whigs and four Democrats], who were well armed and would have seen us [receive] fair play 'at all hazards and to the last extremity,' " and having on hand

facts, documents and living witnesses, on the ground, to have paid him back with compound interest; and in retaliating, we intended taking up the public and private calendar of his numerous exploits, and making just such a showing, as he would depricate [*sic*.] having brought out, to the end of his sinful career. We say this in no spirit of *boasting*, but because the facts were known to more than one hundred men of that ground (*Whig*, September 18, 1852).

The possibility for bloodshed was high, had the issue of veracity been raised. The Parson estimated that from one hundred to two hundred men present were armed. Jones contented himself with a generalization that he had been subjected to slander and abuse. Because he did not identify Brownlow as one of those responsible, the editor did not challenge him and sought no rejoinder. But in the *Whig* he related the affair in detail, giving the names of a number of prominent men he said would have supported his position (*Ibid.*).

The *Whig* editor was not isolated in his refusal to support Scott. A National Union Convention, held at Philadelphia on August 1, nominated Daniel Webster for President. The enfeebled statesman, however, died on October 24. Brownlow, who was the Second District elector for the ticket, pleaded for votes for the Webster electors. The response, however, must have been insignificant, for he printed only scant election returns. But he reasserted his Whiggery, he gloried in the overwhelming defeat of Scott by Franklin Pierce, the Democrat nominee, and he posted on the editorial page immediately the name of Fillmore as his choice for President in 1856.[1]

The death of Webster sent the Parson into mourning for the second time in the summer of 1852. When Henry Clay died on June 28 the *Whig* sighed: "When the mortal remains of Henry Clay were consigned to the tomb, the territories of the dead, on the continent of America, were never honored with richer spoils." As Clay died the signals were flying that the party he had helped found was split to the point where disintegration was certain. Clay had sensed it, and Brownlow forecast a North-South split. Scott had carried Tennessee, but it was by less than 2,000 votes. It was the last time the Whigs won Tennessee in a Presidential election.[2]

Brownlow's course brought hot fire from Scott Whigs. Among them was his old enemy of the 1841 First District congressional race, Thomas D. Arnold, who won the seat over the *Whig's* bitter opposition. When Arnold spoke before the Scott Club in Knoxville, Brownlow was granted a rejoinder and opened with: "I appear before you to-night, in reply to the long and bitter tirade of abuse, blackguardism, and falsehoods, just uttered by the low-flung, low-bred demagogue and calumniator who has just taken his seat." The tone having been set Brownlow went ahead with his speech, and liked it so well that he printed it in the *Whig* in two-column measure and published it in a pamphlet. Indications cropped out months later that Brownlow had agreed with Scott Club leaders to leave national issues alone and confine himself to Arnold. This he did.[3]

In a second speech, this time at the Knox County Courthouse on October 28, 1852, he defended himself against an accusation that he had been bribed by the Democrats to play the independent role. His accusers said he had used the money to pay for a piano and to lift the mortgage on his Cumberland Avenue residence. Brownlow reported that a friend had bought the piano for him in Philadelphia; $100 had been paid down and a balance of $200 remained. The piano was for a Brownlow daughter who was taking music lessons, probably Susan, who was fourteen. The residence had been owned by the Methodist Church, which gave it the name of the "Parsonage." The house had been put up for sale in Chancery Court, and a friend of Brownlow's had bid it in for him. The family occupied it on May 2, 1849. The Parson had been making the payments, borrowing money for the purpose.[4]

In 1851 Knox County was in the Third Congressional District, but was shifted into the Second District by the next legislature. Brownlow took little part in the 1851 race except to hold the *Register* clique responsible for the failure of the party to deliver for Anderson the usual Whig majority. The Parson had a sound, if not partisan reason for supporting Churchwell, who won. The Democrat had proved himself an internal improvement advocate by backing vigorously a bill that provided a $50,000 federal appropriation for navigation work on the Tennessee River. Brownlow was one of five commissioners appointed by the Fillmore administration to supervise this work under the general direction of Colonel John McClellan.

Churchwell and Horace Maynard carried out the 1853 contest on a level that produced a fist fight between the candidates in Overton County. The *Whig* upbraided Maynard for having taken a drink and danced a few steps at a party frolic, and a rash of articles charged Maynard with having written, several years earlier, a number of pieces under the pen name of Zadok Jones. These pieces reflected disdain for the ordinary run of the human race. Years later Temple recalled that Churchwell made "use of money and other means not to be commended."[5]

Tom Arnold also ran for the state senate that year. He gave the *Whig* and its editor "a terrible share of his wrath" in his opener at Newport on June 11 (*Whig*, June 25, 1852). Brownlow waited for Arnold to campaign in the lower part of the district, then dogged him through Blount and Sevier counties. He spit out such challenges as this one at Sevierville:

Gentlemen—this man Arnold, as usual, has his spurs on, and has made his arrangements to deliver a lying and abusive harrangue [*sic*.] of three or four hours and cut out, neither allowing me or his competitors time to say anything. I have attended his appointments, in Blount and Sevier, upon his invitation. He has stated in my absence that I am afraid to meet him in day light [*sic*.], and when I am not surrounded by a Locofoco mob. I have met [him] at Louisville and Maryville, and when he had a huge knife in his bosom, a pistol in his pocket, and a spear cane in his hand as he now has, and I denounced him, as I do now, as a LIAR, a SCOUNDREL, and a COWARD, having no honor, no principle, and no resentment, unless it be in a contest with his wife, a clever, but broken-hearted woman, who has been whipped and abused by him on more occasions than one, as I shall prove today, if he will allow me a showing, and if this can't be had, I shall retire to the grove in front of this Church and do it at once (*Whig*, July 23, 1852).

In his opener Arnold had denounced the Sevier County "Regulators," a vigilante organization that had flogged a number of miscreants, hanged nine and driven twenty-one outside the county. But in the lower counties Arnold found much popular sentiment for the vigilantes and he denied having denounced them, a point upon which Brownlow seized. The Parson had resented bitterly a vigilante movement at Jonesboro in 1845 which threatened to burn his plant and tar and feather the editor, but in the Sevier County movement he found great merit.[6]

The Brownlow piano was purchased in Philadelphia in 1852 for a daughter taking music lessons. Brownlow was accused of taking the instrument as a bribe from the Democrats. In the picture is Mrs. George T. Fritts, great-granddaughter of the Parson. [*Journal* Staff Photograph by Hugh Lunsford.]

Brownlow's furious activity in the Second District congressional race and in Arnold's campaign somewhat overshadowed the gubernatorial contest between Gustavus A. Henry, Whig, and Andrew Johnson in the *Whig*'s columns. The results were mixed. Johnson won by more than 2,000 votes; the Whigs retained a majority in the House of Representatives. They elected five of the ten congressmen. Democrat Churchwell made the last successful race for his party in the Second Congressional District, and Dr. Benjamin Bell, Democrat, defeated Arnold.[7] Brownlow had spun his political wheels in opposite directions and emerged with considerable success. He backed the Whig nominee for governor, a Democrat for Congress, and he had blocked Arnold's election from a Whig district. Brownlow also boasted of a new press, "the largest ever brought to East Tennessee." He installed new and smaller type and enlarged sheet on which the newspaper was printed.[8]

He made an extended defense of his Whiggery; in order to meet the charges he had deserted the party. He traced his party pedigree back to support of Hugh Lawson White for President in 1836 and reviewed his battles as a partisan and editor of the *Whig*. He wrote, not to conciliate his enemies, but, "to set ourselves right with our own friends in the Whig ranks and to guard them against the falsehoods of our enemies." He warned against the perils of division among the Whig members of the General Assembly as they faced the election of a United States senator. Bell's six-year term was nearing an end. As for the Parson, he performed a remarkable acrobatic political feat. He supported Nelson because of friendship, qualifications and the tradition that East Tennessee was entitled to the seat, a precedent which Brownlow had rejected six years earlier in order to support Bell. Now, in a mystifying performance, he exalted the tradition, supported Nelson, and lavished praise on Bell, whom he had been berating furiously a few months before. And he correctly predicted Bell would regain his seat. [9]

Brownlow had washed away his long interlude of bitterness against Bell a few months earlier, without explanation. The editor commented as the senator stopped at the Mansion House on his way to Montvale Springs in Blount County:

> His dignified deportment and politeness, which are uniform, is accompanied by a self-possession which belongs to great minds. We regard him as the greatest man now in the United States Senate of either political party (*Whig*, May 28, 1853).

Bell and Gentry, as mentioned before, had financed the purchase of two presses and other materials for Brownlow's Knoxville opening, at a cost of $900. Brownlow was to be given patronage to enable him to pay the note. Brownlow had paid $7,000 in security debts before leaving Jonesboro and had raised $1,000 from the sale of his print shop equipment there.

Two years later the congressmen remained unpaid, and at Knoxville creditors were threatening legal proceedings to collect a note for $800. The Parson had gone security on this note for his former associate, Valentine Garland, and Garland had failed to pay, throwing the responsibility upon Brownlow. T. W. Humes, one of the *Register*'s backers, and Joe King, also of Knoxville, had bought the note and given it to Lawyer Sneed, also a *Register* underwriter, for collection. The Parson worked out an involved arrangement to meet this peril. Sam Patton, editor of the *Methodist Episcopalian* for which the *Whig* shop did the printing, paid Humes' share of the note, the Parson to pay Patton in printing. Brownlow attempted to meet King's claim with another note, but a bank refused even to discount it. The Parson worked out of this corner by assigning to King a payment of $400 due the *Whig* in Washington for government printing which Bell and Gentry apparently had got for Brownlow's newspaper. This was money that Bell and Gentry had expected to receive as payment of the note they had endorsed for Brownlow, and when they learned it had been diverted to King they were furious. Gentry

wrote me [Brownlow] a letter, reflecting on me, as either wanting in *honesty* or *veracity* in that *I had used funds in Washington for one object which I had promised* to devote to another. I therefore determined that I would raise the money and relive [*sic.*] Bell and Gentry, or I would sacrifice my office and all I have for the nine hundred and interest.

The Parson went to Memphis and obtained a promise he would be lent money for this purpose, probably by his old friend and fellow editor, Dr. Jeptha Fowlkes. In bitter mood he suggested to Nelson he was on the point of leaving the party, although

I suppose there is no man living, as far removed from Democracy as I am in my feelings and sentiments; and certain as I am that I will be one of the last men on earth to go over to Democracy, but I have been badly treated by the Whigs, and I intend to pay them back, if I can, *in some way* or another.[10]

When Brownlow wrote this letter to Nelson more than a year had elapsed without the Parson getting any of the expected patronage from Washington. He had stormed at Bell, "The general government has printing to do in this place amounting to more than one thousand dollars, but this will be given to the *Register* with a view to *buy up its support for those Tennessee* Whigs whose election to Congress, and to the United States Senate, it has hitherto opposed" (*Whig*, February 2, 1850). J. R. Hobbie, first assistant postmaster general, tendered the *Whig* $315 in advertising in January of 1850, which Brownlow rejected as an insignificant crumb. The rejection led to reports that the editor had threatened the administration by letter that he would join the opposition party if he was not given substantial contracts. To counteract this, the editor published Hobbie's letter submitting the business and his fiery return of it (*Whig*, August 17, 1850). His answer to Hobbie had been delayed because

We have had high waters here for six or eight weeks, and *your* carts and mail-riders make it a business not to cross any stream if it has rained the previous night, or if the water is so muddy they cannot see the bottom by moonlight. (*Ibid.*).

As for Hobbie, Brownlow regarded him "as a corrupt, and overbearing Locofoco, who ought to be dismissed from office forthwith." The Parson's tone was that of a mistreated Whig, but still a Whig (*Ibid.*).

Bell had started early in 1850 trying to get patronage for the *Whig* and had obtained promises from several departments. He also wrote Nelson that he was trying to get office or employment for Brownlow "which will lift him above the pursuit of his creditors." The Parson, meanwhile, urged Nelson to put more pressure on Bell and Gentry. Brownlow described them as controlling the Taylor administration. A bill was pending in Congress to appropriate $20,000 for improvement of the river from Knoxville to Decatur, Alabama. Brownlow wanted one of the two top jobs provided for in the measure.[11] This did not materialize and more than a year later Bell was imploring Nelson to advise him how to stop the *Whig*'s fire upon him.[12] When President Taylor died on July 9, 1850, and Fillmore succeeded to the presidency, the *Whig* began to display government advertising. How it came about was not explained, but Brownlow let his readers know Bell was not responsible. The Parson criticized the senator for giving indifferent support to the appointment of Solomon D. Jacobs of Knoxville, who succeeded Hobbie in 1851 as first assistant postmaster general (*Whig*, April 26, 1851) and he announced:

As to Mr. Bell we have not written him a letter in fifteen months, nor have we received one from him. We have no correspondence with him and intend to have none. For the last fifteen years we have been his advocate and friend—we have supported and defended him through evil and good report, and even incurring thereby the displeasure of some prominent men in the state. For all this "labor of love" he has treated us with cold indifference, not to say downright ingratitude, just as others who knew him better than we did told us he would do. We have quit him—not hastily or under the influence of passion—but after the most mature deliberation and after a fair and full trial of his merits. We never again expect to conduct a paper which will directly or indirectly advance his interests. Our influence, however, is but limited, and he can get along in this world without us. If he cannot, and is forced to retire to the shades of private life, the State will sustain no serious injury (*Ibid.*).

Gentry attempted mediation and urged Brownlow to be more considerate of Bell. An understanding that the Parson went in for exaggeration, rather than moderation, in all things, and especially in describing his own fury, moved Gentry to intercede. The *Whig* printed Gentry's letter under the pen name of "Amicus" with a note, "We give this letter more out of regard to the writer than the gentleman written about. There is no man in the District of Columbia for whom we entertain as much respect as we do for the writer of this letter." But Brownlow did not suggest that the latter would alter his course. Years later Oliver P. Temple identified the author as Gentry, and added a sentence which the *Whig* did not print: "Now if I were in Mr. Bell's place, I should write to you and tell you to go to h—l."[13]

The Parson did change. He swung full circle. And in the course of it he suffered utter chagrin. He flew high before he fell. It looked as if he was on top of the world when he boasted:

No one holds a mortgage upon our pen or conscience—WE ARE FREE. Our paper is now PERMANENTLY established, with a circulation larger than any other Weekly political paper in the State, and with more subscribers than all the political papers in Knoxville put together! Ours is the only Printing Office in Knoxville, *situated on its own premises*, and not required *to pay house rent*. And upon enquiry of *Journeymen Printers*, of the *Merchants and Mechanics* of the city, and *Farmers* and *Paper-Makers* of the country, it will be ascertained, beyond contradiction that our office *pays its debts*! Nay, it will be ascertained, that we owe *less*, by *one half*, than any other newspaper establishment in Knoxville! (*Whig*, June 19, 1852).

This sounded like Brownlow's moment of triumph and he must have believed it was. John W. O'Brien, Brownlow's partner, was leaving or had left for Washington, where he was to collect money, probably for government printing. Brownlow sent a letter to him through United States Representative A. G. Watkins of the Second District, directing O'Brien to pay Bell and Gentry all he collected above that amount necessary for his return. The Parson trusted his friends and business associates to the point of carelessness. When O'Brien came home Brownlow asked him if he had "received my letter through Watkins? He said, 'I did—allright.' " The editor did not ask him pointedly if he had paid Bell and Gentry, and after a time he began to have misgivings. By September he learned that O'Brien had pocketed $1,000 and had not paid the members of Congress. The partnership was dissolved on September 11, 1852, and it was announced that O'Brien was to start the *Free Press* at Loudon. The Parson told his readers, "We part with our old associate, in peace and on kind terms," which was not the case, and he wrote Bell an abject, apologetic letter, outlining what had happened. "I state these important facts to let you and Gentry know that I had not used the money for other purposes, and that I have not received one dollar of it and never expect to." The Parson had not forgotten Gentry's reproach when the congressman learned the editor had diverted to Joe King money he had expected to get. In his distress Brownlow shed his arrogance so far as to plead with Bell to help him get a job as a river commissioner under a bill just passed, or failing that, one with the port of entry office to be opened in Knoxville. [14]

Desperate, humble and uncertain as Brownlow was about his material prospects in 1852, he has displayed a slender, wry conviction two years earlier that he expected much more agreeable returns after death. He fell ill at Abingdon, Virginia, where he had gone to attend the Holston Conference, and his condition had worsened so much that his death was anticipated. Bishop William Capers, concerned about the state of the Parson's soul, visited his bedside, prayed with him as to his spiritual state. The Parson later said he was so ill he could not recall his answer but that his friends had credited him with saying: "Well, Bishop, if I had my life to live over again I could improve it in many respects and would try to do so. However, if the books have been properly kept in the other world, *there is a small balance in my favor.*"[15]

The Parson presented himself to his readers in a variety of roles: editor, lecturer, preacher, traveler and commentator, but he also was worth watching for his changing relations with men for the foe of one day might be the friend of the next, as well as the reverse. The times also produced a shattering of old political alignments, as men hestitated, or sought new standards. He had been enraged and embittered at Bell for what he believed was political ingratitude. He had been crushed when Gentry suggested he was guilty of double-dealing, and he had treated Sneed with polite hositility because the lawyer was one of the men who had helped finance the *Register*. But by the middle of the 1850s he was warmly and virogously espousing the political interests of all three. The divisions between the North and the South were shattering to Democrats and Whigs, fatally to the latter. Men groped for new political structures or simply traded parties. James G. Jones, Crozier and Swan turned Democrats. Bell and Gentry leaned toward the American Party but stopped short of declaring allegiance. Brownlow, Nelson, Temple and Sneed became outright Americans.[16]

Bell's name went up on the *Whig*'s editorial page as its choice for President late in 1854, but the Tennessee senator declined to attend the American convention in 1856. He received little or no consideration and the nomination went to Fillmore.[17] Gentry ran for governor against Johnson in 1855, in response to leaders and newspapers throughout the state who were determined to provide opposition. The fragmentation of the Whigs and the dissident Democrats opposed to Johnson presented such a conglomeration that no political umbrella was broad enough to cover this motley group and no convention was held. Brownlow, active in the Sons of Temperance, insisted that the candidate he would support must favor submitting to the people the issue of a "Prohibitory Liquor Law." When he came out for Gentry, he assured his readers this man would meet this requirement, but he also knew his choice would carry a ragged banner in such a cause. Gentry was a heavy drinker. The Parson met this difficulty with some neat prose and an awkward straddle:

Now, although Col. Gentry is not a member of any Temperance Society and his *practice for years past* has been at war with total abstinence principles, still, for an outsider, he concedes a great deal. And those who know the man, know him to be one of the most bold, fearless, frank and reliable men in the State; and whatever he pledges himself to do, he will do it though it defeat him in the election.[18]

Gentry had made an outstanding reputation as an orator, in Congress and out, but while he was accomplished and eloquent, in view of his style and gentility, he could not cope with Johnson's facility with the sledgehammer and dung fork. The governor attacked the Know-Nothing (American) Party for its secrecy, placed it on a level with some contemporary outlaws known as the Murrell gang and termed it reptilian in its repulsiveness. Gentry refused to reply in kind, despite urging from Brownlow and Temple. His failure to do so was construed as unwillingness to support the party that was trying to elect him. Johnson won by more than 2,000 votes but the Know-Nothings elected six of the ten congressmen and took control of the General Assembly.[19]

The Parson, as a zealot of the American Party, fought Roman

Catholicism and foreignism. But in support of Sneed, the American candidate for congress, he went stoutly to the defense of a Catholic who had come to this country from Ireland. Sneed, Brownlow said, had been charged

with *subscribing money to import Catholics* to this country! Now for the facts, as they are, and as we know them to exist.

Old Neddy Lavender, aged about 60 years, has been in this country eight years, from Ireland, and is a *naturalized* citizen. He wishes to *bring his wife*, an old lady, to this country. Calling upon Sneed, among others, for a small charity, he [Sneed] gave him TEN DOLLARS. The old man is the Sexton at Grey Cemetery, employed by the stockholders, by the year, to keep the grounds, trim the trees, and dig all the graves, under the same moderate salary. The old man stood his ground throughout the cholera, and dug one or more graves every day. We assisted him in easing down into their graves different persons, hot and dry as was the weather, and gloomy as were the prospects all around! Had the old man called upon us, we would have contributed something, as little as we desire the increase of foreigners in our country. The old man has been a member of the Order of Sons of Temperance for several years and is perfectly harmless. His poor old wife will not vote in this country, or *raise up voters*. Helping to bury Sneed's little children, as he did, Sneed could have not done less than subscribe and pay $10 to the fund. It is a small affair, when rightly understood, and will only be used in a *desperate* cause (*Whig*, July 21, 1855).

The Parson performed a redoubtable flip in his opinion of Sam Houston. In 1845 the *Whig* had accused Houston, as president of the Republic of Texas, of playing a double game. Brownlow said that Houston represented to President Jackson that he favored annexation to the United States, and to the British that he was against it. When Houston was in Tennessee later in the same summer, Brownlow was more abusive. He recommended that every door in the state should be closed to him. Before the close of the year Brownlow wrote: "We have looked upon Houston for years as one of the most corrupt, despised, wicked, selfish, sordid and disgusting blackguards on earth"; but, he added, those characteristics qualified him very well as a Democratic officeholder. Texas, in the meanwhile, was admitted to the Union, and Houston was elected senator from the new state. The *Whig* reported, "Senator Sam Houston recently passed down the river by Memphis, on his return to Texas, about drunk enough to make an eloquent Temperance speech." In reporting him as a reject of the Democratic National Convention at Baltimore in

SAMUEL HOUSTON.

Samuel Houston [From Benson J. Lossing, *Pictorial History of the Civil War in the United States of America*, Hartford, 1877.]

1848, [20] in the choice of a presidential nominee, the Parson tidied his faults into this bundle:

This old "Military Chieftan" [*sic.*] who abdicated the Government of Tennessee—divorced himself from a decent wife—united his fortunes with an Indian Squaw—undertook to carry out old Burr's scheme against Mexico—fought, bled and died at the battle of San Jacinto—liberated Santa Anna when a prisoner—and came back to the Hermitage to let the "Greatest and Best" die in his arms was *run over* by the baggage wagons, when the first engagement took place, and has not been heard from since. He spoke long and loud through New England for the nomination, but oh! the ingratitude of his countrymen (*Whig*, June 7, 1848).

Brownlow faced about completely when Houston, staying at the Mansion House in Knoxville, condemned the proposed Southern Convention scheduled at Nashville and declared, "Every d--d rascal who attends that convention ought to be hung [*sic.*] with a d--d great rough halter." The Parson, like Houston, saw in this convention the seeds of disunion. Thereafter he was the Parson's bosom comrade. He saluted him with a headline "Three Cheers for Gen. Houston," in reporting his speech in Washington affirming his loyalty to the United States and threatening military warfare from the South against those who favored secession. Brownlow apparently had met Houston when the latter paused in Knoxville during a visit with his sister, Mrs. William Wallace of Maryville. How they buried the scorching vituperation the Parson once had piled upon Houston was not disclosed, but Brownlow later was on record as saying the Texan had spoken very highly of the editor's father. Houston knew him as a schoolmate in Rockbridge County, Virginia.[21]

Brownlow continued to lavish praise and friendliness on Houston. As the Texas senator paused in Nashville on his way to Washington the editor observed, "With a fur cap, a three-cornered cloak, and large whiskers, he steps about like a boy. I think I can see in San Jacinto about as much of availability as is to be found in any of the prominent men of the day." A few weeks later as the Parson spent considerable time in Washington with the senator he reported, "Houston looks well and is behaving well." On the senator's last visit to the *Whig* editor in Knoxville, Houston impressed John Bell Brownlow because the senator was wearing yellowish corduroy pants, a black velvet vest and something resembling a sailor jacket.[22]

In this strange period when old enmities were transformed into friendships, Brownlow was reconciled with Dr. Joe Powell, a former state senator from the First District. Powell was an associate and relative of Landon C. Haynes in his earlier feud with the Parson. In 1856 Powell wrote the *Whig* editor from California, where he was the enrolling clerk of the legislature, a cordial letter inquiring as to the state of political affairs. Overlooking the lurid accusations they earlier had exchanged, Powell and the Parson apparently forgave each other everything (*Whig*, May 24, 1856).

When Dr. Isaac Anderson of Maryville, a Presbyterian leader and educator, died in 1857, Brownlow effected something like a postmortem reconciliation with the preacher he had ridiculed and fought in *Helps to the Study of Presbyterianism* more than thirty years earlier. Of Anderson, dead, he wrote: "He was a useful man, spending his time and his talents in preaching and teaching. We have heard him frequently. While he was a strong preacher, he was the best and most powerful exhorter in the Presbyterian ministry in East Tennessee. His voice was powerful, and his manner was earnest, zealous and unostentatious, and all together made him able and successful."[23]

The Parson even laid aside his animosity to Horace Maynard. In 1857 he supported Maynard in the latter's successful race for Congress. One of his justifications was that most of the Whigs who had fought Temple and nominated Maynard in 1853 had gone over to the Democrats. He even suggested Maynard as a candidate for governor.[24]

Animosity between Brownlow and Governor Johnson, however, flourished, as they fed it with the coarsest exchanges. The times were not ripe for their interests to be joined and they roared at each other from newspaper and stump. When Johnson defeated Gentry in 1855, the former made a victory speech in front of the Coleman House in Knoxville. It so infuriated the Parson that a few weeks later he delivered from the square in front of the capitol in Nashville one of the most searing attacks of his career. His review of Johnson's speech began:

> Gov. Johnson said this new party of self-styled Americans professed to have organized with a view to purify and reform the old political parties. A beautiful set, said he, to reform! The Order of Know Nothings was composed of the worst men in the Whig and Democratic parties. As a sample of these men, he pointed out *Andrew J. Donelson* by name, exclaiming as often as twice, who is Andrew J. *Donelson?* He is a soured, office-seeking, disappointed politician, who has been kicked out of the Democratic Party. To illustrate his view more fully, he told the crowd to imagine a large gang of *Counterfeiters* out there!—and an equally large gang of Horse-thieves out yonder! Take from these two companies the worst men in their ranks, for a third party of these, and you have a representation of this Know Nothing party (*Whig*, October 27, 1855).

Johnson was so arrogant, Brownlow said, that when a member of the audience challenged one of his statements the speaker retorted that he had "heard the hissing of an adder, or a goose."

Brownlow appraised jointly his old foe, E. G. Eastman, editor of the former Knoxville *Argus* and now of the Nashville *Union* and *American*, along with the governor. He described Eastman as a former abolitionist from Massachusetts brought to Tennessee as a hireling to write party propaganda:

> He is a poor Devil, as void of truth and honor as he has shown himself to be of courage and resentment. He edits a low, dirty, scurrilous sheet; and like his master, Gov. Johnson, never could elevate himself above the level of a common blackguard. No epithet is too low, too degrading, or disgraceful to be applied to the members of the American party, by either of these Billingsgate graduates. Decent men shun coming in contact with either of them, as they would avoid a night cart, or other vehicle of filth. As some fish thrive only in dirty water, so the Nashville Union and American would not exist a week out of the atmosphere of slang and vituperation. A fit organ this for all who arrange themselves under the dark and piratical flag of Andrew Johnson and his progressive Democracy. I am the more specific, in reference to *Eastman*, because I understand he is in this assembly! (*Ibid.*).

The Parson recalled some of Johnson's characterizations of the

35,000 to 40,000 Know-Nothings in the state, employed during his campaign:

In his Murfreesborough speech, he asserted that *"the Devil, his Satanic Majesty, presides over all the secret conclaves"* held by the Know Nothings, and that *"they are the allies of the Prince of Darkness."* I quote from his printed speeches from memory, but it will be found I quote correctly. In that same speech, he asserts that all Know Nothings are *"bound by terrible oaths to fix and carry a lie in their mouths!"* In his Manchester speech, I believe it was, he called all members of the new party *"Hyenas,"* and *"huge reptiles, upon whose neck and feet of honest men ought to be placed."* And in this same speech he says he "would as soon be found in a clan of John A. Murrell's men as in a Know Nothing Council. . . ."

On every stump in Tennessee, he held me up as the "High Priest of the Order," representing Col. Gentry as my candidate. Since I came to Middle Tennessee, I have been informed that he pointed to the fancied fact that I was the head of the Order, as an evidence of *its utter lack of respectability (Ibid.).*

Before going to Nashville for his tirade Brownlow sought to set Donelson against the governor by writing him of Johnson's insults. The result was, Brownlow told his audience, that Donelson, former secretary to President Jackson and his nephew by marriage, went to Nashville, where he "was seen walking these streets with a *large and homely stick* in his hand, looking *grim*, as any gentleman would do under the circumstances." However, Brownlow said, the governor *"ingloriously lied out* of what he had said. . . . I, therefore, pronounce your Governor, here upon his own dunghill, an UNMITIGATED LIAR AND CALUMNIATOR, and a VILLAINOUS COWARD, wanting the *nerve* to stand up to his abuse of better men than he himself!" The Parson must have felt he had done a complete job on Johnson—with a proper flick at Eastman—for he made the same speech at Clarksville and Shelbyville and printed it twice in the *Whig.* He expressed surprise that Johnson had denied the statements about Donelson and offered to produce "one hundred respectable gentlemen in Knoxville," who would swear the governor made them. Although the Parson in his Nashville speech set Donelson right as to the governor's insults the latter did not return to Nashville and flog the man Brownlow said had defamed him. [25]

Greater fame, if not political fortune, awaited Donelson. The Tennessee delegation to the Philadelphia convention of the Know-Nothing Party successfully pressed his suit. He was nominated for vice-president, along with Millard Fillmore for chief executive. The Parson, a delegate and chairman of the Credentials Committee, championed the cause of Southern manhood when a dispute arose with the Ohio group over a platform plank. The New York *Times* reported: "Parson Brownlow of Tennessee said he could lick any five of the Ohio delegation, and that five of the Tennessee delegation could kick the Ohio delegation all around the hall." The validity of the Parson's assertion was not tested, for the *Times* added: "All soon became quiet again."[26]

The Parson's zeal and energy in behalf of the American candidates seemed to have no limit. He published in 1856 the two books previously mentioned, he poured out campaign editorials, and he took to the stump in behalf of Fillmore and Donelson. He regretted that he could not meet all the requests for speeches because he was horseless and buggyless, and therefore restricted to appointments where the trains ran. He attained something like a state of rapture during the big American Party rally at Knoxville, billed for Thursday, September 4, 1856, but which broadened to run from Tuesday through Friday. The event drew from 20,000 to 30,000 people from the thirty counties of East Tennessee who lined the roads with their camps, poured from trains, marched in processions, heard interminable speeches mixed with the roar of cannon from Old Methodist Hill, slept out of doors after all the beds in the city were filled—the Parson admonished those who feared they might take cold under such circumstances to *"lay up the gaps"*—and sometimes reveled until 2:00 and 3:00 a.m.[27]

The election returns startled Brownlow. Democrat James Buchanan not only swept the nation to become President, but also carried Tennessee by the largest majority any party had attained in a presidential race since 1840, nearly 7,500. Republican John C. Fremont ran a respectable second, although his vote in Tennessee was insignificant. Fillmore carried one state, Maryland. The reeling remnant of the Whig Party had received its death blow. "We are whipped out— utterly vanquished—demolished—thrown far into the shade of retirement!" the editor moaned as he saw another voyage up familiar Salt River: "one we have been navigating for *eighteen years*, going up every other year and returning as often. . . This trip we aim to *go higher up*, than we have ever done before." The Parson could look with a wry smile on his personal misfortune, but for his friends and for the nation he was alarmed. He had seen how "The strong darkly-rolling tide of fanaticism passed over the Northern portion of the Union—the fierce, hot fires of Disunion swept over the South,—and the result is that the dark, piratical flag of Anti-Americanism, Locofocoism, now floats in triumph." Yet, he held that the nation's will had been "legally and constitutionally" expressed and that each citizen should accept this decision. For Brownlow "Our remedy for the evils of this character is the *ballot box*, and we will not consent to resort to any other." The returns had brought him to the conclusion, "The great body of the Northern people are utterly and irreconcilably opposed to *Negro Slavery*, as it exists in the South, and that they will not favor its extension, if indeed they will tolerate its existence where it is." He had a few deeply prophetic words for Tennessee: "In the day of the Union's greatest trouble and peril, not far distant, she will vindicate her right to the proud name she bears."

The Parson trimmed his business sails by cutting from $1.00 to fifty cents the price on two hundred copies of *Americanism Contrasted with Foreignism, Romanism and Bogus Democracy* remaining in his shop. He did not report if this stimulated sales. Celebrating Democrats had their casualty. Fuller Ryan, ramming the charge into a cannon on Old Methodist Hill, which was being fired in the jubilation over Buchanan's election, was killed by a premature explosion.[28]

The Know-Nothing Party made its final effort in a state race in 1857. It ran Robert Hatton of Lebanon against the democratic choice, the able Isham G. Harris of Memphis. Brownlow unloaded his usual diatribes against the Democratic Party and promoted Hatton.[29] But he liked and respected Harris, and described him as

a man of talents and experience, an able debater, a thorough gentleman, and a man of unblemished private character. His good character and the knightly and courteous demeanor with which he demeans himself toward an opponent are so unlike what Democracy has been accustomed to in the State for several years past that we are not sure it will be acceptable to a large portion of his party (*Whig*, May 16, 1857).

Harris defeated Hatton by 11,371 votes, and the Democrats took control of the General Assembly.[30] This dismayed Brownlow to the point of wavering on his political course, but he managed this denunciation of the opposition:

We recognize in the ranks of the Democratic party thousands of high-minded men, ardent patriots, and true lovers of their country; but before we fall into the support of what we believe to be the reckless and ruinous party—the low flung humbuggery, and villainous designs of this self-styled "National Democratic Party," we would see that unwashed, unterrified, uncombed, uncircumcised, and unregenerate organization as far down in Hell as a Forge-hammer would fall in a thousand years! Let none suppose that this language is too strong, without considering to what sort of organization it is applied. We apply it to the Foreign Catholic, Pauper-loving, Anti-American, Wet nurse Democracy, who, differing among themselves, widely and materially on every question of national policy before the country, nevertheless agree, affiliate, and fraternize in elections for the sake of the spoils—with all the parties, of all colors, and from all claims, and of all religions, embracing in fraternal hug, all the odds and ends of God's creation! (*Whig*, August 29, 1857).

Brownlow's bitterness was compounded when the legislature elected the retiring Governor Johnson to the United States Senate to succeed James C. Jones.[31] Brownlow's hatred and contempt of these men he displayed by giving them the newspaperman's ultimate measure of unimportance, a final paragraph in a brief report of legislative actions, placed below even the election of doorkeepers, that snapped:

The election of United States Senator was gone into, on Thursday, and resulted in the election of *A. Johnson*, the Democratic papers easing the conscience of *Jones*, by eulogizing his patriotic course, and thanking him for the aid he had rendered them in two fierce contests! (*Whig*, October 17, 1857).

Another blow fell on the Parson when the Democratic majority in the legislature, pressing its advantage, voted to send A. O. P. Nicholson of Maury County to the United States Senate when John Bell's term would expire two years later.

The campaign of 1859 found the remnants of the Whig and Know-Nothing parties, with a scattering of dissident Democrats, organized under the forlorn banner of "Opposition." They nominated John Netherland of Rogersville to compete against the unanimous choice of the Democrats, the tried incumbent, Isham G. Harris. Netherland had served in both houses of the legislature and was Whig elector for the state at large in 1848. He was a competent speaker, renowned as a jury lawyer and a man of striking appearance. But he was not as diligent as Harris in preparing for the campaign and seems to have depended more upon wit than detailed information. The *Whig* supported Netherland vigorously, although Brownlow had reasons for disliking him politically. He held Netherland responsible for T. A. R. Nelson's failure to be elected to the United States Senate in 1851, and he believed Netherland was part of a Hawkins County clique which traded with Andrew Johnson in order to get Netherland elected to the legislature. [32]

If the *Whig* lacked its usual enthusiasm for party candidates during the campaign, it also may have been because Brownlow was busy in a number of other controversies that required his close attention. He battled in the courts the trustees of the defunct Bank of East Tennessee. He beat down a spate of civil and criminal libel cases brought by Martin Patterson, the former editor of the *Democratic Eagle* at Kingston. And he gave his friend Nelson every help he could in the First District congressional race where the Jonesboro lawyer would defeat his former law student and the Parson's old enemy, Landon C. Haynes. Another of the *Whig*'s old foes, E. G. Eastman, editor of the Nashville *Union and American*, gored deeply into the flesh of the Netherland organization with harsh satire on its failure to come up with anything better for a party name than "Opposition." [33] Brownlow mastheaded his candidates under the banner of "Whig and American ticket," and he struck lusty blows for Horace Maynard, who was running for reelection to Congress on this slate. The *Whig* found much to approve in Maynard, for he caned the editor of the now Democratic *Register*, James W. Newman, and he was running against James Crozier Ramsey, son of Dr. James G. M. Ramsey, the historian, who had drawn the Parson's fire as one of the trustees of the Bank of East Tennessee. [34]

The *Whig* showed garish enthusiasm over the election of seven out of the ten members of Congress, including Nelson and Maynard. The editor did not seem to suffer severely over the defeat of Netherland, conditioned by Governor Harris' majority falling more than 3,000 below the 11,000 of two years earlier. Nelson won by only 100, but in a district that had been sending a Democrat to Congress, and Maynard's majority was 1,400. The "Opposition" celebrated in front of the Lamar House in Knoxville—Maynard, Nelson, Netherland and even Bell holding forth to the crowd. [35] The Parson, a week earlier at the same spot, speaking briefly because of his afflicted throat, had announced:

I can only speak for myself, and for myself I say most unhesitatingly that I shall fight this Democracy until I die. They may call me a Black Republican, an ally of the North, or what not; I am against the thieving party in power. And if the Opposition shall nominate The Devil Himself With Horns and Tail on, I will take him as a choice of evils, against any of the corrupt, insincere and plundering leaders of this self styled Democratic party (*Whig*, August 13, 1859).

The Parson's sulfurous period to the campaign was in striking contrast to the manner in which the races had been conducted. "Politeness and courtesy" characterized the Nelson-Haynes debates. The sometimes belligerent Maynard's only act of violence was to cane Editor Newman. Netherland and Harris seem to have done no more than to lift a forefinger at each other. Brownlow also racked up personal political triumphs. He was elected an alderman from the Second Ward of the newly established municipality of East Knoxville, in 1856 and 1857.[36]

CHAPTER XI NOTES

[1] *Whig*, July 24, August 14, October 30, November 13, 1852. See also Claude Moore Fuess, *Daniel Webster* (Boston, 1930), 2 Vols., II, p. 351. Hereafter referred to as Fuess.

[2] *Whig*, July 3, 1852; Fuess, II, p. 209; *Whig*, November 13, 1852; Folmsbee *et al.*, *Short History*, pp. 231-232.

[3] *Whig*, September 24, 1852, January 1, 1853.

[4] *Ibid.*, November 13, 1852; reminiscent article by John Bell Brownlow, *Knoxville Tribune*, August 18, 1896.

[5] *Acts of Tennessee, 1851-1852* (Nashville, 1852), p. 293; *Whig*, June 6, July 9, 23, 30, June 26, 1852. For biographies of Maynard and Temple, respectively, see Rothrock, ed., *French Broad-Holston*, pp. 453-454, 496-497; Turner, "The Public Career of William Montgomery Churchwell," pp. 21-23, 25-26; Temple, *Notable Men*, p. 138.

[6] *Whig*, May 21, 28, 1853.

[7] White, *Messages*, IV, pp. 519-522; Folmsbee *et al.*, *Short History*, p. 233; Rule, ed., *Standard History*, pp. 320-321; *Whig*, August 6, 13, 27, September 3, October 15, 1853.

[8] *Ibid.*, August 20, October 1, 1853.

[9] *Ibid.*, September 17, 24, November 5, 1853; Joseph H. Parks, *John Bell of Tennessee* (Baton Rouge, 1950), pp. 211-215. Hereafter referred to as Parks.

[10] Brownlow to Nelson, May 30, 1851. Nelson Papers.

[11] Bell to Nelson, February 25, 1850, Brownlow to Nelson, March 23, 1850. Nelson Papers.

[12] Bell to Nelson, May 5, 1851. Nelson Papers.

[13] *Whig*, July 19, 1851 (The page is incorrectly dated July 5, 1851); Temple, *Notable Men*, p. 236.

[14] Brownlow to Bell, September 7, 1852. Polk-Yeatman collection, Manu-

script Division, Tennessee State Library and Archives. *Whig*, September 11, 1852.

[15] *Parson Brownlow's Book*, pp. 14-15; Rule, ed., *Standard History*, pp. 326-327.

[16] Parks, 302-307, 311-312; Folmsbee *et al., Short History*, pp. 233-245; Alexander, *T. A. R. Nelson*, pp. 54-55; *Whig*, November 4, 25, December 30, 1854, April 7, May 1, July 10, August 31, 1856.

[17] *Ibid.*, October 14, 1854, March 1, 1856; Parks, p. 307.

[18] *Whig*, October 28, December 2, 16, 1854; see also Temple, *Notable Men*, p. 242.

[19] *Whig*, May 5, July 21, 1855; Temple, *Notable Men*, pp. 234-235, 383-385; Folmsbee *et al., Short History*, pp. 235-236; Temple, *Notable Men*, p. 389; *Whig*, November 3, 1855.

[20] *Ibid.*, April 9, 1845. For background see Folmsbee *et al., Short History*, pp. 189-190, 211; *Whig*, July 16, September 16, 1845, September 16, 1846.

[21] *Ibid.*, April 13, August 31, June 29, April 13, 1850; *Parson Brownlow's Book*, p. 16.

[22] *Whig*, January 12, February 23, 1856; John Bell Brownlow's letter, Knoxville *Tribune*, August 16, 1896.

[23] *Whig*, February 7, 1857; Rothrock, ed., *French Broad-Holston*, pp. 367-368.

[24] *Whig*, May 30, August 22, January 17, 1857.

[25] Quotations are from *ibid.*, October 27, 1855. Some italics were omitted in the second printing, *ibid.*, February 9, 1856. The Murrell gang, led by John A. Murrell, killed and robbed in Mississippi and Arkansas until Murrell was captured, convicted and imprisoned. Temple, *Notable Men*, fn p. 385.

[26] Folmsbee *et al., Short History*, pp. 237-238; *Whig*, March 1, 1856; quoted in the Knoxville *Register*, September 11, 1856.

[27] *Whig*, April 12, May 24, August 2, September 6, 13, 1856; *Register*, September 11, 1856.

[28] *Whig*, November 8, 15, 1856; Parks, pp. 311-313; Folmsbee *et al., Short History*, p. 238; Alexander, Thomas A. R. Nelson, p. 59. There is an error in subtraction in Buchanan's majority in the *Whig*, July 4, 1857. See also *ibid.*, August 29, 1857, November 15, 18, 1856.

[29] Folmsbee *et al., Short History*, pp. 238-239; White, *Messages*, V, p. 15; *Whig*, March 21, April 25, May 2, 16, June 27, 1857.

[30] White, *Messages*, V, p. 22; Folmsbee *et al., Short History*, pp. 238-239; *Whig*, August 22, 29, 1857.

[31] Folmsbee *et al., Short History*, p. 239; White, *Messages*, V, pp. 24-25; *Whig*, November 7, 1957.

[32] White, *Messages*, V, pp. 90-92; Folmsbee *et al., Short History*, p. 239. In re missing files see Chapter X, fn 4. Temple, *Notable Men*, pp. 159-161; *Whig*, November 1, 22, 1851; John Bell Brownlow marginal comment, *ibid.*, September 15, 1857, August 16, 1851.

[33] White, *Messages*, V, pp. 92-93, quoting Nashville *Union and American*.

[34] *Tri-Weekly Whig*, April 7, July 12, 21, August 6, July 23, 26, 1859. John Bell Brownlow marginal note, *Whig*, August 13, 1859.

[35] *Ibid*. The political complexion of the First Congressional District was subjected to redistricting in 1852 by the addition of Jefferson, Hancock and Sevier counties to give it a Whig majority and to end Andrew Johnson's domination. White, *Messages*, IV. p. 457-458. The shifting of party lines also produced personal political changes. A. G. Watkins, as a Whig, had represented the Second Congressional District for two terms, from March 4, 1849, to March 3, 1853. The redistricting placed Watkins, who lived at Panther Springs in Jefferson County, in the First District, where he ran unsuccessfully in 1853. Switching to the Democratic Party, Watkins was elected to the Thirty-fourth and Thirty-fifth Congresses, March 4, 1855 to March 3, 1859. He declined to run in 1858. *Acts of Tennessee, 1851-1852* (Nashville, 1852), p. 293; *Biographical Directory of the American Congress*, (Washington, 1961), pp. 152, 156, 163, 168,1781-1782; Alexander, *Thomas A. R. Nelson*, pp. 61-62. Watkins' career also can be traced through the *Whig*, August 16, 1851, August 11, 1855, August 22, 1857.

[36] Alexander, *Thomas A. R. Nelson*, p. 60; Temple, *Notable Men*, p. 168; White, *Messages*, V. p. 96; *Whig*, March 15, 1856, March 21, 1857.

The Whig

"Put None on Guard but Americans."   Chapter No. 12

THE MATERIAL PARSON

The first issue of the *Tennessee Whig* at Elizabethton in the spring of 1839 described itself as a "political journal," a needless explanation since the substance demonstrated that (*Whig*, May 16, 1839). Editor Brownlow soon expanded into the field of religious controversy,[1] and then a third element began to worm its way into the newspaper — items dealing with economic facts of life.

Brownlow had learned early in life that food, lodging and clothing must be paid for in toil, whether it was in the field of the farmer, at the bench of the carpenter, or in the pulpit of the preacher. As already mentioned he suffered the acute pain of material loss when a deputy sheriff levied on him to pay the costs in a libel conviction. The deputy seized a handsome mare, saddle and accoutrements, this depletion leaving the circuit rider unhorsed. To sustain his bride, Eliza, he left off regular preaching and took a job managing the O'Brien iron works in Carter County. After he had agreed to edit the *Whig*, he did so by candlelight and labored for the O'Briens during the day. At first he followed a policy of not going near the printing office at Elizabethton (*Whig*, July 15, 1841), but after six months he moved to town and worked in the atmosphere of the primitive plant. Sitting there, however occupied he may have been with writing, he could not miss a new insight into the lives of farmers, tradesmen, artificers, lawyers and bankers. He could feel closely the pulse of subscribers and advertisers. In time this awareness was conveyed into the columns of the *Whig*.

The early issues of the *Whig* reflected the Parson was concerned principally with the political and social scene, as it did also in his first visit to the East in 1841. But soon items began to appear in his newspaper that showed a recognition of the material needs in the daily lives of the people. He wrote on the state of farming, the conditions of the crops and market prospects. Finally he supplied

some detailed statistics on the economic and professional life of
Jonesboro. These he wrote with a satirical pen, which nevertheless
threw light on the entire life of the town. Jonesboro had four doctors, four lawyers, three churches, two female schools, ten stores,
five saddlers, five blacksmiths, three "boss house carpenters," four
shoe and boot shops, a book bindery, two printing plants, three
cabinetmaking shops, one hatter, a carriage and wagon maker, a sil-
versmith shop, three taverns, two saloons and three cake bakers. The
town received mail three times a week from the east, the west, and
the Carolinas, and by three weekly horse mails. [2] The conditions of
the stage routes, wagon roads, and water courses were vital to the
editor because by them alone came the newspapers and letters that
afforded news of the outside world, as well as necessary supplies,
ink, paper, type, forms, stands and presses. Self-sustaining as such
towns as Jonesboro were, as Brownlow's statistics showed, many
products came from Baltimore, Philadelphia, New York and Charleston. Because merchants bought many of their supplies from these
large centers, the wholesale houses there were advertising customers
of the *Whig*, especially as its circulation grew.

The editor's frugal nature peeped through an approving item he
wrote that President Benjamin Harrison went to market daily before
sunrise with his basket on his arm (*Whig*, April 14, 1841). He was
ambitious to make money, although he was unsuccessful outside of
the newspaper field. These experiences, always unsuccessful, as mentioned before, probably impressed him with the importance of commercial news, for he began to season his dispatches from the cities
and regions he visited with more of these items. He reported and
compared prices, wrote of the progress of manufacturing and railroad
building, stared in wonder at the forest of masts in Charleston Harbor, and noted that the New World was supplying the old with
foodstuffs. When he encountered large droves of swine from East
Tennessee headed for the Southeast markets along the roads near
Yorktown, South Carolina, he jotted down that 6,000 of them were
from Jefferson County. [3] But, if in practice he recognized the importance of business news, in philosophy he minimized it, as his
annual message to his readers after seven years of editing and publishing shows:

We shall advocate Whig Principles—which is but another name for implicit
adherence to both state and national constitutions—the only means of preserving
law and order—and security to public liberty and private rights. Whig principles

teach liberty and equality to all and every free citizen of the United States. A recognition of no other distinction than that of virtue and vice; the improvement of all by the means of education; and elevation of the poor and laboring classes, by keeping open the channels of wealth to all, by encouraging and sustaining industry and enterprize [sic.] and the discountenancing of idleness and vice, mobs, and rebellion. This Whiggery, and this is our creed *(Whig,* May 13, 1846).

A little more than a year later he gave extensive space to a report on the imports and exports of Washington County. Included was a statement that a railroad would stimulate the county's commerce, inspire more manufacturing and utilization of raw products, bring in capital and population and provide outside markets for hay, oats, potatoes and lumber. Brownlow made no editorial comment on this report, but in the meetings and debates of the time on whether to press for macadamized roads, railroads or river improvements in upper East Tennessee, he leaned toward the water routes. He was familiar with the Holston River because he had traveled it often while shipping iron castings for the O'Briens to Knoxville.[4]

The Parson received most instructive, though painful, lessons in the use of economic weapons from the group of wealthy and influential men who backed the *Register* in the newspaper war that erupted when Brownlow brought his *Whig* to Knoxville in the spring of 1849. These men sought to intimidate advertisers. They procured criminal and civil litigation against him, engineered the raising of his rent, bought up unpaid notes on which he remained as security and pressed for collection, and they may have been involved in a plot to destroy his printing office. But when all these tricks and devices had failed, he had learned, as he had in a lesser degree at Jonesboro, that a newspaper which gives its readers sparkling, vigorous material can command circulation, and with circulation advertising and influence followed.

Unlike most of today's newspapers which seek circulation in a tight, concentrated market to interest retail merchants, Brownlow sought subscribers wherever he could get them within the nation. He asserted at Jonesboro and at Knoxville that he could operate without local support. He always played to rural people and to workmen—mechanics was the term for them then. In his maiden issue at Knoxville he offered to take the farmer's wood or grain for subscriptions, and as for mechanics he would exchange his work for theirs. Giving the market price for flour, he added: "Our publishing these facts will not be very acceptable to our citizens and speculators, but we can't help that. We go for the people and the farming interests and we will give them the *true* state of the market, offend whom we may." He drew the line more sharply by characterizing his opposition as the "scrub aristocracy."[5]

One of the finest examples of the Parson's turning an event designed for his downfall into a victory occurred at Clinton, where he had been called for trial on a charge of advertising a lottery. The spectacle of seeing a preacher-editor on trial for a gross material offense, both illegal and immoral, brought a large crowd of the curious. The case was thrown out, and the delighted Parson eagerly responded to cries for a speech. But instead of devoting himself exclusively to a hymn of triumph, he shrewdly delivered a mouth-watering speech on the economic resources of Anderson County and how they could be utilized to bring prosperity to its people. He reminded his hearers of his vigorous support of internal improvements, and he dangled before them the rich prospects for markets which would be available upon completion of the railroad projects being pressed toward Knoxville from two directions. He envisioned the flow of farm products from the lush Powell River valley, dwelt on the availability of water power for manufacturing and called for improved roads and mail routes from Cumberland Gap to Knoxville by way of Jacksboro and Clinton. Time proved this to be a logical travel and communication route. The Parson, of course, was not quite the seer to foresee Norris Dam and the rail and highway routes that have followed the course he traced. Either from vanity, or a desire to gloat over his enemies, or realizing that he had made a lasting impression with the speech, he printed it in full (*Whig*, March 23, 1850).

The *Whig* was in favor of the material progress of the region, but it also was arrayed against the men of money and means in Knoxville. So Brownlow offered as appropriate this message before the end of his first year:

A young man, whose father was a hard working mechanic, either has a moderate fortune left to him, or he marries a few thousand dollars—and forthwith he puts on airs, and assumes an importance, perfectly disgusting to all who are acquainted with the circumstances of his "rise and progress" in the world. Such young men regard as beneath their dignity the vocation of their parents ... .We have even met with some who looked upon the vocation of a humble mechanic, as beneath the dignity of a gentleman, foregoing [sic.], meanwhile, that the taint of the father attaches to the son! ...

There are many young men in our towns and villages [and some young ladies, too!] who seem to be proud of the wealth of their parents—while their own reputations would be soiled by associating with the sons of mechanics. In their strange infatuation, it never occurs to them that their fathers made all their property by down-right stealing, cheating and lying—while their grandfathers were sold at public auction, in our seaports, to pay their passage across the ocean! See the number of young men in our country, who, endowed with scarcely common sense and no sort of love for genuine republicanism, resort to the study of the learned professions, such as Law and Medicine, while every mark about them declares, in terms which cannot be misunderstood, that the God of nature intended them for bricklayers [,] house carpenters and black smiths! Many of these ought now to abandon their professions for the more profitable and equally honorable fields of labor . . . . God deliver us from the bastard arristocracy [sic.] of our little villages, and *Cod-fish* aristocracy of our larger towns!

The course charted, Brownlow tied himself even more closely to the hardworking, humble people with this declaration:

One of us a Printer by profession and the other a House Carpenter by occupation, we were satisfied then, as we are now, to be ranked with that hardy class of men, who eat their bread and meat, and wear their garments, whether coarse or fine, by the sweat of their brow and are content with the avails that industry affords its votaries . . . ." (*Whig*, June 29, 1850).

He lectured even more vigorously and extensively upon this theme as he began his fourteenth year of running a newspaper. Brownlow had detested aristocracy all his life and had "warred upon it, from the pulpit and the press, for a quarter of a century past . . . ." And while he ridiculed what he described as its airs and pretensions, he chided the working people because they had accepted this class line of separation:

By a false law of honor, and an equally false principle of society, the dignity of *indolence*, and the respectability of *splendid poverty*, command both admiration and homage; while the equally imaginary *degradation* of labor, whether upon the farm or in the line of the manufacturer, has excited contempt! In no town in all the South-west is this more true than in the town of *Knoxville*. And the industrial classes are themselves responsible for the disgraceful error; they suffer it to exist—not alone without rebuke, but they connive at, and assent to it. They *creap* [sic.] after men of rank and bow submissively to their inferiors in all that should ennoble human nature. They lend themselves as the *willing instru-*

ments, of base and unprincipled men, who have acquired some property, by a species of *pilfering* that they would scorn to stoop to!

God forbid that we should array ourselves against the necessary and sincere courtesies of social intercourse . . . . Far be it from us, likewise, to array the poor against the rich—though few of the latter are to be found in our midst! But we would have the true men of our country—the sources of our wealth and prosperity—*the better class of society* know and properly estimate their true value (*Whig,* June 19, 1852).

In the years at Jonesboro Brownlow had brought into the *Whig* columns an increasing number of items on market prices at home and abroad, the condition of crops and the importance of means of transportation to carry the products of East Tennessee to the outside. He made a telling point in his last year in this town by reporting that representatives of a Georgia company had sent buyers into East Tennessee. They had purchased 10,000 bushels of wheat and shipped it by water to the terminus of a rail line in Georgia. He offered the illustration to prod Virginia interests into moving more rapidly on a line from that state into Tennessee. After he moved to Knoxville his interest in railroad building appeared to grow, although he never overlooked transportation by water. When he went to Nashville in the fall of 1851 to support Thomas A. R. Nelson for the United States Senate seat he wound up lobbying for the railroad interests. He was delighted that the General Assembly had voted $8,000,000 in state loans to railroad companies. In a short time officials of the East Tennessee and Virginia Railroad, which projected from a junction at the Virginia line with roads leading to the Northeast seaboard, and heads of the East Tennessee and Georgia Railroad, which was to connect with roads leading to the South Atlantic coast, met in Knoxville to select the site for the junction of their routes. They chose a place half a mile north of the existing business district, where the Southern Railway lines now run. Trains on the southern line were running between Loudon, Tennessee, and Dalton, Georgia, the following year. This opened direct connections between Loudon and the seaports of Savannah and Charleston. The first train reached Knoxville on June 22, 1855. Track laying eastward by the East Tennessee and Virginia was started July 4, 1855, destined to connect with Bristol, also the terminus of the Virginia and Tennessee road. Still in the talking and promotional stages were the Rabun Gap road and the Knoxville and Kentucky company. The former was never completed and the latter was completed after the Civil War, after many shifts and starts and reorganizations.[7]

River traffic continued to thrill and engaged the Parson. When a flood tide brought product-laden craft from farther up the state to Knoxville in May 1856, he counted 300 boats lined up along the river bank at Knoxville. Their cargoes of corn, wheat, oats, flour, bacon, salt, iron, casting and lumber were valued at $300,000. Prices went down under the impact of this volume.

Brownlow's appreciation of the importance of commercial and business news grew swiftly after his arrival in Knoxville. He wrote of crops and markets as he found them in the region or wherever he went, and he introduced a "Commercial" column with quotations on grain, flour, meat, fruit, vegetables, cotton, molasses, lard, rice, sugar and feathers, from New Orleans, Charleston, Augusta, Chattanooga, Macon, New York, Philadelphia, St. Louis, Cincinnati and Nashville. He also carried a column of railroad news as well as separate items. His crop reporting grew more extensive and sometimes covered several southern states.

The *Whig* sometimes carried outbursts that it could operate without Knoxville circulation, which might have been taken to mean he disliked Knoxville. Actually, he was deeply concerned for the city's progress, as the trend of his editorial policy showed. He performed as a traveling chamber of commerce for Knoxville as he crisscrossed the South and Southeast. He devoted a lecture in Savannah to the advantages of trade with East Tennessee. He grew lyrical over the advantages of Knoxville as he poured out this praise of his home:

We will soon have the Railroad Cars coming in and going out of our city daily, with freights and passengers, connecting us at once, by steam, with Charleston, Savannah, Augusta, Mobile, Nashville, New Orleans, St. Louis, Louisville and Cincinnati. In a very short time thereafter, we shall have a first-class Railroad completed, connecting us with Lynchburg, Richmond, Norfolk, Baltimore, Philadelphia, New York & Boston, *this* being the greatest thoroughfare on the American Continent. It will then require half a dozen of the largest class Hotels to accomodate even transient customers, saying nothing about regular boarders attached to numerous business houses. Knoxville is the centre of East Tennessee, both east and west, or north and south—aye, it is the *Metropolis* of a territory of some thirty counties, a rich and fertile country, abounding in rich iron ore, coal, salt, hydraulic lime, marble, valuable timber, and other choice materials for manufacturing purposes. Add to these excellencies, a salubrious climate, fine air, and the best water that ever our God sent forth from the hills and vallies [sic.] " to nourish and invigorate his creatures." Add still to these charms the fact that the entire territory of East Tennessee presents to the eye of the paralized [sic.] beholder, a surface of country, not only fertile in the highest degree, but picturesque and beautiful beyond conception. Is it any wonder that we thus calculate on the growth of our already flourishing town? Certainly not. . . .

Our honest opinion is that there is not a more interesting locality, or delightful city in the Union, all things considered, than this aforesaid Knoxville, and hence we are here for life! We have now lived in this world almost a half a century, and in that time, . . . we have met with no locality that holds out more inviting inducements to population, wealth, enterprise, industry and talents (*Whig*, April 30, 1853).

The Parson also forecast the day when he would be editing *Brownlow's Daily Whig* (*Ibid.*). He missed on that prophecy.

Knoxville was once chiefly a depository for agricultural products, but was now moving into such industries as sawmills, flour mills, foundries, planing mills and machine shops that utilized the new steam power. Before 1853 ended, Brownlow urged that the city should get into wider fields of manufacturing. "The time is coming," he wrote, "when all the woolen and cotton goods, hats, shoes, edgetools and farming impliments [sic.] now manufactured in New England and other parts of the world will be manufactured in our midst. We can command the wool and leather now, and the iron and coal, and we have the cotton with far less freight on it than we have at the North" (*Whig*, December 24, 1855).

The cholera epidemic of 1854 brought Knoxville to an economic standstill. But when it was ended and business began to be resumed Editor Brownlow mounted a horse for a survey of the town and found what he described as a surprising amount of building. It was an obvious attempt to encourage the citizens who were depressed by the tightness of money as well as by the scourge of the epidemic. He came back with another boosting editorial—a Christmas message—in which he acknowledged that the fears of economic decay had arisen. But again he cited an increase in business houses and manufacturing plants. The Parson reminded his subscribers that Knoxville had grown from the 2,000 population it had when he began publishing there in 1849 to between 5,000 and 6,000. But in a separate piece he accused the citizens of permitting a low state of morals to exist; he described the municipal government as being laggard, the schools as inadequate and juvenile crime as on the increase. He charged the county with permitting bridges across First Creek to reach such a state of repair that they were not fit to be used by "a sheepkilling dog, a runaway negro, or a returning convict from the penitentiary."[9]

Christmas of 1855 found the Parson in delighted mood regarding the material progress of Knoxville:

A spirit of enterprise is manifested every where; not only do we see it in the number of buildings that are going up, but we also see it in the neat and well designed Business Houses of huge dimensions, the principal ones being on Gay Street. Go where you will, within or without the limits of our Corporation, and new houses are being erected—old ones repaired, or enlarged—while all is activity, stir and enterprise—attracting the notice of the traveler, and drawing from him some words of commendation and praise!

Besides the many evidences of business activity, such as the lighting up of our city with Gas, the cutting down and paving of our streets—all will bear testimony to the fact that the completion of the East Tennessee and Georgia Railroad to this place, the rapid extension of the Tennessee and Virginia Railroad . . . has infused new life into every grade of business . . . . And what a change is perceivable in the advanced price of real estate, such as town lots and lands! So much has our Railroad enhanced the value of lands in East Tennessee that we consider that the Road does not owe the stockholders one dollar of dividends, upon a fair and just settlement! (*Whig*, December 29, 1855).

Again, as in 1854, the Parson found that the material prosperity and a high state of morality did not go hand in hand, for he saw many of the people of Knoxville galloping headlong to perdition. He had observed the holiday by remaining at home for three days, except to deliver a temperance lecture at a Negro church. As for many of the other residents:

Instead of meeting to pray and praise, and to send up offerings of gratitude to God, for that great sacrifice on Calvary, we have, too many of us, attended candy-pullings, frolics, card-tables and cock-pits, where *liquor* has been abundant, and the name of God has been shamefully blasphemed—Others have hung around Groceries, drank and swore, fought and stabbed their fellowmen—sent some, certainly, to Hell, and increased their own chances for the infernal pit, at no distant day! (*Ibid.*).

Even if hell awaited the sinners, the material future looked glowing. The municipal corporation had extended its limits northward to take in the railroad junction, car shops and Gray Cemetery. A few weeks later the *Whig* reported that a steam-powered sawmill at the mouth of First Creek was cutting 6,000 to 8,000 feet of lumber daily. The operator was a Democrat but *"the cleverest kind of a fellow,"* and there was agitation for a bridge across the Tennessee River—still called the Holston at that time.[10] Then the panic of 1857 struck. The times grew so hard that John Fleming of the *Register* suggested that merchants would find it a simple step to suspend business for Thanksgiving, "that matter having been pretty well attended to already." Brownlow drew this picture in the spring of 1858:

> Our once growing city, at present, is almost as dull as if the cholera had arrived, and done its work! There is scarcely any business doing. The spring season is about winding up with the dealers in Dry Goods, and but little is doing by other merchants, while the employment of all is to sit at their doors, smoke cigars, read newspapers or complain to passers-by of hard times! And the newspapers which they read are as void of news as those who read them are of customers.
>
> We are sorry that we cannot say our city is on a *stand*—it is evidently going down hill, for the present. There are very few houses in a course of erection. Many of our mechanics are out of employment, or have but little to do, and cannot get money for what they execute. Money is scarce and daily becoming more difficult to command. Collections are being pressed through officers, and great sacrifices of property must follow . . . . We are sorry to make so gloomy a representation of affairs as this to the public, but this is the light in which we view the state of things here. If anyone will show us the bright side of the picture, we will dwell upon that, at least for a time, for we delight to speak of the prosperity of our city, and of the success of her business men and houses . . . .
>
> What are we to do? Let us dress plainer and cheaper. Let us eat less idle bread, and *make* what we do eat. Let us get out of debt and then *stay out—* (*Whig*, May 22, 1858).

The *Whig*, like other businesses, must have suffered from decreased revenues.

Brownlow also had been required to pay debts for others on whose notes he had gone security, a predicament in which he found himself several times in his life. He made his usual meaningless vow that he would never again endorse for anyone. His outlook grew so gloomy that upon a trip to a Sons of Temperance meeting in Bristol he recommended burning the decaying villages of Kingsport and Blountville. Yet, he saw correctly that Bristol, Knoxville and Chattanooga would be the major cities of East Tennessee.[12] He could not foresee Johnson City for it did not exist. The doleful prospects, however, forced him to scour everywhere for business and economic news. This drove him into an expansion of such items that the *Whig* lost some of its political cast. The issue of November 14, 1857, carried on page 2, where the cream of the news was printed, nineteen items dealing with business, industrial and financial subjects. The topics ranged from reports on the money markets of Paris and London to riots and disorders arising from the panic, and from the market for Tennessee bonds to the price of sugar and molasses. The river was rising and the tide would bring salt boats from upstate; provisions were high, producing protests in the larger centers, but produce prices in Knoxville were declining (*Whig*, November 14, 1857). It was a significant development in newspaper reporting, a turning from the narrow scope of politics, government and religion, with now and then a fist fight or a duel between editors, into the broad and diverse field of business, finance and markets.

The winter of 1857-58 was mild, but the warm weather did not prove to be a boon. In the spring the Parson reported that the ice crop, usually stored in underground caches for summer use, was so scant that "We must all go it next summer on spring and cistern water, and mean whiskey as we find it!" But the Yankee North and the East Tennessee and Georgia Railroad rescued Knoxville. Ice was shipped from Boston by way of Savannah, arriving from that port after thirty-three hours. The Parson trilled, "We are fast approaching that bright destiny which has heretofore lived only in the vision of an inflated imagination. May we not soon expect to realize the fact that ours is the great central metropolis of this once remote and mountain bound region known as the "Switzerland of America."[13] He did not mention the price of ice.

When the East Tennessee and Virginia line was completed on May 14, 1858, linking the tracks between Knoxville and Bristol, the celebration was widespread. Knoxville, the junction of two major railroads, was on a great route stretching from the eastern cities of New York, Boston, Philadelphia and Baltimore to Memphis. Travel time from New York to Memphis was cut to three days and nine hours. Brownlow dwelt on the scenery passengers on this route would enjoy and began to promote the resort advantages of the East Tennessee area, especially the mineral springs.

But his zeal for almost every railroad projected and his devotion to a friend led him into an embarassing situation. Dr. Jeptha Fowlkes, the Memphis editor and plantation owner who had bailed Brownlow out of a tight corner with a loan several years earlier, was a heavy investor in the projected Southern Pacific Railroad, from New Orleans westward. The *Whig* editor became an enthusiastic agent for the sale of stock in the road, but its operations became involved and suspect, and Fowlkes took over as president to straighten out its affairs. When the cloud fell over the company Brownlow quit selling the stock, but even the then friendly *Register*, while absolving the Parson of any taint, suggested that "the evidences of a gigantic fraud are now almost irresistible." Brownlow obviously believed the operation was meritorious.[14]

Brownlow's personal hand in affairs was reflected in the character of his reporting in the big railroad events of 1855 and 1858. His coverage of the arrival of the first train in Knoxville was skimpy. This was probably the result of a snub by those in charge of the combined celebration of July 4, a jubilee over the anniversary of American independence and the railroad's transportation opening. Brownlow's name does not appear on any committee, although he published a list of these dignitaries. So he published only a barebones account of the preparations. He was vigorously engaged in 1855 in supporting Meredith Gentry's unsuccessful race against Governor Johnson, who was seeking reelection, and in advancing the campaign of W. H. Sneed for Congress; but he would have been pleased—in fact probably expected—to be designated for some part in the arrangements and the festivities.[15] That the Parson felt he had been snubbed was indicated in this tart and bitter summary of the event:

In everything but *numbers* our national festival was a failure. We had an immense concourse of people here—we had good order—no accident occurred whatever—and to the honor of the grocery-keepers they closed up their doors.

But we lacked organization—all was confusion . . . There was a Brass Band, and that performed well enough. The trains of cars came and went, according to notices given, and the whistles of the engines blew fiercely. The natives collected from every quarter, and gazed on the sight with profound astonishment! The citizens were liberal, and entertained the people with becoming hospitality. But out and out, the thing was rather a humbug! (*Whig*, July 7, 1855).

The railroad celebration at Greeneville three years later drew the Parson's approval in every respect. He was on the Joint Central Committee from Knox County, and O. P. Temple, a Green County native, was chairman. He promoted the occasion enthusiastically and reported it with gusto. He found it to be "a grand affair, and all, too, that the friends of the enterprise could have desired." The crowd was estimated at 8,000 to 10,000, and the table was 1,800 feet long. It required 7,000 feet of plank, yet all was covered with linen cloth. He praised Greene County for the way the event was carried out and predicted that the "great day . . . will long be remembered by thousands." Temple would write up a long list of speakers. It must have been a big day for John Fleming, *Register* editor, failed to get his account back to the office, and Charles A. Rice, publisher, wrote the story with a rather sharp explanation that he had to fill in for his writer.[16]

Knoxville's business life must have been stimulated by the coming of the railroad, for Brownlow came out with the *Tri-Weekly Whig* on the advent of 1859. He recalled that when he had arrived a decade earlier:

Knoxville was a small and inconsiderable place with a population of about two thousand souls—with no Railroads, no Turnpikes—and no means of getting merchandise to or from the place, but such as were offered by a few, small stern-wheel boats, running about six months in the year. Town property was down at a low rate—real estate was at ruinous prices in all the surrounding country—there was nothing to give encouragement to enterprise, and but little stimulus to commerce (*Tri-Weekly Whig*, January 4, 1859).

Some men of means and influence had contributed to the considerable growth of Knoxville, including increasing wholesale trade and the establishment of several manufacturing plants. Now that business was reviving as the panic's inroads were lessening, "Our capitalists and business men, must not remain idle, or fold their arms and remain quiet." They should resume activity. The *Tri-Weekly Whig* would be a lever in this work and could perform the task of meeting the "increasing wants of our thriving population." As mentioned before, the Parson said *Tri-Weekly Whig* would make little more than expenses for a time. The editor's published reasons for starting the new paper had substance but other factors probably entered into his decision. Rice sold the *Register* and it passed into Democratic hands. If the Democrats revitalized the *Register* they might restore its discarded semiweekly issues. So the Parson may have decided to get into the field first.[17]

Indications appeared that business was beginning to revive. This the editor noted in the first tri-weekly issue, but farmers were getting low prices for their products, and the prediction was that they would drop more [*Whig*, July 31,1859). The Parson's health was declining, however, and after the election of August 1859 he printed this notice:

The shattered condition of our health—the enfeebled state of our system—worn down by inordinate attention to business—long residence in town—excessive mental anxiety—we find ourselves to be an exhausted and sighing invalid, attended by an insupportable sense of weariness and lassitude; and as such, we go to the mountains of Virginia, to seek a *panacea* in the delightful and refreshing baths, and other uses of their curative waters.

He was not entirely debilitated, for he kept a steady stream of spicy, chatty and gossipy dispatches flowing from the resorts. But frothy and amusing as his writings were, he was filled with deep concerns, aside from that over his own health, as he wrote Temple:

My greatest concern in life is to raise and educate my children, and to this point I am directing my attention. John will graduate next June, when I wish him at once to read law with you. James will graduate in two years more, when I desire him either to read Law or Medicine, as he may be inclined. I wish neither of them to meddle in *politics*.

My next greatest concern in life is for the growth and prosperity of *Knoxville*. The town is going down—everything is getting flat—and the prospects ahead are all gloomy. If something is not done to push those cross Roads to completion, and to get up manufacturing establishments there, it is a doomed place . . . .

There is too much of selfishness, too much of a desire to speculate and swindle, and too little of public spirit in Knoxville. Wallace and others go in *clans*, and seek to monopolize all that is on hand, or like to come up.[18]

Brownlow expanded on this theme in an editorial he wrote while at one of the resorts, but without using any names. He rehashed his argument that the city must have manufacturing plants for growth; that prices of building lots and materials were so high they discouraged construction; that banks were demanding exorbitant rates; and that the remedy lay in pressing for completion of the long rail route from Charleston, through Kentucky, to Cincinnati: [19]

The one on the South will give us an outlet to a great commercial mart, and a heavy increase of travel; the one on the North will bring inexhaustible banks of rich ore and beds of superior coal to our doors, and build up foundries and Machine shops, and all manner of Iron manufactories. Unless this is done, we are a used up people, and our town is a doomed one, where *dog-fennel* and *sour-*

dock will take the place of *paved streets* and *elegant side-walks.*

He restated his theme, a month later, urging that Knoxville should put up $50,000 of bonds to help build the Kentucky road, with little East Knoxville adding $25,000 for this purpose, although privately he was not hopeful about the second amount.[20]

The Parson reported his visit to the springs improved his general health (*Whig*, October 15, 1859), but the editor and his beloved Knoxville were destined for the shattering experiences of intense political strife, wretched divisiveness and war.

CHAPTER XII NOTES

[1] Elements of religious controversy appear in Brownlow's quarrels with Landon C. Haynes, but they generally involved internal affairs of the Methodist Church. The major interdenominational dispute that appeared in the *Whig* was with the Rev. Frederick A. Ross in 1846. See also Brownlow's complaint that Roman Catholicism triumphed in the 1844 election of George M. Dallas as vice president. *Whig*, December 4, 1844.

[2] *Ibid.*, March 18, April 7, 1841, May 18, July 6, 1842.

[3] *Ibid.*, April 23, 30, 1845, November 4, 18, 25, 1846.

[4] *Ibid.*, July 7, May 26, July 7, 21, September 29, 1847, January 19, 1842.

[5] *Ibid.*, May 19, June 16, 1849.

[6] For examples of the increase of commercial items see *ibid.*, May 8, 1842, March 12, April 23, 30, 1845, October 14, November 4, 18, 25, 1846, September 29, November 10, December 27, 1847, January 24, 1849.

[7] *Ibid.*, February 7, 1852. Brownlow agreed to make a temperance speech in Lynchburg, Virginia, but announced that he would "wind up on the railroad," *ibid.*, February 28, 1849. Seven years later when the Tennessee General Assembly was considering railroad legislation he proclaimed, "I am the friend of each and every Company railroad in the State," *ibid.*, January 12, 1856, March 27, July 24, 1852; Rothrock, ed., *French Broad-Holston*, pp. 106, 110-112, 228-232. An early mention of the route north from Knoxville and of the Cincinnati to Charleston and Savannah line is in the *Whig*, January 10, 1852 and thereafter with frequency, e.g., October 2, 13, 1852, December 16, 1854, July 9, 1856, April 18, 1857, October 8, 1859.

[8] *Ibid.*, May 17, 1856. The Parson's growing interest in commerce, industry and crops may be traced through *ibid.*, November 27, December 25, 1852, January 1, 1853, May 5, 1855, February 18, 1860, April 2, 16, 30, 1853. For the Savannah speech see *ibid.*, March 26, 1853.

[9] *Ibid.*, October 21, December 30, 1854.

[10] *Ibid.*, December 29, 1855, March 15, April 12, 1856.

[11] *Register*, November 26, 1857.

[12] *Whig*, April 25, May 2, 1857.

[13] *Ibid.*, March 6, April 17, 1858.

[14] *Ibid.*, May 8, 22, 1858; *Register*, May 20, 1858; Rothrock, ed., *French Broad-Holston*, pp. 108-109; Folmsbee *et al.*, *Short History*, pp. 262-263; *Register*, December 10, 1857. Brownlow's efforts in behalf of the Southern Pacific were spread over several years. *Whig*, January 17, May 16, 1857, March 20, May 29, June 6, July 3, 24, 1858, *Tri-Weekly Whig*, January 4, February 10, 12, July 3, 1859, *Whig*, July 17, 1860. Seventy-five years later the Parson's stock selling was held up for critical examination by Vernon M. Queener before the East Tennessee Historical Society, meeting at Maryville. Queener recalled that in May 1859 Brownlow had sold to Blount Countians 300 shares of Southern Pacific stock which proved to be worthless. Queener was an ardent Democrat, and he did not hold Brownlow in high esteem as an editor. His Maryville address was based upon his thesis, University of Tennessee, 1930, and summarized in "William G. Brownlow as an Editor," ETHS *PUBL*. No. 4, pp. 67-82.

[15] *Whig*, May 26, June 30, July 7, 1855.

[16] *Ibid.*, April 17, June 12, 1858; *Register*, June 10, 1858.

[17] *Tri-Weekly Whig*, January 4, 1859; *Register*, June 25, 1857. The *Register* was printing a semiweekly and weekly when Brownlow moved to Knoxville. *Whig*, January 5, 1850.

[18] The springs Brownlow visited are now in the Monroe County area of West Virginia. *Ibid.*, September 10, 17, 24, October 1, 8, 1859; Brownlow to Temple, September 6, 1859. Temple Papers. The Wallace referred to probably was Campbell Wallace of Knoxville, president of the East Tennessee and Georgia Railroad, when it was completed to Knoxville. Rothrock, ed., *French Broad-Holston*, p. 106.

[19] *Whig*, September 3, 1859.

[20] *Ibid.*, October 3, 1859, Brownlow to Temple, September 12, 1859. Temple Papers.

Ⓣⓗⓔ   𝔚𝔥𝔦𝔤.

"To the Union, the Constitution, and the Laws."   Chapter No. 13

1859-1861

The rest at the resorts of Virginia restored the Parson's vigor but left him still suffering from bronchitis and hoarseness. These conditions were painful and limited his expression to the pen, except for brief conversations. When a "valued friend" from the South, who happened to be in New York, learned of the editor's condition he recommended the surgery of Dr. Horace Green in the metropolis and paid the expense of trip and treatment. Brownlow's reason for explaining these personal facts was: "I do not travel for pleasure and have no money to spend that way." Dr. Green's treatments took place before the eyes of waiting patients. The Parson found that while some of the spectacles were unnerving he was impressed with the skill of the surgeon and his assistant. When Brownlow's turn came Dr. Green sliced off a "sort of fungus growth" three inches long, in the region of the epiglottis. The doctor worked so swiftly that the patient felt no pain until soreness set in. Brownlow required daily cauterization with nitrate of silver for several days but the doctor permitted the Parson to return to his hotel room. Lover of good food that he was, he found that the greatest misery following the operation was to sit down to a table "groaning under the weight of everything palatable" and yet be unable to swallow (*Whig*, November 26, 1859).

The after effects of the operation confined Brownlow to his hotel room for a few days. Everywhere he went on his trip he found one "great agitating topic of conversation." John Brown, an angry man from the furious fighting between the free soil and pro-slavery forces in Kansas believed he had a messianic mission to free slaves. He and his tiny army captured and held briefly the United States arsenal at Harper's Ferry before they were overcome by the Marines and imprisoned. The New York preachers infuriated the Parson with their sermons on Thanksgiving Day eulogizing Brown who was doomed to hang on December 2. The Parson said:

The gospel these hypocrites preach is a gospel of rifles, of revolvers, of pikes, of fire, murder, insurrection, and all the horrors of civil war. They do not scruple to proclaim old Brown, though a horse thief and a murderer, a saint and a hero. Several of these pious divines pointed to Brown's hanging tomorrow week, as the sign and symbol in our politics, that the Cross of Christ is in our religion (*Whig*, December 3, 1859).

The Parson, in company with a Baptist preacher from Canton, Georgia, went to Brooklyn to hear one of the most famous clergymen of his day, Henry Ward Beecher. He found Beecher's prayers for slaveholders, slaves and the doomed survivors of Brown's ban utterly abhorrent; yet he was deeply impressed:

I came to the conclusion that he was not a bad hearted man; and crazy as he is, on the subject of slavery, those of our friends in the South who are fortunate enough to get to heaven, need not be astonished to find HENRY WARD BEECHER there! ... He is a rapid speaker, but for one hour he held the large audience spellbound. I was amazed at the novelty of his position, and his utter contempt for anything like system! I was charmed by his eloquence, originality of thought, wit, sarcasm and the vehemence with which he uttered his sentiment. And in turn, I was disgusted with the infidel tendency of some of his doctrines (*Ibid.*).

In previous years the Parson had atrociously abused the clergyman's sister, Harriet Beecher Stowe, author of *Uncle Tom's Cabin*, for her position on slavery and for the book she wrote. [1]

Brownlow had been sickened when he witnessed the hanging of a wife murderer in Knoxville in 1839. But he wanted to see Brown meet his doom and made his plans to be at Charleston for the execution. The curious swarmed in such throngs and the security measures were so tight that he gave up seeing "old Ossawattamie [sic.] pull hemp without footfold, or rather cotton, for a gentleman in Alexandria has furnished the jailor with a new *cotton cord* to hang Brown, the product of slave labor." Yet the reports of the doomed man's last hours led him to admire Brown's calmness and courage as he awaited the scaffold, and he rated him "as game a man as ever lived." Free from derangement, he was "in intellect and courage, ... the superior of four-fifths of the men in Congress .... He has no hopes of any pardon, or even rescue, and really contemplates the gallows that awaits him with the philosophy of a Socrates" (*Whig,* December 10, 1859).

The execution of Brown held special interest for the Parson and the people of the Knoxville area, for the free soil guerrilla leader and his men had murdered three members of a family with a Knox County background. James Pleasant Doyle, who had left Knox County in 1845, wound up on a homestead in what was then Lykins County, Kansas, near Osawatomie. Brown and his men took Doyle and his two sons, William, twenty-two, and Drury, twenty, from the home, hacked and shot them to death, and left their bodies nearby. Brown spared John C. Doyle, fourteen, upon the pleas of his mother, Mrs. Mahala Doyle. The remaining Doyles moved to Chattanooga, and when Brown was hanged, according to a statement given by John, "I had permission from Governor Wise to hang him, but failed to get there on account of a landslide between Morristown and Bristol." Mrs. Doyle also wrote that her son was anxious to see Brown hanged. The Doyles were not slaveowners and the father came from a Knox County area that was rigidly Unionist. But in Kansas the Tennesseeans followed their natural inclination to side with the southern view in the cleavage that bloodied Kansas, and to Brown that meant they deserved destruction. Embittered, John served in the Confederate army from June 1861 until May 1865.[2]

The closing days of 1859 had brought a bristling forecast. A New Yorker was summarily brought before a meeting of citizens at the Knox County Courthouse on the accusation of being an abolitionist. John Crozier Ramsey, lawyer and one of the city's fire-eating southerners, recommended hanging. But the moderates prevailed and the New Yorker, a nursery salesman, was given three days to wind up his business and leave town. A dispute between James Park, pastor of the First Presbyterian Church and a moderate, and Postmaster C. W. Charlton, a Methodist minister and an extremist, reached the point where their supporters drew weapons. Friends restored peace (*Whig,* December 24, 1859).

Brownlow wrote in jubilant mood from Nashville when the Constitutional Union Convention of the state voted to support John Bell for the Presidency (*Whig,* March 3, 1860). Bell came close to being his idol, although a lesser one than Henry Clay. The party also had shed its ignoble designation of opposition. Brownlow's harrowing experience of seeing his son, named for John Bell, tried for murder, must have sucked some of the bounce out of him, but his son was exonerated. His usual ebullience returned and he was an enthusiastic delegate to the national convention that nominated Bell for President with Edward Everett of Massachusetts as his running mate. The platform was a gem of brevity: "The Constitution, the Union and the Execution of the Laws."[3] Brownlow paused in Washington on the way home and heard Senator Stephen A. Douglas, of Illinois, defend "Squatter Sovereignty" and denounce Senator Jefferson Davis of Mississippi, who opposed it. Since this represented the wedge that was splitting the Democratic Party, the Parson relished it and he described how Douglas demolished Davis:

Douglas spoke *three hours and five minutes* . . . . The speech was an able one, both powerful and convincing, for as a debater, I doubt whether he has a superior in American public life. In the private circle, he is vulgar, profane, drunken and low flung. On the floor of the Senate, he is wanting in dignity, speaks to the galleries and the crowd around him, in the true style of a demogogue. But he sways the people, and inspires both friends and foes with admiration for his abilities. I think I never heard such an effort, and I have heard all who speak of it say the same. He literally ruined the Democratic party, and made the Senate Caucus who adopted Davis' resolution condemning Squatter Sovereignty, look like a gang of stupid *Asses* . . . (*Whig*, May 26, 1860).

Brownlow also released this evaluation of Buchanan's Administration:

Corruption, foul and loathsome, wicked and damning, swarms around the White House, in all the Departments, and around the Capitol, daring the gaze and defying the power of outraged constituencies; legislation is bought and sold. Members of the House, in violation of their oaths and honor, have sold their oaths and honor, have sold their votes to carry through the English Lecompton Bill, a favored Administration measure, for a given price, receiving as high as $10,000 for a vote! Senators stagger in the Chamber, from drunkenness, and swear profanely while in session, talking to one another—a disgrace to the Nation and to the State which sent them here. Members of the Cabinet are partners in large contracts, and are engaged in swindling the Government out of millions of dollars. The corrupted villain at the head of the Government is using the people's money to bribe a set of equally corrupt newspaper editors, to defend his villainy and thefts. Better for us, as a people, and for our posterity, better for our peace at home, and our character abroad, that the Congress of the United States should meet but once in ten years, than that the Government should be disgraced by such Senators (*Ibid.*).

The Democrats tried to meet as a unified party, then fractured. The southern wing nominated John C. Breckenridge of Kentucky and the northern wing nominated Senator Douglas of Illinois. The new, northern-based Republican Party nominated Abraham Lincoln of Illinois.

Brownlow and his old Whig comrade, Tom Nelson, believed their Constitutional Union ticket offered a standard to which northern and southern conservatives could rally. They felt that sectionalism hung over all the other aspirants. [4]

Before the campaign reached full fury, the Parson compared his throat with Douglas', the Illinois senator having gone to Dr. Green in New York for treatment:

Our friends are sorry for us, and Douglas' friends are sorry for him, but there is this difference between us. Ours stood the "wear and tare" [sic.] of time, and the warring elements, for 33 years, because we advocated truth, and the best interests of Church and State. Douglas caved in with the labors of 23 years, and what passed through his throat, *coming out*, would have burned and blistered a throat of brass. What has *passed down* was sufficient to have burned out his swallow and windpipe, and to have *carried away the root of his tongue (Whig,* June 23, 1860).

The *Whig* went into the campaign in high gear with new body type and a circulation which jumped from 9,000 to 11,000 in a month. Nelson and Temple stumped for Bell. The Parson's throat kept him campaigning only with his pen,[5] until John H. Crozier, Breckenridge supporter, speaking in front of the Lamar House during the week of the East Tennessee Division Fair, sized up the editor as "meaner than Judas, as going over to the Abolitionists and as a dastard and a coward." This, Brownlow decided, was an insult that required notice and an answer. He had posters printed in large type and armed with a bucket of paste and a brush, he put them up on Cumberland and Main Streets and in the business part of Gay Street. They served notice that he would answer Crozier on the night of October 17, 1860. He had given his version of Crozier's pedigree before. This time he amplified it and asserted that he had thwarted the lawyers' ambition to obtain the Whig nomination for governor in 1853. Further, he had rebuffed a proposal, when Nelson and Jones were fighting for the United States Senate post in 1852, for a Whig-Democratic deal to elect Crozier. He accused Crozier of nurturing an ambition to be a general "in the great Southern Army that is to pull down his government,"[6] and he made this evaluation of his personal character:

He [Crozier] told the crowd that I would not attack anyone; that I would fill a coward's grave! It is folly for me to attempt to prove here to-night *by words* that I am brave. I really can't say whether I am a man of courage or a coward! No man has tried my pluck in Knoxville! . . . If this little scoundrel, who is barking at my heels, desires to know . . . let him make the experiment! I will not say that I fear no man in Knoxville. There is one man in Knoxville, I confess before God and this audience, I do fear, nay, I *dread* him—that man is John H. Crozier. I do not fear that he will meet me face to face and make an open manly attack upon me. Never! But I fear that, as mean and stingy as he is, he will shell out one hundred dollars to some irresponsible vagabond and assassin to shoot or stab me in the dark, or at the dead hour of night, apply a torch to my house and burn it down over my head. This is the pluck of the man, and before God I confess that I fear him (*Ibid.*).

Ridicule was one of the Parson's most frequently used weapons, and he trained it on Crozier, hinting that he made his wife take in sewing, starved his Negroes, made butter from the milk of his cow, and gave a "fashionable entertainment," in blackberry time, serving them the wild growing fruit to be had for the picking. Miraculously, the editor's voice held out for forty minutes. Crozier had made his speech three times and the Parson carried his tirade in the 10,000 copies of the *Whig* (*Whig*, October 27, 1860). Brownlow probably brought on Crozier's attack by criticizing and abusing him for having opposed John Bell in his campaign for President that year (*Whig*, September 29, 1860). It is unfortunate that Crozier's position in his quarrels with the Parson is not to be found in existing records, a fact which makes objective evaluation impossible.

The Parson's throat had been inadequate a month earlier in a confrontation with William L. Yancey of Montgomery, Alabama. Yancey's violent views on secession included a program that he predicted would "precipitate the Cotton States into a revolution." He came to Knoxville on behalf of Breckenridge in the course of a long speaking tour. A friendly account had Yancey arriving in Knoxville under escort of her citizens after what amounted to a "triumphal procession," from Kingston, Georgia. The *Whig* reported that Yancey was met at the railroad station "with two carriages and a music wagon and was escorted to the Lamar House by a very small crowd, three-fourths of whom were Bell and Everett men attracted by the fame of the distinguished visitor."

When Yancey spoke from a stand erected underneath a large oak in the northwest section of the city, a note was sent to him that propounded this question: "If Lincoln should be elected would you consider that a sufficient cause for dissolving the Union, or would you be resisting his inauguration?" The note was signed by Brownlow, Samuel R. Rodgers, O. P. Temple, John M. Fleming and William R. Rodgers, M. D. Yancey called the men to the stand and asked them if they supported Bell's position on slavery. Temple replied that he did, stipulating that Bell's words should be given their full meaning rather than lifted out of context. The three other men echoed Temple[7] but Brownlow elaborated with:

> Yes, I endorse all Bell has said and I will go further than he has gone. I am one of the numerous party at the South who will, if even Lincoln shall be elected under the forms of our Constitution, and by the authority of law, *without committing any other offense than being elected*, force the vile Disunionists and Secessionists of the South, to pass over our dead bodies, on their march to Washington to break up this government! (*Whig*, September 29, 1860).

Yancey's biographer found the encounter an "amusing document," yet he furnished the most inflammatory version available of the reply as given by the extremist from Alabama:

> If my state resists I shall go with her and if I meet this gentleman (pointing to Brownlow) marshaled with his bayonet to oppose us, I will plunge mine to the hilt through and through his heart, feel no compunction for the act, but thank God my country has been freed of such a foe.[8]

The exchange brought tension to the audience but if there was any pistol cocking it was not reported. The incident plagued Brownlow. Yancey, by quizzing his questioners, had kept the initiative, and his bold, extreme reply to the Parson probably delighted the Breckenridge partisans in the audience. Temple barely alluded to the affair. Brownlow's inability to speak must have left him very unhappy. Curiously, the *Whig*'s first account failed to carry Yancey's threat to bayonet Brownlow if the former met the latter in martial conflict. A week later Brownlow mentioned it in this backhanded fashion:

> Wonder if he thought we in Knoxville were such fools as to imagine that he, the redoubtable Yancey, would secede alone if Lincoln were elected, and expecting him to come along by Knoxville, marching with his flag or his bayonet, whistling his own march and commanding no body but his own gallant body, to prevent the inauguration of a President? If he did, he is a far greater fool than he mistook his audience to be. If we never get a bayonet plunged into us till the valiant Yancey does it on such a march as that, we are sure to die some other death (*Whig*, September 29, 1860).

WILLIAM L. YANCEY.

William L. Yancey [From Benson J. Lossing, *Pictorial History of the Civil War in the United States of America*, Hartford, 1877.]

That the Parson felt he had been put at a disadvantage with Yancey is indicated by the way he pounced upon him in the *Whig* following the encounter, an obvious attempt to recover lost ground. The *Whig* of September 29, 1860, carried on two pages items with a dozen scathing allusions to the Alabamian. Aside from the editor's personal chagrin, he may have decided Yancey was a choice whipping boy, for two incidents in connection with his Knoxville appearance damaged the outsider. Senator Andrew Johnson, who knew East Tennessee voters as well as any man, refused to be drawn into a meeting with Yancey, although both supported Breckenridge. Johnson, who passed through Knoxville the day Yancey spoke, said he was too extreme for most Tennesseans. Yancey also made the mistake of assuming that he spoke to an audience of aristocrats,[9] a point upon which Brownlow seized with this comment:

He [Yancey] stated that white women at the North stand over the wash tub and cook—that white men black boots and drive carriages, and perform all other menial services—while at the South, where we were more elevated, we make negroes [sic.] perform these degrading duties! This was a most unfortunate hit for this latitude. It might do in South Alabama, or in the wealthy portions of the Cotton States. But every tenth man he was speaking to did not own a negro [sic.]; while the wives and daughters of all who heard him, wash, cook and milk cows, without ever suspecting that they were performing menial services! . . . No wonder that Gov. Johnson said Yancey was a bad egg, and declined associating with him in a public debate! (*Whig*, September 22, 1860).

The heat and the turbulence were maddening. When the Rev. Anthony Bewley, a native of East Tennessee and once a member of the Holston Conference, was hanged in Texas for being an abolitionist, he drew no sympathy from the *Whig* editor. Instead "he had no business there, meddling with the domestic institutions of the country. And great as is our respect for the friends and relatives of Mr. Bewley, we must be permitted to say that the people of Texas served him right. If he had been our brother, we should say he ought to have been hung [sic.]."

Henry S. Foote, former governor of Mississippi, in denouncing Yancey and his extreme policy, told a crowd on the public square in

Nashville that "the *ropes* were already manufactured with which such *infamous traitors* as Yancey and his associates in Disunion were to be hung [sic.]!" (*Whig*, November 3, 1860).

Parson Brownlow, a fighter for temperance if ever there was one, was taken to task by the Rev. R. M. Hunt, a Lutheran preacher, in a seven-hour debate in Burke County, North Carolina. The Lutheran, taking the negative side in a temperance debate, charged, "William G. Brownlow is a low-down drunkard, and after all he has written about Temperance, during the cholera epidemic of 1844, in Nashville, when all the other Ministers fled, he remained and danced the streets from morning till [sic.] night, with three sheets in the wind and the other fluttering" (*Whig*, October 6, 1860). This was a wretched untruth. As mentioned earlier, the Parson had remained in Knoxville in 1854, not 1844, and not in Nashville. He performed great services as hundreds fled, and there is no likelihood he ever danced, in the streets or on a wood floor. The pressures of the times seemed to throw men grotesquely out of joint, in their actions and in their words.

Ardently and vigorously as Brownlow campaigned for Bell, he indicated that the election of Lincoln would not be a surprise. As the returns came in it did not overwhelm him to report: "The telegraphic dispatches announce—what we have expected—that Abraham Lincoln has carried all the Northwestern and New England states, and he is consequently elected President by the people." Bell carried his state by less than 5,000 votes with Middle Tennessee going substantially for Breckenridge. The unofficial returns gave:

	Bell	Breckenridge	Douglas
East Tennessee	22,320	18,904	1,659
Middle Tennessee	29,006	34,452	2,187
West Tennessee	18,384	11,697	7,548
Totals	69,710	65,053	11,394[10]

Brownlow drew a little comfort from the fact that East Tennessee had clung to the old Whig line, Knox County, for example, giving Bell 2,471, Breckenridge 839 and Douglas 128. But neither the scant satisfaction to be obtained from these figures, nor the dismay at Bell's failure as a national candidate (he ran fourth) could save him from the consuming fear that his country was in peril. It was not a new conviction. He had been filled with it early in 1858 when he had written from Mobile to his friend Temple: "The truth is, there is but little talked of here, but a dissolution of the Union, and all parties are for it. It is so in Mississippi, Louisiana, Arkansas and Alabama, where I have been. The tendency of things is that way." A few days later he spoke to a joint session of the House and Senate of the Alabama legislature, devoting two hours and fifteen minutes to discussing "the question of the North and South." The speech must not have been received with enthusiasm, for Brownlow did not mention the response of the legislators. Had he been greeted with approval or outright bitterness he would have mentioned it.[11] Neither would it have been in character for him to neglect his love for the Union. Now, sensing that extremists would use Lincoln's election to press their demands for quick secession, he laid aside the role of the polemicist, the architect of hyperbole and epithet, and addressed one of the most temperate pleas of his career to "Reasonable Men in the South," at a time when "passion and reason" were locked in struggle:

We are not so vain as to suppose that what we can say will stay the tide of passion in certain quarters in the South, and bring back the impetuous wanderers, to consider facts and principles. Yet, the task of *trying* even those of our countrymen ought not to be shrunk from by conservative and patriotic men of the South, whose Southern birth and raising, and long service in behalf of the Union, and the maintenance of the laws, may be urged as a reason why they are at least entitled to a patient and respectful hearing. It is an ungracious and thankless task to exhort the LEADERS of the Breckenridge party in South Carolina, Georgia, Florida, Virginia, Alabama and Mississippi to calmness, or to a patriotic reconsideration of the perilous position to which, under the apprehensions engendered by the election of a Northern Sectional President, they are plunging under the impulses of passion . . . .

Mr. Lincoln himself is no doubt a patriotic man, and a sincere lover of his country. He is today, what he has always been, AN OLD CLAY WHIG, differing in no respect—not even upon the subject of *Slavery*—from the Sage of Ashland. The great objection with us to his election is the *sectional idea* upon which he was run, the *character of the partisans*, who supported him and will, it is to be feared, to some extent control his administration. But Lincoln is chosen President, and whether with or without the consent and participation of the South will be, and *ought* to be, inaugurated on the 4th of March, 1861. True, as the lights before us indicate, we should say that Lincoln has not received more than one-third to two-fifths of the aggregate vote of the nation. Neither did Buchanan, and yet he, like Lincoln, has been elected by divisions among his opponents. Lincoln, then, has been chosed legally and constitutionally, without either fraud or violence, simply by the suffrages of an enormous majority of the people of the North, who have actually given him more Electoral votes than Buchanan received, who was permitted quietly to take his seat. Against the *manner* of his election, nothing can be urged. It is true, as we have before stated, he was a *sectional* candidate; and it is equally true that, with trifling exceptions in Maryland, Virginia, Kentucky and Missouri, he received no Southern votes. But, do the Constitution or the Laws of our land require a man to receive Southern votes before he can be inaugurated President? Do they compel a candidate to receive votes in every *State* before he shall be declared our Chief Magistrate? Certainly not! Thus there is no just ground for resistance or revolutionary movement on that score.

But the argument of Secessionists is that the administration of a Black Republican President must necessarily be of an aggressive character towards the South, and that the Slave States should forestall such iniquitous policy by withdrawing from the Union. Nay, the election of a man to the Presidency, by a party known to be opposed to slavery, and who heretofore have never been successful in such a contest, is alleged to be a just cause for secession. This view of the subject is so fallacious, and so extremely shallow, that it ought not to mislead anyone. The argument is that the South is exposed to all the wiles and infamy of an abolition government—an argument we cannot accept as legitimate in fact or reason. Did Lincoln receive the suffrages of the North under a pledge that if elected, he would disregard his oath of office, violate the Constitution, and subvert the Union? Certainly not, for had he given that pledge, the day his election was announced, the entire South would have been united in carrying out a most thorough and determined revolution, and thousands of true men at the North would have joined us! But, now that Lincoln is elected, will he execute the purposes of abolitionism? This he cannot do under the solemn oath to be administered at his inauguration. And who will say that he intends taking that oath with treason in his heart, and perjury on his tongue? We have no right to judge of Lincoln by anything but his *acts*, and these can only be appreciated *after* his inauguration. He knows very well that he cannot violate the Constitution in any serious particular, without rendering the dissolution of the Union necessary on the part of the South, and thereby involving the North in alarming trouble and certain ruin . . . .

But, the attempt to break up the Union, before awaiting a single overt act, or even the manifestation of the purpose of the President elect, would be wicked, treacherous, unjustifiable, unprecedented and without the shadow of an excuse. And then again, disunion is not a remedy for any evil in the government, real or imaginary; and it is an uncertain and perilous remedy to be resorted to only in the last extremity, and as a refuge from wrongs more intolerable than the desperate remedy by which they are sought to be relieved. What the people of the

HON. JOHN BAXTER.

Hon. John Baxter. [From T. M. Humes, *The Loyal Mountaineers of Tennessee*, Knoxville, 1888.]

HON. C. F. TRIGG.

Hon. C. F. Trigg. [From T. M. Humes, *The Loyal Mountaineers of Tennessee*, Knoxville, 1888.]

GENERAL JOSEPH A. COOPER

General Joseph A. Cooper. [From W. R. Carter, *History of the First Regiment of Tennessee Volunteer Cavalry in the Great War of the Rebellion, with the Armies of the Ohio and Cumberland, under Generals Morgan, Rosecrans, Thomas, Stanley and Wilson*, Knoxville, 1902.]

ISHAM G. HARRIS.

Isham G. Harris [From Benson J. Lossing, *Pictorial History of the Civil War in the United States of America*, Hartford, 1877.]

Interview of W. H. H. Self with his daughter in Knoxville Jail. [From *Parson Brownlow's Book*.]

Execution of Jacob Harmon and his son Henry. [From *Parson Brownlow's Book*.]

C. A. Haun parting from his Family before his Execution. [From *Parson Brownlow's Book*.]

Parson Brownlow entering the Knoxville Jail. [From *Parson Brownlow's Book*.]

Charles S. Douglas shot by the Rebels while sitting at his window in Gay Street, Knoxville. [From *Parson Brownlow's Book*.]

The County Jail at Knoxville. Brownlow was confined on the lower floor. In the upper story were two immense iron cages, into which the worst criminals were put, and in these some of the most obnoxious Loyalists were confined. Out of this loathsome place several were taken to the gallows. The jail was a block and a half west of the Courthouse and was where the First Baptist Church stands today. [From Benson J. Lossing, *Pictorial History of the Civil War in the United States of America*, Hartford, 1877.]

THE COUNTY JAIL AT KNOXVILLE.[1]

COLONEL JAMES P. BROWNLOW

Brigadier General Turner Ashby, Jackson's dashing cavalry leader. He was long on daring, but short on discipline. [Drawing from *Harper's Weekly* reproduced in *Civil War Times Illustrated*, Vol. XV, Number 7, November 1976.]

Colonel James P. Brownlow. Both Brownlow boys were cavalry officers. [From W. R. Carter, *History of the First Regiment of Tennessee Volunteer Cavalry in the Great War of the Rebellion, with the Armies of the Ohio and Cumberland, under Generals Morgan, Rosecrans, Thomas, Stanley and Wilson*, Knoxville, 1902.]

KNOXVILLE WHIG OFFICE.

Knoxville *Whig* Office [From Benson J. Lossing, *Pictorial History of the Civil War in the United States of America*, Hartford, 1877.]

Judah P. Benjamin [From Benson J. Lossing, *Pictorial History of the Civil War in the United States of America*, Hartford, 1877.]

JUDAH P. BENJAMIN.

Below: letter to Benjamin from Brownlow [From *Parson Brownlow's Book.*]

Knoxville Jail, Dec. 16. 1861.

Hon. J. P. Benjamin:

You authorized Gen. Crittenden to give me pasports, and an escort to send me into the old Government, and he invited me here for that purpose. But a third rate County Court Lawyer, acting as your Confederate Attorney, took me out of his hands and cast me into this prison. I am anxious to learn which is your highest authority, the Secretary of War, a Major General, or a dirty little drunken Attorney, such as J. C. Ramsey is!

You are reported to have said to a gentleman in Richmond, that, I am a bad man, dangerous to the Confederacy, and that you desire me out of it. Just give me my pasports, and I will do for your Confederacy, more than the Devil has ever done; I will quit the country!

I am, &c,

W. G. Brownlow

Upper left: an early engraving of Brownlow made from a daguerrotype. *Upper right*: note the extensive retouching on the same engraving.

This stained portrait of the Parson once hung in the old State Library in the Tennessee State House. The stain was made from tobacco juice spurted upon it by old Confederates. When the new library was built, there wasn't enough room to hang many portraits and the Parson was stored in the basement. Some years ago the portrait was sent to St. Louis for cleaning and the stain was removed. [Tennessee State Library.]

John Bell Brownlow, probably taken in his forties. [*Journal* Staff Photograph by Hugh Lunsford from an original owned by Mrs. John F. Brownlow.]

O. P. Temple. [*Journal* Staff Photograph by Hugh Lunsford.]

Steve Humphrey in the museum of the University of Tennessee's Mechanical Engineering Department examines the steam engine used by the Parson in printing *Brownlow's Knoxville Whig*. Manufactured in Knoxville in 1855, the engine was used during the Civil War to drive machinery converting squirrel rifles into army muskets and later to run machinery in Georgia stamping buttons for Confederate uniforms. After the war it was recovered and resumed its original use in printing the Parson's newspaper. It has since undergone a number of repairs and uses. [*Journal* Staff Photograph by Lin Hudson.]

William G. Brownlow, IV taken in Knoxville September 17, 1974. The Henry rifle
he is holding was presented to Parson Brownlow in 1865 by the New Haven Arms Co.
The rifle probably has never been fired.

Detail of the same rifle. [*Journal* Staff
Photographs by Hugh Lunsford.]

Southern States should do, may be summed up in a single word. PAUSE! Let the entire South, united with the thousands of conservative men North, bury their feuds, make common cause, and in 1864, the National Constitutional men of the country, North, South, East and West will overthrow the Sectionalists and re-store the Government to a better condition than it has been in for a quarter of a century. The night is dark, we confess, and troubled, but there are gleams of light along the line of the horizon. Lincoln is President; but he is nothing more. We trust that he contemplates no mischief, but if he does, he can do none. The Senate, the House of Representatives, and the Supreme Court will hold him in check, and stand by the Constitution, and the rights of all sections. Here, then, is our hope, and here is the platform that all conservative men should occupy, and time and reflection will, anon, inspire a sober second thought in quarters where, at the moment, the blind impulses of passion bear sway (*Whig*, November 24, 1860).

The spirit of calmness and tolerance and the appeal to reason that infused this editorial the Parson did not extend to President Buchanan and his final message. Brownlow printed the half of it that he considered was sufficient for the *Whig's* readers and then condemned it with: "God be praised that its imbecile and corrupt author is never to issue another Annual Message to Congress" (*Whig*, December 15, 1860). The editor also was carrying on a crackling war of words with infuriated Southern extremists who wrote in to cancel their subscriptions. His answers were so harsh and cutting that it must have required an intrepid soul to accompany a notice of cancellation with criticism of *Whig* policy. The extremists accused Brownlow of treason and libel and threatened him with lashings, tar and feathers, and death. As a loyal Unionist and a confirmed believer in the institution of slavery, he was under fire from two directions—and he returned volley for volley. On the Northern front he had reopened his battle with Pryne. From that quarter he was under attack from an abolitionist, while in the South the advocates of slavery charged him with being an abolitionist. Yet his stand on these issues brought him support from both sections of the nation. John Bell Brownlow reported that the *Whig's* circulation doubled after the Presidential campaign of 1860. John Bell and Temple have placed the *Whig's* top circulation at 14,000, but no objective count is, or was, available.[12] Brownlow's forceful, imaginative, hyperbolic style had made the newspaper most readable for years, but at the zenith of its circulation much of its popularity rested upon the sizzling contribution it made to the fury of the times.

Extreme haste showed through the action of Governor Harris in calling a special session of the General Assembly to meet on January 7, 1861. He greeted it on the first day with a message suggesting that the only course for Tennessee would be to go along with the states already moving into a confederacy. The legislators acted swiftly. They enacted a provision on January 19 for a referendum to be held on February 9. The provision submitted two questions to the electorate: should a convention be held to determine whether Tennessee should stay in or get out of the Union, and should it elect delegates in the event of convention approval. The convention, if approved, was to meet in Nashville on Febraury 25. [13]

The electorate was in an agitated state. The Parson was hanged in effigy at Eufala, Alabama. Secessionists, infuriated because Senator Johnson spoke boldly against them, hanged or burned him in effigy in Memphis, Nashville and Knoxville. The Parson, finding his old foe aligned with him in the common cause, applauded with "Lay on Andy." At the same time the *Whig* warned Republicans that the Union men of the South would not submit to the implementation of the party's platform on slavery as adopted at Chicago. Brownlow also raised the possibility that East Tennessee would seek separate statehood and take in portions of Virginia and North Carolina. His voice recovered sufficiently for him to join a band of loyal stump speakers that included O. P. Temple, John Baxter, C. F. Trigg and John Fleming. Temple, Baxter and Trigg were Union candidates for the convention.

The Stars and Stripes was unfurled by the loyalists, and "A tall and magnificent Liberty Pole was raised by the Union men . . . on the corner of Gay and Main streets . . . and such a shout went up as has not been heard in these parts in many a long day!" Another flag was raised at Luke Wilde's brickyard on Temperance Hill in East Knoxville. Brownlow assisted at the ceremony. The *Whig* reported that farmers and mechanics were demanding that business houses indicate their position by flying the flag of the United States if they were loyal, and some other banner if they were not Union men. A hardy secessionist in what was then the Ninth Civil District offered to head a company into Knoxville to hang Brownlow. The Parson suggested that his foes should come the following Monday, for "There will be a Mass Meeting of the party [Union] here on that day and the hanging of the 'notorious Brownlow,' will add greatly to the interest of the occasion." The Parson was not hanged but the meeting stirred up so much enthusiasm that two more Union flags went up, one at municipal headquarters in East Knoxville and the other at a livery stable.[14]

The state went 69,675 to 57,798 against holding a secession convention; 88,803 votes were cast for Union delegates and 27,749 for disunion representatives. It is possible some Union men voted for the convention but against delegates favoring secession. West Tennessee favored the convention, Middle Tennessee was evenly split and East Tennessee reported very large majorities against it. The *Whig*, gloating over the one-sided vote in Knox County, 3,158 against the convention and 391 for it, gigged the secessionists by printing some of their names, including that of the lone East Knoxville disunionist. Temple, cut to the quick because one Sevier Countian balloted against him, explained it on the grounds he had offended the man while examining him as a witness.[15]

Lincoln's inaugural address, a month after the Tennessee election, brought this high praise from Brownlow:

> We endorse the entire Address, as one of the best papers of the kind we have ever seen, and we commend it for its temperance and conservatism . . . . It is, out and out, a Union address, worthy of the approbation of every Union and Conservative man South, as well as the North. Had it been delivered by Jackson, Polk or Breckenridge, even the Cotton States would have declared it to be the height of political perfection. And we unhesitatingly affirm, that if Lincoln's Inaugural is a true indication of the character of his coming Administration, all good and true men may congratulate themselves upon his election to the Presidency . . . . Let us, then, of the Border States, patiently await the developments of the new Administration. We may be much better off under it than under the late profligate Administration of Buchanan—we can't be worsted by four years of Republican misrule (*Whig*, March 9, 1861).

In the false calm between the February referendum and the seizure of Fort Sumter by the already seceded South Carolina, Brownlow burst out with an announcement for governor, a step that remains puzzling. It was unsolicited, made because of "a tardiness on the part of aspiring men in the State to declare themselves . . . and as the people seem a little slow in moving in that direction," and with this explanation:

> I am frank to confess that I desire the position on account of its honor, and as a means of rebuking my numerous Southern caluminators, who are unrelenting in their abusive war upon me because of my Union sentiments, and of my

opposition to their treason. I shall, of course, if elected, hope to serve the interests of the people, of the whole State, irrespective of parties. But not being rich, I would like to hold the office for two years, for the sake of the THREE THOUSAND DOLLARS PER ANNUM. Candor requires these avowals (*Whig*, March 23, 1861).

Perhaps Brownlow thought that through this medium he could gain more widespread attention for the cause of Unionism. Perhaps he believed he could ride into office on what appeared to be a great tide of loyalty for the central government as demonstrated in the February vote, for his seventeen-point platform was essentially a plea for the preservation of the Union. He must have held no serious intention to make the race because a few weeks later he would not permit his name to be submitted to a convention, although he maintained the position of an independent candidate. He wound up supporting with some reluctance William H. Polk, brother of the late President, who was smothered under a tremendous majority for Governor Harris. The vote was 75,300 to 43,495.[16]

The second vote on the question of seceding intervened after the editor announced for governor. It overshadowed all other issues and threw the East Tennessee loyalists into one of the most determined campaigns in the history of the region. The fall of Fort Sumter and Lincoln's call for 75,000 volunteers brought swift changes in Middle and West Tennessee sentiment. Governor Harris quickly called the legislature into session and the members responded to his appeal by calling another election for June 8. This time the question was put bluntly: Separation or No Separation. The act that put this question to the electorate was itself a separation document, and placed the General Assembly as well as the governor on the side of secession. On May 7, the day after enactment of the legislation for a June 8 referendum, the legislature entered into a military compact with the other states of the Confederacy. Negotiations had been carried out by commissioners appointed by the governor even before the passage of the referendum act. Much of the legislation at this time was passed behind closed doors, a fact that Brownlow did not neglect.[17]

This time the campaign brought into operation, in addition to the band of Unionists who had fought successfully in February, an extraordinary team from the halls of Congress: Senator Andrew Johnson, Democrat, and Representative T. A. R. Nelson, an old line Whig. They stumped East Tennessee energetically, fearlessly and ably. Johnson's forthright stand for the Union had brought Brownlow around to a position of admiration for his old enemy—except for some bitterness that Lincoln had placed Tennessee patronage in the hands of Johnson and Emerson Ethridge—and he needed no move from Nelson to applaud and support his course. Johnson received a taste of southern venom at Lynchburg, Virginia, on his way home from Washington. A mob hooted and hissed him as he went from one railroad station to another, and one man boarded the train and attempted to pull the senator's nose. This indignity led Johnson to display his revolver, whereupon the car was emptied rapidly.[18] The Unionists of Middle and West Tennessee lost heart, either from intimidation or despair. Public sentiment in these divisions of the state was enthusiastically behind the governor and the legislature. Troops were being raised on every hand, and a little group of men who once had been stalwart Unionists issued a statement at Nashville that must have shocked East Tennessee. It commended Governor Harris for his defiant refusal of President Lincoln's call for volunteers, condemned the President's policy, deplored secession and advocated a neutral position for Tennessee. The governor had abandoned neutrality already. Among the signers was John Bell. A few days later he abandoned neutrality.[19]

The defection of the Nashville group had little effect on East Tennessee sentiment. The Unionists campaigned with fervor and fearlessness, for Confederate troops were moving through the area by train and other units for the Southern army were being organized and drilled in Knoxville and elsewhere.[20] Alabama soldiers, while passing through Knoxville, attempted to pull down the Stars and Stripes in Luke Wilde's brickyard. They desisted when Miss Lucy Wilde grasped the flag rope and defied them, and her brother appeared on the scene with a shotgun loaded with buckshot. When the train carrying the several hundred troops pulled through East Knoxville, a number of rifles were fired at the brickyard. The act evoked this comment from the *Whig*: "This was a gallant charge upon a gang of unarmed women and children, and it was the first instance of bad conduct upon the part of many troops passing through here. If these were some of the flower of the Alabama youth, God in his mercy save East Tennessee from being visited by the 'rag, tag and bobtail' of their population." As thousands of Confederates passed through the town, enemies of the Parson haunted the trains and encouraged the men to "call and groan for Brownlow." Some were incited to the point where they brandished revolvers (*Whig*, May 11, 1861).

Bloodshed on Gay Street was averted on April 27, 1861, as Johnson spoke from a stand. A Monroe County brass band first tried to
drown out the senator. Then "two military companies, with drums
and Secession flags flying started toward the Union meeting." Two
Confederates, Colonel David H. Cummings and Joseph A. Mabry,
"acted the part of gentlemen, and through their influence, and active
exertions, they silenced the Band, and kept the men from advancing
upon the Union crowd," where many men were armed. The Parson
was quite sure some firebrands had been urged on the band and the
companies. At the time of the near confrontation he had leaped
upon a chair and warned the audience that the "interruption was the
work of Secessionists, and that they were instigated by SCOUN-
DRELS and VILLAINS residing in Knoxville." Nelson also spoke
and Brownlow acclaimed the Congressmen for having given "Two
Noble Speeches."[21]

The following week two men died as the result of a quarrel between Charles S. Douglass, an outspoken Unionist, and Captain G. W.
(Wash) Morgan, with Confederate troops stationed at Knoxville. The
quarrel arose at a flag raising at the corner of Gay and Main streets.
Partisans of Morgan, angered at what Douglass said, fired nine shots
at the latter. One bullet inflicted a minor wound in Douglass' neck,
but another killed an unoffending countryman at the door of a store.
Douglass, apparently a storekeeper, obtained a gun at his place of
business. Morgan returned to camp where soldiers prepared to march
back to the town, armed. Knoxville citizens persuaded them to desist. The following day, according to Union accounts, Confederate
soldiers entered the Lamar House by the "Ladies Entrance," and
from the hotel fired across Gay Street, killing Douglass as he sat in a
window, his wife beside him. No prosecution followed. Brownlow
said that the Rev. Mr. Humes, "was proscribed for daring to attend
the funeral and officiate, at the request of the widow." Humes credited Colonel David Cummings, Confederate officer from Sevier
County, who had helped avert the near collision of the previous
week, with having "relieved the occasion [the funeral] of its reproach in the eyes of unfriendly observers, by magnanimously joining on horseback the officiating minister in leading the sad procession."[22]

Nelson and Johnson were of different political metal, but they had
fused into a forceful and effective weapon for Unionism. Their con-
trasts were striking, outside of politics. Both were bold but where

Johnson was coarse, artful and of meager literary skill, Nelson was precise in language as well as in courtesy, elegant in his rhetoric and skillful in composing rhyming couplets, as well as in the drawing of legal papers. Each, in his own way, was a superb speaker on the stump. Nelson exerted the widest influence because he had long been a leader and laborer in Whig affairs in a region predominantly Whig; Johnson could talk the Democratic line to his partisans, an area where persuasion was sorely needed for the tendency of the party members was to accept the hotly secessionist party doctrine out of Nashville. Nelson's words fell on sympathetic ears; his task was to stiffen resolution. Johnson's work was more difficult. In most cases he sought to overturn long-held convictions.[23]

Back in the *Whig* office at Knoxville, where Brownlow had adjusted his mind and his pen to praise the efforts of an old enemy as well as those of a long and cherished friend, the editor believed he had discovered a plot to murder Johnson. The exhausting schedule of the two top speakers for the Union had carried them across East Tennessee and as far west on the Cumberland Plateau as Jamestown. Their last engagement was at Kingston, forty miles from Knoxville on June 7, the day before the election. Young John Bell Brownlow picked up a report that two or three men had left Knoxville for Kingston for the purpose of stirring up Confederate soldiers to kill Johnson as the senator rode the train from Loudon to Knoxville. It had been established that a troop train carrying 2,000 soldiers would arrive in Knoxville on June 8. Parson Brownlow dispatched his son to Kingston in a horse-drawn buggy, armed with a Sharp's rifle and two revolvers, and with another youth as companion. Years later John Bell Brownlow wrote this account:

We got to Kingston while Johnson was speaking. Trigg & Nelson had already spoken. A stand was erected in a fine grove. Nelson was sound asleep in the stand on the floor of which was a big tin bucket of whiskey punch. Nelson had had too much of it & Johnson had all he could bear & talk. After the speaking Nelson, Johnson & C. F. Trigg were about to start immediately for Loudon in a carryal [*sic*]. Nelson was so tight he had to be assisted into the vehicle. Nelson & Trigg went to Loudon that night—7th of June & next morning went on to Knoxville & on the train were two thousand rebel soldiers. I told Johnson, in the presence of Trigg, that I had brought a buggy to take him to Knoxville because 2000 rebel soldiers would be on the train next morning & I believed they would assassinate him. He swore "he was not afraid, said he owned $12,000 in the stock of that Rail Road & he would be d——d if he would be driven from it by the traitors of the Cotton States." But on reflecting a moment he concluded he would go with me & we travelled all night getting to Knoxville about 6 or 7 A.M., June 8th. After Breakfast Johnson crossed the river & went in buggy to Greeneville & thence as fast as he could to Barbourville, Ky.

Young Brownlow did not reveal whether his father and Johnson met or where the senator ate breakfast, but he added this comment:

I believe it possible Johnson would have been assassinated if he had not gone to Knoxville in the buggy & I now believe it would have been best for the South & country if he had been and best for his own fame.[24]

Nelson and Johnson earlier had experienced obstructions and perils. More than forty citizens of Democratic Sullivan County had petitioned the two not to speak at Blountville. These people feared violence after the home of a Union man had been burned. Their difficulties were compounded when they spoke at Jonesboro early in May. Because County Court was in session they were forced to speak in the street. Nelson was heard with some order, but Johnson was "greeted with cheers and groans . . . . But owing to the unfavorable weather, the crowd having to stand up, together with the noise made by the drilling of volunteers, the banging of a couple of drums and the squeaking of a fife or two—it was impossible to hear with the satisfaction that attends good order." When Johnson tried again to speak he was interrupted by galloping horses and yelling men and rainfall. He finished his speech in the courthouse basement. [25]

More than half a century later John Bell Brownlow, in a letter to Andrew Patterson, grandson of Andrew Johnson, threw fresh light on the reported attempt to kill Johnson, and linked one of the plotters to the murder of Douglass. John Bell wrote that after the rescue of Johnson from the soldiers he learned "that two citizens of Knoxville . . . had gone to Loudon for the express purpose of inciting soldiers to assault Johnson." One of the men, a lieutenant in the Confederate army at the time and later a lieutenant colonel, John Bell wrote, "was utterly unprincipled and later was *partici* [sic.] *criminis* in the murder of Charles S. Douglas, a Johnson Democrat and Union man of Knoxville." John Bell added, "The disloyal hated Johnson far more bitterly than Nelson or Trigg and while the latter two could travel on that train without being assaulted it might have been different with Johnson." The implication is that the soldiers considered Johnson, a Democrat, as an outright turncoat.[26]

A clash between Confederate soldiers on a passing train and a great

Union mass meeting at Strawberry Plains on May 5, 1861, produced gunfire from both sides. A. S. Meek, owner of the land where the Unionists met and through which the train passed, said the shooting began after a Confederate threw a rock at him and another, or the same one, fired a revolver at him. Temple, who along with Representative Horace Maynard and John Fleming was to speak, said bullets whistled above the stand where they waited. Armed Unionists (and there must have been many of them) returned the fire. The Confederates apparently were well protected by the boxcars in which they were being transported, and they must have aimed above the heads of the crowd, which included women and children. The Unionists threatened to tear up the tracks but were dissuaded by cooler counsel among the leaders. No one was hit, but the shooting must have heated up the oratory that followed, if anything was needed to that end.

The *Register*, ardently secessionist, reported: "There was an outrage perpetrated, but it was by the armed adherents of Brownlow, who waylaid a train and without any sufficient provocation fired with rifles and guns nearly a hundred shots at the unarmed volunteers." The *Register* also charged that the first shot was fired by the Unionists "waiting near the railroad with guns cocked and pointed, for the purpose of provoking a disturbance with the passing troops." This account was not documented, as the *Whig*'s had been, and listed no names of informants. In a later issue the *Register* carried an account signed by D. S. Latham, a North Carolinian teaching at Strawberry Plains High School, which was in line with the newspaper's anti-Unionist version of the affair. [27]

The election of June 8 was marked by calm, in contrast to the fury of the campaign. The outcome was complete disaster for the Union cause. The state went overwhelmingly for separation. The vote:

	For Separation	*Against Separation*
East Tennessee	14,780	32,923
Middle Tennessee	58,265	8,198
West Tennessee	29,127	6,117
Military Camps	2,741	0
Totals	104,913	47,238[28]

The *Whig* praised Knox County for having "gloriously breasted the storm" by voting 3,196 against separation. Two versions of the number of ballots cast by residents in favor of separation exist. Historians have assumed Knoxville citizens voted for separation, 777 to 377, which was the total given by the *Register* and was obviously incorporated into the official returns which reported the Knox County vote as 3,196 against separation and 1,216 for. Brownlow, however, reported that the vote in Knoxville, which consisted of three precincts, Courthouse, Market House and East Knoxville, was 372 against separation and 325 for, with this explanation: "We have not named, in this calculation, the votes of 462 troops at a special precinct, as we do not know where they hail from and do not consider votes from other counties legal, although authorized by our late mobocratic legislature." Brownlow refused to carry these 462 votes into the county total, as did O. P. Temple in his *East Tennessee and the Civil War*. Temple did not mention the soldier vote in Knoxville. The *Register*, unlike the *Whig*, gave separately the vote of the three city precincts and listed East Knoxville as having gone 462 to 5 for separation.[29] This was the Parson's precinct and the report may have represented a mischievous and malicious plot to humiliate him. This would not have been surprising, because the editor had unmercifully gigged the secessionists for their small vote in February. The secessionists had complete control of the election machinery in June and were in position to have engaged in just such a manipulation by letting the East Tennessee Regiment, drilling at Camp Cummings, the Fair Grounds site, vote in East Knoxville where Brownlow did.[30] The Parson must have been terribly hacked, for he never again referred to the humiliation.

Brownlow had given a pledge, and he said when he made it that he was speaking for the Union men of East Tennessee: "If the State, through her citizens, at the ballot-box, shall vote to Secede, Union men, however opposed to it, will bow to the will of the majority with the best grace they can. But if fraud is practiced at the ballot-box, and the Union men are intimidated and kept from the polls, the Union men of East Tennessee will rebel, and take the consequences, if they are even death and utter ruin!" (*Whig*, May 25, 1861). With the election lost, the editor vigorously resorted to the qualification in his statement and penned this defiance:

The election is over, and the fell spirit of Secession, and its accompanying outrageous tyranny, in Middle and West Tennessee, have forced these portions of the State out of the Union . . . .

The election in Middle and West Tennessee has been a perfect *farce*. There was the show—an empty show—of a popular vote upon the ordinance of secession, when the military forces stationed at important points, intimidated timid men, and, themselves voted, in and out of the state, in violation of the Constitution, and of every law enacted in pursuance thereof. The Union leaders of Middle and West Tennessee, from considerations of *cowardice*, bowed before the storm of anarchy, and either sealing their lips in disgrace, or with the polluting offer of spoils, derived from offices and contracts, gave in their adhesion to the heresy of Secession. The *Press*, as a general thing, knocked under to the storm of jacobinism and anarchy, and for a consideration in hand paid, gave in their adhesion to the tyranny established over the souls of the people. We sincerely mourn for Tennessee. A majority of her citizens are opposed to Secession, but they have been over-run by an insulting minority—they have been tricked, cheated, duped, swindled, lied and betrayed out of their rights and liberties (*Whig*, June 15, 1861).

The Parson made a swift foray into sarcasm. He conceded, "It is folly for *us* to fight longer, and therefore we shall devote our columns to the publication of Literary, Agricultural and Miscellaneous matter, including the current War news of the day." Then, in one of his disconcerting and unpredictable reversals of mood, he wrote in deadly earnestness:

In doing this, we take back nothing we have said against Secession and a Southern *Confederacy* and in favor of the Government of the United States. Nor do we abandon a single principle we have advocated in connection with this great question. We are opposed to a Northern Republic, a Southern Confederacy, a Central Government and a Northwestern Empire. We are not for *thirty-four* nations, but only one nation—one great, grand and glorious, free and independent nation, extending from the Atlantic to the Pacific, and from the Gulf to the Lakes. Hence we shall die in opposition to Secession, and in favor of the Union, and even a war intended to perpetuate it inviolate (*Ibid.*).

Nelson shared Brownlow's belief that Middle and West Tennessee Unionists had been intimidated, their views suppressed and falsehood and illegality resorted to by the legislature and its secessionist leadership. He found in the Greeneville Convention, held on June 17-20, a means by which to express his convictions. The convention had arisen because a group meeting at Knoxville decided that in the event the state voted for separation provision should be made for an organization to express the views of East Tennessee.[31]

After the first session of the convention, held at Knoxville on May 30-31, the Parson praised the speeches of Nelson and Johnson, and in another of the remarkable reversals Brownlow gave warm approval to a fiery Union speech by Thomas D. Arnold at whom Brownlow had often cast his most elaborate personal villification. Arnold's effort, the *Whig* reported, was "well received by the Convention and he was listened to with a degree of attention that any man might esteem as a compliment. We have been hearing the General, off and on from a quarter of a century, and we considered he was making the best speech of his life (*Whig*, June 1, 1861).

Discretion, rather than violence, now marked movements of some of the loyalists. Johnson, whose status after the June 8 election became that of an official of a warring government, slipped out of East Tennessee into Kentucky by way of Cumberland Gap, and therefore missed the Greeneville Convention. Brownlow traveled by horse and buggy to Bull's Gap, instead of taking the train from Knoxville to Greeneville. He had charged that a plot was under way to create an uproar if the convention met at Knoxville, and to shoot the leaders. Therefore, Nelson had selected Greeneville for the meeting. Both sides were arming. As the Parson drove through Sevier and Jefferson counties, he saw two companies of Unionists drilling. Resistance was high in the countryside.[32]

Resistance was strong at Greeneville, also, and the boldest, angriest and most articulate spirit was the convention's president, T. A. R. Nelson. He drafted a burning "Declaration of Grievances" and a set of resolutions breathing independence of the balance of the state and petitioning the legislature to grant East Tennessee separate statehood. Moderates succeeded in cooling some of the more heated language, but the hot spirit of defiance remained. It was incorporated into the memorial prepared by the commissioners appointed for this purpose, Temple, John Netherland of Hawkins and James P. McDowell of Greene, and presented to the assembly. There it had no possibility of acceptance by the inflamed secessionist legislators. A committee's recommended rejection of the request was anything but harsh, yet it carried a superior, almost contemptuous tone. The committee said it was not satisfied that the memorial represented the sentiment of East Tennesseans, that the balance of the state was unaware of the desire of the memorialists and consequently the legislators and constituents of Middle and West Tennessee were out of communication on the subject. They further stated that the question should be left to the succeeding assembly members who would come "fresh from the people." A gesture of conciliation was made in the final paragraph of the report in the expression of a hope that irritation between sections of the state would soon be removed and that the divisions would fall solidly into unity.[33] That was a vain hope. The petition continued to be ignored.

Union sentiment had one more opportunity to play a political hand. This was in the election of August 1, 1861, when members of Congress and state officials were elected. Also submitted to the electorate was the question of a Confederate state constitution. The strictures upon the East Tennessee loyalists were tighter than on June 8 when troops were encamped in or moving through the area. In August the muzzles of Confederate rifles were only a few feet from the ballot boxes, for units were stationed in such loyal counties as Claiborne, Campbell, Morgan and Roane. Brownlow described East Tennessee as occupied territory. The people wanted the old Government, but faced with hostile military power, they submitted to the new with such grace as they could summon, permitted the Confederate flag to "float unmolested" and took down the Stars and Stripes "to avoid further annoyance." He expected help from the North but until that development he advised: "Let the thousands of Union men in East Tennessee, who belong to the 'Home Guards' drill regularly, keep up their organizations, and hold themselves in readiness to strike for their independence, and to defend their right whenever called upon, and driven to that dread alternative!" This did not sound like submission, and it is not surprising that East Tennessee secessionists were clamoring for forces to put down the rebellion.[34]

Governor Harris was reelected and the Confederate constitution was ratified, but East Tennessee clung to and expressed its Union convictions. The voting was conducted under the auspices of a Confederate state, in fact if not technically in law, but in the first four congressional districts of the state Union men were elected. They had no intention of going to Richmond, and they were aware that their determination to serve in the Congress of the United States, although elected from districts in a seceded state subjected them to arrest in the Confederacy. These loaylists were Nelson, Maynard, George W. Bridges of the Third, and Andrew J. Clements of the Fourth. All escaped and served at Washington except Nelson, who was captured on August 4, by a band of thirty Confederate horsemen in the southwest corner of Virginia, only a few miles from Kentucky, where he would have been safe from arrest. As president of the Greeneville Convention Nelson had called another meeting to be held at Kingston on August 31, 1861. Because he was in Confederate custody and because the South was tightening its hold on East Tennessee this meeting was not held.

The legislature elected was overwhelmingly for the South, and the East Tennessee delegation, largely Unionist, was helpless and stultified because the members were required to swear allegiance to the Confederacy before they could take their seats.[35] The alternative for these men was to leave their districts unrepresented.

Lonely hours settled upon the *Whig* editor. The outcome of the June election was depressing in itself, but out of the campaign had come a melancholy personal incident. John Bell came to East Tennessee apparently believing that in his new role as rebel, rather than Unionist, he could influence some of his old friends to soften or drop their fierce loyalty to the Washington government. A small crowd heard him at the courthouse, and Brownlow treated his talk with deference marked by regret to find his old friend tarnished by an ignominious position. After Bell spoke he met some old friends in Temple's office. Among them was the Parson. The occasion was delicate, awkward and even tremulous. Bell made it more so by observing that none of his old friends had gone to hear him speak. This aroused the *Whig* editor to respond that their absence was deliberate because "We did not wish to witness the spectacle of your being surrounded by your enemies, who a few months ago were denouncing you as a traitor. We did not want to hear these men shouting for you and see you in such a position." The editor then broke into a tirade against secession, to which Bell made no reply. But, Temple recalled, "no one uttered a word of censure or an unkind remark about him [Bell] personally." They parted in sadness, and Bell's biographer wrote that his defection from a Unionist position set the sun of his "influence and public service."[36]

The August aftermath brought heavier burdens on Brownlow. Nelson was in custody. Maynard had escaped but his voice in Washington reached his constituents feebly, strained by such passage as it could make through the Confederate lines. The rousing voices of the courageous band of stump speakers were silenced by fear of Confederate military authority and personal reprisal. The ballot box issues were gone. Only Brownlow was left with a voice, and the *Whig* and its readership were being decimated by the blockade and the malicious efforts of mail clerks and postmasters who feared no prosecution if they destroyed or mislaid the Parson's newspaper. Confederate authorities had no time, if they had the inclination, to police the postal system to enforce the delivery of a newspaper whose editor denounced the South. That put him in the role of traitor, so far as those loyal to the government at Richmond were concerned. And angry hands were reaching for the throat of the *Whig*, eager to throttle it into silence.

CHAPTER XIII NOTES

[1] Brownlow accused Mrs. Stowe of being a *"deliberate liar,"* of writing "shameful and unmitigated falsehoods," in *Uncle Tom's Cabin*, and of being considerably less than virtuous during a Paris trip. *Whig*, February 5, 12, October 29, 1853.

[2] *Ibid.*, November 19, December 31, 1859; Mrs. Mattie Turnley, "Survivor of a John Brown Family Raid," *Tennessee Historical Magazine*, Vol. 7 (October, 1921, Nashville), pp. 231-232; Stephen B. Oates, *To Purge This Land with Blood* (New York, 1970), pp. 119, 122-123, 134-135, 143, 344-345. The Doyle family has been influential in Knox County Republican politics for years, many of its members living in the area south of the Tennessee River, a Republican stronghold. A. E. (Ebb) Doyle was county register from 1922 to 1930, and Miss Mildred Doyle was county school superintendent from 1946 to 1976.

[3] *Whig*, May 19, 26, June 9, 1860; Parks, pp. 351-355.

[4] *Whig*, June 30, August 25, September 1, 1860; Alexander, *Thomas A. R. Nelson*, pp. 67-68.

[5] *Whig*, July 14, August 25, July 28, September 1, 29, October 6, 1860.

[6] *Ibid.*, October 27, 1860.

[7] *Ibid.*, September 22, 29, 1860; Humes, *The Loyal Mountaineers*, pp. 81-85; John W. Du Bose, *Life and Times of William Lowndes Yancey*, 2 vols. (Birmingham, 1892), II, pp. 494-496, hereafter referred to as Du Bose; *Whig*, October 13, 1860. Temple, who was present and participated in the encounter with Yancey made only a vague reference to it in his two books dealing with the times.

[8] Du Bose, II, pp. 494-496; Humes, *The Loyal Mountaineers*, p. 84.

[9] *Whig*, September 29, 1860.

[10] *Ibid.*, October 6, 13, November 10; Folmsbee *et al.*, *Short History*, p. 316, citing the Nashville *Patriot*, November 26, 1860. A slightly different figure is given in White, *Messages*, V, p. 270.

[11] *Whig*, November 10, 1860. Other examples of the editor's deep concern for the nation's future may be found in *ibid.*, November 17, 1860, Brownlow to Temple, January 26, 1858. Temple Papers. *Whig*, February 13, 1858. The Parson admitted during his northern speaking tour in 1862 that his reception at Montgomery was chilly. *Ibid.*, February 6, 1864.

[12] *Ibid.*, December 15, 1860, February 16, June 29, 1861; *Parson Brownlow's Book*, pp. 37-48, 65-74, 75-80. Examples of letters written to Pryne, *Whig*, January 14, February 25, May 12, November 10, 1860. John Bell Brownlow use the 14,000 circulation figure on the margin of a copy of Temple, *Notable Men*, in the McClung Collection, p. 42. Temple obviously got his figure from John Bell Brownlow, with whom he carried on an extensive correspondence. Temple Papers, *passim*. See also Temple, *Notable Men*, p. 276.

[13] Folmsbee *et al.*, *Short History*, pp. 317-318; *Whig*, January 19, 1861; White, *Messages*, V, pp. 254-271; *Acts of Tennessee, First Extra Session, 1861* (Nashville, 1861), pp. 15-17; Temple, *East Tennessee and the Civil War*, p. 170.

[14] *Whig*, December 24, 1859, January 28, 1860, quoting Rochester (New York) *Advertiser*, *Whig* January 5, 19, 26, February 2, 9, 2, 9, 1861.

[15] White, *Messages*, V, p. 272; Temple, *East Tennessee and the Civil War*, p. 176; Folmsbee *et al.*, *Short History*, p. 319; *Whig*, February 16, 1861; Temple, *East Tennessee and the Civil War*, pp. 176-177.

[16] *Whig*, April 27, May 11, July 13, 20, 1861; Folmsbee *et al.*, *Short History*, pp. 325-326.

[17] *Ibid.*, pp. 320-321; White, *Messages*, V, pp. 278-294; Folmsbee *et al.*, *Short History*, pp. 319-321; White, *Messages*, V, pp. 287-288; *Whig*, May 4, 11, 1861.

[18] Alexander, *T. A. R. Nelson*, pp. 75-78; *Whig*, April 27, May 4, 25, 4, April 6, 1861.

[19] *Ibid.*, April 27, 1861; Parks, pp. 397-399; White, *Messages*, V, p 273.

[20] *Register*, May 2, 24, 1861; *Whig*, May 4, 1861; Temple, *East Tennessee and the Civil War*, pp. 186-188; Humes, *The Loyal Mountaineers*, pp. 100-102.

[21] *Whig*, May 4, 1861; Temple, *East Tennessee and the Civil War*, pp. 185-187, *Notable Men*, pp. 399-401; Alexander, *T. A. R. Nelson*, pp. 75-77.

[22] *Parson Brownlow's Book*, pp. 278-279, illustration p. 192; Humes, *The Loyal Mountaineers*, pp. 100-101, appendix, p. 347; *Whig*, May 11, 18, 1861; *Weekly Register*, May 16, 1861; *Daily Register*, May 23, June 6, 1861.

[23] Temple, *Notable Men*, pp. 399-400, 451-467, 167, 172; Alexander, *T. A. R. Nelson*, pp. 75-77.

[24] *Ibid.*, p. 79; Temple, *East Tennessee and the Civil War*, pp. 197-198; Alexander, *T. A. R. Nelson*, pp. 75-77; John Bell Brownlow to Temple, August 14, 1893. Temple Papers. *Whig*, June 1, 1861.

[25] Clipping from Jonesborough *Express*, May 10, 1861, Scrapbook No. 13, Nelson Papers. Alexander, *T. A. R. Nelson*, p. 77; Patton, *Unionism and Reconstruction in Tennessee, 1860-1869* (Gloucester, 1966), p. 53, hereafter referred to as Patton, *Unionism and Reconstruction*.

[26] John Bell Brownlow to Andrew Patterson, May 12, 1915. John Bell

Brownlow Papers. University of Tennessee Special Collections. *Particeps criminis* means an accomplice.

[27] *Whig*, June 1, 1861; clippings from *Tri-Weekly Whig*, June 6, 1861; Scrapbook No. 13, p. 100. Nelson Papers. Temple, *East Tennessee and the Civil War*, pp. 192-195; *Register* clipping, June 1, 1861, Scrapbook No. 13, pp. 100-101. Nelson Papers.

[28] *Whig*, June 15, 1861; *Register*, June 11, 1861; Folmsbee *et al.*, *Short History*, p. 322.

[29] *Whig*, June 15, 1861; Rothrock, ed., *French Broad-Holston*, p. 129; *Register*, June 11, 1861; White, *Messages*, V, p. 304; *Whig*, June 15, 1861; Temple, *East Tennessee and the Civil War*, p. 199. Brownlow later acknowledged that the official vote for separation in Knox County was 1,226, and he listed the military vote, camp by camp, but with no mention of Camp Cummings at Knoxville, which further suggests that its vote was incorporated into the Knoxville returns. *Parson Brownlow's Book*, pp. 221-223.

[30] *Register*, May 2, 16, 1861.

[31] Temple, *East Tennessee and the Civil War*, p. 341; Alexander, *T. A. R. Nelson*, p. 78; White, *Messages*, V, p. 311.

[32] *Whig*, June 22, 29, 1861; Alexander, *T. A. R. Nelson*, pp. 84-85.

[33] *Ibid.*, pp. 85-87; Temple, *East Tennessee and the Civil War*, pp. 343-360, appendix, pp. 565-571; *Whig*, June 29, July 6, 13, 1861; White, *Messages*, V, pp. 314-315; Temple, *East Tennessee and the Civil War*, pp. 360-361.

[34] Brownlow pointed up the strange, dual character of the election: "By the law of Tennessee in full force, unrepealed (Code section 825) the people on that day are to choose Representatives to the *Congress of the United States*. By the proclamation of Isham G. Harris, the Governor, they are at the same time to choose Representatives to the *Congress of the Confederate States*. Between the two, Tennessee will be well represented! Of course the Secessionists will vote for candidates to represent them in *the Confederate Congress*; and the Union men will vote for candidates to represent them in the *Congress of the United States.*" *Whig*, July 13, 1861; *O.R.*, Series IV, 1, Landon C. Haynes to Confederate Secretary of War L. P. Walker, July 6, 1861, L. Polk to President Davis, July 9, 1861, William G. Swan to President Davis, July 11, 1861, pp. 346-347.

[35] White, *Messages*, V, pp. 330-332; Folmsbee *et al.*, *Short History*, p. 326; Alexander, *T. A. R. Nelson*, pp. 88-89; *Whig*, August 10, 1861. See oath required of members of the assembly, *ibid.*, October 26, 1861. See also Fleming's dilemma, Temple, *Notable Men*, p. 119; *Whig*, July 20, August 10, 24, 1861.

[36] *Ibid.*, June 15, 1861; Temple, *East Tennessee and the Civil War*, pp. 233-235; Parks, pp. 402-405.

[37] *Whig*, March 3, May 4, June 6, 29, July 13, 27, August 3, 10, 1861.

Brownlow's Knoxville Whig,
and Rebel Ventilator.

"To the Union, the Constitution, and the Laws."   Chapter No. 14

CRUSHED AND EXILED

Brownlow acknowledged immediately after the election of August 1, 1861 that the *Whig* was in serious trouble. The voters reelected Isham G. Harris governor and adopted the constitution of the Confederate States. The Parson dropped the *Tri-Weekly Whig* and sharply reduced the total content of the weekly by cutting it from eight columns to five and increasing the size of the body type.

But owing to the falling off of advertisements, the amount of reading matter will not be diminished in equal ratio. This necessity arises from the diminished income of the office, growing out of the stagnation of business generally, the blockade, cutting off Northern advertising, the discontinuance of the mails, and the wholesale robbery of my letters, while the expenses of my business are increased (*Whig*, August 3, 1861).

Advertising revenue, from North and South, was down, and many newspapers were increasing their subscription rates as well as issuing half sheets. Brownlow estimated his weekly losses at from $20.00 to $40.00, but he vowed he would try to "weather this storm" even though temporary suspension might become necessary, for:

At this most critical period in the affairs of the country, let us keep under way a Union paper, that will dare to publish other than Secession accounts of what is transpiring.

I only ask that the expenses of publication be met, and that I get my meat and bread. I am willing to labor in the cause without one dollar in the way of profits. I ask no favor of Secession—I expect none—they may continue their proscriptive course toward me—and I shall alike scorn it and their vile principles (*Ibid.*).

Fortune, however, granted the Parson a favor. Brigadier General Felix K. Zollicoffer, the former Nashville editor who had got his newspaper training in Knoxville and who had been a fellow Whig, was directed to take charge of the military district of East Tennessee. He took over the post late in July.[1] The general prepared a firm, yet conciliatory statement in which he recognized two sources of alarm to the Confederacy and sought to remove them:

Can there be recreant sons of Tennessee who would strike at their brothers while thus struggling for Southern honor and independence? Or who would invite the enemy over the border to inaugurate war and desolation among our own fair fields? There can be but few such. If any, it were better for their memory had they perished before such dishonor (*Whig*, August 10, 1861).

Zollicoffer's statement reflected the concern, even alarm, of Confederate civil authorities. Influential citizens such as Landon C. Haynes and William G. Swan of Knoxville, were clamoring for Southern troops to offset the threatening militancy of the Unionists. The rugged terrain of the area afforded coves and mountain tops where some loyalists were known to be training, while others were slipping along the ridges and passes into Kentucky to join the Union army. Amid this, reports persisted that Northern forces were about to invade East Tennessee.[2] An ardent Unionist who lived through the period suggests that at the time of the Greeneville Convention, when Southern troops were passing through the town, the delegates were unmolested because "the Secessionists of East Tennessee were at that time in greater fear of the Union men than the latter were of them."[3]

Zollicoffer wanted his statement to obtain the widest distribution and as a newspaperman he knew the *Whig* would reach and influence more East Tennessee readers than any other medium. He probably reached an understanding with the Parson, for the *Whig* of August 10, 1861, carried the notice, "We publish, at the request of Gen. Zollicoffer, his address to the people of East Tennessee, his command embracing this division of the state. It is our only hope of getting this issue of our paper before the public. The mercenaries of the Confederacy in charge of the Post Office and mails probably will let this paper pass in order to circulate this address." Brownlow knew, or guessed, that word went out through Confederate channels to see that this issue of the *Whig* went to each destination without fail. The Parson got into this issue returns from Knox and other East Tennessee counties showing that the Unionists had expressed their loyalty at the ballot box on August 1 by electing Nelson, Maynard and Bridges to the United States House of Representatives. He sought to arouse their ire by reporting the arrest of Nelson and his being taken in custody to Richmond, where "when they cast into their filthy city prison, THOMAS A. R. NELSON, they will have more brains, patriotism, honor and chivalry, in their Prison, than can be found in their Rump Congress!" (*Whig*, August 10, 1861). He explained why the *Whig* was not being delivered and why it was operating at a loss:

Our exchange papers are kept back and not allowed to come to Knoxville. Our letters are broken open and robbed, in all directions, and our newspaper packages are laid aside or destroyed. . . . At Cumberland Gap, or the office near there, we are informed upon reliable authority, there is a large pile of letters, to say nothing of papers addressed to us, which Secessionists will not allow to come forward. These letters no doubt, mostly from Kentucky, contain several hundred dollars for subscriptions. At Bristol, we are informed, our paper is thrown aside, and not allowed to go further East (*Ibid.*).

The editor predicted the *Whig* had only a short time to live. Either it would be suppressed on orders from Richmond or local mobs would destroy his plant and office. Then his pen scratched out these words designed to arouse greater Union bitterness:

Leading men of the Union party, of unblemished character, must be rudely seized by an armed band of men, to gratify the malice of leading Secessionists in Knoxville, torne [*sic.*] from their families and rushed off upon the cars to Richmond, and there thrown into a loathsome prison! The only Press they have must be muzzled, its batteries silenced, and its readers and friends required to take the false statements of Secession papers for the news of the day! Large bodies of armed men must be thrown into our country, and put in possession of all the principal towns and thoroughfares of the country, but no wrongs are to be inflicted upon the people of East Tennessee, nor are they to be deprived of any of their rights!

Can all this mean anything less than a declaration of war against East Tennessee? Is it not opening the ball, and inviting bloodshed in East Tennessee? What the effect of all this will be, we are wholly unable to say. It will either depress the Union forces of this end of the State, and cause them to cower like dogs, or it will make them frantic in defense of their gallant leaders, down-trodden because of their principles, and arouse a thirst for vengeance and brave deeds! What Union leader, after all this, can any longer meet his friends and urge them to peace, and moderation, as we know they have been doing?

So far as we are concerned, we can suspend our publication, in obedience to the dictates of tyranny and intolerance—we will yield to the demands of an

armed mob—turn over to them our office and what little property we have—
deprive ourselves and a helpless family of small children the necessary means of
support—and beg our bread from door to door among the Union men who are
able to give—but we shall refuse, most obstinately refuse, to the day of our death
to think or speak favorably of such a Confederacy as this. . . . And whether our
humble voice is hushed in death—whether our press is muzzled by the spirit of
intolerance at Richmond . . . we beg all who may come after us and our paper to
credit no Secession falsehood that may represent us as having changed our
principles from those of exalted devotion to the old AMERICAN UNION, and
of undying hostility to those who would perpetrate its dissolution (*Ibid.*).

General Zollicoffer's earnest but more formal appeal to East Tennesseeans to submit with good grace to the Confederate government
made the front page—perhaps this was part of the bargain—or the
Parson may have decided its presence there would help insure delivery of the *Whig*. But Brownlow's flaming declaration on page two
must have offset much of the effect sought by the general (*Whig*,
August 10, 1861). Yet events upon the battlefield and in the government circles at Richmond lent strength to the efforts to restore
order, if not peace, to East Tennessee. The defeat of the Union
forces at Bull Run depressed Brownlow and Nelson, and the considerate and deferential treatment given the latter at Richmond—he
was not cast into a "loathsome prison" but was permitted liberty
under parole—had its effect on both men.[4] Nelson, on the third
attempt, framed a letter that President Jefferson Davis found acceptable and granted his release. Upon his arrival in East Tennessee Nelson made an extended statement that was a marvel of ingenuity in
deferring to the Confederacy, under which he was forced to live if he
remained in East Tennessee, without approving of it.[5] The intensely secessionist *Register*, with some justification, found Nelson's skillful exposition "modeled after the style of Mark Antony's speech in
Shakespeare's Play, or, to quote a distinguished East Tennessee
orator—'it is sorter so and sorter not so, but a little more sorter not
so than so.' "[6] Brownlow had executed a less subtle shifting of
position by announcing that he had expected Nelson's release, as the
result of efforts of two of his friends who had gone to Richmond,
John Baxter, the Knoxville lawyer who was easing into something of
a secessionist, and Dr. Jeptha Fowlkes of Memphis, a peace commissioner of the state government to East Tennessee. Both of these men
had met Nelson at Abingdon as he was being taken to Richmond in

custody. The editor also noted that Nelson had "committed no offense."[7]

Brownlow's editorial policy also shifted toward a much more moderate course regarding leaders of the Confederacy. But he did not relent in his denunciations of the Knoxville secessionists, for he blamed them for stirring up bitterness and clamoring for troops to be stationed in the area in order to avenge personal differences. The Federal government had a responsibility to put down rebellion, but the East Tennessee Union men were against an invasion of the area by the North and had not applied to Washington for arms, men or money. They had even considered a mission to the North's capitol to present their views. Brownlow even said that the reports of "large numbers" of Unionists slipping through the mountain passes into Kentucky to join the Northern army were exaggerated. He suggested, in a neat bid for some rebel nods and chuckles, that East Tennessee would never be invaded until the Union armies fought better along the Potomac, and that if these forces, with their overwhelming resources, failed to subdue the South, "the only Government then remaining in America, entitled to respect, will be that of the Southern Confederacy. And Union Men, will fall into its support whatever contempt they may have for those who control it, and originated this Rebellion." The devotion of East Tennessee loyalists was to the government, not to Lincoln, he argued, and had they not "been so grossly misrepresented by Secession leaders, so shamefully abused, tyranized [sic.] over and then threatened, as they have been by the base, corrupt and cowardly leaders, such as control matters in Knoxville, and other towns, there would be at this time less of bitterness among them, and more of a disposition to harmonize with the other portions of the State." The Union leaders, so unjustly accused, had in fact tried to calm the citizenry, he argued (*Whig*, August 17, 1861).

The Parson's tongue must have made his cheek protrude as he wrote this editorial. He obviously designed it to lull the Confederacy into removing some of the troops from the area, a step that would further infuriate Knoxville Secession leaders, who had been demanding them for protection. Nelson's abdication from a position of Union leadership to one of neutrality provided a splendid backdrop against which to lay this new and amazing position of the *Whig*, even though it appeared in print a week before the lawyer's statement. The Parson praised Zollicoffer as "a man of fine sense, of great firmness of character and of true courage; and like all men of this cast, our citizens will find him generous and reasonable—not disposed to oppress anyone because he may have the power to do so, and is really desirous of avoiding any collision with the people of East Tennessee" (*Ibid.*). Zollicoffer's policy of conciliation appeared to be working. He expressed in a formal order carried by the *Whig*, gratification "at the preservation of peace, and the rapidly increasing evidence of confidence and good will among the people of East Tennessee." He called upon those under his command to exert "scrupulous regard for the personal and property rights of all the inhabitants. No word or act will be tolerated to alarm or irritate those who though heretofore advocating Federal Union now acquiesce in the decision of the State and submit to the authority of the Government of the Confederate States." Fowlkes stopped in Knoxville and drew praise, not only for helping in the release of Nelson, but for having "done more, perhaps, than any other man, toward restoring peace in this end of the state." When reports got out that rebellion was being threatened in Union circles, seventeen men, among them such known and staunch loyalists as John Baxter, O. P. Temple, Brownlow, Connally F. Trigg, John M. Fleming and R. H. Hodsden, counselled in an open letter to Zollicoffer against armed revolt. They assured the general that if troops were required elsewhere he need have no fear that their removal from the East Tennessee area would result in disorder. The general replied that with this assurance he would retain no more troops than necessary to maintain "the peace and safety of the community."[8]

The course of Brownlow and the other Union leaders at this time was a shrewd one. They were old Whigs and they had been partisan comrades of Zollicoffer for many campaigns. The secession leaders in Knoxville were mostly Democrats who undoubtedly viewed the rapprochement with alarm and bitterness. J. A. Sperry, editor of the *Register*, a militant secessionist and Democrat, was unable to conceal his anger at the situation and the frequency with which secessionists from other parts of the state called upon Brownlow and engaged in extended conversations with him. The Parson needled this sensitive nerve in Sperry by recalling the remark of Henry A. Wise, former governor of Virginia, that old Clay Whigs "knoweth each other by the instincts of gentleman," a form of response which the Parson was sure would lead none of them to Sperry's office. The *Register* editor had the reputation of being "*a base and cowardly liar, a drunken and degraded scoundrel, and the mere cat's paw of meaner men than himself.*"[9] Brownlow, who probably glowed at the effect of the wedge he was driving between the Zollicoffer command and the Knoxville Secession leaders, laid on this further lick:

> The Government of the Confederate States at Richmond has suffered in this quarter, by being viewed *through this Register and those associated with it*. This ought not to be. A distinction should be kept up between the Government and the *base men* who represent it here and constitute the *Sperry Clique*. The Confederate Authorities at Richmond have become elevated in my estimation, since I have been informed by gentlemen, directly from there, that they *wholly disapprove the base forgery in Knoxville of letters in the name of Senator Johnson*, with a view to injure him upon a false issue, and so steal money from others! And whenever the Confederate Authorities shall lay aside such *depraved villains* as hang upon their skirts here, they draw to their standard a better class of men (*Whig*, August 24, 1861).

The forgery mentioned had been reported by the *Whig* in mid-July. The Parson published letters signed Andrew Johnson and addressed to Amos Lawrence, a wealthy Bostonian known to be a contributor to free state causes. Lawrence had a deep feeling for the border state Unionists and a high regard for Johnson's loyalty. When he received a letter signed "Andrew Johnson," and asking for funds to support East Tennessee loyalists he responded with a draft for $1,000 enclosed to Johnson, and sent to Knoxville as the senator was campaigning against secession in the June 8 referendum. A second letter to Lawrence, carrying Johnson's name, said the signer was afraid to cash the draft, but that $5,000 to $10,000 in "New England currency" would be safe. Lawrence's letter and draft found their way into the hands of Governor Harris and were published in the Richmond *Enquirer*. Johnson obtained from Lawrence copies of the letters bearing his name. He denounced them as forgeries and said he was many miles distant from Knoxville, campaigning, when they were mailed from that post office. The purpose of the letters, the senator said, was to injure him and the cause of the Tennessee Unionists. The Confederates, also, could have made use of the money, Johnson laid the forgeries and trickery on the Knoxville postmaster, C. W. Charlton. He did not mention Charlton by name.

Brownlow also charged the forgery against the Knoxville post office. He noted that the *Register*, "edited and published in the buildings where the post-office was kept during this *diplomatic and financial correspondence*, and familiar with the turpitude of the whole affair, nevertheless, paraded the correspondence before its readers as a wonderful discovery, and as evidence of Johnson's corruption and Abolitionism." But he first accused W. G. Swan, Confederate congressman, one of his old enemies, of having forged Johnson's name.[10]

When the Union army seized the archives of the Tennessee Confederate government at Augusta, Georgia, three years later, letters from Charlton to the then Governor Harris were found. They revealed that Charlton had been opening Brownlow's mail and forwarding it to the governor, along with the postmaster's alarmed reports on the strength of union sentiment in the area. Charlton acknowledged he had forged the letters to Lawrence "to reach their purposes and plans at the North," and he was vexed with Dr. Jeptha Fowlkes of Memphis for bringing the Lawrence letter to Brownlow. Charlton's conscience may have twinged him for he wrote Harris: "*I am the guilty man, if there be guilt in it.*" Charlton had resigned as postmaster under the Lincoln administration early in the spring, but he must have continued to operate the office, apparently on the theory that he was running it as an agency of the Confederate government, even before Tennessee voted for separation.[11]

Fowlkes was one of the secession leaders among the old Whigs who tried to get Brownlow to cast his lot with the South. In furnishing the Parson with the Lawrence letter, he may have been trying to show that the central Confederate government could be trusted and lacked the deep hostility that existed against the *Whig* and its editor on the part of the Knoxville leaders. From the outcries of the *Register*, the Knoxville clique was fully aware of the efforts of Fowlkes and others and was enraged by it. The *Whig*, delighted at the anger being generated among its old foes, took notice of reports that Brownlow had turned secessionist, denied the charge, and restated its Union loyalty. But the editor acknowledged that his side had been overpowered in Tennessee, first at the ballot box and next by the South's army, and hence he had retired to a "position of neutrality." Because East Tennessee had failed to set itself up as a separate state and the Lincoln Administration had not come to the rescue of the region, the opportunity to resist had been lost. In this unusual role as a neutralist, Brownlow wrote: "So far as I am individually concerned, I will not be a party to any mad scheme of Rebellion, gotten up at this late day, or to any insane attempt to invade this end of the State with Federal troops." The enraged *Register*, in an article Brownlow described as aimed at Zollicoffer and Brigadier General W.

R. Caswell, counselled "the hanging of Union men, and protests against showing any quarters [*sic.*] to the leaders in East Tennessee." The *Register* acknowledged it was being so harsh it was keeping Union men from coming "into line gracefully. . . ," but

We are willing to accord to men the most unlimited time to wheel into line, provided they do not obtrude themselves before the people as candidates for their confidence until they have at least given some earnest of the sincerity and permanence of their conversion. But for the friends of Brownlow to ask time for him to change front, and to put on the Southern garb gradually, as if he would be in danger of taking cold by throwing off his extreme Northern vestments, excites our risibility. The fact is patent to every observer, that while he means to keep his promise to the [word illegible], and to keep under his Lincolnism, it is ever in his heart, as it ever has been.[12]

However stoutly the Parson needled his enemies he surely underwent inner turmoil and torment. Before the June election he had revealed he was under pressure to switch to the South. Family, as well as friends, may have tried to influence him to change course, for after the Parson's departure to the North the *Register* charged:

It is a notorious fact in this city that Brownlow's children repeatedly declared here that they had done all in their power and used every exertion to induce him to espouse the cause of the South. A gentleman who was Brownlow's intimate friend and the adviser of his family in his absence has asserted upon our streets that he knew the fact that he would have advocated the Southern cause had it not been for the attacks[?] of the Knoxville *Register.*

R. N. Price, the gentle Methodist historian and friend of Brownlow, wrote years later that the *Whig* editor was on the point of "renouncing the Union and aligning himself with the leading politicians of the South." But the Parson tore up an editorial that he had written to this purpose when the *Register* "pre-announced it with ridicule and as an impugnment of the motives of the man." Baxter, who probably was the "intimate friend and adviser" mentioned by the *Register*, years later in the Reconstruction period when he fell into a furious personal and political controversy with Brownlow, accused the latter of having "in substance said that he had made up his mind to abandon the Federal cause and support the Confederacy, and that as soon as he could, with due respect to public opinion, he would change his position. Baxter claimed that he had heard him say this in his own home, in the presence of Fowlkes and John S. Sanborn, a Mississippian. Fowlkes, meanwhile, had died and Sanborn was unavailable. Brownlow not only denied Baxter's charge but also produced a letter which he said he had displayed at that time asserting he would not change. Included also was testimony of a witness who was in the next room and heard him say: "I will die at the end of a rope before I will support the Southern Confederacy." The charges made by the *Register* and by Baxter were born of hatred and bitterness, but the Parson had earlier acknowledged that he had been under a terrible strain in 1861.[13] When he resumed publication of the *Whig* in 1863 he wrote:

When the Rebellion was inaugurated, there were thousands among us, who were half inclined to regard the attempt to quell the outbreak as hopeless, and who were more than half inclined to end the war by conceding the independence of the bogus Confederacy, although they knew it had originated in, and was based upon the GREAT SOUTHERN PLATFORM of falsehood, perjury, and treachery (*Whig*, November 11, 1863).

Brownlow's close friend and contemporary, Temple, declared that the Parson never wavered in his devotion to the Union, but he was silent on the struggle the editor underwent.[14]

Brownlow accepted, with surprising restraint, the arrest and temporary imprisonment of his oldest son, John Bell, for having in his possession Hinton Helper's *The Impending Crisis*. The author was a former slavery advocate who had turned abolitionist. The Parson described the work as "mischievous" but hardly in the class with other incendiary documents and works in his library, such as the Constitution of the United States, the Declaration of Independence and "five copies of the Holy Bible." It turned out that the book had been lent to John Bell by William G. McAdoo, a secessionist. The military authorities had arrested the youth, but Confederate Judge West Humphreys released him. The editor, in branding as false reports that both father and son had been arrested, complimented Zollicoffer for having thrown two hundred troops into the city to guard the *Whig* office, patrol the town and close liquor shops when threats were made to demolish the newspaper building. As mayor of East Knoxville, Brownlow also commended the prompt action taken by officers when he complained that cavalrymen were riding their mounts upon the board sidewalks.[15]

Newspapers throughout the South operated under great difficulties. One estimate was that four hundred had suspended and twelve hundred had reduced their size. Because the *Whig* was the only newspaper in the South that spoke against the Confederacy, it faced the resentment and reprisals of those handling the mails. The Confederate postmaster general assumed a hands-off position so far as the *Whig* was concerned. He left the responsibility for the distribution of its 7,500 copies in the hands of hostile state officials. Brownlow also was told by Fowlkes that the *Whig* would be suppressed. The Parson admitted he was meeting more trouble in operating on his reduced scale than when he was printing a tri-weekly as well as a weekly. To get in all the cash he could, he sent out young William Rule, who was employed in the *Whig* office and was destined for a significant future in the Knoxville newspaper field, to collect accounts. He protested to Postmaster Charlton that his newspaper was not being delivered in Union, Blount, Roane, Anderson and Sevier counties, while the *Register* was reaching its subscribers with regularity. This situation, Charlton replied, "is certainly remarkable . . . for thus far, I have tried to do my whole duty in properly distributing your paper." The editor also fired off to the Confederate postmaster general a list of points at which his newspaper was not distributed and cited the service to Sevier County as being so bad that citizens were sending a courier to Knoxville to pick up the *Whig*.[16]

A discouraging development was Baxter's decision to run for the Confederate Congress. Brownlow, in a labored editorial, explained that although Baxter once had held staunch Union convictions, he had reached the conclusion that the North could not win and that East Tennessee's logical course lay with the South. He gave this justification for the lawyer's candidacy: "In view of these considerations, and the fact that in his opinion the Union was dissolved, and that he could do nothing to arrest the result, he deemed it a duty to yield, and did so, and from that period till [*sic*.] the present has favored the idea of doing all he could to give a sound, constitutional, and healthy direction to the new Government, and to bring the war to a speedy and satisfactory conclusion. . . ." He stopped short of endorsing Baxter, although he considered him preferable to W. G. Swan, who was elected.[17]

East Tennessee was not at peace, whatever efforts leaders on both sides may have been making. Twenty-five persons were arrested in McMinn County, twenty of whom were released by Judge Humphreys. Among them was a Methodist preacher, the Rev. William H.

Duggan, who was accused of praying for the United States Government. Some Confederate volunteers made a foray into Unionist Sevier County. They arrested five men, but were overtaken by a larger force of Union men and forced to kneel in the mud and beg for mercy. The offenders were reproved by military authorities, but these events indicated that the resentment on both sides needed only a spark to set off blows and bloody reprisals. [18]

Brownlow was hemmed in by the obstructions placed on the distribution of his newspaper, cramped by reduced revenue, and confronted by hostile civil and military authorities and deepening social ostracism. So he resorted to a weapon that cut agonizingly into the pride of the Secessionists; he taunted them for the failure of prominent men and their sons to enter military service.[19] Perhaps the most incisive and mocking editorial he ever wrote was headed "To Arms! To Arms! Ye Braves!" and continued:

Come Tennesseeans, ye who are the advocates of Southern Rights, for Separation [*sic.*], and for Disunion—ye who have lost your rights, and feel willing to uphold the glorious flag of the South, in opposition to the Hessians arrayed under the Despot Lincoln, come to your country's rescue! Our gallant Governor, who led off in this State, in the praiseworthy object of breaking up the old rickety Government in the hands of the Black Republicans, calls for 30,000 Volunteers, in addition to the 55,000 already in the field. Shall we have them? If they do not volunteer, we shall have our State disgraced by a *draft*, and then we must go under compulsion. Come, gentlemen, many of you promised that "when it becomes necessary" you will turn out. That time has come, and the *necessity* is upon us. Let us show our *faith* by our *works*. We have talked long and loud about fighting the Union-shriekers, and the vandal hoards [*sic.*] under the Despot, Lincoln! Now we have an opening. Some of us have even said we were willing for our sons to turn out and fight Union men. We have a chance at a terrible array of Unionists in Kentucky—let us volunteer, and Gen. Sidney Johnson will either lead us on to victory, or something else! Come, ye braves, turn out, and let the world see that you are in earnest in making war upon the enemies of the South! Many of you have made big speeches in favor of the war. Not a few of you have sought to sell the army supplies. And thousands of you are willing to stoop to fill the *offices* for the salaries they pay, and you have been so patriotic as to try to get your sons and other relations into offices. Some of you have *hired yourselves out as spies, understrappers*, and *tools*, in the glorious cause, at two to four dollars per day! Come, now, enter the ranks, as there is more honor in serving as a private. Come, gentlemen, *do* come, we insist, and enter the army as volunteers. You will feel bad when *drafted*, and pointed out as one who had to be *driven* into the service of your country! Let these Union traitors submit to the draft, but let us who are true Southern men *volunteer.* Any of us are willing to be Judges, Attornies [*sic.*] , Clerks, Senators, Congressmen, and campfollowers for *pay* when out of danger, but who of us are willing to shoulder our knapsacks and muskets, and meet the Hessians? Come, gentlemen, the eyes of the people are upon you, and they want to see if you will pitch in. This is a good opening! (*Whig*, October 12, 1861).

A week later he printed another scathing editorial under the heading "Who Will Volunteer?" but this time suggesting the wealthy and influential avoided military service, although they "are in comfortable circumstances, and could leave their families enough to live on. Not so with the poor laborers and mechanics they are urging to turn out.—Their wives and children, during a hard winter, would be obliged to suffer." The Parson's taunts were on target, for Dr. J. G. M. Ramsey, one of Knoxville's most belligerent Secessionists, wrote President Jefferson Davis at Richmond, early in November, that the volunteering spirit was very low.[20]

When Brownlow printed his last issue of the *Whig*, October 26, 1861, he ran again and on the front page those two trenchant editorials, citing them as examples of "treasonable articles" for which he had been told he was to be indicted in Nashville. Dr. R. H. Hodsden, Sevier County representative then in Nashville, sent Temple the following note:

I have just learned from Judge Briant [*sic.*] , this morning, that in addition to Brownlow, Col. Trigg, Col. Jno [.] Williams and yourself, are to be indicted in federal court here, this week, for Treason. I have barely time to write this much.

Yours Truly
R. H. Hodsden

Judge Brian [*sic.*] told me about it in confidence—Thornburg will be released today.

R. H. H.

The "Judge Briant" or "Judge Brian" probably was John S. Brien, a former chancellor and Nashville lawyer. Brien, originally a Whig and a Unionist, had followed John Bell's lead in the election on the question of separation. The indictments were not returned, and Judge Humphreys freed Dr. John M. Thornburg, who had been arrested in Knoxville and taken to Nashville.[21]

Suddenly, two weeks after he had published the first of the two taunting editorials, some of the fire went out of the Parson's pen. In a depressed farewell piece, he acknowledged that he was forced to suspend the *Whig*. He was crushed. The labor of more than twenty years in which he had brought the *Whig* to the point where it was a money maker, its influence wide and with the largest circulation of any weekly in the South, now counted for nothing. Its end had been brought about without any formal order of suspension from the Confederate government. He was beset by enemies who had silenced his voice and now sought his liberty and his life. Dispiritedly he wrote, "I am prepared to lie, in solitary confinement, until I waste away because of imprisonment, or die from old age. Stimulated by a consciousness of innocent uprightness, I will submit to imprisonment for life, or die at the end of a rope, before I will make any humiliating concession to any power on earth!"[22] Then, after his resignation to what he saw as a wretched fate, he wrote with approval of his course:

I have committed no offense—I have not shouldered arms against the Confederate Government, or the State, or encouraged others to do so—I have discouraged Rebellion, publicly and privately—I have not assumed a hostile attitude toward the Civil or Military authorities of this new Government. But I have committed grave, and I really fear unpardonable offenses. I have refused to make war upon the Government of the United States; I have refused to publish to the world, false and exaggerated accounts, of the several engagements had between the contending armies; I have refused to write out and publish false versions of the origin of this war, and of the breaking up of the best Government the world ever knew; and all this I will continue to do, if it cost me my life. Nay, when I agree to do such things, may a righteous God palsey [*sic.*] my right arm, and may the earth open and close in upon me forever!

The real object of my arrest and contemplated imprisonment is to dry up, break down, silence, and destroy the last and only Union paper left in the eleven seceded States, and thereby to keep from the people of East Tennessee, the *facts* which are daily transpiring in the country. . . . It is not enough that my paper has been denied a circulation through the ordinary channels of conveyance in the country, but it must be discontinued altogether, or its Editor must write and select only such articles as meet the approval of a pack of scoundrels in Knoxville, when their superiors in all the qualities that adorn human nature, are in the Penitentiary of our State! (*Whig*, October 26, 1861).

In an uncharacteristic moment of self aggrandizement he likened himself to John Rogers dying at the stake for his principles. In less agonizing days the Parson had built himself up to an exaggerated stature, only to deflate this creature with a shaft of humor. There was no humor lying about at this juncture; he was more than sixty years old and "life has lost some of its energy." He turned to his subscribers and assured them that if the opportunity came he would make up the loss to those who had made advance payments. He forecast for the people days of "wanton" and "outrageous wrongs" but from which their traditional resolution would rescue them. As for himself, "Exchanging with proud satisfaction, the editorial chair, and the sweet endearments of home, for a cell in the prison, or the lot of an exile, I have the honor to be,&c.,

WILLIAM G. BROWNLOW

Editor of the Knoxville Whig (***Ibid., Oct. 24, 1861***).

Brownlow's editorials on the tardiness of Southern youth to enlist and the tendency of the wealthy to hold back while urging the men of less means to join the armed services cut deeply. Temple wrote that it produced a "cry of rage" against the editor. His family entreated him to leave Knoxville. His presence imperilled their safety. He tried to reach Kentucky by the mountain passes along the border of the two states. The Parson turned back when he was warned they were closely guarded by Confederate forces. This effort he made two or three days after he issued the final *Whig*. This act showed that he was aware of the peril to himself and to his family as long as he stayed in Knoxville. He remained home briefly, then, "Mounting an old iron-gray horse" on November 4 or 5, 1861, and accompanied by an old friend and Methodist preacher, James Cumming, he set out for Blount and Sevier counties. His justification or pretext was that he intended to collect accounts owed him. Some he collected.[23] While the Parson was absent from home a new and frightening peril to the Confederacy in East Tennessee and north Alabama burst. It shattered what rapproachement, uneasy at that, that might have been building between Unionists and Secessionists.

An elaborate and daring scheme had been conceived, developed and approved during the summer and fall of 1861. The plan called for the burning of nine vital railroad bridges on the lines that connected Virginia with the central and western South. The architect of the plan was the Rev. William B. Carter. He had been educated for the Presbyterian ministry at Princeton but gave up preaching because of his health. He managed the extensive farming interests of his wealthy family in Carter County. He was a man of striking appearance. Legend puts a strain of the blood of Pocohontas in the famous Carter and Taylor families of East Tennessee. He was one of the firebrands who lined up with T. A. R. Nelson at the Greeneville Convention in the summer of 1861. Soon after the meeting Carter worked his way to the North and laid his plan before President Lincoln, Secretary of State William H. Seward and General George B. McClellan. He persuaded them of the plan's feasibility, obtained funds for the project, and received assurance of a supporting military operation. The East Tennessee preacher-farmer, who had turned saboteur, then went over his plan with Brigadier-Generals William T. Sherman and George H. Thomas in Kentucky. He then slipped back into East Tennessee to complete arrangements with his agents. He proceeded without any further communication from the two generals, and he was unaware that Sherman had decided the East Tennessee operation which was to coincide with or follow the railroad disruption was impossible. Carter's men went ahead and burned the bridges across the Holston, at what is now Bluff City, across Lick Creek near Greeneville, the Hiwassee at Charleston, and two across Chickamauga Creek near Chattanooga. An attempt to burn the bridge across the Holston at Strawberry Plains was one of four failures.[24]

The Confederate military in the area was chagrined because the efforts to restore order by conciliation had failed, and because the exploit, while not entirely unanticipated, caught officers off guard. Zollicoffer, who had been specifically directed to keep the railroads open, was not unaware of the peril. He had written Governor Beriah Magoffin of Kentucky, "For weeks I have known that the Federal commander at Hoskins' Cross-Roads in Kentucky was threatening the invasion of East Tennessee, and ruthlessly urging our people to destroy their own railroad bridges."[25] It is doubtful that the general anticipated anything on the coordinated scale that followed. When he had moved north to Cumberland Ford and was preparing to advance farther into Kentucky, he had left an inadequate force, very short on weapons, at Knoxville, "and at the various railroad bridges the unorganized Fourth East Tennessee Regiment, totally unarmed."[26] Fury and panic replaced whatever apprehension the Confederate leadership may have felt before the bridge burning. Railroad officials, fearful of further destruction, demanded help to make repairs and to provide protection from sabotage.[27] Colonel W. B. Wood, also a Methodist minister, who commanded the post at Knoxville, forwarded reports to Adjutant General S. Cooper that Union men were organized into fighting units near Strawberry Plains and in Sevier and Hamilton counties and at Watauga bridge.[28] Zollicoffer sent a regiment to Knoxville, and other Confederate forces were moved from West Tennessee, Alabama and North Carolina.[29] Colonel S. A. M. Wood, commanding the Alabama troops, reported upon arriving in Chattanooga: "All in confusion; a general panic; everybody running up and down, and adding to the general alarm," and sized up Brigadier General W. H. Carroll, commanding troops arriving from Memphis, in this tart appraisal: "He has been drunk not less than five years. He is stupid but easily controlled."[30]

Zollicoffer was completely disillusioned. He ordered Colonel Wood at Knoxville to disarm all Unionists, seize the leaders and hold them as prisoners. His bitterness at what he considered outright deceit led him to tell Wood: "The leniency shown them has been unavailing. They have acted with base duplicity, and should no longer be trusted."[31] Wood advised Confederate Secretary of War Judah Benjamin on November 20, 1861, that the rebellion had been put down in some counties and would be suppressed in the balance in two weeks. Among prisoners taken in the general roundup of Unionists was Judge David T. Patterson, Senator Johnson's son-in-law, and State Senator Samuel Pickens of Sevier County. The prisoners deserved hanging but Wood wrote:

There is such a gentle spirit of conciliation in the South, and especially here, that I have no idea that one of them will receive a sentence at the hands of any jury impaneled to try them. . . .

I have to request, at least, that the prisoners I have taken be held, if not as traitors, as prisoners of war. To release them is ruinous; to convict them before a court at this time—next to an impossibility; but if they are kept in prison for six months it will have a good effect.[32]

The East Tennessee Unionists, excited and thrilled by the bridge destruction, engaged in some mobilization in Carter, Sevier, Greene and Hamilton counties. But they were dispersed quickly by Confederate forces. The alarm spread by the reports of their organization was in excess of their significance.[33]

Parson Brownlow would have been suspected of having a hand in the plot to burn the bridges had he been in Knoxville at the time. But his absence increased the convictions of his foes, if they needed it, that he was a conspirator. He preached in Sevierville on Sunday and Wood sent a squad of soldiers from Knoxville to arrest him. A little band of Unionists—O. P. Temple, C. F. Trigg, E. J. Sanford and John Baxter—met at Baxter's home on West Main Avenue, probably at the urging of Mrs. Brownlow. They decided to send young William Rule to warn the Parson. Rule had worked for the *Whig* since 1860, and he was a native of the Knox County area through which he must pass before entering Sevier County. Rule was rowed across the river that night. Martial law had been declared in Knoxville, and he would have been required to take the Confederate oath of loyalty to have been passed by the military. He obtained a horse and galloped part of the way that night. The next day, as he rode through Sevier County, he saw hundreds of armed men. They were frequently father and son, ready with their hunting rifles and shotguns to repel any Southern soldiers attempting to arrest Brownlow or any others suspected of taking part in the bridge burning. That day Rule reached Brownlow at the home of Valentine Mattox in Wear's Cove. He told the editor that the Confederate cavalrymen were understood to have orders to shoot him in sight. Rule "found Mr. Brownlow cool, free from anything like excitement and seemingly perfectly indifferent to the threats being made against him." He also "disavowed any knowledge of the plan to burn the bridges."[34]

The cold and rugged mountains offered a refuge for men marked for arrest by the Confederates. The little party that climbed to a haven above the east fork of the Little River included "members of the legislature, preachers and planters," Brownlow wrote of his refugee companions.

As the Unionists struggled up the stream's gorge a quite different caravan set out from Knoxville to meet the rumored assaults of Sevier countians a second time against the bridge at Strawberry Plains. The bridge defenders included two hundred infantrymen, a company of cavalry, and a motley force of one hundred citizens. Among these last marched John Baxter, at whose home a few nights earlier the arrangements were made to warn Brownlow of his peril. Now, in an astonishing turnabout, Baxter marched with his double-barrelled shotgun on his shoulder, a militiaman for the Confederacy. The bridge and the mountain hiding place were thirty or forty miles apart. Home guards kept watch in a cove below the refuge, friends brought provisions for them, and one of the refugees killed a bear. Secluded as the Parson and his comrades were, their general location seemed to be known and they decided to separate into pairs. Brown-

low and the Rev. W. T. Dowell went to a house six miles from
Knoxville, and there began to negotiate with the Confederate military authorities.[35]

The events that followed produced a tangle of facts, personalities
and negotiations, interwoven with bitterness, hostility and intrigue,
through which the Parson threaded his way with a combination of
guile, craftiness and defiance. He assured Brigadier General Carroll,
by letter, that he had left Knoxville because his presence invited
insults and threats to the very door of his home. He went on to say
that his family believed his absence would lessen this torment, that
he had no part in the bridge burning and that he had kept his pledge
to Zollicoffer to "counsel peace." He declared himself "ready and
willing to stand a trial upon these or other points before any civil
tribunal; but "I protest being turned over to *any infuriated mob of
armed men* filled with prejudices by my bitterest enemies."[36]
Carroll forwarded a copy of Brownlow's letter to Benjamin and the
same day sent this message to the Parson:

Head-Quarters, Knoxville, Nov. 28, 1861.

REV. DR. BROWNLOW:—

It is my business here to afford protection to all citizens who are loyal to the
Confederate States; and I shall use all force at my command to that end. You
may be fully assured that you will meet with no personal violence by returning
to your home; and, if you can establish what you say in your letter of the 22nd
instant, *you shall have every opportunity to do so before the civil tribunal, if it
is necessary,*—PROVIDED YOU HAVE COMMITTED NO ACT THAT WILL
MAKE IT NECESSARY FOR THE MILITARY LAW TO TAKE COGNI-
ZANCE.

I desire that every loyal citizen, regardless of former political opinions, shall
be fully protected in all his rights and privileges; and to accomplish which I shall
bend all my energies, and have no doubt I shall be successful.

Respectfully,&c.,

Wm. H. Carroll
Brig.-Gen. Com[37]

The Parson prepared another letter to Carroll, dated December 4,
1861, in which he enclosed an affidavit bearing his name and that of
two Methodist ministers, James Cumming and W. T. Dowell, "that
we had no knowledge whatsoever of any purpose or plot, on the part
of any persons or party, to burn the bridges: had we been apprized
of such a movement, we should have protested against it as an out-

rage." Brownlow, who had been gone from home a month, also protested the seizure of his printing plant by Carroll for the alteration of arms. He expressed fear that the general's letter did not give him protection, for "If you mean by *loyalty* faithfulness and fidelity, I can scarcely hope for protection. I am loyal to the Government of the United States, and that is the only Government I consider as having an existence in this country." The letter was not delivered as other events intervened.[38]

Baxter, in another shift, laid aside his shotgun and took up for the Parson the role he had played in getting Nelson out of Confederate custody and into a neutral position. He was making a definite play to obtain influence at Richmond. Whatever underlying motives Baxter may have had, he produced some results in Brownlow's behalf. In November 1861 Baxter was in Richmond and obtained an interview with President Davis and Secretary of War Benjamin. He urged a more moderate policy toward the East Tennesseeans who were favoring the North. In this meeting he also grasped the opportunity to ask for a passport for Brownlow. The following day Benjamin supplied Baxter with a note to Major General George D. Crittenden at Cumberland Gap. Benjamin expressed a firm desire to get Brownlow out of the South and authorized Crittenden to issue the passport "if you are willing to let him pass."

Crittenden was willing, for when Brownlow and Baxter presented him with Benjamin's note, he authorized a pass into Kentucky for Brownlow under military escort. At this stage of the negotiations the Parson had made two grave mistakes: he obtained permission to leave Knoxville on December 7 instead of December 6, as Crittenden had suggested. This gave his enemies time, if they needed it, to get out a warrant against him. He also assumed Crittenden would insulate him against arrest by the civil authorities. How Brownlow could accept these assumptions is difficult to understand, for he had written Carroll that he was prepared to stand trial "before any civil tribunal." Carroll reiterated this line of agreement in his reply. The general wrote that if Brownlow could establish his innocence of any action against the Confederacy "you shall have every opportunity to do so before the civil tribunal if necessary." When Crittenden succeeded Carroll in command at Knoxville he told John Bell Brownlow, acting for his father, that if the Parson returned to his home "he must submit to the civil authorities." Crittenden knew that the civil officials were going to arrest the editor. In fact, he seems to have given leave to Confederate Commissioner R. B. Reynolds to issue the warrant and a pledge that he would not interfere in this procedure. If both sides were playing a cat-and-mouse game, the Parson became the mouse. Just before sundown on December 6 he was arrested on a warrant issued by Reynolds, upon the oath of Confederate Attorney J. C. Ramsey, son of the historian, and charged with treason

against the Confederate States by then and there within said district of Tennessee and since the 8th day of June last publishing a weekly and tri-weekly paper known as Brownlow's *Whig*; said paper had a large circulation in said district and also circulated in the United States and contained weekly divers of editorials written by the said Brownlow which said editorials were treasonable against the Confederate States of America, and did then and there commit treason and prompt others to commit treason; by speech as well as publication did as aforesaid commit treason and did give aid and comfort to the United States, both of said Governments being in a state of war with each other.[39]

Brownlow fired off this sharp note to Crittenden that he penned while in the custody of the marshal but apparently before he was jailed:

KNOXVILLE, December 6, 1861.

Major-General CRITTENDEN:

I am now under an arrest upon a warrant signed by Messrs. Reynolds and Ramsey upon a charge of treason founded upon sundry articles published in the Knoxville *Whig* since June last. I am here upon your invitation and promise of passports; and claiming your protection as I do, I shall await your early response.

Very respectfully,

W. G. BROWNLOW

The following day an aide to the general replied that "in view of all the facts of the case . . . he [Crittenden] does not consider that you are here upon his invitation in such manner as to claim his protection from an investigation by the civil authorities of the charges against you which he clearly understood from yourself and your friends you would not seek to avoid."[40]

When jail doors closed behind the Parson, he must have regretted his sweeping assurance, given while free, that he had no dread of civil prosecution. For now, as a prisoner and subjected to these authorities the prospect was gloomy indeed. It was made even more grim when he was denied $100,000 bail proffered by his friend Temple.[41] Ramsey supplied an account of the background and arrest to Benjamin. It suggests that an important aspect of the motive in jailing Brownlow was to appease the clamor from Southerners, soldiers and civilians, not only for punishment but to prevent his being sent North. Demands expressing these sentiments were sent to President Davis by Dr. J. G. M. Ramsey, and by Confederate Congressmen Swan and William H. Tibbs. Prosecutor Ramsey indicated that he had limited proof. But he argued that the case deserved investigation and he submitted as his best thought that the military should have sent the Parson to a military prison, where hundreds of other Unionists had been confined. Brownlow, in his account of the arrest, accused Ramsey of having relied upon a *Whig* editorial of May 25, 1861. Brownlow had printed it before Tennessee voted to secede. The editorial could not have constituted treason against either the state or the Confederacy, because on that date Tennessee was a part of the United States.[42]

That editorial had reported a conspiracy was under way for the arrest, after the June election, of Johnson, Baxter, Temple, Trigg, Nelson, Maynard and George W. Bridges. The last three were elected to the United States Congress. These men, the editorial predicted, would be taken to Montgomery, Alabama,

and either punished for *Treason*, or held as hostages, to guarantee the quiet surrender of the Union men of East Tennessee! The thousands of Union men of East Tennessee, devoted to the principle, and to the right and privileges of those who fall unto the hands of these conspirators, will be expected to avenge their wrongs! Let the Railroad on which citizens of Tennessee are conveyed to Montgomery in irons, be eternally and hopelessly destroyed.

Confederate officials read into Brownlow's broad suggestion a link to the bridge burning. They overlooked several other forms of reprisal he had suggested. Had Ramsey known then what was printed in one of Temple's books thirty-eight years later he would have had a damaging bit of circumstantial evidence. The Sevier County men who had attempted to burn the Strawberry Plains bridge, and failed because their matches had been misplaced or lost, fled to a refuge in the Great Smoky Mountains. They selected the same gorge to which Brownlow and other refugees repaired. The inaccessability of the retreat probably attracted both groups, but the fact that they had joined would have given Ramsey's case more substance. Brownlow surely realized this and was motivated by it to leave and take his chances with officialdom.[43]

Brownlow's biographer wrote that "he was no bridge-burner." Neither was he the first to mention railroad destruction. Nelson had suggested it several weeks earlier. The *Register* had chided him for this at the time of the Strawberry Plains encounter between Unionist civilians and Confederate soldiers on a troop train.[44] Nelson had been silenced. Brownlow remained a roaring nuisance, for when he galloped into the mountains the search emphasized his importance as an enemy of the South and as a living, vociferous symbol for the Unionists. While Southerners in East Tennessee wanted Brownlow punished, Secretary Benjamin in Richmond preferred to have him removed to the North. Benjamin expressed this view at the beginning of correspondence with Confederate military officials at Knoxville and confirmed it when he reviewed the facts.

This difference of opinion helped the Parson in overcoming to some extent the blunder he had made in declaring himself ready to submit to civil prosecution. The editor's enemies, eager for his punishment, pounced on this opening with the warrant for his arrest. In turn, the arrest left Benjamin aghast. In his note sent by Baxter to Crittenden he took no cognizance of civil prosecution, in fact, had not anticipated such a development. When Crittenden replaced Carroll at Knoxville he inherited a complex situation, Carroll's correspondence with Brownlow and Benjamin's note. Had Crittenden been more familiar with the Knoxville background he might have steered a less inflammatory course. As it was, he followed Benjamin's direction and notified Brownlow he could have a passport. But at the same time he knew civil officials were planning to arrest the editor, and interposed no objection. The chagrined Benjamin called upon Ramsey for an account of the circumstances leading to Brownlow's arrest, and then sharply demanded his release by civil authorities.[45] While Benjamin was reviewing Ramsey's report, the Parson demonstrated that the walls and bars of the Knoxville jail had not rendered him inarticulate. He fired off this trenchant, biting note:

Knoxville Jail, Dec. 16, 1861

Hon J. P. Benjamin

You authorized Gen. Crittenden to give me pasports [*sic.*], and an escort to send me into the old Government, and he invited me here for that purpose. But a third rate County Court Lawyer, acting as your Confederate Attorney, took me out of his hands and cast me into this prison. I am anxious to learn which is your highest authority, the Secretary of War, a Major General, or a dirty little drunken Attorney, such as *J. C. Ramsey* is!

You are reported to have said to a gentleman in Richmond that, I am a bad man, dangerous to the Confederacy, and that you desire me out of it. Just give me my pasports [*sic*.], and I will do for your Confederacy, more than the Devil has ever done, I will quit the country!

I am, etc,

W. G. Brownlow [46]

Benjamin's letter to Ramsey did not mention Brownlow's cutting message. He concerned himself entirely with getting his government out of a possible implication of breach of faith with the Parson. The secretary had acted upon Baxter's representation that Brownlow was safely concealed from Confederate officials, but was willing to surrender upon promise of safe delivery to the North. The other side of the picture, Benjamin wrote, was:

If Brownlow had been in our hands we might not have accepted the proposition but deeming it better to have him as an open enemy on the other side of the line than a secret enemy within the lines authority was given to General Crittenden to assure him of protection across the border if he came to Knoxville.

It was not in our power nor that of anyone else to prevent his being taken by process of law. . . . This has been done, however, and it is only regretted in one point of view—that is, color is given to the suspicion that Brownlow has been entrapped and has given himself up under promise of protection which has not been firmly kept. . . .Better that even the most dangerous enemy, however criminal, should escape than that the honor and good faith of the Government should be impugned or even suspected. [47]

Benjamin's sensitiveness on the subject of Brownlow's arrest did not extend to the bridge burners. He demanded that they be caught, hanged and their cadavers left suspended near the railroads so that passengers might see and profit. Brownlow was told, while in jail at Knoxville, that the bodies of Jacob M. Hensie and Henry Fry were left where train passengers could, and did, strike them with their canes. He vowed, as he wrote in his prison diary, that he would have an illustration drawn of this brutal scene. It appeared later, that while the bodies were in view of passengers passing through Greeneville, they were too distant for blows. Three others were hanged at Knoxville, C. A. Haun and a father and son, Jacob and Henry Harmon. [48]

Hanging those found guilty by drumhead court-martial did not satisfy Benjamin's zeal for punishment. He ordered the following steps to be taken against the men still held as traitors, but who could not be proved to have been bridge burners:

All such as have not been so engaged as bridge burners are to be treated as prisoners of war and sent with an armed guard to Tuscaloosa, Ala., there to be kept imprisoned at the depot selected by the Government for prisoners of war. Wherever you can discover that arms are concealed by these traitors you will send out detachments, search for and seize the arms. In no case is one of the men known to have been up in arms against the Government to be released on any pledge or oath of allegiance. The time for such measures is past. They are all to be held as prisoners of war and held in jail until the end of the war.[49]

The Confederacy had placed Colonel Danville Leadbetter in charge of protecting the railroads of East Tennessee. He went at his task with ferocious zeal. Leadbetter, a Maine native, was educated at the United States Military Academy at West Point, but had turned militantly Southern after marrying "a refined lady of the South." When Fry and Hensie were hanged at Greeneville, he wrote, "The execution of the bridge-burners is producing the happiest effect." He pursued Unionists with such relentlessness that farmhouses were emptied of males, while "The women in some cases were greatly alarmed throwing themselves on the ground and wailing like savages. Indeed the population is savage." He ordered the horses of Union men and provisions to be impressed with payment only to those who became loyal to the South. This course was to be followed "until quiet shall be restored to these distracted counties, and they can rely upon it that no prisoner will be pardoned as long as Union men remain in arms." The colonel concluded that the people generally were being treated "with great kindness."

Benjamin's policies were sending a stream of prisoners to Knoxville and beyond. Brigadier General Carroll reported on December 11, 1861, that a total of 150 prisoners remained at Knoxville after forty-eight had been sent to Tuscaloosa. When Colonel Leadbetter arrived and took command in Knoxville on January 7, 1862, he found 130 prisoners, with the number increasing. He coped with this situation by dissolving the court-martial, applying his harsh Greeneville policies and asking for more prisoners to be accepted at Tuscaloosa. Benjamin, on November 30, 1861, directed the military at Knoxville to ignore writs of habeas corpus issued by the civil courts. Meanwhile Confederate Attorney Ramsey, on November 25, 1861, plaintively inquired why he wasn't getting any of the action in the prosecution of the bridge-burners. The secretary, plainly unimpressed with the attorney, snapped back with: "I am very glad to hear of the action of the military authorities and hope to hear they have hung [*sic.*] every bridge-burner at the end of the burned bridge."[50]

Lawyer Temple watched with alarm and mystification "long lines of wasted Union men, many of them three score and ten years of age, and some only mere boys, being driven through our streets on their way to the cars which were to carry them to Tuscaloosa." Brownlow, in the jail less than a block from Temple's office, also watched. His fears and gnawing bitterness were fed by the sights he saw and the news filtering into the jail from the lips of prisoners constantly being thrown into its stench and filth. In Powell Valley cavalry captured between 400 and 500 young men from Jefferson County who were fleeing north to escape conscription by the Confederacy. The soldiers marched them to the jail at Knoxville and then took them by rail to prison. "They were driven across the creeks and past the springs without being allowed to drink, on their long and hurried march of nearly fifty miles, then confined all night without food and drink," until they resorted to lapping water from puddles, the Parson wrote a short time later.[51]

Ramsey dismissed the civil charge against Brownlow, at Benjamin's insistence, but this failed to bring freedom to the Parson. Captain G. H. Monsarrat, commanding the Knoxville post, sent him back to jail as a necessary measure "for his own safety and in order that the public peace might not be violated. I infer from your letter to the district attorney that Brownlow is entitled to a safe-conduct beyond our lines and with reference to this I await your further instructions. It was two months before the Confederate bureaucracy ground out the order by Benjamin to escort the Parson to the North.[52] The secretary was running the South's war machine and nettlesome as Brownlow was he had other decisions to make.

According to a number of sources [*see* 53], the harsh policies and the reprisals that followed the bridge burnings intensified the anguish and suffering of the Unionists. "It is a fact which no one could dispute that a heritage of hatred for the Confederate element was burned into the hearts of the East Tennesseans, a heritage which Parson Brownlow was to capitalize to the fullest extent," his modern biographer has concluded. It has been estimated that from 2,000 to 3,000 "non-combatant, unarmed Union people in thirty-one counties" were shot, hanged or slaughtered "in cold blood," in addition to the "despoilment of personal property." A Unionist who remained in Knoxville during the war, thus described the repressive steps taken after the bridge burnings:

In the whole history of the war nothing can be found so blind, so infatuated, so absolutely devoid of wisdom and statesmanship, as the conduct of those who dictated the policy of the Confederate authorities toward the Union people of East Tennessee. . . .But madness ruled the hour. Folly held its high carnival. Personal and political animosity were in the saddle. . . . And all this was done under the advice of home leaders. It was not the work of Mr. President Davis, nor the Confederate authorities.

Inside the jail where Brownlow found 150 inmates, the fears and uncertainties of the imprisoned men were intensified by the wretched conditions in which they were forced to exist. So crowded were the quarters that men had to take turns sleeping and standing. The space would not accommodate, stretched out or huddled, all of the prisoners. Two tubs, sawed from one barrel, were the only toilet facilities and these often overflowed. Water was brought in by a bucket dipped in a hogshead in which the guards washed their hands and faces. Water carriers for the prison were required to dip from the river at a point downstream from a Confederate army abbatoir. The slaughterers, who processed pork for the soldiers dumped offal and refuse into the stream. The room on the second floor where Brownlow was held was about ten feet square and contained no item of furniture until the brigade surgeon, who drew the Parson's commendation, obtained rude benches and tables. The jail food was wretched but Brownlow ate well. One of his sons brought him meals from his home. He shared the food with the ill and the elderly, among whom were two Baptist preachers, both more than seventy years old. One had prayed from his pulpit for the President of the United States; the other had cheered as men on horseback bearing the Stars and Stripes had passed his home. The Parson attributed the Confederate decision to let ample food supplies to be sent from his home to a hope that it would save the South expense, and that the inmates who shared the editor's basket would "eat him out of house and home." Soldiers jailed for drunkeness were tossed into the room with the political prisoners. This created uproars, and guards sometimes taunted the Unionists by "accidentally" firing into the room. The Parson's old foe, bronchitis, beset him.[53]

Fear gripped the prisoners constantly for they had no intimation of the fate awaiting them. Three times the death cart, carrying upon it the coffins for the convicted bridge-burners, rolled to the jail door. The victims were called out for their ride to the gallows, sometimes with brief warnings of their fate. Jacob Harmon went through the torture of seeing his son, Thomas, hanged before he was taken to the gallows, on December 17, 1861. Others were marched away to die in Confederate prisons, or as a result of their imprisonment. Among those imprisoned was Dr. William Hunt, who had married Mrs. Brownlow's only sister. Few were tried. Some Confederate citizens and officers protested vainly against this vicious policy.[54]

Brownlow concluded he would be hanged and prepared a gallows speech for such a development. If the Parson's expectation was born of a hallucination, as his biographer suggests, his mental disorder was on target with the facts. On the outside his bitterest foes met in Ramsey's office and discussed three ways to dispose of him: outright hanging, release him to Confederate soldiers who would kill him, or imprisonment in some state farther south. Joe Mabry, a Secessionist but Brownlow's friend, who had helped talk down the Gay Street confrontation between Monroe County troops and Unionists earlier in 1861, sat in on these meetings. He objected to the designs against the Parson and in court testimony later revealed the plot. The conspirators included Ramsey and Reynolds, both civil officials, and Crozier and Sneed, both men of wealth and influence in the Confederacy. Intent was there if success did not follow. Perhaps these enemies of the Parson were, as he charged, behind the incitement of a mob threatening to lynch him early in 1862 after he had been removed from the jail to his home because of his health. W. A. Camp, who as a major in the Confederate army had charge of the guard around Brownlow's home while the editor was under house arrest, deposed in a suit brought against Mabry in Knox County Circuit Court after the war, that Mississippi troops threatened to mob and hang the Parson. Camp kept a guard of one hundred men convenient to the residence, while Mabry, mounted on his horse, mixed with the mob for more than an hour until it subsided. Mabry also urged a railroad official to move the Mississippians out of town as rapidly as possible. The Parson also charged that he came within one vote of being sentenced to death by a drumhead court-martial, but no corroborative evidence has been found. [55]

While the Parson's foes on the outside schemed to take his life, he played a role in saving from the gallows Harrison Self, who was convicted of participation in the burning of the Lick Creek bridge in

Greene County. The day set for the execution, December 27, 1861, authorities permitted Elizabeth Self to see her father. Brownlow and the other prisoners wept as they watched the farewell embrace. At the daughter's request Brownlow wrote for her a pleading telegram to President Davis. Two hours before the time set for the execution Davis wired a commutation of the death sentence. Whatever part his daughter's plea played in this extension of mercy remains uncertain. The members of the court-martial who had found Self guilty had unanimously recommended clemency. A. T. Bledsoe, chief of the Bureau of War at Richmond, who reviewed the testimony, decided that Self should not be hanged. Brownlow's telegram probably got most of the credit for the commutation, which followed quickly upon the heels of the wire. The Parson told what he had done in *Parson Brownlow's Book*. He did not mention the plea for clemency made by members of the court-martial; perhaps he did not know of it. Temple, however, writing many years later, reported the merciful position taken by the officers who heard the testimony, and by twenty-five other persons, private citizens and members of the armed forces, but "All proved unavailing," until the daughter's message. Brownlow owed Self a favor. A few hours earlier the doomed man had refused to purchase his life by making a statement that he had been instigated and paid to engage in the bridge burning by Brownlow, Trigg, Baxter and Temple.[56]

Imprisonment broke the Parson's health to the point where, upon advice of his personal physician, authorities removed him to his home under guard. But nothing daunted his spirit. He seemed to thrive upon defiance, whether he was in jail or under house arrest, for he even contemplated an attempt to escape. His course differed from that of his friend Nelson. The latter had resorted to his expertise as a lawyer to avoid prison and prepared a statement, reflecting great ingenuity, cunning and skill, something resembling the plea of *nolo contendere*. Without acknowledging guilt he pledged to offer no resistance to the Confederacy, a device that got him his liberty but at the price of silence. Brownlow never was silenced. He rejected the proposal of General Carroll to obtain his freedom by pledging allegiance to the Confederacy with the assertion, "I would lie here until I died with old age before I would take such an oath." Carroll's suggestion was made on December 14, 1861, and an accompanying incident must have cut the Parson deeply. It was the harsh comment of John Baxter, his lawyer and a man he believed to be his friend. When Brownlow refused to take Carroll's offer Baxter snapped:

"Damn him, let him lie there."[57] Baxter's angry burst may have been born of his exasperation at his client's refusal to accept the arrangement. Baxter may have worked hard to persuade Confederate officials to agree to the deal, and for the Parson to have rejected it must have offended his pragmatic mind. Or, Baxter may have believed he could achieve favor with the Confederates by this reproach to the Parson. He also acted upon impulse. What the impulse was we cannot be certain.

The relationships of the men had been close, even intricate. While Baxter was in Richmond, and probably currying favor with the authorities there, he obtained Benjamin's approval for a passport. The day before Carroll wrote to Benjamin that he had seized Brownlow's printing plant for the use of the Confederacy the Parson conveyed the entire property, real estate, building, engine presses, print shop equipment and furniture, to Baxter. The contract (it was not described as a deed) was recorded on November 26, 1861. Baxter paid Brownlow $5,000 "in currency bankable at Knoxville." Out of this Baxter was to pay $1,200 plus interest on a note held by Phillip Shetterly against the property. Baxter also was security on the note.[58]

As a going concern the *Whig* property was worth much more than $5,000, but since publication had been suspended and the military had seized the entire property its value was greatly diminished.

Captain Monsarrat, commander of the Knoxville post, issued the order to remove Brownlow from the jail to his home at the close of 1861. His action drew the Parson's commendation. The former editor's physical surroundings were now much more comfortable but he was irritated by his guards. He charged that they were rude, demanding, insolent and destructive of household furniture. Colonel Robert Vance, Monsarrat's successor, gave the Parson and his household some relief and Brownlow dubbed him "a gentleman of character." The Parson was ready to travel north on February 27, 1862. But he was doubly apprehensive when Captain Monsarrat, again in charge, told him that Brigadier General John H. Winder, in charge of the defense of Richmond, had called for the Parson to be delivered to him. Brownlow protested to Benjamin on February 27 that he wanted to go out by way of the Cumberland Mountains. The secretary granted the request and added "or any safe road." On March 3 Monsarrat sent the Parson on the way to Nashville. Joe Mabry showed up again. Brownlow credited him with having exerted his influence to get railroad routing in the direction of Nashville. Brownlow was treated with such deference that he was permitted to select the officers in charge of ten soldiers to escort him. He chose Colonel Casey H. Young, who had protested against the harsh treatment of East Tennessee Unionists, and Lieutenant John W. O'Brien, a cousin of Mrs. Brownlow's. The Parson's sons, John Bell and James Patton, and Samuel H. Rodgers, a lawyer friend made up the civilians in the party.[59] Deference gave way to antagonism along the route. Confederate soldiers on furlough attempted to rush the passenger car in which the Brownlow party was traveling, and military commanders created delays until it was March 15, 1862, before the group entered the federal lines. At the sight of swarming blue uniforms, Rodgers recalled, the Parson's wrinkles seemed to disappear and he exclaimed: "Glory to God in the highest, and on earth peace, good will toward all men, except a few hell-born and hell-bound rebels in Knoxville."

The former refugee from Confederate wrath, who had endured the horrors and hardships of the Knoxville jail and feared the possibility that he would be hanged, now moved swiftly into another world. There he met warm and welcoming handshakes, unstinted admiration, cordiality and the polite and deferential reception of General D. C. Buell, commander of "ninety thousand men here, and more arriving every day." A lady sent a bouquet to his hotel room and pressed by officers and civilians he made a speech, despite the soreness of his throat.

Generals Ulysses S. Grant and William T. Sherman, moving relentlessly south, had transformed Nashville, reluctant as most of its citizens were to be under Union domination. Governor Harris and the members of the legislature had fled in haste. When the House adjourned *sine die*, in Memphis, the maker of the motion must have been cackling with delight inwardly. He was Dr. R. H. Hodsden, the redoubtable old Unionist from Sevier County, who had warned Temple and Brownlow that indictments were being prepared against them in Nashville, and who in turn was arrested but was released on orders from Judge Humphreys.[60]

Old friends greeted Brownlow, among them Horace Maynard, Emerson Ethridge and Connally F. Trigg. So did an old and bitter enemy, Andrew Johnson, now military governor of Tennessee. The exiled editor and the governor, who for a quarter of a century had dredged the language for invectives to hurl against each other, now found themselves, by the fortunes and exigencies of war, comrades. They met and embraced, physically and politically. A chronicler of the times has written that they "wept like women,"[16] If they shed tears upon each other's necks it watered their friendship for only a few years.

CHAPTER NOTES

[1] *Whig*, August 10, 17, 1861; *Register*, August 3, 1861; Humes, *The Loyal Mountaineers*, pp. 122-123; O. R., I, 4, pp. 374-375.

[2] *Ibid.*, pp. 364-366, 372-376. The great exodus of Union men from East Tennessee began early in August 1861. Temple, *East Tennessee and the Civil War*, p. 368.

[3] *Ibid.*, p. 357.

[4] *Whig*, August 17, 24, 1861; Alexander, *T. A. R. Nelson*, p. 92.

[5] *Ibid.*, pp. 90-93; *Whig*, August 24, 1861.

[6] *Register*, August 23, 1861.

[7] *Whig*, August 17, 24; Alexander, *T. A. R. Nelson*, pp. 90-91.

[8] *Whig*, August 24, September 21, 1861.

[9] *Ibid.*, August 24, 1861; *Register*, August 23, 1861.

[10] *Whig*, July 13, 17; Barry A. Crouch, "The Merchant and the Senator: an Attempt to Save East Tennessee for the Union," ETHS *PUBL.*, No. 46, pp. 53-72, hereafter referred to as Crouch; *Whig*, July 13, 27, 1861; *Parson Brownlow's Book*, pp. 122-133; Humes, *The Loyal Mountaineers*, pp. 129-131.

[11] *Whig*, June 28, 1865, March 13, 1867. Charlton resigned as United States postmaster in March, *Register*, March 7, 1861.

[12] *Whig*, August 24, September 7, 1861; *Register*, August 23, 1861.

[13] *Whig*, May 11, 1861; *Register*, May 20, 1862; Price, *Holston Methodism*, III, pp. 323-324; *Whig*, May 15, 1867.

[14] Temple, *Notable Men*, p. 203.

[15] *Whig*, September 7, 14, 1861.

[16] *Ibid.*, September 14, 1861, quoting Nashville *Banner of Peace*; *Whig*, August 24, 1861, May 15, 1867, September 21, July 31, August 24, September 28, 1861.

[17] *Ibid.*, September 28, October 10, 1861; Temple, *Notable Men*, p. 71; White, *Messages*, V, p. 356.

[18] *Whig*, September 28, October 12, 1861; *Parson Brownlow's Book*, pp. 135-36, illustration opposite p. 144.

[19] *Whig*, August 3, September 7, 1861.

[20] *Ibid.*, October 19, 1861, O. R.., 1, IV, pp. 511-512.

[21] R. H. Hodsden to Temple, October 23, 1861. Temple Papers. Temple, *East Tennessee and the Civil War*, p. 369; *Whig*, October 26, 1861.

[22] *Ibid.* See also Temple, *Notable Men*, pp. 305-308; *Parson Brownlow's Book*, pp. 249-255.

[23] *Ibid.*, p. 415; Temple, *Notable Men*, 305, 308-309; *Parson Brownlow's Book*, pp. 280, 416.

[24] Accounts of Carter's background, his trips to Washington, into Kentucky and into East Tennessee for the purpose of carrying out the bridge burning are found in Temple, *East Tennessee and the Civil War*, pp. 370-385; Temple, *Notable Men*, pp. 88-93, 309-310; *O. R..*, I, 4, p. 284, Adjutant General L. Thomas to Brigadier General W. T. Sherman, with enclosure, October 10, 1861, pp. 299-300; Brigadier General O. M. Mitchel to Brigadier General George H. Thomas, October 10, 1861, pp. 301-302; Sherman to George H. Thomas, October 12, 1861, pp. 305-306; L. Thomas to Secretary of War Simon Cameron, October 21, 1861, pp. 313-314; W. B. Carter to George H. Thomas, October 22, 1861, p. 317, October 27, 1861, p. 320; George H. Thomas to Brigadier General A. Schoepf, October 29, 1861, p. 323; Sherman to George H. Thomas, October 31, 1861, pp. 324-325; George H. Thomas to Sherman, November 5, 1861, pp. 338-339; Major General George B. McClellan to Brigadier D. C. Buell, November 7, 1861, p. 342; Sherman to George H. Thomas, November 12, 1861; pp. 353-354.

[25] *Ibid.*, Zollicoffer to Governor Magoffin, September 14, 1861, p. 195; *ibid.*, II, 1, Landon C. Haynes to Confederate Secretary of War L. P. Walker, July 6, 1861, p. 824.

[26] *Ibid.*, I, 4, Zollicoffer to Lieutenant Colonel Mackall, assistant adjutant general, Nashville, September 28, 1861, pp. 424-425.

[27] *Ibid.*, John R. Branner, president of the East Tennessee and Virginia Railroad, to Secretary of War Benjamin, November 9, 1861, p. 231; RO [*sic.*] L. Owen, president of the Virginia and Tennessee Railroad, to Benjamin, November 11, 1861, pp. 235-236; J. W. Lewis, superintendent of the East Tennessee and Virginia Railroad, to President Jefferson Davis, November 11, 1861, p. 235; Colonel W. B. Wood to Adjutant General S. Cooper, November 11, 1861, p. 236.

[28] *Ibid.*, Wood to Cooper, November 11, 1861, pp. 236-237; Branner to Benjamin, November 13, 1861, p. 243; Zollicoffer to Cooper, November 14, 1861, p. 243; Temple, *East Tennessee and the Civil War*, pp. 388-389; *Parson Brownlow's Book*, p. 259.

[29] *Ibid.*, pp. 259-260; *O. R..*, I, 4, pp. 240-241, 559.

[30] *Ibid.*, Major General Braxton Bragg to Benjamin, November 17, 1861, enclosure Colonel S. A. M. Wood, commanding Seventh Regiment Alabama Volunteers, to Bragg, November 17, 1861, pp. 248-250. Carroll was the son of William Carroll who had enjoyed a distinguished military and political career, serving six years as governor. Temple, *East Tennessee and the Civil War*, p. 396; Folmsbee *et al.*, *Short History*, pp. 138-139, 142, 163-164, 184-185. The son had a reputation for being dissolute. Humes, *The Loyal Mountaineers*, p. 147; *Parson Brownlow's Book*, pp. 304-305.

[31] *O. R.*, I, 4, Zollicoffer to Wood, November 12, 1861, p. 242; Temple, *East Tennessee and the Civil War*, p. 390; *Parson Brownlow's Book*, pp. 261-262.

[32] *O. R.*, I, 4, Wood to Benjamin, November 20, 1861, pp. 250-251.

[33] Temple, *East Tennessee and the Civil War*, pp. 385-387. A Union company was organized in Greene County prior to the bridge burning. T. H. Reeve to Rule, February 5, 1887. Rule Papers.

[34] Sketches by William Rule, Rule Papers. Temple, *Notable Men*, p. 310; *Parson Brownlow's Book*, pp. 280-281; *O. R.*, I, 4, Wood to S. Cooper, November 11, 1861, pp. 236-237.

[35] *Parson Brownlow's Book*, p. 281; Temple, *Notable Men*, p. 72; *Whig*, August 29, 1866, May 15, 1867. Baxter's changing role is mystifying unless it is accepted that he was a brazen opportunist. He was a militant Unionist; he helped extricate Nelson from Confederate custody; he marched like a zealous Confederate to the Strawberry Plains bridge after the false report Unionists were preparing to attack it again, and then appears as Brownlow's friend and attorney, getting Brownlow a passport to the North. In the Reconstruction period when Brownlow was governor he lashed Baxter with some of the harshest charges he made in his career. He accused Baxter of trying to ingratiate himself with the Confederate government, trying to get a commission as a brigadier general and giving Confederate Senator Louis T. Wigfall of Texas a $300 saddle horse. Baxter published one issue of a Knoxville newspaper supporting the South, he entered into a law partnership with Confederate Senator Landon C. Haynes, and the Parson said that correspondence found in Haynes' office when Federal troops took over Knoxville revealed that Baxter had proposed to bribe northern newspapers to favor the Confederacy, if given $500,000 for the purpose. See later chapters for details.

[36] The letter to Carroll is from *Parson Brownlow's Book*, pp. 282-283. Slightly longer is the same letter in *O. R.*, II, i, pp. 902-903. Variations frequently appear between the communications in *Parson Brownlow's Book* and *Official Records*, which may be attributed to the extreme haste with which the Parson wrote, or from lack of copies, the author relying on his memory. Punctuation in *Official Records* also is sparse compared with the Parson's generous use of it.

[37] *Parson Brownlow's Book*, p. 284; *O. R.*, II, 1, pp. 903-904.

[38] *Parson Brownlow's Book*, pp. 284-286, 288; *O. R.*, II, 1, Carroll to Benjamin, November 26, 1861, p. 903. The affidavit, but not the letter, appears in *ibid.*, p. 905.

[39] *Ibid.*, II, 1, Baxter to Benjamin, November 30, 1861, p. 904; *ibid.*, enclosure A, Benjamin to Crittenden, November 20, 1861, pp. 921-922. There is an error here because it is out of the question for Benjamin to have written to Crittenden authorizing a passport for Brownlow ten days before Davis and Benjamin met with Baxter. *Ibid.*, Crittenden to Benjamin, December 13, 1861, pp. 908-909; *Parson Brownlow's Book*, pp. 294-296. See also *O. R.*, II, 1, warrant against Brownlow, p. 922.

[40] *O. R.*, II, 1, Brownlow to Crittenden, December 6, 1861, p. 922; *ibid.*, Harry I. Thornton, Aide-de-Camp, to Brownlow, December 7, 1861, p. 923. The items cited are enclosures D and E in *ibid.*, Brownlow to President Davis, without date but marked "Entered 'Received January 2, 1862,' " pp. 919-923.

[41] *Parson Brownlow's Book*, p. 296; Temple, *Notable Men*, p. 313.

[42] *O. R.*, II, 1, Ramsey to Benjamin, December 7, 1861, pp. 907-908; *ibid.*, Swan to Davis, J. G. M. Ramsey and William H. Tibbs to Davis, December 7, 1861, pp. 905-907; *Parson Brownlow's Book*, pp. 298-299.

[43] Temple, *East Tennessee and the Civil War*, pp. 382-384.

[44] Coulter, p. 169; Alexander, *T. A. R. Nelson*, p. 77; *Whig*, June 15, 1861, quoting *Register*.

[45] *O. R.*, II, 1, Benjamin to Ramsey, December 22, 1861, pp. 916-917.

[46] A reproduction of the letter is in *Parson Brownlow's Book*, between pp. 318-319. A slightly different version is on p. 318; also with more correction in *O. R.*, II, 1, p. 910.

[47] *Ibid.*, Benjamin to Ramsey, December 22, 1861, pp. 916-917.

[48] *Ibid.*, Benjamin to Wood, November 25, 1861, p. 848; *Parson Brownlow's Book*, pp. 269-270 (picture between pp. 301-302); Temple, *East Tennessee and the Civil War*, pp. 393-394, 399.

[49] *O. R.*, II, 1, Benjamin to Wood, November 25, 1861, p. 848.

]50] *Ibid.*, Jno. Withers, assistant adjutant general, Special Orders, No. 216, November 11, 1861, p. 841; Temple, *East Tennessee and the Civil War*, p. 394; *Parson Brownlow's Book*, pp. 420-421; *O. R.*, II, 1, Leadbetter to General S. Cooper, November 28, 1861, p. 849, Leadbetter to Benjamin, November 30, 1861, p. 851, Leadbetter to "The Citizens of East Tennessee," proclamation, November 30, 1861, pp. 851-852, Leadbetter to S. Cooper, December 8, 1861, pp. 852-853, Carroll to Benjamin, December 11, 1861, pp. 854-855, Leadbetter to S. Cooper, January 7, 1862, p. 869, Benjamin to Captain R. F. Looney, November 30, 1861, p. 851, Ramsey to Benjamin, November 25, 1861, p. 848, Benjamin to Ramsey, November 25, 1861, p. 849.

[51] Temple, *East Tennessee and the Civil War*, p. 392; *Parson Brownlow's Book*, pp. 309-321; Temple, *East Tennessee and the Civil War*, pp. 424-425; *Parson Brownlow's Book*, p. 453. For additional accounts of the Parson's experiences and the persecution of Unionists see *Whig*, March 5, 1864, January 9, September 13, December 27, 1865, February 7, August 1, December 19, 1866, April 1, July 15, 1868.

[52] *O. R.*, II, 1, Monsarrat, approved by Leadbetter, to Benjamin, December 27, 1861, p. 917, Monsarrat to Benjamin, December 29, 1861, p. 919, Benjamin to Monsarrat, March 1, 1862, p. 928.

[53] Coulter, pp. 174-175; Humes, *The Loyal Mountaineers*, p. 307, appendix, p. 392; Temple, *East Tennessee and the Civil War*, pp. 421-422; *Parson Brownlow's Book*, pp. 305-307, 417-422; *Whig*, September 13, 1865; Temple *Notable Men*, p. 313; the Parson's testimony before Congressional Investigating Committee, *O. R.*, I, 16, pt. 1, p. 674; *Parson Brownlow's Book*, pp. 305-307, 325, 418; *Whig*, February 7, 1866; *Parson Brownlow's Book*, pp. 325-326, 321, 320.

[54] *Ibid.*, pp. 312-313, 319; Temple, *East Tennessee and the Civil War*, pp. 392-396; *O. R.*, II, 1, Carroll to Benjamin, December 11, 1861, p. 854; *Parson Brownlow's Book*, pp. 313-314, 317; Temple, *East Tennessee and the Civil War*, pp. 404-408, 413-420; *O. R.*, II, 1, J. J. Craig to Benjamin,

January 3, 1861, pp. 923-924, H. C. Young to D. M. Currin, December 19, 1861, pp. 857-858, Robertson Topp to Robert Josselyn, Esq., October 26, 1861, p. 834, H. R. Austin to President Davis, marked "Received War Department, December 28, 1861", p. 869.

[55] *Parson Brownlow's Book*, pp. 330-337; Coulter, p. 192; *Whig*, February 7, November 7, 1866, September 25, 1867. Temple believed Brownlow was marked for assassination. *Notable Men*, p. 308; *Whig*, February 7, 1866.

[56] *Parson Brownlow's Book*, pp. 326-328; Temple, *East Tennessee and the Civil War*, pp. 397-398, O. R., II, 1, account of Self's trial, pp. 858-859; *Whig*, February 7, 1866.

[57] *Parson Brownlow's Book*, pp. 337-338; Temple, *Notable Men*, p. 314; *Whig*, May 15, 1867.

[58] W. G. Brownlow (by attorney) to John Baxter, *Knox County Deed Book*, A3, p. 171; Green, *Bench and Bar*, pp. 58-59.

[59] *Parson Brownlow's Book*, pp. 337-338; O. R., II, 1, Brownlow to Vance, February 15, 1862, pp. 926-928; *Parson Brownlow's Book*, p. 361; O. R., II, 1, Brownlow to Benjamin, February 27, 1862, p. 928; *Parson Brownlow's Book*, pp. 367-368; O. R., II, 1, Benjamin to Monsarrat, March 1, 1862, p. 928, Monsarrat to Benjamin, March 3, 1862, p. 928; *Whig*, May 15, 1867; *Parson Brownlow's Book*, pp. 370-371; Temple, *Notable Men*, pp. 314-315; *Whig*, February 7, 1866. See Young's appeal for kinder treatment of East Tennesseans, O. R., II, 1, pp. 857-858; Temple, *East Tennessee and the Civil War*, p. 414.

[60] *Parson Brownlow's Book*, pp. 371-377, 380; Temple, *Notable Men*, pp. 315-316; *Parson Brownlow's Book*, pp. 380-393; Folmsbee *et al.*, *Short History*, pp. 331-333; White, *Messages*, V, p. 372; *House Journal, Thirty-Fourth General Assembly*, comp., *Tennessee Historical Commission* (Nashville, 1957), p. 479.

[61] Temple, *Notable Men*, p. 316; *Parson Brownlow's Book*, pp. 381-384.

"The union of lakes—the union of lands—The union of   Chapter No. 15
states none can sever—The union of hearts—the union of
hands—And the flag of the Union forever."

THE PROFITS OF EXILE

Exhilaration and excitement surrounded the Parson from the moment the surprised and admiring Union soldiers greeted him five miles south of Nashville. He reveled in the company of old friends and responded as well as his shattered voice would permit to the clamors for speeches. He was warmed by the officers who pressed to meet him, he was flattered by an interview with Major General Don Carlos Buell, whose troops were pouring south from Nashville, and he basked in the serenades from regimental bands. Amidst this adulation and freedom the Parson's store of indignation swelled. He trained a fiery batch of it on preachers who cast their lot with the South, especially if they were Methodists. Yet, he was deeply comforted to learn that Bishop Soule, who had given him his first circuit riding assignment, remained at the age of eighty and living near Nashville, "a staunch advocate of the Union and of the Constitution of his country." Most gratifying of all was the opportunity to denounce before appreciative audiences the hideous, evil men of the Confederacy, especially those who had been his bitterest foes in Knoxville. When he spoke at Fort Donelson, where the arms and legs of the battle's victims still protruded from the shallow graves, he presented this snapping synopsis of life in East Tennessee:

I am just from the land of oppression, where there are no constitutional guards left for the protection of the rights of the citizens—where they have abolished the *habeas corpus*, provided county dungeons for Union men, the sweets of which I have tasted; where they have instituted *lettres de cachet*, violated the mails, disarmed communities and individuals, quartered drunken troops on private families, hung [sic.] men for not being Secessionists, shot down others in their fields for adhering to the Stars and Stripes, muzzled the press, silenced free speech, debauched the pulpit, tortured women and children, and brought into service, at two to four dollars per day, a pensioned band of depraved spies and informers.[1]

254

Yet, as the Parson enjoyed liberty of speech and of movement as well as the enveloping limelight, he must have felt a gnawing fear for the safety of his family. He indicated as much in assuring the troops he would return to his home when they repossessed the land. His accounts written at the time ignore, perhaps for reasons of security, any mention of the departure of his sons or the routes they took from Nashville. James P., the younger son, quickly headed for Cumberland Gap where with other men he helped organize a company that became a unit in the First Tennessee Cavalry Regiment, U.S.A. This unit was also called the First East Tennessee Cavalry Regiment.[2] John Bell, now the family guardian, was back in Knoxville before many days. He had already been entrusted with looking after the interests of the family when the Parson had fled into the mountains. During the negotiations for a passport he accompanied John Baxter in visits to military officials. He had supported Baxter's statement to these officials that the lawyer had bought the *Whig* plant. General Carroll confided to Benjamin that he not only believed the sale was not genuine but that Baxter's loyalty to the Confederacy was not to be trusted. Yet the sale was genuine and some of the Parson's bitterness at the loss of his plant may be laid to his resentment at being forced to sell the mortgaged property to Baxter for what he considered half its worth.[3]

The path of restoration for the Parson, however, lay to the north and there he hastened. He arrived in Cincinnati on March 27. The hero-starved North embraced him, feted him, besought him for speeches and replenished his finances. Book publishers wooed him, and he accepted the offer of George W. Childs of Philadelphia. This agreement led to the publication of *Parson Brownlow's Book*.

Brownlow began his speaking tour in Cincinnati on April 4, 1862, in Pike's Opera House. Three hundred and seventy-two children sang his praises. The president of the Chamber of Commerce, Joseph C. Butler, introduced him, and two other dignitaries, General S. F. Carey and Lieutenant-Governor John F. Fisk of Kentucky, rounded off the evening with speeches. The packed house brought the Parson receipts of $1,125. This auspicious night initiated a train of events that made Brownlow the man of the hour, more publicized than generals and was highly remunerated financially. His voice seemed to improve with every speech. The editor's flamboyance with facts, his acid treatment of his foes and his colorful and incisive prose delighted the Northerners. He told them what they wanted to hear about the South even more expressively than they could imagine it. Yet he gave his audiences large doses of candor. He approved of Andrew Johnson as military governor of Tennessee, but he acknowledged having fought him "perseveringly, systematically and terribly for a quarter of a century in Tennessee." Brownlow came from a line of slaveholders and he had been robbed by the Confederate cavalry on a Sabbath, of "a valuable boy . . . worth about one thousand dollars." The anti-slavery agitators of the North he said, were as appropriate candidates for the gallows as the disunionists of the South. Yet if the preservation of the Union was narrowed to the issue of slavery or its prohibition, then, said the Parson, slavery would have to go. The South, he conceded, had held the advantage of the North in political offices and favorable legislation, yet had brought on the conflict deliberately. And he furnished chilling accounts of what he saw and endured in the jail at Knoxville.[4] Always a Unionist, Brownlow went back to the days when South Carolina had threatened nullifi- cation and was stopped dead by Andrew Jackson. Tracing his loy- alty, he said he had abused and castigated Jackson, alive and as a corpse, although Brownlow credited him with the proper course in stifling nullification. Now he gave old Hickory this rousing tribute:

I would have resurrected him, if I could have done so, two years ago, and placed him in the chair disgraced by that mockery of a man, Buchanan, and had him to crush out this rebellion. Jackson was a true patriot, and a lover of his country, and a Union man; and if he had been living when this rebellion broke out, he would have hanged the leaders and prevented this unnatural war.[5]

Brownlow wound up the first leg of his lecture tour at In- dependence Hall in Philadelphia, April 18. He had delivered his speech and been received with official honors and acclaim in Indian- apolis, Chicago, Columbus, Pittsburg, Altoona and Harrisburg. Gover- nors sought him out and were pleased to introduce him. The Ohio legislature met in joint session to hear him. He rode in the cab of a locomotive across the Allegheny Mountains.[6] If he had a rival in splendor it was the aurora borealis.

The Parson declined an invitation from President Lincoln to visit the White House. He gave as his reason the necessity to hasten work on his book, but it is also possible he was vexed with Lincoln for not sending troops to the rescue of the East Tennessee loyalists.[7] He took refuge in the home of Robert E. Peterson at Crosswicks, New Jersey, and there he wrote, clipped and pasted together the hodgepodge that the abbreviating binders labelled *Parson Brownlow's Book*. Haste was important for the book to be placed before the eager northern market that had been stimulated by the wide and worshipful attention Brownlow was getting from newspapers, magazines and the platform. The author penned some of the chapters. Others consisted of strings of editorials he had written at the approach of war and before he suspended the *Whig*, his jail diary and his personal memoirs. Illustrative of the devices employed to hurry the manuscript was the Parson's use of his speech as it was carried in the Cincinnati *Gazette* rather than to set it down himself. He completed the writing in May, two months after he had left home. By September an estimated 100,000 copies had been sold.[8]

The Parson's flaming rhetoric at Cincinnati had the effect of driving his family out of Knoxville and into his arms at Crosswicks. His old foe from the litigation over the collapsed Bank of East Tennessee, W. M. Churchwell, was now a colonel and provost-marshal in Knoxville. He interpreted Brownlow's speech to mean that the Confederacy was holding Mrs. Brownlow and her family as "hostages for the good behavior" of the Parson. Churchwell gave Mrs. Brownlow and her family thirty-six hours to leave. Mrs. Brownlow protested she needed more time, was granted an extension, and left Knoxville on April 25. John Bell Brownlow; her daughters—Miss Mary Brownlow and Mrs. Sue C. Sawyers; and her grandchild—Mrs. Sawyers' son—accompanied her. They were out of the Confederacy by the last of April. Churchwell ordered Mrs. Horace Maynard and her family out at the same time. The Confederates required the Brownlows and the Maynards to pay their transportation to Norfolk and Fortress Monroe. Behind all this was Confederate rage at a statement the Parson had made in his Cincinnati speech but which he did not mention in *Parson Brownlow's Book*. John Bell Brownlow, thirty years later, wrote that when he went to the office of the Confederate commander in Knoxville, General E. Kirby Smith, to protest against the expulsion, the general showed him a copy of the Cincinnati *Gazette* reporting the speech. The newspaper quoted the Parson as saying, "A rebel has but two rights, a right to be hanged and a right to be d–d." It also reported the exiled editor was very severe on graduates of the United States Military Academy who went with the South. Kirby avowed, "The family of no man shall stay within my lines who would make such a speech."[9]

John Bell was soon in Cincinnati, and may have helped his father during the speaking tour and in preparing *Parson Brownlow's Book*, for he did not enter military service until August 1863.[10]

When the Parson completed the manuscript for his book he returned to the demanding and lucrative lecture circuit. He was in New York for ten days, beginning May 13. There he picked up from $1,200 to $2,500 a speech, along with subscriptions to the *Whig*, upon its resumption. He spent a week in Boston and then moved on to North Bridgewater, Salem and Lowell, Massachusetts; Portland, Maine; Dover, New Hampshire; Roxbury, Massachusetts; Providence, Rhode Island; Norwich and Hartford, Connecticut; Springfield, Amherst and Worcester, Massachusetts; and finally back to Philadelphia. He next visited seven cities in New York State, returned to Philadelphia, and in September headed for Michigan and Illinois. This tour included county fairs, the Michigan Republican State Convention in Detroit, and a huge Republican rally in Chicago. He closed out his speaking labors at Monmouth, Illinois, on November 3.

The Parson's participation in these partisan affairs put him down as having lost all dread of being called a "Black Republican." Although he may have been vexed with Lincoln for not having sent troops to the rescue of East Tennessee Unionists, he was now aligned in support of the Washington administration. He had not come completely around to a position acknowledging that slavery as an institution was dead, but he was approaching it. He had told his Cincinnati audience that in the last analysis, if he had to choose between the preservation of the Union and slavery, the Union must come first, but he added this suggestion:

> Let the Federal Government now guarantee to all loyal men in seceded States the right and title to their property, including negroes [*sic.*], and protect them in the enjoyment of the same; but let the title held by rebels seeking to destroy the Government be annihilated, both as to negroes [*sic.*] and all other property.

Lincoln's Emancipation Proclamation must have caught Brownlow by surprise; for at the Kent County Fair at Grand Rapids, Michigan, on October 7, 1862, while speaking to an audience of 10,000 persons he endorsed it "As a military measure . . . but in no other sense." He saw it as a sop to abolitionists and as utter unenforceable. He held, "The rebellion must first be put down before the government has any power to put down slavery in the rebellious states. Till the rebellion is crushed by the sword it is idle to talk of what is to be done with slavery. Let us do one thing at a time."[11]

The removal of the Brownlow family from Knoxville failed to blot out its members, especially the head of the house, as news items for their old neighbors. The *Register* and its editor, Sperry, had always found the Parson wicked and malignant, but fascinatingly so, an almost hypnotic evil. This tendency was reflected in the famous editorial in the *Register* that extolled Brownlow's skill in obtaining his release to the North. It took off with:

We do not desire to be understood as attaching undue or extravagant importance to the discharge of Brownlow from the custody of the Confederate authorities. The writer of this has known this individual for years. He is, in few words, a diplomat of the first water. Brownlow rarely undertakes anything unless he sees his way entirely through the millstone. He covers over his really profound knowledge of human nature with an appearance of eccentricity and extravagance. If any of our readers indulge the idea that Brownlow is not '*smart*' in the full acceptation [acceptance] of the term, they should abolish the delusion at once and forever. Crafty, cunning, generous to his particular friends, benevolent and charitable to their faults, ungrateful and implacable to his enemies, we cannot refrain from saying that he is the best judge of human nature within the bounds of the Southern Confederacy.

In procuring from the Confederate authorities a safe-conduct to a point within the Hessian lines, he has exhibited the most consumate skill. . . .

Brownlow! God forbid that we should unnecessarily magnify the importance of the name; but there are facts connected with the character of the man which a just and discriminating public would condemn in us did we not give them due notice.

In brief, Brownlow has preached at every church and school-house, made stump-speeches at every cross road, and knows every man, woman and child, and their fathers and grandfathers before them, in East Tennessee. As a Methodist circuit-rider, a political stump-speaker, a temperance orator, and the editor of a newspaper, he has been equally successful in our division of the state.

Let him but reach the confines of Kentucky, with his knowledge of the geography and the population of East Tennessee, and our section will soon feel the effect of his hard blows. From among his old partisan and religious sectarian parasites he will find men who will obey him with the fanatical alacrity of those who followed Peter the Hermit in the First Crusade. We repeat again, let us not underrate Brownlow.[12]

Everyone who knew Sperry, or who read his newspaper, was aware of his hot hatred for the Parson, and most of them knew he spoke for a group of influential secessionists in Knoxville who wanted the former *Whig* editor hanged or sent to a remote and secure prison in the Deep South. The chagrin of these men was intensified because Brownlow had eluded the fate they desired for him by the decision of the military on their own side. It was more humiliating and frustrating than if President Lincoln had marched a Union army into East Tennessee and snatched up Brownlow. Sperry held up the Confederate officials and officers to scorn and ignominy, but in doing it he paid Brownlow one of the greatest tributes ever set in type. The *Register* continued to follow the blazing trail of the Parson across the North. It castigated and denounced him, but never subjected him to neglect. It reported his profits and described him as "the grand attraction of the 4th of July celebration at the Fair Grounds at Louisville." It gloated when Confederate prisoners hissed the Parson when he attempted to speak to a group. It denounced him, along with Andrew Johnson, for approving Lincoln's Emancipation Proclamation, and noted that he was recommending extermination of the South's population. It had him swooping into Washington like a vulture after carrion, as leading a regiment of blacks into East Tennessee, and finally upon hearing of the suicide of Abram Pryne it granted him this capsuled detestation:

It is not surprising that Pryne has left the world in disgust. Brownlow's infamy so far transcended his own that he has "curled up and quit." The one was false only to his God, the other to both God and his country. Pryne had become a lunatic, Brownlow was born morally insane.

The anger of the *Register* against "our tender-hearted military" had burst out earlier in 1862 when the editor protested that too much tolerance had been shown to those loyal to the old government. He flared out with:

Unionism here has never felt the heel of proscription. *The exact opposite is the truth.* In the entire length and breadth of the Confederate States, East Tennessee is the only place where Toryism or, if that term be too harsh to the delicate ears of those for whom we particularly write—Unionism, has been tolerated.

The liberty of the press and the freedom of speech were enjoyed here in their most unbridled license and wanton abuse. There was in all the South but one paper that advocated the maintenance of the old government and the overthrow of the new. That sheet was, thrice a week, under the very guns of the Southern army, published in Knoxville. Unmolested, it assaulted in every possible form of falsehood, popular sophistry, detraction and vulgar slander, our government, its officials and friends, until, from sheer exhaustion, it could no longer insert an untruth, pervert a fact, blacken a character or insert a fang into a sensibility. If this infamous sheet had been published in Memphis . . .; or in Nashville . . .; its office would have been demolished, and its editor, perhaps, ridden upon a rail, instead of being escorted, by a guard of honor, *brim-full of intelligence*, to the enemy... East Tennessee was the paradise to tories—the only spot in all the South where Union men were allowed free discussion.[13]

The *Daily Southern Chronicle*, which appeared in Knoxville on June 28, 1863, and which lasted only a few months, ridiculed rather than belabored the Parson. It printed a captured letter of Brownlow to his wife, dated July 6, 1863. It was seized by troops of the Confederate cavalry leader, General John H. Morgan, in a northern raid. Brownlow had written it at Nashville, where he was assistant special agent for the United States Treasury Department. The *Chronicle* published it on August 4, 1863, a month before Union forces moved into Knoxville. The letter conveyed a warning to Mrs. Sue (Susan) Sawyers, widowed daughter of the Brownlows, not to permit the attentions of a Union officer, named Reece. Sue, the mother of a son, was a redoubtable soul. She had defied, with rifle or pistol, Confederate soldiers who had threatened to tear down the Stars and Stripes floating at the Brownlow home on East Cumberland Avenue. A couple of pamphlets had been written about her exploits and she had travelled with her father on his speaking tour of the North. Nevertheless, she was a member of the Parson's household, then living at Covington, Kentucky, and he held her to be under his dominion and control. He warned her (through her mother) that the suitor was no good:

Gen. Burnside will muster him out of service in disgrace. He has made an ass out of himself; he is a petty tyrant, full of self-conceit, and has no *common sense*. Say to Sue, for me, that she must not be seen walking with him or conversing with him. And she must receive nothing from him, in letters, or presents. She must either go with me or him—she can't go with both, and he will end up his career in disgrace and bankruptcy and will be so published in the army records. I know what I am talking about.

The same letter also revealed the Parson's efforts to see that his children were well garmented. Father Brownlow laid down dress goods, as well as the law for Sue and the other children. He wrote:

The silk I bought for the girls, I will describe to you. For Sue and Mary, plaids with stripes of red, brown and green. For Fannie, 9 yards of checks, white and blue, like apron check, very pretty. Sue's piece has 15½ yards—Mary's 15 yards. They are good and handsome, and I get them for less than *one dollar per yard*. For the little Tads I have a bolt of brilliants and a bolt of linnen [*sic*.] with black stripes.

Sue bore up very well under the stricture on her suitor. In less than three years she married Dr. Daniel T. Boynton, who practiced medicine from the Parson's home after the marriage.[14]

The *Chronicle*'s jibe at Brownlow and his family may have afforded the Knoxville secessionists one of their last pleasant moments of the summer. Union armies were moving southward toward East Tennessee, and soon after the middle of August Confederate authorities started moving supplies and troops south. Most outspoken southern sympathizers took the same direction. Knoxville suffered a strange hiatus. With troops and officers gone the city was left without governmental authority, and "A vague and yet terrible sense of insecurity and uncertainty filled the minds of all." Then, on a sunny afternoon, September 1, 1863, a brigade of cavalry commanded by Colonel John W. Foster, galloped up Gay Street from the north. It concentrated about the Lamar Hotel and occupied the city. Two days later General Ambrose Burnside made his formal entry.[15]

Brownlow's Knoxville Whig reappeared on November 11, 1863. It brandished the additional title of *and Rebel Ventilator*, a capsuled declaration of the Parson's program for his foes. The Union army brought the Brownlow and Maynard families to Knoxville from the Cincinnati area and provided the Parson with substantial help in getting the *Whig* going. It supplied him with $1,500 cash, five wagons to haul paper and printing supplies from Cincinnati, and probably with a printing press. Brigadier General James G. Spears seized a press, type and other equipment at Alexandria, a small town in Middle Tennessee, and ordered the material sent to Knoxville for Brownlow. The Parson did not, as might have been expected, take over the printing office and equipment of either the *Register* or the *Chronicle*. That of the former was sold through an order of the United States District Court, and Treasury Department aides working under Brownlow auctioned off what apparently was the property of the latter. The *Whig* resumed operations at its old stand, after necessary renovation, with a hand operated press. Brownlow published a duplicate newspaper at Cincinnati for northern subscribers, of whom there were from 15,000 to 20,000. The Knoxville circulation was limited, for regular mails did not exist and subscribers were required to get their *Whigs* at the Knoxville post office or at the *Whig* shop.[16]

Ventilation was a rather mild term for Brownlow's ferocity

against the secessionists remaining in the area. He recalled in his opening address that he had predicted: "the South will be whipped and driven in disgrace back into the Union, and *made* to yield to the laws and constitution of the United States." He also recalled his prediction that the heaviest blows of the North would fall upon the Border States, who were pressed into the conflict by the more insulated sisters of the Deep South. He did not linger on these points because "The *past* is with the reader, and we have only to speak of the *present* and of *what is to come*." Thus looking ahead the Parson recommended that while the government and the military authorities should

deal in the most liberal spirit toward the deluded masses, and for the patriotic who were conscripted, we urge the punishment of intelligent traitors, and insist that the *halter* should be summoned to do its appropriate work among the leaders! . . .

The *guerrilla warfare* which the rebels delight in and threaten Union men with cannot long be maintained when once the war is ended, or when rebel soldiers are driven from a State. Self-preservation will lead good men everywhere to unite with the Government in closing it out. No mercy will be shown to such thieves and assassins, if they continue their ravages, when their armies have laid down their arms. They have no claims under the laws of warfare; they are out of the pale of their protection, placed there by their own reckless violation of those laws. This picking off of men here and there, and these guerilla raids upon families and villages, where murder and plunder are the only motives, and not in any sense the furtherance of the objects of war, should be punished with death, without even the forms of a trial. Let no such men be taken as prisoners. Let a stern vengeance be taken upon every guerrilla that falls into our hands. . . . (*Whig* November 11, 1863).

Only a shade less evil than guerillas, in the Parson's book, were clergymen who had promoted the rebellion:

They have aided in the work of devastating the country; they have contributed to fill the land with mourning; they have caused tears of tens of thousands of widows to flow; they have done their full part, in handing down to posterity an army of orphan children; they have aided materially in filling thousands of graves with the best citizens of the country, North and South; and fearful to relate, they have mainly contributed to send thousands to hell, who might have been redeemed by the blood of Christ, but for this war!

He endorsed President Lincoln's policies in full, with a reservation:

"The Federal Government has been too lenient, and too slow to punish rebels, and to crush out this most abominable, wicked and uncalled for rebellion." He favored what he described as *"mediation"* with *"cannon and the sword"* to the point of subjugation or extermination. Only loyal men, he wrote, "are to be heard in the casting up of accounts of men who have done the amount of mischief these leading rebels have!" He offered to his enemies, provided they were honorable, "decent respect" and forgiveness *"provided they have not been the persecutors of Union men."*

Brownlow now swung full circle on the subject of slavery, an institution he had once argued enjoyed divine approval. It was gone, abolished by the war. He wrote that the masses of Southern people had never favored it, but opposed emancipation "because of the repugnance of negroes to labor, and of the demoralized state of society that must follow." This was a bold step for the slave-holding Parson. Fifteen years earlier he had noted without a trace of compassion, "The contents of the vaults of the Rogersville Bank passed through here [Knoxville] this week in the shape of 170 negroes," [*sic.*] on their way to the Mississippi market. The Parson was indignant because the bank had loaned money to slave traders who were his political enemies. He manifestated no compassion for the human creatures being marched along Gay Street as property, like a herd of cattle or a drove of hogs.[17]

The evidence that Brownlow owned slaves just before the Civil War is conclusive, although the Knox County tax records of the period do not reflect such ownership. It is conceivable that the property assessor found reasons, best known to himself and to the Parson, to favor the latter in making his returns. Brownlow asserted his ownership in *Parson Brownlow's Book*. He mentioned specifically a Negro boy carried away by the Confederate cavalry, and listed the slave's value at $1,000. The widow of John F. (Jack) Brownlow, the Parson's grandson, recalled two Negro women in the household of the editor's widow who had been slaves. Felix A. Reeves, who read law along with John Bell and James P. Brownlow, just before the war, listed the Parson with Andrew Johnson and Horace Maynard as slave owners.[18]

The Parson had ventilated the rebels with only two issues of his reestablished *Whig* when he was forced into a move that must have chagrined him. Along with other prominent Unionists he fled north to escape possible capture by the South. On September 19 the Confederates soundly defeated the Union army under General William S. Rosecrans at the Battle of Chickamauga. General James S. Longstreet was dispatched with a Confederate force to dislodge Burnside at Knoxville. Union officers were uncertain they could hold Knoxville and they advised a group of loyalists to leave.

After a lapse of six weeks Brownlow resumed publication on January 9, 1864. He missed the Battle of Fort Sanders, and he almost ignored it in the *Whig*. It was fought on November 29, 1863. When his newspaper finally reported it as a Union victory it was in its edition of January 30, 1864. He ran "A Rebel Account" taken from the Augusta *Constitutionalist*.

The Unionists who fled with the Parson included O. P. Temple, Thomas A. R. Nelson, John M. Fleming and M. M. Miller of Knoxville, and John Netherland and Absolom Kyle of Rogersville. Brownlow must have been deeply hacked on the ignominious journey. During a stop at Clinton a patriotic matron, who was unable to believe that the party was on the run, who did not recognize the Parson in the darkness, taunted them with: "I expect the next thing I hear will be that old Billy Brownlow is running, too." The editor counselled immediate departure from the scene. The *Whig* offered this justification for the flight:

True, when the seige set in, and the prospect was that the rebels would take the place, we made it convenient to pass beyond the Ohio River.

We are not aware that we are especially timid, but we are certainly not brave enough to want to encounter one of the lousy, filthy and cold prisons of the South. We are not brave enough to seek to live on their *diet*, or to hang on one of their trees (*Whig*, January 9, 1869).

The Parson had been in prison once. He did not care to risk a return.

Compassion moved Brownlow on that northern trip as he watched thousands of loyalists flee from Longstreet's army. They struggled on foot, on horseback or by any conveyance they could find, through the difficult defiles of the Cumberland Mountains to find a refuge in Kentucky. To some he opened his purse. Yet the trip produced economic benefits for him. While he was in Cincinnati Brownlow was granted, as assistant special agent for the Treasury Department, authorization for release to Knoxville retailers of more than $100,000 worth of goods. Among those granted permits was the Parson's good friend, O. P. Temple, who reciprocated by advertising his store in the *Whig*, and by inserting in his card as an attorney,

"Reference—W. G. Brownlow."[19]

The Parson's power in the area occupied by the Union forces was sweeping. He was the hero of the North and the fierce foe of the secessionists. He had a complete understanding of the people, the geography and the economic and cultural facts of life. These qualifications undoubtedly gave him the keen and respectful ear of the military officers. As editor of the *Whig* he could condemn or praise with powerful effect. As treasury agent he held the sole authority to grant permits to trade, a power he thus summarized:

To regulate the sale of goods, seize all goods smuggled into East Tennessee without regular permits, and to seize and confiscate all the goods, wares and merchandize [*sic.*] —the loose and perishable property left by rebels who have abandoned their homes and gone with the rebel army for protection (*Ibid.*).

Early in 1864 Brownlow's power was extended to include "All houses, tenements, lands and plantations, excepting such as may be required for military purposes, which may have been or may be deserted."[20]

Bitterness, threats and demands for vindication and vengeance flowed from the pen of the Parson. Longstreet's ragged and often barefoot forces retreated slowly into upper East Tennessee, but made occasional forays into such Union counties as Blount and Sevier. Because of this the Knoxville secessionists, who still hoped for a resurgence by the Confederate general, failed to display the submissiveness that Brownlow considered appropriate. He found them "insolent." Spirited Confederate women, who refused to assume the garment of repentance, irritated him. He taunted some of them because they were living on "the patronage of the Lincoln army" by running boarding houses that catered to "Yankee officers and soldiers." The *Whig* raged at atrocities reported against Union men and families above and below Knoxville.[21] Loyalists who attempted to intercede for those so accused drew the editor's fire:

And yet, when those imps of Hell are arrested, Union men come forward, impose upon the authorities, and procure their release. God forbid that we should ever to be found endorsing for one of these scoundrels, or those baser villains on our streets, who exult over their deeds of carnage, and are daily smuggling letters through our lines to the enemy!

The Knoxville *Register*, which was published briefly at Atlanta and which apparently based its report on information from friends in Knoxville, wrote:

The ferocity of Brownlow is fearful. . . . He evidently deems himself master of the situation and expects to reign a lordly potentate in East Tennessee . . . Brownlow . . . declared he not only was in favor of arming every negro in the South but that he would turn loose wild beasts to prey upon the population of the country.[22]

Prejudiced as Sperry was, his appraisal had some justification. Brownlow, as Treasury agent, not only followed rigidly the orders that trade permits should be granted only to loyal citizens, but also had a finger in the extension of loans and credits. He was a director of the First National Bank that was established in the summer of 1864 with a capital of $100,000. The bank directorate included such staunch Unionists as Perez Dickinson, Samuel R. Rodgers, O. P. Temple, S. P. Carter and William Heiskell, one of Brownlow's Treasury aides. The requirement that only loyal persons should be granted trade permits undoubtedly stimulated the signing of loyalty oaths during the winter of 1864. Some of these signers, Brownlow told his readers, took the oath with mental reservations and planned to do all they could to aid the South regardless of their sworn pledges.[23]

Brownlow adopted with cold fury, a policy which he said the rebels had promulgated when they were in control in East Tennessee: only one side could live in the area. Now that Union men were in control "Their persecutors would do well to leave." He named, among others, W. H. Sneed, William G. Swan, John H. Crozier, C. W. Charlton, Editor Sperry and Landon Haynes. He declared that they could never live in East Tennessee: "Indeed, we regard Union men who have suffered at their hands, and because of their counsels, as justified in shooting them down on sight, before or after the war terminates . . ." When Ephraim Dodd, a Texan, was hanged as a spy after a court-martial held at Knoxville, Brownlow envisaged a rich field for the gallows. He delivered this opinion:

There are at least 25 citizens of Knoxville, resident spies, who ought to hang, one by one. As the work has commenced, let it go on! . . . until compensation is had, in part, for the hundreds of cold-blooded murders perpetrated in East Tennessee.

When protests were made that Dodd's sentence was harsh,[24] the Parson retorted that the protestors had been unmoved by compassion at the hangings of Fry, Hensie and the Harmons:

When Union men were shot down in the woods, put in irons, and sent by hundreds to Southern prisons, while their families were insulted and plundered, these infernal hypocrites said it was all right! They are now seeing the other side of the picture. Let us crowd the traitors, thieves, and assassins, and make them cry out, in the bitterness of their sufferings, "That mercy we to others show, that mercy show to us" (*Whig*, January 16, 1864).

Confederate troops which were reported to have violated the rules of war or had committed outright atrocities, drew this denunciation:

> Had we our wish, we would throw hell wide open, and place all such beast-like officers and men upon an inclined plane, at an angle of forty-five degrees, grease the plane with hog's lard six inches thick, with a wicket at the bottom, and send them, as one stream of traitors, robbers and assassins, into the hottest part of the infernal regions.

The Parson also offered this merciless recommendation for "The Spring Campaign" of 1864 by Union forces:

> Let us have a half million of fresh troops, and let us start the plough-share of ruin into the Cotton States, sub-soiling as we go, and letting the first dash of the plough be over the handle in the "sacred soil of the South."—Lay these Cotton States waste; make a howling wilderness of the cotton, rice and grain growing plantations of the South;—starve out, and drive out the population; and introduce honest laborers, who are loyal, and will answer the end for which they were created (*Whig*, February 20, 1864).[24]

The conscription of Union men into the Confederate army created the most intense bitterness among the loyalists. The task of conscription often was assigned to Union men. Some acted from duress and others at the request of neighbors who believed it preferable to have the hateful work done by a considerate friend than by a dreaded enemy.[25] Brownlow divided these Unionists into those who

> were mild and kind in the discharge of their odious office. . . . It was their misfortune to be appointed. To refuse to accept was to defy the rebel government and probably bring ruin on his head who dared to do it.
>
> But there was a different class of enrolling officers, who forced that law with the most heartless cruelty. There were men who delighted in surprising Union families in the dead hours of the night, and forcing the father, husband or son away from home with the point of the bayonet, and in many cases tied or handcuffed. Some of them accompanied these with wanton insults, and with mockery of the cries and anguish of the wife and children. Often the conscript was shot down in the presence of his family. He was *always* abused and insulted.

He was worse than a slave after he was put in the army—he was treated as a *dog*.

Now, we say, let justice be done. These traitors have had their day; now we have ours. Let everyone who voluntarily aided in this infamous system of forcing Union men to fight against their government be made to atone for it in his purse and property. They have boasted that all the wealth of the South was on their side.—Then it is time the wealth was changing hands. Strip them a little, by a few judgments for damages, and perhaps they won't feel quite so aristocratic. . . . It is well that there should be a change of property. The peace of the country hereafter demands that those who inaugurated this hellish war should be curtailed of their majestic proportions, and forced into poverty and obscurity. After their terrible crimes, if they are permitted to live, even in poverty and obscurity, they may thank God for the mercy and unmerited forbearance extended to them. It will be an act of pure clemency (*Whig*, March 5, 1864).

The sufferings of the East Tennessee Unionists had been intense. The East Tennessee Relief Association was organized at Knoxville early in February 1864. Dr. Thomas W. Humes was president. A petition to President Lincoln from the association drew this picture of the plight of the Unionists during the two years of Confederate occupation:

Union citizens were disarmed—arrested without warrant, and for alleged military offenses, imprisoned at the pleasure of petty military tyrants in violation of all law—forced to take oaths against their consciences and in derogation of their allegiance to the United States—taxed with illegal costs to support corrupt officials—the property seized for public and individual uses. Their fields were laid waste; in some instances, houses were burned over the heads of families as a punishment for their loyalty, and in other instances, *not a few*, men patriotically sealed their devotion to their country with their life-blood, either butchered by a lawless soldiery or officially murdered by a military court.

Nathaniel G. Taylor, a wealthy citizen of upper East Tennessee who became a Methodist minister after his sister, Miss Mary Taylor, was killed by a bolt of lightning at a camp meeting, aided by Edward Everett and other influential men of New England, engaged in raising funds. Their efforts brought $250,000 to the aid of the impoverished region. Brownlow was on the committee that signed the petition to the President, along with Humes as chairman, William Heiskell, John Baxter, O. P. Temple and John Fleming.[26] But for the Parson's personal contribution on the horrors of occupation for the columns of the *Whig* he required more horrendous language. He used the letter of Secretary Benjamin to Colonel W. B. Wood, commander at

Knoxville, as a starting point to describe the punishment to be given
East Tennessee prisoners of war:

It will be seen that BENJAMIN divides the Union population into two classes:
First, those who participated in the bridge burning, and all these were to be *hung*
[*sic.*] *on the spot.* Second, those who had not so participated in the bridge burning; and all those were to be held as prisoners of war and sent with an armed guard
to Tuscaloosa, Alabama. Now, if history can produce any act of tyranny more
atrocious and revolting than this, we cannot recall it. Over thirty thousand men
were doomed by this imperial tyrant to hanging or imprisonment (*Whig,* March
5, 1964).

The hanging of Jacob and Henry Harmon brought a special sense of
horror to Brownlow. He mentioned it twice in his book and expanded on it in the *Whig,* recalling:

The father, an old man, was forced to sit upon his coffin and witness the hanging
of his son. The rope broke, and a second time the half lifeless son made that
fearful leap through the trap door of the scaffold. . . .

To all the conclusive and irresistible arguments used by the defendants' counsel, showing that the court had no jurisdiction in the case and therefore could
not punish, the only answer was the ukase of Benjamin. He had ordered them
hung [*sic.*], and therefore they *must* be!. . .Finally they ceased to try at all.
All who were suspected were arrested, thrown into jail, held until they had
collected a *drove* of one or two hundred, and then marched off to Tuscaloosa.
Hundreds, yes, thousands, were thus sent away without charge, without a trial,
without proof, upon the bare *suspicion* of being Union men. . . .Need we recall
the fact that four hundred and fifty men, many of them mere boys, who were
fleeing to Kentucky to escape the ruthless persecutions at home, were overtaken
by Ashby and his murderers, and caught, and all sent in a body, with one or two
exceptions to the charnel houses of the South? Their crime was that they sought
the protection of the stars and stripes.—And who that saw will ever forget the
sight witnessed, as that body of men were marched under guard through the
streets of Knoxville, when one by one they would *stealthily* stoop and with the
hand scoop up the filthy water from the streets to allay their burning thirst?
They were DRIVEN across the creeks and past the springs without being allowed
to drink, on their long and hurried march of near fifty miles, then confined all
night without food or drink.—No wonder then, that as they set forward on their
gloomy march to their Southern houses of death, they stooped and lapped up
the slimy water. And will anyone who saw ever forget—(*ought any one ever to
forget?*)—the infernal joy that gleamed in the countenance of Ashby[27] as he
rode and pranced at the head of these four hundred and fifty men, on a sum-

mer's day, and as he looked upon their bare heads, their sore and bleeding feet, their parched lips, their famished forms and their tremblimg limbs? Others who looked idly on, although at the time they grew sick at heart, and perchance dropped a tear, may forget, but those injured patriots will never *forget or forgive*.

Well and faithfully was the stern edict of the Jewish Nero, to kill and imprison, kept and obeyed. *Zollicoffer, Carroll, Woods* and *Leadbetter* gladly obeyed it. The army and all its followers everywhere willingly obeyed it. The court martial, with the fiendish *Campbell* [28] as Judge Advocate, with extreme joy obeyed it. The Confederate Court, with the madman *Humphreys* on the bench, and the imbecile *Ramsey*, at the bar, earnestly obeyed it. The Knoxville *Register* joyfully [oh how joyfully!] obeyed it and daily cried and begged for more blood. *Heiskell, Swan* and *Tibbs* in Congress, obeyed, and demanded of Nero a new *ukase* and fresh victims. *Sneed, Crozier, Wallace, McAdoo*, and some who daily walk our streets, obeyed and shouted for a hecatomb upon the altar. *Harris* and his *Legislature* obeyed, and snuffed the air for the sweet odor of fresh blood. And everywhere, throughout the State, the hell-hounds of the rebellion whined, and cried, and howled for blood.—And day by day was the fresh pure blood of innocent patriots lapped up by the inmates of the infernal kennel, and still they whined, and snarled, and whetted their fangs for more. And as each fresh victim fell, they leaped, and snarled, and howled, and yelled afresh, and grew more insatiate for blood. And as these demons grew drunken with blood, they serenely smiled, and talked complacently in the legislative halls, in the council chamber, in the camp and in the pulpit, on the bench and at the bar, on the streets and in the press, by the fireside, *at the gallows, and in their houses of death*, of their *forbearance* and *lenity*, and of the *magnanimity* and *clemency* of their great government (*Ibid.*).

This magnificent example of the Parson's ability to overlay some solid facts with lurid hyperbole was written while he was under intense strain. He was editing his newspaper, carrying on his Treasury job, and he was the target of hundreds who sought his influence or his advice in the shifting times. As a stern but doting father he must have had constantly on his mind the fearful risks his two sons were taking as they led their cavalry units against the enemy. They were "frequently in the East Tennessee area where as sons of the *Whig* editor they surely were marked men for the enemy."[29]

Yet, in the midst of this life and death struggle, Brownlow's sardonic wit flashed through an exchange of letters with Sam Wallace. The latter was a Blount Countian who had fled South and left a young and charming wife at home. Wallace's letter, written from Augusta, Georgia, on September 21, 1864, set the tone of the correspondence:

> *W. G. Brownlow, D.D.*—DEAR SIR: I have heard that in your issue of the 10th of August, you have a letter from me to my wife, said to have been captured. I have not seen the paper, but suppose the letter is correctly reported, and as there may be others *via* "underground" that might fall into your hands, I will say, *if it suits you as well*, leave off many items that an *old man would be likely to write his young wife*; but anything that is contraband, why "ventilate," of course.
>
> I have quit writing letters and turned my attention to writing the history of *Guberdom.*
>
> I have further heard that Mrs. Wallace is a tenant of yours. She is a mighty clever woman, and I hope your terms will be liberal.
>
> You will please send her word I am well and doing well, eating sweet potatoes and gubers, and fighting mosquitoes by way of exercise.
>
> > With due respect,
> > Sam Wallace
>
> P.S.—I would be glad [if] you would make old Abe quit his "foolishness," as I want to go home (*Ibid.*, October 26, 1864).

The editor replied in a letter dated October 21, 1864, that he had omitted, in the *Whig*, all intimate expressions and detail Wallace had written, then offered these observations:

> It is true that Mrs. Wallace is a *tenant* of the Federal Government—not of mine—though I am the agent of that Government, and rent to her, almost upon her own terms, the fine farm you so foolishly abandoned. She had called to see me, and I believe you when you say "she is a mighty clever woman"—nay, she is a lady, and I treated her as such.
>
> As she doubtless sees every issue of my paper, I will have no occasion to send her word that you were well at the date of your letter.
>
> You desire me to "make old Abe quit his foolishness, so as to enable you to get home." Make your bad man, Jeff Davis, "quit his foolishness," and cease fighting against a Government that will eventually crush him and all who are in arms against it, and you will soon be able to come home. I think you have seen enough of the destruction of life and property in the "Sunny South," to agree with me that it was the perfection of "foolishness" for the South to have plunged into this war. If you have not made *that* discovery hold on through another season, "eating sweet potatoes and gubers, and fighting mosquitoes," and you will yet make the discovery.

That you have, yourself, been guilty of greater "foolishness" than old Abe has, I think you are prepared to admit. It was the very climax of folly in you, living in comfort, to join a set of the worst men that ever God permitted to live, in a villainous war upon a Government that never did you any harm but had protected you, and secured to you, life, liberty and property—even the peacable [sic.] possession of the *everlasting nigger*. But to run from "a young wife," of great personal beauty and domestic charms, was a degree of madness that no one but a deluded secessionist could be guilty of! For this folly you deserve to be annoyed by mosquitoes, bed-bugs, seed-ticks and Confederate *lice*, in your down-lyings and your uprisings, at least during the war. And sweet potatoes and gubers are too good for a rebel.

Hoping to hear from you again, I am very truly, &c.,

W. G. Brownlow (*Ibid.*).

Even the editor's closest friends must have been astonished when he endorsed the consumption of a barrel of confiscated "rebel whiskey" by a regiment of newly organized "Citizen soldiers." Brownlow not only approved of the treat but added that "if the regiment had got drunk and hung [sic.] all the rebels in Knoxville who are giving the enemy information and inviting those raids into the country that would have met with our sanction also." General Joseph Wheeler had just raided East Tennessee with his cavalry units and caused some consternation.[30]

But the glory and the glitter had gone out of Confederate arms. In the fall of 1864 General U. S. Grant took command at Chattanooga and General Sherman reinforced him with troops from Mississippi. By the close of November the Union soldiers under this new command drove the Confederates from Lookout Mountain and Missionary Ridge. Grant was called to Virginia and given command of all the northern forces. Sherman, left at Chattanooga, prepared for the campaign of 1865 which would see the capture of Atlanta and his march to the sea. Generals Nathan Bedford Forrest, John H. Morgan, and Joe Wheeler made brilliant and harassing raids into Tennessee with their cavalry units, but they produced no change in the declining fortunes of the South. Longstreet pulled out of East Tennessee and joined Lee in Virginia.[31]

The arrival of Burnside and his army had precipitated a huge celebration in Knoxville by the loyalists. The celebration was dimmed temporarily during the siege of Knoxville, but revived after the Battle of Fort Sanders. Gradually the old routines of the community began to take shape and activity, with some new developments. Brownlow led the field. He filed suits for damages against "the villainous leaders in the rebel ranks," and beckoned to others to follow this course. They did. Prices shot up and agitation was renewed to resume work on the barely started Knoxville and Kentucky railroad. The *Whig* called for hotel accommodations. The Federal army bridged the Tennessee River. County elections were held and Union candidates won. A "Liberty Pole," eighty feet tall, was brought from South Knoxville, and the same flag which had earlier flown defiance to the South and which had been carefully preserved, was raised again. A brass band played and Governor Andrew Johnson spoke. The Lamar and Franklin houses prepared to reopen. The military began directing the cleaning of rubbish from the town. The courts began to grind out orders for publication and notices of attachments and sales, profitable grist for the *Whig*'s advertising columns. By September 1864 abundant crops began to appear despite the scarcity of laborers and horses. Vacant houses were unavailable. The fledgling First National Bank, in business five months, declared a dividend of five percent.[32]

The military struggles on Tennessee soil were nearly ended. Political conflict waited in the wings.

CHAPTER XV NOTES

[1] *Parson Brownlow's Book*, pp. 380-394, 396-399.

[2] *Tennesseans in the Civil War, a Military History of Confederate and Union Units Available with Rosters of Personnel*, Civil War Centennial Commission (Nashville, 1965), 2 vols., pt. 1, p. 318; R. W. Carter, *History of the First Regiment of Tennessee Volunteer Cavalry in the Great War of the Rebellion, with the Armies of the Ohio under Generals Morgan, Rosecrans, Thomas, Stanley and Wilson, 1862-1865* (Knoxville, 1902) pp. 19-20; hereafter referred to as Carter.

[3] *O. R.*, II, 1, W. M. Churchwell to Major H. L. Clay, April 23, 1862, p. 930; *ibid.*, Clay to Lieutenant Joseph H. Speed, April 24, 1862, p. 930; *ibid.*, pass issued by Churchwell, April 25, 1862, p. 931.

[4] *Parson Brownlow's Book*, pp. 399-400; Coulter, pp. 213-235; "The Public Speaking Career of William Gannaway (Parson) Brownlow," dissertation by Royal Forrest Conklin, University of Ohio, 1967 pp. 195, 162-174; hereafter referred to as Conklin; *Parson Brownlow's Book*, pp. 400-425. Brownlow may have made more than $60,000 from the sale of his book, Coulter, VIII, introduction by James W. Patton. In a letter to this writer on December 9, 1971, Patton was unable to fix a specific authority for the

statement of the Parson's profit from the sale of the book, but wrote that
when he was engaged in research in 1934 for *Unionism and Reconstruction in Tennessee, 1860-1869*, he talked to three of the Parson's grand-
children and William Rule. He suggests his information came from them.
Parson Brownlow's Book, pp. 409-410, 411-414, 412-413, 417-422.

[5] *Ibid.*, pp. 409-411. See also Brownlow's speech at Grand Rapids, Michigan,
      on October 7, 1863. *Whig.*, February 6, 1864.
[6] Conklin, pp. 167-169; Coulter, pp. 216-221; *Parson Brownlow's Book*, pp.
      425-442.
[7] Coulter, p. 223; *Parson Brownlow's Book*, pp. 453-454.
[8] *Ibid.*, p. 444; Temple, *Notable Men*, p. 317; Coulter, pp. 234, 239.
[9] *O. R.*, II, 1, Churchwell to Mrs. W. G. Brownlow, April 21, 1862, p. 929;
      ibid., Mrs. Eliza Brownlow to Churchwell, April 21, 1862, p. 929; John
      Bell Brownlow to Temple, February 16, 1892. Temple Papers; *O. R.*, II, 1,
      Clay to Speed, April 24, 1862, pp. 930-931; *ibid.*, Churchwell *pass*, April
      25, 1862, p. 931, *ibid.*, A. T. Bledsoe, Assistant Secretary of War, to Major
      General Benjamin Huger, April 28, 1862, p. 931; *Parson Brownlow's
      Book*, pp. 446-452; *Whig*, February 7, 1866; John Bell Brownlow to
      Temple, February 16, 1892. Temple Papers.
[10] John Bell Brownlow to Temple, January 24, 1891, Temple Papers; *Ten-
      nesseeans in the Civil war*, pp. 2, 342-343.
[11] Conklin, pp. 168-174; Coulter, pp. 223-234; *Parson Brownlow's Book*, p.
      413; *Whig*, February 6, 1864.
[12] The editorial appeared while Brownlow was under house arrest. *Parson
      Brownlow's Book*, pp. 342-345. It must have appeared prior to January 3,
      1862, for a copy of it was enclosed in a letter written on that date; J. J.
      Craig to Benjamin, January 3, 1861, but incorrectly dated because it en-
      closed other items from the *Register* dated December 7, 13; *O. R.*, II, 1,
      pp. 923-926.
[13] *Register*, May 20, June 22, April 22, October 1, November 22, 1862,
      January 3, April 26, 1863, October 16, 1862, March 12, 1862.
[14] *Daily Southern Chronicle*, August 4, 1863; *O. R.*, I, 23, pt. 2, p. 524;
      Frank Moore, Comp., *The Rebellion Record: a Diary of American Events
      with Documents, Narratives, Illustrative Incidents, Poetry Etc.* (New York,
      1861-1868), I, p. 109; Major W. D. Reynolds, Miss Martha [*sic.*] Brown-
      low; or , *The Heroine of Tennessee* (Philadelphia, 1863). A copy is in the
      McClung Collection. The Philadelphia publisher also got out a German
      version under the title *Miss Maude* [*sic.*] *Brownlow order Die Helden von
      Tennessee*. Sue married Dr. Boynton on January 17, 1866. Roscoe
      d'Armand and Virginia d'Armand, *Knox County Marriage Records,
      1792-1900* (Knoxville, 1970), p. 99. See also Zella Armstrong (comp.),
      Notable Southern Families, 5 vols. (Chattanooga, 1918) I, p. 43; *Whig*,
      October 17, 1866.
[15] Temple, *East Tennessee and the Civil War*, pp. 471-475.
[16] *Whig*, November 11, 1863; *O. R.*, I, 30, pt. 3, Secretary of War Edwin M.
      Stanton to W. G. Brownlow, Esq., September 19, 1863, p. 745. Women of
      the Brownlow family had been living in Covington, Kentucky. *Whig*,

---

[17] *Ibid.*, November 11, 1863. A marginal note by John Bell Brownlow mentions his father's opposition to the Hawkins County slave traders. *Ibid.*, October 27, 1849.

[18] *Parson Brownlow's Book*, preface, 7, and 358, 413-414. That the Brownlow family had two domestic slaves, Rhoda and Curtis, was told this writer by Mrs. John F. (Jack) Brownlow, widow of the Parson's grandson, in an interview at her Knoxville home on April 27, 1972. Mrs. Brownlow came to Knoxville as a bride, lived with her husband in the home of his father, John Bell Brownlow, for eleven years, and Mrs. Eliza Brownlow, the Parson's widow. She was told that the two slaves remained in the Brownlow household after they were freed. A young student, who lived in the Brownlow home while reading law just prior to the Civil War, described the editor as a slave owner. Felix A. Reeve, "East Tennessee in the War of the Rebellion," a pamphlet containing a speech delivered on December 3, 1902, at a stated meeting of the Military Order of the Loyal Legion of the United States, commandery of the District of Columbia, War Papers. A copy of this pamphlet is in the files of the Western Reserve Historical Society, Cleveland, Ohio. A fellow townsman described the Parson as a slaveholder. Samuel Heiskell, *Andrew Jackson and Early Tennessee History*, [Nashville, 1920-1921], 3 vols. III, p. 212.

[19] Humes, *The Loyal Mountaineers*, pp. 245-246; Temple, *Notable Men*, p. 282; *Whig*, January 9, 1864.

[20] When Brownlow returned to Knoxville he retained his post as an assistant United States Treasury agent which office he had filled at Nashville (see fn. 13). *Whig*, November 11, 18, 1863, January 9, 16, February 20, 1864, and thereafter. See also Folmsbee *et al.*, *Short History*, p. 342; *Whig*, April 16, 1864.

[21] Seymour, p. 13; *Whig*, January 16, February 6, 29, August 24, November 18, January 16, August 17, 1864, November 11, 1863, January 9, 1864, November 11, 1863, January 11, 25, 1865.

[22] *Register*, October 23, 1863. The *Register* was published in Atlanta until it was suspended in the spring of 1864. *Whig*, April 30, 1864.

[23] See "Treasury Regulations," *ibid.*, January 9, 1864, June 4, October 2, November 5, January 30, 1864.

[24] *Ibid.*, January 9, 1864. Intercession for Dodd, originally a Kentuckian, was made by members of the Masonic order. Humes, *The Loyal Mountaineers*, pp. 289-292; *Whig*, January 16, 30, February 20, 1864.

[25] Temple, *East Tennessee and the Civil War*, p. 429; Humes, *The Loyal Mountaineers*, pp. 165-167; *Whig*, March 5, 1864; James Welch Patton, *Unionism and Reconstruction in Tennessee, 1860-1869* (Chapel Hill, North Carolina, 1934), p. 60; hereafter referred to as *Unionism and Reconstruction*.

[26] For organization of the East Tennessee Relief Association and the petition to Lincoln, see *Whig*, February 13, 1864; Humes, *The Loyal Mountaineers*, pp. 301-303, 307-308, 313-392; Temple, *East Tennessee and the Civil War*, pp. 408-410. "Determining to hold the region at all costs, the Confederates inaugurated a reign of terror. Vigilance committees prowled over the country, armed to the teeth, arresting men on suspicion of hostility to the

new government, and shooting down others. . . A civil and guerilla war was thus begun, the horrors of which almost defy description." Patton, *Unionism and Reconstruction*, p. 63.

[27] Captain H. M. Ashby was in command of the Confederate cavalry which captured the Unionists attempting to flee to Kentucky. In the fight in Campbell County, Ashby reported killing thirty and wounding an equal number, then marching the survivors to Knoxville, where most of them were sent to southern prisons. *O. R.*, II, 1, p. 860; Humes, *The Loyal Mountaineers*, pp. 165-166; Temple, *East Tennessee and the Civil War*, pp. 424-425; *Whig*, March 5, 1864.

[28] T. J. Campbell was judge-advocate of the court-martial convened at Knoxville to try men for the bridge burning. *O. R.*, X, 5, pt. 1, pp. 649-650.

[29] "While the editor wrote all the editorials for this paper, he faithfully discharged the onerous duties as agent of the Treasury Department, personally supervised the work of reorganizing & building up the *loyal* Methodist Church, made many Republican speeches of which no notice was taken in this paper for want of space & was visited by many loyal people all over East Tenn. of all sexes. His labors were prodigious." Marginal note by John Bell Brownlow, *Whig*, September 21, 1864.

[30] *Ibid.*, August 26, 31, 1864.

[31] Folmsbee *et al.*, *Short History*, pp. 337-339; *Whig*, April 31, 1864.

[32] Temple, *East Tennessee and the Civil War*, pp. 475-482; *Whig*, January 9, 1864, March 1, 1865, July 2, February 13, September 7, 1864, February 11, 1865, May 14, March 5, April 9, March 12, April 16, May 23, June 4, July 23, 1864 and thereafter. See also November 5, 1864.

Brownlow's Knoxville Whig,
and Rebel Ventilator.

"The union of lakes—the union of lands—The union of states none can sever—The union of hearts—the union of hands—And the flag of the Union forever."

Chapter No. 16

THE PARSON'S ADVOCATE

At the prompting of President Lincoln, Governor Johnson made futile attempts to restore civil government in Tennessee in 1863 and early in 1864. He then hit upon the device of reconvening the Greeneville Convention of 1861. This body reassembled in Knoxville on April 12, 1864, and fell into such disagreement that after four days it adjourned without taking action on either of two sets of resolutions offered. The discussions, however, forecast the direction political lines would take. O. P. Temple noted, "The old leaders of the Greeneville Convention, such as Nelson, Baxter, Spears, Heiskell and Fleming found themselves confronted by a new set of men who to a large extent belonged to the army, and who had imbibed by suffering and persecution, feelings quite unlike those of the men who had neither suffered nor entered the army." This latter group and Parson Brownlow made common cause.[1]

On the heels of the convention's failure a mass meeting was held in Knoxville. Johnson engineered it and was billed as the chief speaker. The meeting adopted a resolution requesting the governor to call a constitutional convention. The delegates would be required to be loyal men and pledged to the abolition of slavery. Another resolution praised President Lincoln and Johnson and endorsed their administrations, and another demanded the complete subjugation of the South. Some neat political footwork preceded the meeting. Johnson had the resolutions drawn, but since they lauded him, it would have been most indelicate for them to have been presented bearing his name. The governor took them to his old foe, Brownlow. The Parson found them satisfactory and agreed to offer them under his name. But because the Parson's voice was inadequate, he enlisted his friend Temple to read them. Temple did, but made an objection to the plan calling for a constitutional convention. He preferred that this task be performed by a legislature. Johnson, in his speech, found great merit in the "Brownlow" resolutions and reiterated his position that "treason must be made odious, and traitors be punished and impoverished." The *Whig* closed this circuitous operation by describing the resolutions as "having been offered to the meeting by the editor of this paper." The newspaper also complimented the governor on his speech.[2]

This temporary Brownlow-Johnson axis again operated successfully at the Union Party Convention held in Baltimore in June. Tennessee won admission of its delegates after a sharp fight that arose over whether the state was in or out of the Union. Convention delegates learned that Parson Brownlow was in the hall on the night of June 7 and prevailed upon him to speak. He urged them not to commit the error of regarding Tennessee as a state in rebellion because "We don't recognize it [secession] in Tennessee. We deny that we are out. We deny that we have been out." As an additional inducement to seat the Tennessee delegation, he indicated that the state would nominate Andrew Johnson for Vice-President. When Johnson was nominated as Lincoln's running mate, the *Whig* paid tribute to him "as a man who stood firm in the defense of his country when his old party associates South were going over to the enemy."[3]

Johnson was determined that the ticket on which he was running with Lincoln should carry Tennessee. He had a record of winning which he wanted to maintain, and the stakes were the highest in his career. In East Tennessee Brownlow battled furiously for the Union Party ticket. But many of the old Whig and Unionist leaders of the area, possibly a majority, refused to support Lincoln. Instead they swung in behind the Democratic nominee, General George B. McClellan, who favored an immediate peace. But McClellan supporters were disfranchised. A Radical State Convention (also known as the Union State Convention) recommended a stiff test oath, which Johnson may have devised. The governor embodied this requirement in a proclamation which directed voters to swear that they would "cordially oppose all armistices or negotiations for peace with rebels in arms." Immediate peace was what the Democratic platform had pledged. Ten Tennesseeans petitioned Lincoln to set aside the test oath, but he found no reason to interfere. The *Whig* published the President's letter in full, and noted, "Mr. Lincoln is good on a reply, and had given this self-constituted Tennessee Committee the sort of a reply they merited." The *Whig* also reported that the names of T. A. R. Nelson and A. Blizzard on the petition were not authorized. Lincoln's reply left the McClellan supporters helpless and they withdrew their electors. [4]

The Lincoln-Johnson ticket, with the opposition destroyed, carried the state. But Congress held that Tennessee was in rebellion and refused to recognize the vote. The returns, while conclusive, were scarcely gratifying to the Radical Unionists, for they were extremely light. Reliable reports as to the exact vote are not to be found. The *Whig* reported early returns showing that ten East Tennessee counties had cast 10,279 ballots, all for Lincoln and Johnson. A week later the paper reported that 40,000 votes had been counted at Nashville, half of them from East Tennessee. Succeeding issues of the *Whig* failed to carry supporting figures, which suggests that if additional returns were available they did not justify the previous claims. Thousands of East Tennessee loyalists were in the Union army and unable to vote, and parts of the state remained a battleground. Fighting continued in upper East Tennessee and General Hood moved north into Middle Tennessee. These conditions were unfavorable for a normal vote, even without the stricture of disfranchisement. [5]

The dust of the campaign had barely begun to settle when the *Whig* carried a call for a preliminary convention to be held at Nashville on December 19, "to form a ticket to run for a Constitutional Convention by the loyal men of the State, the Governor designating the day for the election by proclamation after the preliminary Convention makes out the ticket." The call also invited Middle and West Tennessee to "act in concert" by getting up their delegates. Three men from Knox and one each from Greene and Roane counties were on the "Executive Committee for East Tennessee," which issued the call. The committee based its authority on "the heavy loyal vote cast in Tennessee which shows the sentiments of the people and their desire to put down the rebellion and restore Civil Government."

Tennessee's interests also suffered because the state lacked the two senators and eight representatives in the United States Congress which readmission would give it. This was a point of urgency (*Whig*,

November 16, 1864). The mass meeting of loyal men in Knoxville had asked the governor to call such a convention and the maneuvering by the "Executive Committee" seems to have come down channels from him, especially since the governor's son-in-law, David T. Patterson, was a member of the group that issued the call. Patterson was a former circuit judge who had suffered a brief arrest by the Confederate military during its occupation of East Tennessee. The chairman was Samuel R. Rodgers, Temple's law partner. Rodgers had accompanied the Parson to Nashville when the editor was escorted out of the Confederacy in 1862. Rodgers also had signed the call for the Knoxville-Greeneville conventions, assemblies also summoned to deal with critical public conditions as their justification for existence. R. K. Byrd, a Roane County farmer and slaveholder, also was a member of the Greeneville Convention. He fled North in 1861, organized the First Tennessee Infantry and as its colonel led the regiment in a number of engagements. Perez Dickinson was a staunch Unionist of New England birth who had accumulated wealth in the mercantile business in Knoxville. When he was indicted by the Confederate Court in Knoxville on a charge of treasonable conduct, he had been North on business. Judge West Humphreys had released him under $10,000 bond to guarantee good behavior. Dickinson had rejected an offer to obtain his release without bond if he would take the oath of allegiance to the Confederacy. Brownlow's name was in third place on the committee, but he was elevated to the chairmanship when the same five men reconstituted themselves into a group requesting the loyal men of East Tennessee to meet in Knoxville on December 5 to select delegates to the state convention.[6]

The East Tennessee Convention represented the bulk of the Union vote in the state, and it put up Brownlow as a candidate for governor. Chairman Rodgers, in his official account of the proceedings, said the Parson told the delegates, "If chosen for that office, he would use the whole power of the state to rid East Tennessee of all rebel thieves and robbers, and took his seat amid prolonged applause." The warm response to Brownlow's pledge was reported in an issue of the *Whig* that carried several stories of atrocities by Confederate soldiers and guerillas, including the killing of forty-one Union men in Polk County (*Whig*, December 7, 1864).

The advance of General John B. Hood's Confederate army into Middle Tennessee delayed the meeting in Nashville. Two battles were fought before the session was possible. Franklin, fought on November 30, saw Union General John M. Schofield retreating to Nashville, but Hood was hurt by many casualties. He remained outside Nashville until General George H. Thomas moved upon him with a much larger force and decisively defeated him in the Battle of Nashville, fought on December 15 and 16. The delegates then met in the capital on January 9, 1865, and debated furiously the question of the convention's power. On the sixth and final day, the convention nominated and approved unanimously Brownlow.[7] The Parson dashed off a three-paragraph acceptance that included a pledge:

And God being my helper, if you will send up to Nashville, on the first Monday of April, a Legislature that will re-organize the State Militia, and enact other necessary laws, I will put an end to this infernal system of guerilla warfare and private and public robbery, if we have to shoot and hang all concerned, in East, Middle and West Tennessee (*Whig*, January 25, 1865).

The convention's arrogation of power went far beyond the announced and expected task of preparing a slate of delegates. This development Brownlow had not anticipated until he arrived in Nashville. On the eve of the meeting in Knoxville he still saw the assembly as functioning to elect delegates, "who, if chosen by the people, are to amend the Constitution of the State, perhaps elect a governor, besides other civil officers." He recommended swift action "so as to avert any effort to remand our state into a territorial condition. This may be done by the Congress about to meet, and in that event, our civil organization may be set back several years."

Historical writers, including Temple, who was a delegate, insist that the body was a mass meeting, and acted far in excess of whatever authority it had, certainly of that outlined in the call. It resolved itself into a political convention by nominating Brownlow, and into a constitutional convention by preparing amendments to the basic charter. One would abolish slavery and another offered a "schedule" to repeal the legislative acts which took Tennessee out of the Union and into the Confederacy. The proposed constitutional amendments and the repeal of the legislative acts, a curious combination in itself, were to be submitted to the electorate on February 22. The election of governor and members of the General Assembly was recommended to be held on March 4. The six-day session produced some marvels of shortcuts. Johnson often is given responsibility for them, but Brownlow acquiesced in them.[8] He explained, after conceding that the delegates had gone far afield from the purpose stated in the call:

I expected that [the preparation of a ticket for a constitutional convention] would be the work of this Convention; but the call was only suggested as those who called it had no authority to say what the Convention should or should not do. But the best legal minds on this floor have admitted that to agree upon the amendments here is just as lawful as to agree upon them in a Convention hereafter elected. This is the shortest cut, and the most direct route to the port we are aiming for. . . . What we do here is to be passed upon by the people at the ballot-box . . . and if not acceptable to them it will be rejected, leaving us just where we started (*Ibid.*).

The Parson, in pragmatic mood, warned that a constitutional convention would cost between $75,000 and $100,000. The state treasury had been stripped when Confederate state officials fled from Nashville. The cupboard was bare (*Ibid.*).

The convention sealed the outcome of the February 22 referendum by imposing another strict oath (only men of unconditional loyalty were excused). It required voters to sign their ballots and mark them for "Ratification" or "Rejection." Fewer than one hundred men had the hardihood to record themselves against the proposal, and it carried by 25,000 or 26,000 votes. This fulfilled President Lincoln's requirement that a state must cast one-tenth of what it did in 1860 to qualify for recognition from Washington. Armed with this authority, Johnson proclaimed that the election of a governor and members of the legislature would be held on March 4. Brownlow's election was assured since he had no opposition on the ballot and the legislative slate was carefully tailored. The convention nominated most of the men for the seats, half of them members of that body. In East Tennessee the committee which had started the ball rolling filled in the names for some counties.[9] The vote, ridiculously one-sided, was short of a triumph, for Brownlow received 3,000 or 4,000 less than had been cast on February 22. The franchise was limited, but in both elections arrangements were made for Tennessee soldiers in the Union army to cast ballots, and 1,328 of them encamped near Knoxville went on record for the Parson and the legislative slate. Confederates made efforts to break up the election at some places. At Greeneville, on February 22, the Fourth Tennessee Infantry (U.S.) repelled a band of 250, but at Rutledge cavalry carried off the ballot box. On the day of the second election some polls in McMinn County failed to open because of the fear of guerilla raids.

The House and Senate canvasses of the vote, as reported by Secretary of State E. H. East, found 23,222 for Brownlow and 35 write-ins. Yet the official canvass listed returns from only forty-four counties, less than half of those in the state. Among the missing counties were a number in East Tennessee where a substantial vote for Brownlow and the slate could have been expected. Among the missing counties were Blount, Greene, Carter, Sullivan, Unicoi, Washington, Hawkins and Hancock. Secretary East certified that he had examined the returns and found a full contingent of legislators had been elected, including a number of counties where no vote for governor was reported. No county-by-county list of returns for the legislative slate was reported in the canvass. The election of senators and representatives from counties where no vote was reported was certified because all were running at large, and were voted in by ballots cast outside their districts.[10]

Brownlow must have been plied with incorrect information on what returns from throughout the state were showing. Two weeks after the ratification election he predicted that the total would run close to 60,000 and would be even greater in the election for governor and members of the General Assembly. He must have regretted this exaggeration when the correct results were known. Perhaps, with everyone knowing he would be governor, favor seekers were trying to ingratiate themselves by telling him what he wanted to hear (*Whig*, March 8, 1865).

The Parson's election required new arrangements for the operation of the *Whig*. The Parson, John Bell Brownlow, and T. Haws set up a three-way partnership. Haws looked after the business end of the newspaper. The responsibility of editing fell upon the son.[11] The father, in a nostalgic announcement, pledged himself to continue writing about state affairs, "and shall not consider it beneath the dignity of a governor to correspond weekly for a paper of such large circulation, and of such principles, hopes and aims." He reviewed briefly his rugged and exciting career, then turned

to those we have long advised, and acted with, many of whom we may never again see in this life, we take this occasion to say, the consciousness of duty well performed, the complacent rememberance [*sic.*] of good deeds done, and of high moral achievments [*sic.*] won, should encourage, comfort, gratify. But the ghost of misspent hours, all hideous grinning, rise to terrify you through life, and reproach your [*you*] for not having moved more rapidly and to more purpose. So says

The Old Editor (*Whig*, March 29, 1865).

Underneath *Brownlow's Knoxville Whig*, on page one, in the first column, the line of type that for years had read "W. G. Brownlow, Editor" was pulled by the printer and replaced by "Published by Brownlow, Haws & Co." (*Whig*, February 15, 1865).

John Bell Brownlow was a busy young man. He was lieutenant colonel of the Ninth Tennessee Cavalry (U.S.); he was editor of the *Whig*; and he also stepped into his father's shoes as assistant special agent of the Treasury Department for East Tennessee. He wound up this labor early in 1866. It probably required the influence of the governor-elect to get the military to permit John Bell to hold two other jobs while still in the service. Obviously such arrangements were made, for the son was not mustered out until September 11, 1865, more than five months after he had taken over the two outside posts. The Parson had complained frequently that newspaper production costs were increasing, but he equipped the *Whig* plant until Brownlow, Haws & Co. boasted of having three modern presses, and an old one, all driven by steam and with "the best job office ever opened in East Tennessee." Mails were opening and postmasters were moving into their offices.[12] John Bell Brownlow and the *Whig* were ready to take over the role of the Parson's advocate.

The *Whig* of April 12, 1865, under the direction of the new editor, presented pages reflecting the unity and vigor of the Nashville-Knoxville connection. The governor reported the events of April 5, including his inaugural address in full. The *Whig* also published accounts of the day's ceremonies taken from three Nashville newspapers. One reporter described the governor as "an old man, palsied in limbs, but vigorous in intellect, and filled with stern determination." Brownlow's pen was not palsied, however, for he sent back a rather complete account of the organization of the legislature and some special touches on his inauguration. This ceremony, he wrote, came off "before the most [*sic.*] large and brilliant assemblage I ever saw in the Capitol—consisting of the civil and military population.—There were three Major Generals, five Brigadier Generals, each with his staff in full uniform. . . . My voice was fortunately good, and I was distinctly heard by the entire assembly." An auspicious addition to the fluttering flags and brass band was "the roar of cannon in honor of the fall of Richmond and Petersburg." The news of General Lee's surrender occupied the foot of the first column on page two below the accounts of the inauguration.

Cannon that heralded the Union victories also boomed in Knox-

ville that Monday night.[13] John Bell Brownlow wrote with triumphant pen that in compliance with a military order the next day:

All the public offices and buildings were brilliantly illuminated, and for several
hours Knoxville did not hide her light under a bushel. The Franklin house, and
most of the private residences in the city were all ablaze and presented a goodly
sight. One thing struck us particularly as a sign of the coming good times, and
that was the sharing of many of our citizens, who have always sympathized with
the rebellion, in these manifestations of joy over the downfall of Richmond.
May their blazing candles prove the types of the relighting of the fires of true
patriotism in their breasts (*Whig*, April 12, 1865).

If these Southern sympathizers had expected that the war's end
would bring also a cessation of bitterness and reprisals, they were
soon disillusioned. The wires from Nashville brought word of the
enactment of restrictive legislation against them, and at home they
felt distrust and hatred from their neighbors to a point that Knoxville soon became untenable for many of them. Lieutenant William
Rule, on his way to be mustered out at Nashville, heard in Cincinnati
the reports of the Union triumph, and thought happily of peace and
home. But for many on the other side, it did not bring peace. Six
months later, again employed by the *Whig*, Rule made his final entry
in his well-worn notebooks on his Civil War experiences: "We have
heard it from reliable authority that there are three hundred families
making preparations to leave Knoxville for a more congenial climate."[14]

John Bell Brownlow was well and signally qualified to step into his
father's chair as the avenging spirit dedicated to the punishment of
Confederates who had gone with the South voluntarily, and who
showed no signs of penitence for their acts as secessionists. Turbulence had touched John Bell from the embryonic stage onward.
While Eliza was carrying the child and the Parson was putting in his
first year as an editor the mother was prostrated with fear and grief
when Jack and Robert Powell rode to the O'Brien Iron Works for the
purpose of physically punishing Brownlow because of his political
opposition. The young editor fought back. Shots were fired. But he
broke off and entered the house when his mother-in-law entreated
him to comfort his wife. As John Bell neared the age of ten, an
assailant cracked his father's son with a club. The family's alarm at
this misfortune just as the editor was preparing to move his newspaper to Knoxville must have made a deep impression on the boy. In

1860 he killed a taunting and bullying fellow student at Emory and Henry College. As lieutenant of the Ninth Volunteer Cavalry (Union) Regiment he led his troops in dashing and bloody expeditions.

He had soaked up politics almost from birth, in the Parson's household, and he had tagged along with his father to visit Tom Nelson when the lawyer came to Knoxville to argue cases before the sessions of the Tennessee Supreme Court. In Nelson's room at the Mansion House the inevitable course of conversation was politics. Important men of the times—preachers, politicians and soldiers— streamed through the hospitable Brownlow residence at what was then 213 Cumberland Street. The large frame house, which stood above the east bank of First Creek, more than a block west of the present Civic Auditorium and Coliseum, constantly received visitors. They ranged from Methodist bishops to soldier-statesmen such as the Tennessee-Texan, flamboyant Sam Houston. Senator John Bell, one of the state's great leaders, and a man of national renown, once persuaded his young namesake to bring him French brandy from a Gay Street drug store to relieve his thirst in the Parson's spiritless house. He also learned at the family altar how preachers mingled politics and religion. A revered Methodist preacher, and a Democrat, while visiting at the Brownlow home was invited by the Parson to lead in the nightly worship. When the visitor prayed he petitioned for the election of James K. Polk, a Democrat, as President. Brownlow interrupted with: "May the Lord forbid." Unabashed, the visitor broadened his plea, asking the Almighty to remove Brownlow's Whiggery. At this the Parson interrupted: "May the good Lord forbid."

In 1855 young John Bell was thrilled by the eloquence of the famous Whig congressman and orator, Meredith P. Gentry. His introduction to extended political stump speaking came in 1861. He traveled with O. P. Temple, elector for John Bell, the forlorn hope of the southern Unionists in the fateful year when Lincoln was elected President. As was the custom Temple stumped the Second District, and the listening and watching youth was impressed with the ability of his father's close friend. He found himself loathing, perhaps it was an intensification of an established dislike, John Crozier Ramsey, a member of the illustrious Democratic family of Knoxville. When Temple spoke at Blaine's Cross Roads one of the listeners was R. Barnwell Rhett. The South Carolina secessionist and his daughter were staying at a nearby resort. Ramsey escorted them. John Bell feared that Miss Rhett would get the impression that East

Tennesseeans were rude, ill-mannered and repulsive, because Ramsey "spit tobacco juice all over his shirt front," and "changed his shirts as often as once in two weeks and bathed as often as once a month." John Bell's recollection of Ramsey was written thirty-four years later.[15] It may have been tinged with bitterness for as Confederate district attorney Ramsey had signed the treason warrant against Parson Brownlow that resulted in his arrest and imprisonment.

Young Brownlow's experiences continued to broaden. He was made lieutenant colonel of the Ninth Tennessee Cavalry Regiment in 1863 and was "cultivated" by Military Governor Johnson. The governor and the young officer, in 1863 and 1864, cozily drank whiskey from Johnson's demijohn after the state's chief executive had locked his office for the day. They talked politics as they drank, the governor "partaking very freely, myself sparingly." Flattered as the officer was by this attention he realized that Johnson had some purpose in these meetings. Years later he observed that the governor may have expected that the Brownlows would be useful to him in his political career after the war.

By September 1864 John Bell was truly a soldier. He spent hours in the saddle, often with no food, and slept on the ground with one blanket for warmth. As commanding officer of the Ninth he was proud of his men for the resolute way that they faced their first fire in the counties northeast of Knoxville. He had in full measure the Brownlow trait of helping his friends by every means. In reply to a plea by O. P. Temple he arranged to impress teams, drivers and wagons of farmers on the side of the Confederacy to haul 6,000 pounds of the lawyer's tobacco from his farm near Bull's Gap to the railroad for shipment to Knoxville. He justified this operation with:

At all events I will get the property out without it costing you anything. You have done a great deal for Uncle Sam and there is no reason why he should not do something for you. . . .

Nothing can be made for our cause by attempting to conciliate rebels. The only way to restore *peace* is to kill and subjugate them.

Their wagons, mules, horses, corn, oats and every aspect of property should be made subservient to the convenience and interests of loyal men.

John had inherited his father's tendency to speak and write more harshly than he would have acted, but he was also filled with an accumulation of bitterness. The treatment of his father, his family, and the thousands of Union men who had been persecuted by Confederate authorities and Confederate citizens created this feeling. John wrote this callous report of the events surrounding the killing of the Confederate cavalry leader, General John Hunt Morgan, in a surprise attack by Union forces at Greeneville on September 4, 1864:

> At Greeneville, Morgan's force was at least 1,600, I think more; our force was less. Notwithstanding this we routed them completely, and I had the pleasure of seeing the lifeless carcass of their fallen chief.
>
> In ten minutes after he was killed, I met a sergeant with his body thrown over the neck of his horse, with his head and face covered with blood. I pointed the men of the 9th to the corpse, assuring them it was the veritable John Morgan. They made the welkin ring with shouts of applause.

Lieutenant Colonel Brownlow saved for himself a souvenir of Morgan's death: "a large wooden pipe, with a splendid plaster of paris picture of Morgan on it that was found in the room where the Confederate general slept his last night.[16]

About 1912 John Bell Brownlow told a highly respected Knoxville lawyer that his regiment and two others were stationed at Bull's Gap with "their principal duty . . . to occupy enough East Tennessee territory to enable the November election to be held and give the electoral vote of Tennessee to Lincoln and Johnson." The troops at Bull's Gap were under the command of Colonel Alvin C. Gillem, who had been acting adjutant general under Military Governor Johnson. The governor had urged President Lincoln to promote Gillem to brigadier general. The President complied but the Senate Military Affairs Committee held up on recommending confirmation. Gillem had never commanded troops and several hundred other colonels who had seen combat service were favored for promotion.

A fourteen-year-old country boy, carrying home a sack of meal from a mill, was deprived of his food by Confederate cavalrymen on the afternoon of September 3, 1864. The boy heard the Confederates say they were going to stay in Greeneville that night. He reported this fact to Gillem at Bull's Gap, and the colonel called a council of his officers. They favored a surprise attack at daybreak. Gillem didn't but he yielded to the view of his officers. Brownlow led the attacking column; Gillem was at the rear. The Unionists learned that Morgan was staying at the home of Mrs. Catherine Williams on the main street of Greeneville. After Morgan was killed Gillem rode up and Brownlow gave him the details. Using the telegraph office at Bull's Gap Gillem sent the following message to Governor Johnson:

Last night while at headquarters at Bull's Gap I received information that General John H. Morgan and his command was at Greeneville. I made a forced march, starting at midnight, surprised Morgan and his command at daylight, have scattered his troops and they are fleeing toward Jonesboro. We killed General Morgan and have possession of his body.

Johnson relayed the message immediately to Washington and the next day the Senate committee reported favorably on Gillem's promotion. It was confirmed at once by the Senate.[17]

Early in May 1865 the *Whig* published an issue that was the embodiment of Brownlow fury. Father and son, with assistance from the now President Johnson, all contributed to it. Johnson proclaimed that the assassination of Lincoln was the result of a plot engineered by Jefferson Davis, former president of the Confederacy, and a number of other men. He offered rewards totalling $335,000 for the arrest of these suspects. The Tennessee General Assembly directed Governor Brownlow to offer a reward of $5,000 for the "apprehension and delivery" of Isham G. Harris, Tennessee's governor before and during the state's secession,[18] and Brownlow elaborated on the resolution with:

The aforesaid refugee from justice, without the authority of law, and in violation of all law, human and Divine, was the chief instrument in thrusting upon Tennessee this terrible rebellion, and its inumerable [*sic.*] evils; a rebellion which has stormed the very citadel of order, every defense of virtue, every sanctuary of right, and every abode of decency. When those villainous but frantic efforts were astonishing mankind with her success, as much as appaling [*sic.*] them with their atrocity; when the fairest portion of this great Commonwealth had been made hideous by the triumphs of this arch-traitor and his corrupt and treasonable associates, and their prelusive orgies had profaned our churches, like dastards they ingloriously fled, upon the approach of the national flag of beauty and glory, carrying with them to the heart of treason the funds and other valuables of this State. . . . Said Harris has been periodically visiting the border counties of this State, issuing bogus proclamations, and collecting revenue, falsely pretending to be the Governor of Tennessee.

This culprit Harris is about five feet ten inches high, weights [*sic.*] about one hundred and forty-five pounds, and is about fifty-five years of age. His complexion is sallow—his eyes are dark and penetrating—a perfect index to the heart of a traitor—with the scowl and frown of a demon resting upon his brow. The study of mischief, and the practice of crime, have brought upon him premature baldness and grey beard. With brazen-faced impudence, he talks loudly and boastingly about the overthrow of the Yankee army, and entertains no doubt but the South will achieve her independence. He chews tobacco rapidly, and is inordinately fond of liquor. In his moral structure he is an unscrupulous man—steeped to the nose and chin in personal and political profligacy—now about lost to all sense of humor and shame—with a heart reckless of social duty and fatally bent upon mischief.

If captured he will be found lurking in the rebel strongholds of Mississippi, Alabama, or Georgia, and in *female society*, alleging with the sheep-faced modesty of a virtuous man, that it is not a wholesome state of public sentiment, or of taste, that forbids an indiscriminate mixing together of married man and women. If captured the *fugitive must* be delivered to me *alive*, to the end that justice may be done upon him here, upon the theatre of his former villainous deeds! (*Whig*, May 10, 1865).

Young John's contribution to this inflammatory page of the *Whig* was a suggestion that returning East Tennesseeans, who had been militant secessionists, should not be permitted to return to their old homes to live. He cited the example of Robert C. West, a former slave dealer. West had accumulated wealth in his field, and according to John Bell, observed with "much pleasure" the hanging of Union men near Knoxville, and had "knocked down and cruelly beat with a club Isham Alley, a feeble man, sixty-five years of age." West fled before the Union forces arrived in Knoxville, but had returned. Alley, taking his turn, assaulted his tormentor with such vigor that he cracked West's skull. To those who demanded the prosecution of Alley, the *Whig* replied that it approved of his course in assaulting West, predicted that he would never see the penitentiary, and hinted that there were a number of men in the area "who have no more right to live here than Jeff Davis." The young editor's second target was Robert M. Barton, a former Circuit Court judge who also had been a member of the 1861 legislature. John held that that body was responsible for "widows and orphans . . . being dispersed throughout East Tennessee." The *Whig* recalled that the judge *"openly declared that Union men should not be permitted to live in East Tennessee,"* and had approved extreme punishment of the loyalists, including their killing. John Bell stamped the editorial with this suggestion to his old troopers:

A few days since Judge Barton returned to his home in Jefferson County, in the midst of a loyal community, nearly every young man of which served under us in the gallant 9th Tennessee Cavalry. If *he* is permitted to live within the

territory of the United States, there ought to be a general amnesty to traitors.
There is not a penitentiary in the United States that does not contain *better men*
than Judge Barton (*Ibid.*).

The Brownlow legislature faced a task unique in the history of the
state. It had to rebuild the political, economic, and social structure
from the ruins left by war. The executive, legislative, and judicial
functions of the state had fallen into chaos except for such caretak-
ing measures as had been taken by Military Governor Johnson. The
state treasury and records were gone, carried off when the Harris
administration and the General Assembly of 1861 had fled from
Nashville. Communication and transportation had been disrupted.
These facilities had been used by the military forces. Fields had been
torn and ravaged by the conflicting armies, provisions seized, and
stock driven off or confiscated. Financial institutions had been crippled or ruined. Many citizens, especially the old, the women, and the
children, were left helpless and destitute. Churches had entered into
the fray with ministers taking sides and congregations dividing,
especially in East Tennessee. Because classroom doors had been
closed for four years, large numbers of a generation moving toward
adulthood were in a state bordering on illiteracy. The unshackled
slaves groped in unfamiliar freedom for which they had not been
prepared. They were puzzled and confused, anchorless unless they
worked out a new arrangement with their old masters. The white
population of East Tennessee was racked by divisions and hatreds,
the fruits of occupation by both Confederate and Union armies with
the accompanying advantages taken by civilians for reprisal and gain.
In this rugged, mountainous region of the state not only were secessionists and Unionists filled with hatred toward each other, but the
loyalists also were split. The Radicals demanded retribution, proscription, and vengeance. The Conservatives proposed tolerance to
those who had gone with the South, and the restoration of their
former right and privileges.[19]

The composition of the Brownlow legislature represented the
power that had been seized by the Radicals. Its members were overwhelmingly from the ranks of the old Whig Party. They were loyalists; a majority were farmers or planters, and fifteen were lawyers,
eight of whom were in the Senate. Six of the legislators had become
refugees during the war because of their Union convictions, eight had
suffered imprisonment by the Confederates, and twenty-three had
seen military service. Very few of these men were seasoned legis-

lators. Yet they included some men of considerable talent, although they sorely lacked the professionalism of the prewar assemblies. The substantial leavening of men who had served in the Union army or who had been imprisoned or arrested, showed that here was a group of men inclined to view with hostility any move to conciliate secessionists. [20] The assassination of President Lincoln by John Wilkes Booth on April 15, 1865, could only have inflamed this hostility. The members of the assembly condemned those responsible for the deed and laid emphasis on the martyred President's "humanity," [21] a theme upon which the *Whig* elaborated:

> We believe that history will pronounce Mr. Lincoln to have been an eminently honest and merciful man. No expression of harshness, or of personal ill-feeling, can be found in all his voluminous public writings. How marked the contrast with the writings of Mr. Davis, or even of General Lee. The messages of Davis abounded in falsehoods and malignant slanders. It is true Mr. Lincoln sometimes exercised powers that, in time of peace, would have been of doubtful constitutionality. But he did so on all occasions to preserve the Government, and not to *destroy* it. We justify him in nearly all he did. There was nothing of the tyrant or usurper about him. As a man and as a ruler he was generous, merciful, conscientious, and forgiving, almost to a fault. It is reported that he had already prepared a proclamation offering amnesty to all rebels. Whether the rebels will have cause to rejoice over or mourn his untimely end will be seen in the future (*Whig*, April 19, 1865).

The President's death produced a large amount of news in the *Whig*, along with the traditional turning of the printers' rules to bordering the columns with heavy, black lines. Ironically, the *Whig*'s first reference to Lincoln, an oblique one which did not mention his name, was a delighted comment by the Parson in 1846: "Our old Locofoco brother, Parson Peter Cartwright, was beaten by a Whig for Congress, in Illinois, by 1,500 votes." The Whig was Lincoln. [22]

Several bills of an intensely spiteful nature were introduced in the assembly but failed to pass. One would have prohibited returning Confederates from wearing their uniforms, possibly the only clothing they had. Another would have stripped ministers who had been secessionists of some of their traditional privileges in the performance of rites, such as marriages. None of these had the support of the governor or of his newspaper. Brownlow's recommendations in the field of law enforcement, however, were followed with the enactment of measures providing capital punishment for guerillas, robbers, armed prowlers, horse thieves, housebreakers, burglars, and house and bridge burners. Sheriffs were given additional power to maintain posses, which could consist only of men of established loyalty.[23] The bill upon which the Radicals and the governor placed the most importance, and which was fought vigorously in the House before it was enacted, stripped almost all of the returned Confederate soldiers and southern sympathizers of the franchise. The only exceptions were of Union men who had been conscripted. It also eliminated many Conservative Unionists. The measure, in disfranchising Confederates, also built what was considered a base for the continuation of Radical power. The governor expressed pleasure at the passage of the franchise measure, but he was distressed because representatives from Hawkins, Hancock, Cocke, Knox, Monroe, Hamilton, and McMinn counties voted against it. Among these was Speaker William Heiskell, who had been one of Brownlow's Treasury Department aides. In his enthusiasm to report the passage of the bill and to condemn East Tennessee representatives who voted against it, John Bell published two separate roll calls, one immediately below the other, with different tallies. The young editor meant to eliminate one item, but somewhere along the lines the purpose was not accomplished.[24] This type of error still appears in modern newspapers, much to the chagrin of executives.

The governor had other triumphs to celebrate. Near Augusta, Georgia, the Union army had captured archives of the Confederate legislature and $600,000 in state funds. When the captured property was returned to Nashville, Brownlow and his secretary of state, Andrew J. Fletcher, proudly rode from the railroad depot to the capitol on the wagon carrying these items. On one of the boxes of archives sat "the plainly but decorously garbed Governor, holding a gold-headed cane, and looking placidly on the caskets of coin which were his footstool." The seizure also included the letters which exposed the treachery of C. W. Charlton, the postmaster at Knoxville, who had intercepted and read Brownlow's mail preceding Tennessee's secession (*Whig*, June 7, 1865).

An editorial feat by the *Whig* was the publication of a letter from "A Candid Rebel," J. C. Gallaher, a former Knoxvillian who became a major in the Confederate army, lost an arm at Vicksburg, was captured and later exchanged. The letter, addressed to Governor Brownlow, expressed indignation at secession leaders who had urged their countrymen into war, but remained at home, holding civil office and obtaining contracts[25] by which

they might *swindle soldiers* and soldiers' families, and even rob the infant Government of its swaddling clothes. . . . 'Twas they who declared that if the South seceded, Union men could not live in East Tennessee. And it was they who first bowed obsequlously [*sic.*] to Federal masters, and now, sycophants like, ask to be taken into full Federal communion. And in great agony do they writhe under the disfranchisement of the Legislature. I think myself, that, the Union party, and the Legislature particularly (if it is their purpose to conciliate and reconcile the discordant elements, and establish that harmony which once did and ought exist) might, to facilitate these ends, have with profit acted with more magnimity [*sic.*]. But an act most just in all its bearings, and under the circumstances, could not have been conceived of. I, sir, for one, together with all other Southern men of Tennessee, if we had succeeded, would have favored the passage of such laws that would have forever precluded from citizenship men who left their homes and took up arms against us. And I cannot reprobate in others what I would have considered just in myself (*Whig*, June 28, 1865).

Major Gallaher's position was an isolated one but it lent point to the *Whig*'s policy. The great mass of secessionists wanted to recover the franchise in the state which four years earlier had tried, with force of arms, to detach itself from the United States. Strong voices, although in the minority, spoke for them in the assembly, especially in the House. There a determined, but unsuccessful effort was made to enact only moderate restrictions on the exercise of the franchise by former Confederates. Opposing this common position of the Conservative Unionists and the defeated Secessionists were the Radical Unionists, headed by the governor. Thus were the lines drawn in one of Tennessee's bitterest political struggles. At the voter level the Radicals were a minority, when compared with the unrestored Secessionists and the Conservatives. They may have been outnumbered by the latter.[26] But the Radicals held the political power of the state government, and they did not propose to release it, a condition almost the invariable rule in public affairs.

The first test came on August 3, 1865, with the election of eight members to the United States Congress. At stake was the validity of the franchise law, of public opinion of the Brownlow administration, and the position on loyalty of the congressmen to be elected. If the delegation lacked men of unquestioned Unionism their seating might be in jeopardy. The legislature had elected Joseph Smith Fowler and Patterson of Greene County to the United States Senate. The latter was the son-in-law of President Johnson.[27]

Some Conservatives were reported to be planning to ignore the new constitution and elect a new governor and legislature under the constitution of 1834. This would permit all white citizens twenty-one years of age to vote. The report of this move brought quick denunciation from the Parson, who had returned to Knoxville and was writing editorials under the signature of the "Senior Editor." Such a step, the governor wrote, would produce "armed rebellion, civil war, personal violence, and a general disturbance of the peace." Further, any such effort "will be treated as *rebellion*." Brownlow also resorted to one of his traditional positions. He praised the country people for their loyalty and described the towns as centers for rebellious talk. He also revived the story of the firing from a train load of Confederate soldiers on a Union meeting at Strawberry Plains in 1861.[28] By proclamation he called attention to the rigid provisions of the franchise law and demanded that civil authorities "arrest and bring to justice all persons who, under the pretense of being candidates for Congress, or other office, are traveling over the State denouncing and nullifying the constitution and the laws of the land, and spreading sedition and a spirit of rebellion." He supplemented the proclamation with an "Address to the People of Tennessee," in which he charged that even "disfranchised rebels" were being elected to office, and launched into a defense of the "validity and constitutionality" of the state government. The military forces of the United States, he wrote, had won the war on the battlefield, but Washington had placed a civilian, Andrew Johnson, in the governor's seat. When the war was ended the governor, acting under authority from the United States, had shaped and fostered the new state constitution. This the federal government had full right to do, and the convention which adopted the basic charter for the state a few months earlier "was the initiatory means chosen by the National Administration through its civil agent." Perhaps the constitution was dictated,[29] Brownlow acknowledged:

Certain it was forced upon the rebelhous [*sic.*] majority of the State. So was the authority of the United States forced upon them, and at the point of the bayonet, and just so the nation had a right to force upon them a republican form of Government, for nothing but force is recognized by the. . . .

Finally, it is said that the law is harsh and wanting in magnanimity. By law, the crime of the disfranchised is treason, and the punishment death and confiscation of property. All this is waved [*sic.*] and it is said to be cruel to refuse them the privilege of voting for a few years. Magnanimity requires that they should go to the ballot box and with bloody hands deposit their ballots, and by force of numbers seize the reigns of the government they have tried to destroy—elevate their baffled leaders to power—renew their persecutions of Union men, and at last have the victory in the State (*Ibid.*, July 19, 1865).

The election returns disconcerted the Brownlow organization. Only three unquestionable Radicals were elected. They were Horace Maynard of the Second District, W. B. Stokes of the Third and Isaac Hawkins of the Sixth. Hawkins' position was not entirely clear because he had not expressed it in detail. Nathaniel G. Taylor, elected from the First, was somewhere between a lukewarm Radical and a moderate Conservative. He was not a Brownlow man, for the Parson had criticized him sharply when his name was mentioned for the United States Senate in opposition to Maynard. The Parson accused Taylor of having made a substantial profit in funds raised for the destitute of East Tennessee, and of having gone over to the South in 1862. In the remaining four districts men of Conservative bent were elected. Dorsey B. Thomas defeated Samuel R. Arnell, Radical leader in the lower house of the Brownlow assembly, who had sponsored and pressed to passage the franchise law. The vote was Thomas, 2,805; Arnell, 2,350. On the basis of reports furnished to the governor on his demand there was some evidence of misunderstanding or outright violation of the law in the district. He threw out the votes of five counties. This made Arnell the winner, 1,546 to 521. Brownlow's policy was inconsistent. In some counties where reports were inadequate or violations were cited he accepted the returns, in others he did not; in another where violations were reported he let the vote stand, as he also did in some counties which made no reports. Inconsistent or not, the governor accomplished the practical purpose of giving a faithful, demonstrated Radical a certification of election that entitled him to a seat in the United States Congress. This gave the Radicals four members of their party in the delegation that sought admission to Congress. Taylor turned out to be a Conservative.[30]

The Parson returned to Knoxville late in the summer of 1865 to find East Tennessee plagued by threats and violence. Black Union soldiers had killed two white cavalrymen of East Tennessee units. One of the victims was from the Ninth, John Bell's old regiment (*Whig*, August 30, 1865). The *Whig* deplored any war upon the colored troops because they are in uniform with guns on their shoulders. . . . But we are opposed to the freedom with which they use their bayonets and level their muskets at white men (*Ibid.*).

Former Confederates complained bitterly that they were not being given equal protection under the law. A threatening letter signed "Many Rebels" had been sent to Circuit Judge E. T. Hall, Attorney General David K. Young, and Sheriff Marcus D. Bearden, all Unionists.[31] Unless the one-sided state of law enforcement was corrected, the signers warned:

We, many so-called rebels, will take the law into our own hands, and avenge the outrages committed upon our friends, by dealing summarily with the perpetrators and officials. . . .

We are hunted down and driven from our homes, not by the authorities, but by the vulgar, cowardly and unprincipled men who never placed themselves in danger where other men had an equal chance, and you have never tried to suppress it, but we will suppress it, if we have to suppress their worthless lives (*Whig*, September 13, 1865).

The governor, in the role of "Senior Editor," responded in characteristic style. He had just returned from Greeneville where he had visited the oak where Fry and Hensie were hanged

upon a false and groundless charge of bridge burning. They were buried in a common grave just under the tree. And it is that class of murderers, hanging such men, and leaving their widows and orphans to mourn the loss of that we are now called upon to treat with leniency! (*Whig*, August 30, 1865).

In an adjoining column the editor acknowledged many complaints of personal intimidation, torture and death, especially in East Tennessee. They were lodged chiefly by "Union men and rebels whose relatives are the sufferers." Indiscriminate flogging should be stopped and disputes taken to the courts, the Parson advised:

Quiet and peaceable rebels, who never oppressed loyal men, never persecuted them, and never participated in their arrest and imprisonment, and who are behaving themselves, ought to be let alone, and even protected. Rebel soldiers and citizens, who have taken the oath, and are living up to it, trying to obey the laws and make good citizens, ought not to be disturbed, and are entitled to protection. Rebels during the rebellion, who were kind to loyal men and their families—and there were many such in East Tennessee—rebels who actually assisted loyal men to escape from the conscript officers, and treated their families kindly in their absence, should not be ill-treated for simply having been in the rebellion (*Ibid.*).

This editorial, entitled "Shooting and Hanging Men," then launched into a description of several classes of rebels for whom the Parson could ask no favors. He included the men responsible for the conscript laws which led thousands to flee across the Cumberland Mountains, the military officers who pursued and captured them, and treated them harshly; those who sat on court-martials; the Confederates who flogged and beat Union men; those who strung up loyalist women in an effort to wring from them information of their husbands, brothers and sons; and those who confiscated provisions of the farmers and burned their homes or buildings; informers who pointed out loyal men and were the instruments through which they were sent to prison and sometimes to their deaths; and the applauding spectators at the hanging of Union men. Brownlow could have expanded this gruesome category, but having paused he added significantly:

The natural protectors of these families have, in part, returned after having served in the Union army for three years, and they know the guilty parties. Does anyone in his sober senses suppose they can escape killing, or such a beating as will disable them for life? If they are acting under this delusion, their erroneous notions will be corrected by the development of *time*!

To these "active leading rebels and bad men" in East Tennessee the editor offered blunt advice: go elsewhere. He suggested moderation, if not silence, for those who had been complaining of their treatment. The Knoxville Brownlows, father and son, had been threatened with assassination, as had Judge Hall, Attorney General Young and Sheriff Bearden, along with other leading Unionists. If the rebellious element wanted another war, "they can have it, and have it to their heart's content." The legislature had given sheriffs additional power to swear in posses, and Adjutant General James P. Brownlow, at the order of the governor, was in Washington applying for arms for the state. Federal forces were leaving Tennessee, and the state was expected to look after its own affairs. So far as the governor-editor was concerned "no threats from any quarter can intimidate me, or cause me to join in the outcry against what is maliciously styled an 'East Tennessee Mob.' "

The Parson decided it was an appropriate time to publish a copy of the warrant upon which he was arrested in 1861, and to condemn as outrageous the plans of some returning Confederates to try to regain through the courts their confiscated properties. He also favored reverse litigation, such as the action in which the heirs of Sam Pickens, former state senator from Sevier County, had obtained judgment for $10,000 against W. H. Sneed, John H. Crozier and R. B. Reynolds, the latter Confederate Court commissioner, for persecution and death of Pickens in prison. As Pickens was being marched away to prison, according to the Parson, Sneed snarled that the punishment was inadequate, "God d-n him, he ought to be hung [sic.] and quartered." Brownlow had obtained judgment for $25,000 in Circuit Court against the same three men, and he urged more suits of this nature.[32]

A stickler for fine points in classifying violence, the governor drew a distinction "between men who are resenting injuries done to them and their families, and bands of robbers who seek to live without work." He had plenty of material to sort, but most of it went into one basket. A justice of the peace near Bristol, while acting in his official capacity, had been beaten by a band of "Virginia rebels." In Blount County Union men had the upper hand and were using it. To them he suggested that rebels who were the target of what he called justified retribution for their "high-handed" course when Confederate units were scouring the country, should leave and "stay away until these men who were driven out of the country, and had their families all robbed, *die of old age*." He loosed a shaft at rebel women. He blamed them for creating moral decay as well as rebellion, and summed up with: "The devil is unchained and the women are taking advantage of his 'loose reign.'"

Murder, compounded by a lynching, erupted at the Knox County Courthouse, as the Brownlows crowded the pages of the *Whig* with tirades. The killing arose from a grudge between a Union and a Confederate soldier, Will Hall of the Second Tennessee Cavalry (U.S.) and Abner Baker, who had served three years in the Confederate forces. Hall, a nephew of Judge E. T. Hall, apparently was bitter at Baker because the latter had once drawn a pistol on him to halt a dispute that the Unionist was having with a secessionist. An encounter occurred at the clerk's office. As they met, Hall must have believed he saw Baker draw his revolver. Hall broke his cane upon Baker, the two grappled and the southerner put a bullet through Hall's head. Baker was arrested immediately and jailed. Authorities, including Judge Hall, urged calm. Their pleas were unavailing, for that night a thousand or more men stormed the jail and hanged Baker to a tree in the jail yard. Sheriff Bearden and the jailer, the only officers available to resist the mob, were powerless. Brownlow, in his capacity as governor, called on the sheriff to double his guard, and acknowledged criticism with this bristling observation:

There are those in town, who are perfectly shocked at these outrages, and are asking why the Governor does not interfere? The Governor is here and regrets that men who served in the rebel army for more than three years, are parading the streets loaded down to the guards with revolvers, swearing they have been overpowered but not convinced! The Governor regrets that Union men are shot down by them, and that their friends in turn, are hanging them in violation of law. The Governor is as powerless as any other citizen, in all such cases. The Governor is not so much horrified as many others. He was shocked four years ago when innocent Union men were taken from his side, out of the jail, *two at a time, and hung [sic.]* by the other party, and the she-devils threw up their white handkerchiefs in approbation! The Governor may have been a *little used to scenes* of this kind, and not feel as deeply as he ought on this solemn occasion.[33]

Supporters of the Confederacy, and perhaps some others, found double reason to be horrified over the lynching. The victim's father, Dr. James Harvey Baker, was killed by Union raiders on June 19, 1863. The accounts, as usual, were conflicting. The secessionist newspaper in Knoxville, the *Southern Chronicle*, described the "Murder of Dr. H. Baker by the renegades and Yankees in their late raid," as "the assassination of this high-toned and chivalrous gentleman," as "one of the most cold-blooded and diabolical acts that has come to our knowledge during the war." The *Whig* reported that Dr. Baker and other rebels fired on the federal troops, drawing return fire that killed the doctor. The killing took place at the Baker home on Kingston Pike west of Knoxville.[34]

The outcry against the lynching must have been strong and persistent for the *Whig* in its second issue after the hanging carried an uncharacteristic proposal to "look at both sides of the question." The newspaper repeated its opposition to mob law, but reviewed again the severe treatment of Union men in jail four years earlier, but with this repetitive barb:

The leading rebels could have prevented all this, and liberated these men, but believing their punishment just, they refused to turn a hand in their favor. Their love of civil law was not then as great as it is now.

The governor and his newspaper thus outlined their position that enforcement of what the Confederates considered law and order under their administration was bogus. Brownlow held that the South's government was an illegal one, an outlaw organization, and to defy it or to burn its bridges did not constitute a violation of law but was a demonstration of supreme loyalty. All repression of Union supporters and sympathizers was illegal as well as unjust. He threaded this theme with more accounts of the brutal treatment of Union men crowded into the squalid jail at Knoxville and of tortures and whippings outside. Five times the editorial recounted separate acts of repression and punishment. At the conclusion of each, Brownlow hammered down with a sentence that Confederate officials then had lacked the keen sense of justice that now moved them. He touched upon an incident that was gall to him, the efforts of his captors to persuade doomed men to purchase their lives by falsely stating that he and other Union leaders had had a hand in the bridge burning. He capped this recital of an old agony with this fourth chorus:

All this could have been prevented by the leading rebels of East Tennessee, but they were not then *afflicted* with a sense of justice, or they had not fallen in love with the law and courts of this country (*Whig*, September 13, 1865).

The *Whig* put the responsibility for law enforcement upon local officials. This could mean only that local sentiment would determine the course of justice, a concept that would vary considerably between the mountain counties of East Tennessee and the planter dominated areas of Middle and West Tennessee. The editor recognized this in the following forecast of trouble under two-way justice:

Rebel juries will not give Union men justice, nor will they convict rebel outlaws for any offense, no matter what the testimony may be. Letters come to the Executive Department at Nashville every day, complaining that no relief can be had for Union men from rebel juries. Poor women whose husbands were imprisoned and murdered are told by lawyers that the war is now over, and old matters must not be revived. In Middle and West Tennessee the rebels are in the majority, and they have the money and property to enable them to pay out, and they will do it, from the indications we have. Not so in East Tennessee—the Union men are the controlling power, and they do not intend it shall be otherwise. They will not suffer any class of men on earth to run over them, or deprive them of their rights. They have learned by the rebellion what confidence to place in rebels, and in future they will not only assert a "higher law" when imposed upon, but in the language of the Bible they "will be a law unto themselves" (*Whig*, September 20, 1865).

As Tennessee was racked by Reconstruction pains, the *Whig* chronicled the death of William L. Yancey of Montgomery, Alabama. Yancey had met Brownlow and other Unionists in a confrontation in 1860 on the issue of loyalty to the Union. Yancey, who served in the Confederate Congress, had turned upon President Davis, and in a violent argument with another member was knocked across a desk and suffered injuries that led to his death a year later. The *Whig* printed an account of his death, noted that the news of the fight in the Confederate Congress had been kept secret for months, but did so without a word of reproach or condemnation for Yancey's course (*Whig*, October 4, 1865). The *Whig* was too busy with living foes to spend time on dead ones, as it had years earlier when Andrew Jackson died.

CHAPTER XVI NOTES

[1] An attempt to hold a state election in the fall of 1863 was disrupted by the defeat of General Rosecrans at Chattanooga, and another effort calling for the election of county officers on March 5, 1864, resulted in disorder and confusion in most counties. Patton, *Unionism and Reconstruction*, pp. 37-42; Coulter, pp. 258-259; White, *Messages*, V, pp. 377-383. Knox County elected a full slate of Union Officials, but the vote was less than half that usually cast. *Whig*, March 12, 1864; Temple, *Notable Men*, p. 407; Patton, *Unionism and Reconstruction*, p. 45; Coulter, p. 259; *Whig*, April 23, 1864.

[2] Temple, *Notable Men*, pp. 407-409; John Bell Brownlow to Temple, March 9, 1891, Temple Papers; *Whig*, April 23, 1864.

[3] *Ibid.*, June 11, 18, 25, 1864; Patton, *Unionism and Reconstruction*, pp. 45-46.

[4] Temple, *Notable Men*, pp. 165, 408; Alexander, *Thomas A. R. Nelson*, p. 115; Patton, *Unionism and Reconstruction*, p. 46; *Whig*, August 17, 24, 31, September 21, 28, October 12, 26, November 5, 1864; Patton, *Unionism and Reconstruction*, pp. 46-47; Temple, *Notable Men*, pp. 413-414; White, *Messages*, V, pp. 384-386; Alexander, *Thomas A. R. Nelson*, p. 117; *Whig*, November 5, 1864.

[5] Folmbsee, *et al.*, *Short History*, p. 345; White, *Messages*, V, p. 386; Patton, *Unionism and Reconstruction*, p. 48. The reported vote in these counties was Knox, 2,537; Anderson, 760; Bradley, 1,024; Campbell, 649; Roane, 900; McMinn, 1,000; Greene, 800; Sevier, 1,174; Blount, 1,225; and Morgan, 250, round figures suggesting these were estimates. *Whig*, November 11, 13, 16, 23, 30, 1864; Folmsbee, *et al.*, *Short History*, p. 338.

[6] Temple, *East Tennessee and the Civil War*, p. 403; *Parson Brownlow's Book*, p. 270; *O. R.*, II, 1, Wood to Benjamin, November 20, 1861, Benjamin to Wood, November 25, 1861, pp. 845, 847-848; Temple, *Notable Men*, pp. 19, 53; Temple, *East Tennessee and the Civil War*, pp. 340-341; Temple, *Notable Men*, pp. 79-80, 114-115; *Parson Brownlow's Book*, pp. 139-140; *Whig*, November 16, 1864.

[7] *Ibid.*, December 7, 1864; Folmsbee *et al.*, *Short History*, pp. 338-339; Patton, *Unionism and Reconstruction*, pp. 48-49; *Whig*, December 30, 1864, January 25, 1865.

[8] Temple wrote that the method employed to get Tennessee back as a state in the union was "the most irregular that could have been chosen," and that "the instrument adopted was always a source of discontent to many loyal people of the state." He criticized Johnson for his part in taking the short cuts but did not censure Brownlow for acquiescing in them. Temple, *Notable Men*, pp. 409-411. See also Patton, *Unionism and Reconstruction*, p. 49; Alexander, *T. A. R. Nelson*, pp. 118-119; Folmsbee, *et al.*, *Short History*, pp. 346-347; White, *Messages*, V, pp. 386-389.

[9] *Whig*, January 25, 1865. The vote is given as 28,865 to 67 in White, *Messages*, V, p. 389, and as 25,293 to 48 in a much earlier work. Charles A. Miller, *The Official and Political Manual of the State of Tennessee* (Nashville, 1890), p. 48; White, *Messages*, V, p. 369; Alexander, *T. A. R. Nelson*, p. 120, 119; *Whig*, February 15, 22, 1865.

[10] *Ibid.*, March 1, 8, 15, 1865; *House Journal of the First Session of the General Assembly of the State of Tennessee, 1865* (Nashville, 1866), pp. 15-16. House and Senate *Journals* do not give numbers for this session which is generally known as the "Brownlow Legislature." Names of the members are given in White, *Messages*, V, pp. 432-436; *House Journal, 1865*, pp. 228-229, and *Senate Journal, 1865*, pp. 195-196; *Whig*, March 1, 15, 1865; *House Journal, Brownlow Legislature*, pp. 3-5, 15-16.

[11] *Whig*, February 15, 22, March 1, 8, 15, 29, 1865. The partnership included W. G. Brownlow, John Bell Brownlow and Tilghman Haws. The son's role as a partner was implied but not spelled out until the partnership was limited to the elder Brownlow and Haws. *Ibid.*, February 20, 1867.

[12] *Ibid.*, May 17, 1865; *Tennesseeans in the Civil War*, p. 343. The cost of labor and newsprint doubled after publication of the *Whig* was resumed, the weekly bill for the latter reaching $240. But the Parson purchased a new steam-operated press, and by the following August his advertising volume required sixteen of the *Whig*'s twenty-four columns. The telegraphic bills were so high that the editor paid for them from his pocket, rather than from newspaper revenues. The price of newsprint went from $8.00 a ream to $11.00 in five months, and the *Whig* raised the old annual subscription rate of $2.00 to $3.00, early in 1865. *Whig*, May 13, June 4, August 24, October 12, 1864, February 1, July 5, 12, 19, 1865.

[13] *Ibid.*, April 12, 1865. Major General George H. Thomas headed the military group.

[14] Entries for April 10, 27, December 3, 1865, in the Civil War diary of Lieutenant William Rule, adjutant of the Sixth Tennessee Infantry,

unclassified. Rule Papers. Father Abram Ryan, Roman Catholic priest and militant secessionist, wrote from Knoxville that the town "is worse in scenes of blood and violence than ever Nashville was. Scarcely a day passes that is not signalized by some murder or other crime. . . . All decent people are leaving as rapidly as they can. No one can live here safe and secure that does not swear by Brownlow." Ryan to Mr. and Mrs. Mc-Crissy, Clarksville, August 12, 1865. Manuscript Division Tennessee State Library and Archives.

[15] John Bell Brownlow to Temple, January 31, 1894, February 5, 1891. Temple Papers. Letter from John Bell Brownlow to Knoxville Tribune, August 16, 1896. Unclassified memorandum. Rule Papers. John Bell Brownlow to Temple, January 24, 1891. Temple Papers. Temple, *Notable Men*, pp. 17-18, fn 17.

[16] John Bell Brownlow to Temple, February 16, 1892. Temple Papers. *Ibid.*, September 9, 1864 (two letters), September 18, 1864.

[17] Memorandum prepared by W. T. Kennerly, Knoxville lawyer with a bent for history, after an interview with John Bell Brownlow. Special Collections, University of Tennessee. A member of the Seventh Ohio Volunteer Cavalry, writing from Knoxville, noted, "There is a son of Brownlow here who is a Lieut. Co. of the Ninth East Tenn. Cavalry. He takes pains to inform every one that Parson Brownlow is his father." Landon Crabb to "My Dear Mother," October 15, 1863. Letter personal property of this writer.

[18] Governor Brownlow's Message to the legislature. *Whig*, May 10, 1865; Alexander, *Political Reconstruction*, pp. 72-73.

[19] *Ibid.*, pp. 44-66; Patton, *Unionism and Reconstruction*, pp. 71-74, 95-96, 100-101; Humes, *The Loyal Mountaineers*, pp. 301-331; Temple, *Notable Men*, p. 323; Folmsbee *et al.*, *Short History*, pp. 352-353.

[20] Thumbnail sketches of members of the Senate and House were first published in the Nashville *Times* and then in the *Whig*, April 12, 26, 1865. For appraisals of assembly members see Alexander, *Political Reconstruction*, pp. 69-71; Patton, *Unionism and Reconstruction*, pp. 88-89; Folmsbee *et al.*, *Short History*, p. 363; White, *Messages*, V, p. 398.

[21] *Whig*, April 19, 26, 1865.

[22] *Ibid.*, April 19, 1865. Marginal note by John Bell Brownlow, *ibid.*, September 16, 1846.

[23] Alexander, *Political Reconstruction*, p. 73; Patton, *Unionism and Reconstruction*, pp. 92-93; White, *Messages*, V, pp. 427-429.

[24] Alexander, *Political Reconstruction*, pp. 73-76; Patton, *Unionism and Reconstruction*, pp. 97-102; White, *Messages*, V, pp. 428-438; *Whig*, June 7, 1865.

[25] *Ibid.*, June 28, 1865. For Gallaher's service record see *Tennesseeans in the Civil War*, I, pp. 302-303, II, p. 164.

[26] Patton, *Unionism and Reconstruction*, pp. 97-101; Alexander, *Political Reconstruction*, pp. 74-75; White, *Messages*, V, pp. 430-435.

[27] Patton, *Unionism and Reconstruction*, p. 107, 204; Alexander, *Political Reconstruction*, pp. 76-77; *Whig*, May 10, 1865.

[28] *Ibid.*, June 28, July 12, 18, June 28, July 5, 1865; Patton, *Unionism and Reconstruction*, pp. 109-110.

[29] *Whig*, July 12, 1865. Brownlow was dubbed "Old Proc" because of the many proclamations he issued. White, *Messages*, V, fn p. 444. The Parson did not mention that as military governor of Tennessee, Johnson held the rank of brigadier general.

[30] Alexander, *Political Reconstruction*, pp. 79-92; Patton, *Unionism and Reconstruction*, pp. 110-114; White, *Messages*, V, pp. 450-451. See Brownlow's statement on throwing out the votes, *Whig*, November 29, 1865; his denunciation of Taylor, *ibid.*, March 16, 1865.

[31] Reference to the threatening letter is in *ibid.*, August 30, 1865, the text was printed, *ibid.*, September 13, 1865.

[32] *Ibid.*, August 30, 1865. Horace Foster of Blount County was awarded judgment for $25,000 against eight men whom he accused of instigating the seizure of his farm products, shooting him and forcing him to walk bleeding through a creek in water up to his armpits. *Ibid.*, March 1, 1865.

[33] *Ibid.*, September 6, 1865. The editorial on the killing of Hall and the hanging of Baker, although referring to the governor in the third person, undoubtedly was written by the Parson.

[34] Katherine Baker Johnson, typewritten manuscipt, comp., "Odds and Ends of Family History," (1944) two vols., V, 1, pp. 54, 58, McClung Collection; *Southern Chronicle*, June 28, 1863; *Whig*, November 11, 1863.

"Yielding up the other cheek/Dropping humbly
on the knees; Closing lips when dared to speak/Will
not do in times like these."

Chapter No. 17

THE PAINS OF RECONSTRUCTION

The first General Assembly of Tennessee under Governor Brownlow dealt only with the most pressing matters. When the adjourned session met at Nashville on October 2, 1865, the governor submitted a comprehensive message. He recommended legislation to: 1) stimulate immigration from Germany, Switzerland and the northern states to help in the rebuilding of Tennessee. 2) A thorough investigation of the defunct Bank of Tennessee and vigorous efforts to collect its assets. A total of $446,719.20 in gold and silver had been recovered and invested in United States bonds that yielded annual interest of $45,135.25. 3) The replenishing of the gutted school fund by any further resources to be found. 4) Development of ways and means to meet state debt payments of $1,213,719.66, and of interest on the railroad bonds amounting to $3,768,509. 5) Ways to help the railroads complete the work of renovation, now well under way. 6) Financing of repairs on the state-owned Hermitage, neglected during the war. 7) Investigation of the state penal system and facilities. 8) Relief for tax-burdened owners of real estate to avoid its concentration in the hands of a "monied aristocracy." 9) A confiscatory tax on alcoholic beverages.[1]

The governor's greatest concern was what to do about the freed slaves, a subject that raised emotional as well as economic and political problems. The Parson's complete turnabout on the slavery issue was a rending experience for him. He changed from being a vociferous advocate of slavery to the rejection of this view, if such was necessary to save the Union. Finally, he accepted and endorsed emancipation. When he had made this complete reversal, he denounced slavery as the curse of the southern states and said that the South's obsession with it was the underlying cause of secession. A personal experience probably entered into his thinking. He revealed it as he wrote an extended piece, "The Negro Question Again." This piece was a denunciation of the freed slaves who were flocking into the towns as idle, insolent, averse to work, and expecting the Government to provide for their needs. He said black soldiers not only lacked discipline but displayed great arrogance toward white people. This had reached such an extent that in East Tennessee, where a majority of the population viewed blacks with dislike and distaste, a collision was building.[2] Some time earlier, the governor recalled, two black soldiers

in full uniform . . . upon a narrow sidewalk in this city [Knoxville] knocked the writer of this article into the gutter, throwing him upon his hands and knees. He was trying to get out of their way, and they saw it, but being feeble and leaning upon a staff, he moved too slow [sic.] for their idea of progress. I made no complaint, but concluded that these colored ruffians had not learned to respect the uniform of the army, and I went my way, not rejoicing—but feeling . . . that I was worsted by the outcome, which I had not brought about but sought to prevent. Soldiers and officers, wearing the Federal uniform ought all to be gentlemen. . . but the only two colored soldiers I ever encountered did not prove to be of that stripe. I have no wish to try them again—I might light upon others less refined who would run me through with the bayonet! (Whig, September 27, 1845).

Throughout the years the Parson had shown callousness and contempt for the black man as a race.[3] Surely this mortifying experience was in his mind as he wrestled with the question of extending the franchise to this suddenly liberated and uneducated race. The returning soldiers he disposed of quickly. The young and deluded should be pardoned generously and freely upon their showing genuine reassumption of loyalty. "Guilty rebels" should be required to wait five or ten years before being permitted to vote, while the original conspirators and leaders were entitled to "neither mercy nor forbearance." The stimulation of immigration, he predicted, would provide a class of substantial citizens and would offer

a far more safe and rational process of regenerating the South than any sudden and compulsory admission of the blacks to the ballot box . . .The indiscriminate grant of the right of suffrage to the colored population would increase the evils that keep the South depressed, and exasperate those who, under other circumstances, would become devoted friends of the Government and accept the emancipation of the slaves as an event not at all offensive.

The Parson's mind roved restlessly on the subject of the blacks and the vote. A realistic, political approach weighed heavily in his thinking. Two senators-elect and eight representatives awaited admission at the door of the United States Congress. Failure on the part of Tennessee to grant the black man the right to vote might weigh the scales against the admission of the Tennessee delegation. The governor wanted these men seated, for it would add to the prestige and influence of the state. Its congressmen would be placed where they would have a voice in the affairs of the nation and where they could speak directly to Washington on the needs of Tennessee and their constituents. Yet Brownlow could not shake free of some of his old beliefs and convictions, and this forced him to conclude:

I am free to admit that, for the present, we have done enough for the negro, [*sic.*] and although negro voting cannot suit my natural prejudices of caste, there is a class of them I would be willing to see vote at once. A large class, ignorant, docile, easily led by designing men, and not safely trusted with political power, I am not willing to see at the ballot-box; but as even these have been faithful among the faithless, if rebels are to be restored to the right of the elective franchise, I would say let us no longer deny these political rights to the slaves. In my judgment a loyal negro is more eminently entitled to suffrage than a disloyal white man.

The black man would get the franchise eventually, Brownlow saw, but "the time has not come when the ballot box should be turned over to the emancipated slaves of this state, and the thousands who would rush into Tennessee from the Cotton States on this account." It would be well, the governor concluded, to delay granting the ballot to the black until he has been emancipated from "ignorance and poverty, social and political disfranchisement." The legislature should move slowly, because immediate action would leave the great mass of freed slaves open to influence by secessionists "to vote against the Government." Only when the black proved his worthiness would Tennessee extend to him the ballot. Yet the governor was free to confess that if it became necessary to enfranchise the blacks, in order to keep control of the country out of the hands of rebels and traitors, "I am for the measure." Blacks were now persons and no longer property. Therefore Brownlow advocated giving them the right to testify in court, without reservation. But Brownlow held that the black was not the equal of the white, and the best solution to the problem involved in the two races attempting to live together would be to separate them. The blacks should be granted their own nation in some spot like Texas or Mexico after the removal of all the Caucasians.[4]

Historians still offer varying evaluation of this message. One, who has been accused of strong bias, found it a "cross between a political harangue and a Thanksgiving sermon. Inasmuch as the Parson was at present a politician and formerly a Methodist minister, possibly he possessed qualifications in each field." Another, more objective, while failing to praise it in substance, described it as "lengthy and detailed, writen in a relatively quiet tone." Brownlow had spent long hours over it in his study at Knoxville and probably thought well of it. His son John published in the *Whig* high compliments of it taken from friendly newspapers, notably the Cincinnati *Gazette*. The *Gazette* printed most of the text which must have tickled the Parson's fancy as he read:

Such is the peculiar style of the writer that this message will be found very entertaining reading, even to those not specially interested in the topics discussed. Many of the comparisons and illustrations are in the Governor's richest vein (*Whig*, October 11, 1865).

The *Gazette* had sound financial reason to applaud the message. It had invested one hundred dollars to have the material parts of the governor's production telegraphed to Cincinnati, and found the money well spent. It sold 8,000 extra copies of the issue carrying it. The Parson's piquant language, however, was lost upon the South's newspapers, which the *Whig* charged, "by common consent, agreed to attack him from every point of the compass." The General Assembly, out of deference to the governor, or because it was impressed by the message, ordered 15,000 copies printed in English and 5,000 in German. The Parson had found that immigrants from this northern European country were uniformly for the Union.[5]

The assembly had lost some of its most talented members. Brownlow had appointed two of his senators to the bench. His old friend, Samuel R. Rodgers, he appointed to be chancellor of the Eighth Judicial Circuit, and R. R. Butler of Johnson County he named judge of the First Judicial Circuit. The Parson displayed vigor in getting the courts moving. By February 1866 he had appointed a majority of all the judicial officers in the state, and thereby drew some criticism for not having called elections for this purpose. The *Whig* dismissed the critics with two observations: 1) the governor had no intention of yielding to the pleas of "copperheads" and let rebels be elected to the bench, and 2) the legislature had rejected a number of petitions calling for elections to be held. [6]

Whether it was from a lack of leadership or a reluctance to grapple with the issues, the legislature moved slowly. The Senate passed, ten to nine, a bill to permit persons of African and Indian descent to testify in court. The aversion of many East Tennesseeans toward the blacks threatened to block passage of the bill in the House. To counteract this sentiment the governor issued a statement "To The East Tennessee Loyalists," in which he asserted the measure was basically right. It would end the need for the Freedmen's Bureau, where to many whites, the scales appeared to be tipped in favor of the black man, and it would cut two ways. It would gratify the blacks and head off more drastic steps by Congress, possibly granting the franchise to freedmen. The strategy worked. The House passed the bill on January 26, 1866. [7]

The legislature enacted some important legislation. But in the House a "little Rebellion" erupted when an attempt was made to tighten the restrictions on voters. Some members filibustered. Four spoke for a total of thirteen hours against the measure, while proponents occupied two hours. Several absented themselves and other resigned. It was impossible to get a quorum and legislative business was effectively stalled. The *Whig* described the minority as displaying "the true rebel spirit," and Speaker William Heiskell, who opposed the bill, and gray-haired James Mullins, who sponsored it, called on the Almighty to damn each other. Heiskell reinforced his appeal by hurling the gavel at Mullins. No one was hit. Because legislative action was halted, Governor Brownlow called a special election for March 31 to fill the vacancies created by resignations. [8] Adding to the intensity of the times, and certainly with political calculation, the Conservatives called a convention to be held in Nashville on Washington's birthday. Among the listed purposes was one to further the state's restoration to the Union and to approve President Johnson's reconstruction policy that now drew Democratic support. Representative Maynard, who was invited to attend, sent a letter. In it he cautiously approved, in general, Johnson's course, but also restated his own Radical views. Representative Stokes, who spoke after the convention had adjourned, blistered it in a fashion the *Whig* relished. [9] The paper printed this report from a Nashville correspondent:

Look at this Convention! They had made a McClellan man President—they opened their exercises with prayer by a rebel preacher who had been sent through the lines by Gen. Rosecrans—they appointed a man Secretary who had cast the vote of a Congressional District for Jeff Davis and Stephens! They had no stars and stripes in their convention—they made no mention of the martyred Lincoln—they made no allusion to the United States Army and Navy—they passed no eulogy upon Gen. Thomas for saving this city—they had no good words to utter in favor of the brave officers and soldiers who saved the Union! And yet, said Stokes, this professes to be a loyal Union Convention. True, they adopted resolutions censuring the majority [Radical] in Congress—they hissed General Joseph A. Cooper when he attempted to speak, although he was one of the gallant defenders to Nashville but little more than a year ago! They endorsed Andrew Johnson, and they clapped and shouted his veto of the Bureau bill, but it was not because they loved Johnson, but because they rejoiced over the prospect of a quarrel between him and Congress, and the party that elected him (*Whig*, March 7, 1866).

Stokes referred to a fusion of political forces that was under way, a merger of the Conservative Unionists and the disfranchised Confederates. They would be a formidable power if combined, and an overwhelming one if the Confederates gained more access to the ballot box. This added to the governor's anxiety to put on the books a franchise law that would enable him to keep the state government in Radical hands.

The Radical Congress and the President were headed for intense struggle on the issue of reconstruction. It was inevitable in Tennessee that the Conservatives and Democrats would support the President, and that the Brownlow administration would line up with Congress. [10] Early in 1866 the Parson served notice that he could go along with Johnson only if he adhered to his policy as military governor, and if he still stood on the Baltimore convention which nominated Lincoln and Johnson. He told the German Union League at Knoxville on March 24 that Johnson had gone back to the Democratic Party, the party that was responsible for secession and the war. Thus, they were separated. The resumption of roles as antagonists by these two men who earlier had fought long and furiously must have seemed more natural to both than the common path into which they were thrown by their allegiance to the Union. The Parson remained respectful toward Johnson in a speech at the Knox County Courthouse on April 2.[11] It had been only four months since John Bell Brownlow had written from Washington:

The simon-pure men of East Tennessee have in Andrew Johnson a steadfast friend . . . . the health of the President was never better than now. Long may he live to administer our glorious government on the principle of justice and universal freedom (*Whig*, November 29, 1865).

Skillful politician that Johnson was, he had flattered young Brownlow. He had received him immediately upon arrival at the White House, and talked with him at some length. Nor could the impressionable stripling editor refrain from gloating in print at his reception, and casually recalled that he had been very close to Johnson when the latter was military governor (*Ibid.*).

The *Whig*, without explanation, dropped from underneath its name on the front page "And Rebel Ventilator." The change permitted a few more inches of space for the newspaper's thriving advertising custom (*Whig*, February 28, 1866). It continued to ventilate rebels.

At this seething moment in Tennessee affairs the *Whig* printed a letter that was an obvious hoax, but in substance and execution was an example of political surgery. Its style, and its skill in cutting in several directions, suggested that it was the Parson's handiwork. The letter was addressed to "John Webb," described as a former Confederate colonel, and the signature telegraphed its phoniness: "C. Seshon, *Late Gen. C.S.A.*, now M.C. elect." The first part of the letter was designed to infuriate Southerners, scare Unionists from linking with Democrats, and suggest to Johnson the error of his ways.[12] It recommended this course for Southern men:

Remember then, Colonel, first and foremost, that we are all "Johnson men." I know you hate old Johnson as you do the devil. But I tell you I believe we can get him (not the devil but Johnson) to carry out our plans . . . . This is the Lord's doing, and it is marvelous in our eyes. I always believed the Lord was on the side of the Confederacy. We all tell Johnson that we are completely reconstructed and thoroughly loyal. We have thrown dust in his eyes completely, and the old fool is as blind as a bat to our schemes. Never, therefore, allow yourself to say one word against Johnson. Praise him to the skies, and in the same breath curse the Radicals to the devil. This takes well with Johnson.

In the next place, always pretend to be intensely loyal, and enthusiasically devoted to the Constitution. Don't mind the inconsistency of a rebel Colonel, who tried to overthrow the Constitution, now worshipping it as the decalogue of politics. Consistency to the winds. Swear that you are glad the war is ended; and that you are in favor of the "Constitution as it is and the Union as it was." . . . Say that you are in favor of the Constitutional Amendment, and that you are glad the negroes [*sic*.] are free. (But the moment we get into power, the moment our state is reconstructed, we will, you know, pass laws to suit ourselves on the negro subject, and we'll attend to those poor Union whites, too.) (*Whig*, April 4, 1866).

This last whiplash by the phony general's ghostwriter was a reminder to the East Tennessee mountaineers that in the event of a Confederate-manipulated Conservative victory they would be in line for punishment because of their adherence to the Union. It was made clear that it would be best for them to smother their prejudice against the blacks, and accept the Radical line of granting them benefits. The writer approached the theme of Negro equality from another direction. He urged constant denunciation of it and spared no exaggeration of what it might do:

The ends will justify the means. If we can only keep alive this prejudice against the negro [*sic*.] and make the whites believe the Radicals are in favor of social negro equality, we are safe, and the good old Confederacy will rise out of her ashes more glorious than ever. God speed the day! How fortunate for us that these Union people are such ignorant fools as to believe all we say about these Radicals and negro equality.

Editors were to be duped or bribed to follow the lines suggested by the writer. Some Union editors could be bought very cheaply. Religious newspapers should be included. Congress remained an obstacle and must be treated with contempt. The campaign was summarized in this paragraph:

But praise Johnson, curse Congress, denounce the negro, [*sic*.] eulogize the Constitution, and leave nothing undone to unite the South upon another war, and divide Union men . . . . The rebel debt will yet be paid, we will get compensation for our slaves, and keep them as slaves afterwards; and as for these poor, contemptible, ignorant White Union men, when we get in power again, they will find the terrors and sufferings of the late war a paradise compared with what our wrath will heap on their heads. We will smile on them and give them our hands, until we get their votes, but then may the devil speedily get them! (*Ibid.*).

A much more potent force than this sarcasm-laden letter had been set in motion a few weeks earlier, revival of the separate statehood movement. It was started because "The conduct of the rebels of Middle and West Tennessee, in their course toward Union men and the Federal Government is increasing the desire to be separated from them . . . ." The *Whig* also tossed off the observation, "Taking the ballot from a rebel has the effect of extracting the *sting* from a bee. It renders him powerless for mischief." In developing the move to split East Tennessee from the rest of the state, the *Whig* quoted from the Nashville *Banner*. It described it as "a vile organ of treason," edited by a pair of rebels who thus sized up Unionists:

BUT IN HONEST TRUTH, THE MAJORITY OF THE SO-CALLED UNION OR LOYAL MEN OF THE SOUTH WERE THE MEREST TRASH THAT COULD BE COLLECTED IN A CIVILIZED COMMUNITY, OF NO PER-SONAL CREDIT OR SOCIAL RESPONSIBILITY.

The *Whig* quoted this diatribe to turn East Tennesseans against the men who had stood with the Conservatives on the franchise bill. Nothing can be found to indicate this purpose was accomplished. It does reflect the bitterness and contempt certain segments of Middle Tennessee felt for East Tennessee.

The *Whig* vigorously pressed the movement for a separate state. It printed an extended article from a correspondent on the advantages of separation. At a Union meeting held at the Knox County Court-house that was addressed by Brownlow and others one of the resolutions spelled out the purpose of the statehood movement:

Rather than to submit to the domination of traitors, in the event of the defeat of the Franchise Bill now before the Legislature of the State, we are in favor of the formation of a new state, to be composed of the Eastern Division of this State, to be called the STATE OF EAST TENNESSEE.

An East Tennessee Convention that met at Knoxville on May 3 and 4 appointed a committee to memorialize the legislature to grant the separation. The Senate, goaded by this pressure, passed the franchise bill the first day of the convention at Knoxville. The agitation for separate statehood subsided.[13]

It remains a curiosity of East Tennessee politics that one of the spirited speeches for separation made at the convention was by Thomas A. R. Nelson. As a leader of the Greeneville Convention of 1861 he was firmly on record in favor of separate statehood. But in 1866 he was furthering the cause of the Radicals and of Brownlow, with whom he no longer acted and against whom he soon would be in vigorous opposition. Nelson knew the real purpose of the meeting. He was on the Resolutions Committee which spelled it out in the recommendations it submitted. He made an "eloquent and impressive" speech and he was appointed to a "Central Committee" for East Tennessee to keep the movement alive, if needed. [14] The need, of course, was removed.

The results of the March 31 election must have been disturbing and nettlesome to Brownlow, although the *Whig* found "treason has been routed in Tennessee." Twelve of the men who had resigned were returned, and two were replaced by other Conservatives. Four Radicals were elected, two of whom replaced Conservatives. A bitter pill for the *Whig* was the reelection of Pleasant Williams from Carter by seventeen votes. This happened after one opponent retired and another entered late. Williams had supported the first franchise bill, but he fought the second one. He told his constituents that it would deprive some men who had served under duress in the Confederate army of the vote and enfranchise blacks who had served in the Union army. This was a sensitive point in East Tennessee.

When the members-elect appeared in Nashville to claim their seats the House declined to seat fifteen Conservatives, but approved three Radicals. A quorum was declared present, and the house passed the franchise bill on April 12, by a vote of 41 to 15. Williams presented a separate case. He had absented himself on some of the votes before the special election, and his name appeared as one of the signers of a statement by twenty-one members that they were resigning. Williams had asked for a leave of absence, but when his name appeared on the list of the twenty-one the governor declared his seat vacant and called for a special election in Carter County, along with the others. [15]

Williams had served in the Union cavalry for eighteen months before being honorably discharged for disability. He displayed vindictiveness early in the first legislative session by introducing a bill to punish ministers who had sided with the South by stripping them of their immunity from poll tax payments and serving in the militia and denying them the privilege of performing marriage ceremonies. The House killed the bill. It did not appear in the Senate. The House members, however, must have liked Williams. After the franchise bill was passed the House adopted a resolution restoring him to membership and stipulating "that his seat has never been vacant." He also was granted permission to have the journal show that if he had been seated his vote on the franchise measure would have been negative. [16]

Passage of the franchise law gave the Radicals tremendous political muscle for the next election. It perpetually disfranchised all persons who had borne arms voluntarily for the Confederacy; all who had sought or voluntarily accepted any office or attempted to exercise the functions of an office under the authority of the Confederacy; and all who had supported any government, power or authority against the United States. Complete authority was given the governor to appoint county registration commissioners. County Court clerks had formerly performed this function. The Conservatives had made a clean sweep of county offices in Middle and West Tennessee in the last election. The Radicals were not about to let Conservatives control voter registration, especially in these areas, where Radicals already were at a great disadvantage. As a clincher, Brownlow could remove his own commissioners, if they did not suit him. The *Whig* found the measure magnanimous, with the disabilities "imposed upon rebels . . . very moderate. They should be thankful if allowed to live in this state and follow the usual avocations of life." [17]

The *Whig* was annoyed by the militant stand taken against the franchise bill by three East Tennessee legislators. They were Heiskell and Williams in the House and Senator Beriah Frazier. The latter was elected from Knox and Roane counties when Speaker Rodgers accepted the appointment as chancellor. Early in the first session Brownlow had written a Knoxville friend, "Col. Heiskell is clear over on the Copperhead side, and is governed by letters he receives from your city." [18] Yet animosity never appeared in the personal relations of the governor and Heiskell. When the speaker took leave of absence from the House the *Whig* gave him this friendly salute:

When he left Nashville . . . he was on terms of personal cordiality with every Radical member of the House even including Mullins, at whom he threw his mallet. But for the instances in which party prejudices get [got] the better of his reason, he would have made an unexceptionable presiding officer (*Whig*, August 21, 1867).

Heiskell defended his course as correct because he was elected from the state at large. He believed that he should reflect the overwhelming statewide sentiment for the Conservatives, rather than the Radical majority in Knox County. [19] Senator Frazier, who fought the

Radical program from the moment he took his seat, offered a different line of reasoning. He conceded that the bill to permit blacks to testify in court had merit, but

I know the sentiments of my constituents, and am well assured that such a law would startle the whole community. The Union masses of East Tennessee accepted abolition, not because they loved slavery less, but their country more. As to their love for the negro [*sic.*], I believe no portion of the State has such deep and settled prejudice against him as they have. And I for one am not ready to disregard those prejudices.

The *Whig* now carried on a constant war against Frazier. It accused him of having given the impression during the campaign that he was a Radical, but when seated, "he voted and acted generally in favor of the rebels, and against the Union Party and the interests of those who elected him." Whatever statements Williams made to justify his position do not appear in the *Whig*. It did not neglect him, however. It continued to castigate him.[20]

East Tennessee's prejudice against blacks, bluntly noted by Senator Frazier, flared into the lynching of a Union soldier in Knoxville early in 1866. The black soldier was guarding a door during an army surplus sale. He fired upon and killed a respected and popular Grainger County farmer, Calvin M. Dyer, who had been a lieutenant colonel of the First Tennessee Cavalry (U.S.) In company with other men, Dyer was entering a door to pay for purchases when the guard killed him. No justification for the killing appeared. An officer ordered the soldier to his quarters under guard, but he escaped, apparently with the connivance of his custodians. The town was jammed with several hundred former Union soldiers, many of whom had served under Dyer. When they learned that another officer was attempting to spirit the guard to Chattanooga they formed into a mob and frightened the officer into helping search out the fugitive. The soldier attempted to run when found and was wounded by gunfire; when the mob sought to hang him, he struggled so furiously that he broke the rope. A second noose was found and he was hanged in front of the office of the Freedmen's Bureau.

As editor of the *Whig*, John Bell Brownlow was in a difficult and delicate situation. The hanging of the soldier in front of the Freedmen's Bureau office reflected the strong prejudice of East Tennesseeans against blacks. It fell at a time when the Brownlow forces in the legislature were fighting strenuously to place black men on an equal footing with white men in litigation. The young editor and the *Whig* were committed to the administration's course, but John also suffered intense sorrow and indignation over Dyer's death. He had known Dyer intimately, and when Colonel James P. Brownlow was hit in the hips by a Confederate bullet near Nashville, Dyer assumed command of the regiment, "and most gallantly did he bear himself." John cautiously worked his way through an account of the hanging and deplored the choice of the site for the lynching. The spot, he reasoned, was selected because the vengeful former soldiers believed the bureau officers were trying to get the black out of Knoxville, and did not constitute an insult against the Government. The editor concluded his article with this adroit and expedient phrasing:

A more atrocious murder [of Dyer] was never committed in Tennessee, and no event has caused more excitement in Knoxville than the tragedy referred to. While no circumstances can make lynch law *defensible*, if there ever was a case in which it was excusable, this is the case.[21]

Brownlow and the Tennessee Radicals had moved the state away from slavery and granted the blacks more advantages than they had ever known. This was done in the face of furious but impotent opposition. But the Congressional Radicals wanted more from Tennessee. They knew that President Johnson wanted his home state restored to the Union, and they proposed to make him pay a price for it. Since Johnson was opposed to granting suffrage to the Negro, the Radical majority saw a way to stuff the Fourteenth Amendment down his throat. They also knew that this was an operation the governor of Tennessee would relish. They made ratification of the amendment a condition of Tennessee's restoration.

The governor called the Tennessee legislature to meet on July 4, 1866, to act upon the amendment. However the governor may have felt in again reversing himself on the question of suffrage for the blacks, he could point to equal inconsistency on the part of the President. Johnson was now traveling along a path that led back to the Democratic Party, a course lined with applauding former Confederates. The times were chaotic, and altered or reversed positions were almost the rule. The *Whig* found the Memphis *Argus* showering praise upon Johnson in 1866 and recalled that in 1861, under the same editors, it had printed this diatribe: "We should like to see Anderew Johnson's lying tongue torn from his foul mouth, and his miserable carcass thrown out to poison mad dogs with, or hung upon

a gibbet as high as Haman, to fed [feed] the carrion buzzards."
Editor G. E. Grisham of the Jonesboro *Union Flag*, who had been a
captain in the Union army, stopped at a Bristol hotel and found a
notification

by fifteen members of the reconstructed admirers of "My Policy" that he would
be allowed *two* hours to leave in! He *fortified* himself and gave notice that the
first man who approached him should go upon the double quick to some other
country. The consequence was that *fourteen* out of the fifteen backed down,
and the remaining young man did not feel called upon to remove Grisham from
the place!

When the Jonesboro editor reached home he met a demand with
which he could not cope so successfully, the *Whig* reported:

Captain Grisham, of Jonesborough, has been turned out of the post office at
that place because he dared to believe "My Policy" was wrong, and Congress was
right in its course. If men expect to hold Federal offices in Tennessee, they must
subscribe to the infaliability [*sic.*] of the President, and the superiority of rebels
over Union men.[22]

When the legislature met, the opposition made some ineffective
moves in the Senate. One of them, by Frazier of Knox and Roane
counties, was a concession to East Tennessee's prejudice against
blacks. It went directly in the face of the will of Congress. It proposed to reverse the very purpose of the amendment by denying the
blacks the right to vote and forbidding them to sit on juries or to
intermarry with whites. Frazier lost, and the amendment was ratified, 14 to 6. The *Whig* accused Frazier of having attempted to "keep
Tennessee out of the Union." It neglected the prejudicial aspect of
the senator's move. The stand the *Whig* took was more palatable to
its readers than an assault on Frazier for trying to withhold full
citizenship from the black man. House foes of the bill again resorted
to absenteeism and for several days kept the body impotent for lack
of the quorum of fifty-six. The ensuing uproar was described as a
"mass meeting of political maniacs." General George H. Thomas considered the level of excitement so high he feared an effort would be
made to "break up the legislature." The Radicals knew they had the
votes for ratification if they could get a quorum, and after six days
of frustration, they directed Speaker Heiskell to issue warrants for
eight bolters. The deputies of Sergeant at arms William Heydt arrested Pleasant Williams at his remote home in Carter County and A. J.

Martin at Jackson and brought them to the capitol. There they were held under guard in a room that adjoined the House of Representatives.

A quorum was ruled present and weird parliamentary maneuvers followed. One of the points debated by the legislators was whether the representatives in custody, who frequently peeped through a door to watch proceedings, were on the floor. The Radicals held that the two men were present, and won their point by numbers. When the amendment was ratified, 43 to 11, Speaker Heiskell ruled a quorum was not present because, in his opinion, Williams and Martin were not on the floor. The decision of the chair was appealed. This brought the following discussion, as reported by the Nashville *Press and Times*: "Mr. Arnell said that Mr. Martin was then present, but refusing to vote, whereupon Mr. Martin indignantly responed [*sic.*] that he wasn't present at all.

"The House looked as incredulous as doubting Thomas, as they . . . beheld the 'wery identical indiwidual' who had denied the doctrine of the 'real presence.'" The House reversed the speaker. It held that a quorum was present when the vote was taken. It acted none too quickly. Soon a posse of twenty-five men acting under the Davidson County sheriff, who was carrying out orders of Judge Thomas N. Frazier of the Criminal Court, released the two representatives from custody. The posse arrested Heydt and took him before Judge Frazier, who fined him $10.00. Judge Frazier, brother of Senator Frazier, subsequently was impeached, convicted, removed from office, and disfranchised. A later legislature removed these disabilities.

Ratification put the Parson in jubilant mood. He had defeated the President in the struggle. He had aligned himself firmly with the Radicals in Congress. And he had placed the state in a position to be received again into the Union, and her representatives to receive full standing as congressmen. He fired off several telegrams of notification, among them this famous one:

Nashville, July 19, 1866. John W. Forney, Clerk of the Senate, Washington, D.C. A battle fought and won. We carried the constitutional amendment in the House. Vote—43 to 11, two of A. Johnson's tools refusing to vote. My *compliments* to the 'dead dog' in the White House. W. G. Brownlow. [23]

Congress gave final approval to the delegation on July 23. The Senate paused for a brief inquiry into Patterson's tenure as judge of a

Confederate court, a step that had required him to take the Confederate oath of allegiance. However, his loyalty to the Union was widely known. He had served as a judge while Tennessee was in the United States, and under Confederate occupation he was taken into custody and threatened with prison. It was apparent he had served as judge under the Richmond government in order to be helpful to the people of his circuit who were overwhelmingly for the Union. They probably would have fared much worse under a diehard southerner. The *Whig* and the governor apparently accepted this view, for Patterson escaped the terrible rain of invective the Brownlows were throwing at his father-in-law in the White House.[24] They accused the President of stirring up the "bolters" in a

fierce contest of loyalty and principle against patronage, corruption and treachery most foul, backed by an apostate President, who has placed himself in the shoes of Jeff Davis, striving to bring on another rebellion . . . .

It has now come to light, on authority from Washington, that Andrew Johnson has laid his plans for superseding Gov. Brownlow, by the appointment of *Gordon Grainger*, as Military Governor, so soon as the constitutional amendments were defeated. Part of the plot was to *use Judge Frazier's* decision against the House . . . . Let him appoint a Military Governor, if he dare. His impeachment in Congress will follow this usurpation, and a disgraceful expulsion will follow . . . .Let him rant and rave; he can't intimidate Union men in or out of Tennessee. He has no party, he has no strength, and he commands only the respect of rebels and rebel sympathizers (*Whig*, July 25, 1866).

The old Brownlow-Johnson animosity raged with renewed vigor and from higher ground than before, for the former was governor and the latter was President. The Parson listed and condemned Johnson's moves in turning away from the Radicals and moving back into the Democratic Party, and forming ties with former rebels as well as with Conservative Unionists. He displayed resentment over Johnson's denial of troops to "protect the legislature and its legal officers from mob violence" at the July session of the General Assembly, when the Fourteenth Amendment was ratified. He accused Johnson of plotting with the "traitors at the North, and the rebels of the South, to involve this country in another bloody war," and predicted that "the first blow will be struck in Tennessee" (*Whig*, August 22, 1866).

The Parson drew considerable attention at the ten-state Loyalist Convention of 1866, at Philadelphia. The convention was a prelude to the fight the Radicals were to make in the off-year election to increase their power in Congress. He was cheered and he made a brief speech. In it he recommended that if war did break out, the rebel population should be decimated, its property confiscated, and sold to men "who will honor this glorious banner." He gave his pledge to accompany Radical groups preparing to follow Johnson in his campaign for members of Congress friendly to his reconstruction policy. He kept his pledge, although a reporter found him

so thin and stooping, that I am filled with awe, as seeing something that belongs to the grave, every time I look at him . . . . The man is worn out and broken down. He is able to walk but a few steps, and sits up less than half the day. Will, unconquerable will, is all that keeps him from death . . . . Hopelessly shattered in body, he is as stout and fierce in mind as ever. [25]

Yet the Parson sent back several dispatches to the *Whig* and made a few speeches. At Erie, however, he fainted, took several days of rest, and went on to Chicago. There, at the home of Lieutenant Governor Bross, he watched a dramatic partisan parade:

From this vantage point, Brownlow resembled an oriental ruler reviewing his subjects. As each unit of the procession passed, it stopped to salute the patriarch. Even President Johnson had not experienced such honor on his "swing around the circle." That evening a crowd gathered before the Tremont House and called for a speech from Brownlow. He accommodated the crowd by reiterating the remarks he had delivered throughout the campaign.

The governor returned to Nashville on October 13, after having spent two months on a campaign trail that included the midwestern states, New York, New England, and New Jersey. [26]

A Knoxville citizen who wrote to the Nashville *Banner* that Johnson stood high with the city's voters, needled the Parson with an accompanying statement that the *Whig*'s circulation was below its level prior to the Civil War. This, the editor acknowledged, was true, because East Tennessee and its people had been impoverished by the conflict, schools suspended, homes, churches and schools burned, wives widowed, children orphaned, and men killed or disabled. All newspapers "which existed before the war do much less business now than formerly," the *Whig* reported, but it was still self-sustaining:

Had we supported Johnson we could have received Government advertising and *money out of the secret service fund* as the several Johnson papers in Tennessee have done, including the dirty little *Commercial* of this city. Nay! more, *the hat would have been passed around*, among rich rebels for our benefit. Besides this we could now have had high position in the "Bread and Butter Brigade" of Andrew Johnson. Three times, during the months of October, December and January, the President, unsolicited, cordially invited us to accept office under him (*Whig*, October 24, 1866).

The Radicals won in the nation and in Tennessee. They returned to Congress with a majority of more than two-thirds, and in Tennessee captured enough seats in by-elections to assure a full quorum of Radicals. The second adjourned session of the General Assembly met in Nashville on November 5, 1866, and received an extensive message from the governor ten days later. He revealed an inner struggle on the question of extending suffrage to the black, but he was ready "to act in harmony with the great body of the loyal people of the Union." He failed, however, to make an outright recommendation for giving the vote to blacks. When the assembly failed to move on the issue he submitted an additional message, early in 1867, in which he expressed the hope the legislature "will not close its present session without the passage of a bill granting suffrage to all loyal males, properly qualified by age and citizenship."[27]

The *Whig* offered a far more tart justification of Brownlow's change in position on blacks voting:

There is not one man in the United States in every hundred who occupies the position on the everlasting negro [*sic.*] question that he did before the war. The great social and political revolution through which the country has passed has entirely changed the relations of the races in the South and North, and as a matter of necessity men must change with the progress of inexorable and uncontrollable events (*Whig*, November 14, 1866).

Brownlow wanted to follow the course of the northern loyalists, who believed that the South should give the blacks the vote, but he was still faced with the inner conflict of his instilled prejudice against the black race. Necessity, shown by arithmetical logic, prevailed, as this analysis in the *Whig* revealed:

In Tennessee there are forty thousand loyal black men, sixty-five thousand loyal white men, and EIGHTY THOUSAND of the rebel camp whose faces are white. Because of the difficulty of enforcing the franchise law in Middle and West Tennessee, where the rebels are in the majority, there is great danger that the state will pass under the control of Isham G. Harris and the minions of Jeff Davis.—There is no truly loyal man who would not desire to avert this calamity.

This we are agreed upon. Then let us agree as to the manner by which we shall escape rebel tyranny and the rebel rule (*Whig*, December 19, 1866).

The threat of rebel seizure of the state government had been mentioned frequently by the *Whig*, sometimes obliquely. But in Governor Brownlow's message to the legislature on November 15, 1866, he spelled out his fears and asked for authorization to create a state militia, "subject to the call of the Executive, to suppress insurrection or protect the ballot-box." Whether the governor sincerely believed rebellion was being plotted, or viewed a militia as a helpful adjunct to continuing the Radical Party in power, he got what he asked. The assembly enacted a law authorizing a "State Guard."[28]

Pressure for the passage of the State Guard bill mounted after the assassination of Senator Almon Case near his home in Obion County on January 24, 1867, by a young man he had previously helped. Dr. Case had served as a surgeon in a Tennessee Union regiment, was present at the Fort Pillow massacre, and had testified before a committee investigating the killing of black soldiers by the Confederates. The *Whig* charged that his murder was "an invention to get the Senate below a quorum. By assassinating two more senators they can prevent the passage of any law at the present session." The senator's death followed by three or four months the murder of his sixteen-year-old son. A letter from Obion County to another member of the legislature described the senator's assassin as Frank Ferris, a guerrilla who had slain another Unionist on the public square of Troy a few hours earlier.[29]

The Republican State Convention (the term *Radical* was appearing less frequently) met at Nashville on February 22, 1867. It nominated Brownlow for governor, a step so cut and dried that the designation of the Parson for this office was only an item in the long report of the Resolutions Committee, rather than a separate motion. The enfeebled governor made a brief acceptance speech. He confessed to inability to carry on a canvass. A few days later he was at home in Knoxville recovering from a bilious attack.[30] The *Whig*, meanwhile, geared itself for a spirited campaign. It cut its annual subscription rate to $2.00 and appealed for 5,000 more subscribers:

We are entering upon a four month's campaign, which for bitterness, fierce and terrible work, has never been equalled in Tennessee. The State will be flooded with speakers on both sides, and every inch of ground will be contested. And why? Because a governor is to be elected, eight Congressmen are to be chosen, as well as all members of the General Assembly. The contests in these elections will be between the friends and the enemies of the Union—between Patriots and Traitors—and one party or the other goes under in Tennessee the first Thursday in August next (*Whig*, March 6, 1867)!

The *Whig*'s prediction of a heated and violent campaign was correct. The disfranchised Confederates viewed with fury the prospect of being forced to stand aside while the men they had formerly enslaved were invited, even urged, to vote for Radical candidates. Blacks were given the patronizing help of Brownlow's appointees to registration and election posts, and protected by the bristling rifles of the governor's State Guards. A forecast of the tension that would develop between Radical and Conservative appeared in a *Whig* report of a Conservative meeting at Athens, in lower East Tennessee. The newspaper quoted a speaker as saying:

If Governor Brownlow *dare* to call out any portion of the militia, the people (meaning the Johnsonites) would rise and wrench their arms from their hands and *exterminate* them, and he . . . [the speaker] advised them to do so.

This fiery statement, reminiscent of Yancey's threat of bayoneting the Parson's breast in his 1861 speech at Knoxville, brought an equally explosive reply from the *Whig*:

Follow the advise [*sic.*] of the lawyers and politicians who counsel you to rebellion, as they did in 1861, and who, in the next war as in the past, *will take special care to keep (if they can?) their precious carcasses out of harm's way*. We repeat, follow their advise [*sic.*] if you desire; do it if you DARE and Hell will contain so many of you the devil will have difficulty in finding enough muster rolls to regularly classify you in companies and regiments. Gov. Brownlow does not come before you as a suppliant, offering compromises and *beseeching* you to abstain from rebellion. HE DARES YOU TO ENGAGE IN IT.[31]

Both parties sought the vote of the newly enfranchised black man. The Radical Republicans held the edge, for their party was responsible for the ratification of the Fourteenth Amendment and state legislation giving the blacks the vote. The party also had a mighty weapon in the Union League, a highly partisan organization which was started in the North in 1862 and moved into Tennessee in 1864. It organized across the state, and when the blacks were enfranchised, it began a vigorous campaign to enlist their vote. The league elaborated its rituals and ceremonies to attract the credulous and easily influenced former slaves. The Conservatives, in nominating Emerson

Etheridge, of Dresden for governor undoubtedly counted on his reputation as an excellent campaigner. But Etheridge was handicapped by publicity given a statement he was accused of having made in 1865:

The negroes [sic.] are no more free than they were four years ago, and if any one goes about the country telling them that they are, shoot him: and these negro [sic.] troops, commanded by low and degraded white men, going through the country, ought to be shot down.

The Radical newspapers of Nashville carried the story of the statement consistently. There it was expected to have an adverse effect on Conservatives trying to woo black votes. In East Tennessee, where the white population viewed the blacks with distaste, the *Whig* made no spectacular display of the statement. Horace Maynard, one of the Radical speakers stumping the state for the incapacitated governor, said Etheridge was acquitted by a military court of having made this and other alleged disloyal statements. Major General George H. Thomas, however, disapproved the findings of the military commission, but said it would not be reconvened because the "present state of society in West Tennessee does not require that further action should be taken in this case, or further restraint be placed upon the accused." [32]

The Conservative leaders made efforts to head off the application of the franchise law, resorting to legal opinions from private lawyers. In Knoxville, when a citizen asked if the law applied in a city election John M. Fleming, a Conservative, said it was "unconstitutional and ought to be so held by every judicial officer." Fleming went further and said that in the city election the judges on the precinct boards had authority to pass upon the legality of the act. Thomas A. R. Nelson, John Baxter, who had parted company with the Parson and was fighting him venomously, and George Brown, a former circuit judge who had been elected over the Parson's opposition, concurred in Fleming's opinion. The *Whig* expressed amazement that an attorney as astute as Nelson should be found in such a role, observed that the lower courts had held both for and against the law, and reported that in the Knoxville election the four-lawyer opinion had generally been disregarded. In midsummer John C. Gaut, chairman of the Conservative Party's Central Committee, took a much more drastic step. Gaut advised county courts to appoint the election judges. He held that this power was vested in registration commissioners only if county courts failed to act. Gaut did not question the validity of the act, because by this time it had been upheld by the State Supreme Court. But he said that when the law was construed with other sections of the code, it authorized registration commissioners to make the appointments only when the county courts failed to act.

The governor proclaimed that this construction was "false and rebellious." He ordered the county courts "not to act upon the advice of this committee of seditionists," and directed General Joseph A. Cooper of Knoxville, in command of the State Guard, "to enforce the Franchise Law in its letter and spirit, without regard to the threats of seditionists." The *Whig* pithily warned that the governor intend to carry out his enforcement pledge, and "If to do so it becomes necessary that there shall be violence and bloodshed, so be it." Five days later Brownlow issued an even more drastic proclamation and ordered the State Guard to arrest Gaut or his agents if they were found advocating the policy outlined in the opinion. The Conservative must have backed down after he learned of the Parson's warning, for on the day the first proclamation appeared he advised the Davidson County Court to obey the governor. This the court voted to do, 22 to 15.[3]

The tremendous power of the Brownlow forces insured their success in the election. The charges of Baxter, who could not vote, Etheridge's splendid oratory, the smoldering wrath of the frustrated former Confederates, the reports spread of the governor's impending death, and the revelation of an unauthorized transfer by State Treasurer R. L. Stanford of $518,250 of state school funds from his office to a Memphis bank, his acknowledgement, resignation, and suicide were ineffectual against the Brownlow machine and its built-in advantages. The Republicans elected the eight congressmen, all of the state senators, and all but three state representatives.[34]

The overwhelming victory brought some editorial variations in the *Whig*. Etheridge had portrayed the Radical Party members as "paying no taxes, riding poor horses, wearing dirty shirts, and having no use for soap . . . . It turns out that a man's vote with a dirty shirt counts as much as the vote of the purse-proud aristocrat." Brownlow had always been a stickler for personal cleanliness, but now he predicted, "The common laborers of the country, who wear dirty shirts, intend to rule." He had for years pictured himself as the champion of the workingman and the farmer, but to applaud the "dirty shirt" crowd was a departure, even though it applied to politics rather than personal grooming (*Whig*, August 7, 1867). The *Whig*'s approach to the blacks, whose votes had swelled the Radical majorities, underwent spectacular change. It extolled them for industry and viewed the plight of the blacks with this eloquent bit of compassion:

The history of the world furnished no nobler example of honesty, industry and good conduct than the negro [*sic.*] has afforded, when we reflect upon the hundreds of years he has been in chains and slavery, degraded to the level of the brute, sold as cattle in the market, torn by cruel laws from his wife and child, deprived of the God-ordained rites of marriage, robbed of the fruits of his toil and that of his ancestors for hundreds of years, and then turned upon the cold charities of a selfish world, without a dollar for a shelter to protect him from the storm (*Ibid.*).

Political expediency had produced this reversal.

The *Whig* reported, with obvious pleasure, that Brownlow had defeated Etheridge, by 1,540 to 802, in President Johnson's home county of Greene. It gave a nostalgic but embittered touch to a three-county rally at Bull's Gap, where the Parson spoke briefly and recalled that in the crowd were members of the Self and Harmon families, some of whom had been the governor's jail mates at Knoxville. Two Harmons were led out of this jail before the Parson's eyes and taken to the gallows. So sharp and intense had been the division in Greene County that in a race for constable six weeks earlier the contestants had lined up for Brownlow or Johnson. Brownlow's man won by twenty-six votes.

Disturbances were reported at Franklin and Rogersville during the campaign. Two or more men were killed and several were wounded. A pitched battle at Rogersville, that broke out after Maynard and Etheridge spoke separately, led the *Whig*'s correspondent to send this wire from Greeneville:

Two men seriously wounded and one man by name of J. York killed, and one mule killed and several horses wounded. Did not learn the names of the wounded, or who it was that shot. They estimate about 150 shots were fired in the crowd. The Conservatives were first to fire. Everything very quiet this A.M. . . .

R. G.

LATER

The fight occurred by the rebels firing at the niggers as they were marching from the speaking, and I understand made them run in every direction, and loose [*sic.*] some of their colors.

Election day was quiet everywhere. [35]

When the results were known Tennessee seethed with hatred. The Radicals were in control and stronger than ever. Their leaders were committed to a policy of imposing a double penalty on former Confederates: denial of the franchise and extension of it to the former slaves. It is difficult to estimate which stung the most. The Radicals viewed the former Confederates as men who had turned traitor to the United States, had sought to secede by bloodshed and devastation, and could not be permitted to resume their former citizenship as though nothing had taken place but an innocuous interlude. The men who had gone with the South wanted back what they had lost.

Hostile armies had whipsawed the people of the state and their properties. In secessionist Middle and West Tennessee Union forces took over in 1862. In Unionist East Tennessee the Confederacy had exercised military rule, often ruthlessly, from June 1861 until September 1863, when Federal troops arrived in Knoxville.

Samuel G. Heiskell, the son of a Unionist who turned against Brownlow and became a Conservative and who in his own right attained prominence in the Democratic Party, wrote in 1920 that the Parson as governor was

bitter, but everybody was bitter in that vast contest of war . . . . In Eastern Tennessee, occupied as it was successively by the Confederate and Union armies, there was infinite bitterness, followed by reprisal on both sides, and with Brownlow's terrific denunciation of disunion men, it has always been a wonder to me he was not killed a hundred times.[36]

A general impression probably existed at the conclusion of the Parson's first term that he would retire from public office at the close of his tenure in two years. A hint of this lay in the *Whig* announcement soon after the 1867 victory that new quarters for the plant and office were to be built on the West side of Gay Street a few doors north of Clinch Avenue. The *Tri-Weekly Whig* also was to be resumed. This impression was heightened by the extremely feeble appearance the governor made at his inauguration. It seemed reasonable to assume that he would drop the burdens of public office and return to Knoxville to resume general direction of his beloved newspaper.

When Brownlow appeared before the General Assembly to make his inaugural address, he entered the chamber supported by two members, and looked "emaciated, pale and feeble." He sank into an arm chair and heard his speech read by his secretary. In this brief address he implored the members of the legislature to spare him as many burdens as possible, because of "the feeble state of my health." But the Parson was a man of surprises. Six days later, on October 15, 1867, he asked the legislature to elect him to the United States Senate for the term beginning on March 4, 1869, when the seat held by Senator Patterson would become vacant. The governor commented that while he was not as "robust" as in former years, he expected to stage a recovery because the prospects for a peaceful administration were much greater than previously. The truth as to the Parson's health, John Bell Brownlow wrote in 1892, was that when he was elected senator "he was sick in bed and in worse health than he had ever [been] before or than he had for years afterward." But tottering as he was on the edge of the grave, Brownlow won on the second day of balloting, defeating United States Representative William B. Stokes, 63 to 39.[37] Brownlow had many months remaining to serve as governor before he assumed his seat in the United States Senate. They were not peaceful, as he had suggested in his inaugural address. They were tumultuous and terrifying.

In the struggle that followed the former Confederates came up with a new, effective and frightening weapon, the masked, hooded, and horseback-riding Ku Klux Klan. The order had started in Pulaski, Tennessee, in December 1865, by half a dozen former soldiers of the South who were looking for entertainment. Its mystery, secrecy, and grotesque regalia and forms of communication offered such a powerful weapon to intimidate the ignorant and gullible former slaves that it was seized upon by the former Confederates. It reorganized at the Maxwell House in Nashville, in April 1867, in complete secrecy under the nose of the Brownlow administration. It soon became powerful in Middle and West Tennessee, where white men had long dominated the blacks and understood very well how to play upon their fears and superstitions.[38]

Brownlow denounced the Klan bands as "roving organizations of marauders and outlaws," who terrorized "several counties in Middle and West Tennessee" in the spring of 1868. The *Whig*'s columns began to be filled with reports of Klan outrages. Many of the accounts were clipped from the Nashville *Press and Times*, the outspoken Radical newspaper at the capital. The Memphis *Post* contributed to the exposure of the Klan, and printed what purported to be its constitution. It described the regalia which had been seized in a raid in which a score of men were arrested as members of the order.

The *Whig* obtained from the New York *Tribune* and reproduced copies of Klan handbills that portrayed the garish symbols employed by the organization.

The split in the old Union ranks was reflected in the contrasting policies of the *Whig* and the Conservative Knoxville *Daily Press and Herald*. One of the editors of the daily was John Fleming, former editor of the *Register*, who had once been Brownlow's collaborator in the Whig Party and a notable spokesman for the Union in 1861. The *Press and Herald* denounced the Governor as

a poor, palsied old man, trembling upon the verge of the grave, for which his long life of violence and envenomed personal warfare has poorly prepared a man who has been on every side of every question that has ever been discussed amony [among] the people, always managing to leave an unpopular cause just when its fortunes were failing, and bespattering his opponents always with the filth and billingsgate which his own vile nature so readily propagates.

The *Press and Herald* did not limit its warfare to name calling. It set its course firmly against the black race and mocked at reports that the Klan existed. In announcing a meeting at the Knox County Courthouse in preparation for the forthcoming Democratic National Convention, the *Press and Herald* asserted it was for "White men of Knox County, who believe that white men and not negroes [*sic*.], are the proper persons to direct the government of affairs in this state." By midsummer the newspaper threw out a challenge:

If a war of races is to be inaugurated by the Governor of Tennessee, *the White people of the state will not shirk* from the responsibility of the contest . . .. self-preservation is the first law of Nature. The White men of Tennessee are not all dead yet.[39]

The Klan grew slowly at first. It was regarded as "a manifestation of boyish exuberance of trivial importance." But early in 1868, after it had received widespread newspaper display, it began to achieve social and political power. It grew bolder. It issued manifestos and threats. Its members paraded on horseback with beast and rider grotesquely costumed to prevent identification as well as to terrify. Bands of Klansmen engaged in pitched battles with defiant blacks and stubborn sheriffs. At Columbia the confessed killer of a dentist was taken from jail by Klansmen and hanged. A white man, friendly with blacks, was murdered on the streets of Franklin after a black man had been hanged for the rape of a white woman. In Memphis, mounted, robed, and hooded Klansmen rode up to police head-quarters, confronted lined-up police, and challenged the officers to arrest them and collect the reward Governor Brownlow had offered. Both sets of men were armed and the police chief wisely told the Klansmen: "You can go on."

The disfranchised Confederates found in the Klan an instrument with which to exert tremendous influence on the gullible, the super-stitious, and the fearful. They frequently accomplished their purpose by threats and intimidation without the necessity of direct physical violence. The voteless Klansmen thus found a way to keep the blacks from utilizing the ballot. The order's most successful operations were in Middle and West Tennessee, where Conservative domination of county offices gave the hooded bands almost certain assurance that they would not be prosecuted by local officials. In its essence the Klan was the reply of frustrated, voteless men to the restrictions imposed upon them by the Brownlow administration. Denied the ballot, for reasons which they considered unjust, and willing to use violence to recover it, they resorted to a mystic hoodlumism to keep the despised blacks from exercising theirs.

Governor Brownlow's response was to propose new and more re-strictive measures. U.S. Representative S. R. Arnell, who owed his office to the Parson, provided the governor with the occasion for calling a special session of the legislature. Arnell wired that in June 1868 the Klan had searched for him on a train, "pistols and rope in hand," near his Columbia home. The governor appealed to General Thomas at Louisville for more regular troops. Some were already stationed in Tennessee. Thomas replied that the state had sufficient authority to cope with the situation. When the assembly met, alarmed Conservatives attempted conciliation. Thirteen former gen-erals of the Confederate army, including Nathan Bedford Forrest, the head of the Ku Klux Klan, petitioned the legislature to adopt meas-ures to remove all citizenship disabilities as a way to "heal all the wounds of our State." The generals disclaimed being behind any effort to overthrow the state government and predicted that the creation of a state militia would bring on additional strife. This sug-gestion contained in itself the hint of a threat. The *Whig* called the proposal insincere. It reported that three days after the presentation of the petition, William A. Quarles, one of the signers, made a vi-cious, insulting attack upon the governor and General Thomas and hinted at reprisals.[40] The *Whig* continued to carry columns of vituperation against the former Confederates, the Klan, and Conservatives.

The failure of the United States Senate to sustain the impeachment of President Johnson on May 26, 1868, had left the Brownlows in a most unhappy mood, especially since the newspaper had predicted that Senator Fowler from Tennessee would vote to sustain. It was taken for granted that Senator Patterson would not vote against his father-in-law, but Fowler had led the Radicals to believe he would go along with them. The *Whig*, in castigating Fowler, cited a number of instances in which he had declared in favor of sustaining impeachment, and added, "And yet, Mr. Fowler's most inexplicable vote saved the President from conviction" (*Whig*, May 20, 1868).

The legislature created a Joint Military Affairs Committee which found that bands of armed men were terrorizing blacks and some whites with hangings, shooting, whippings, ejection from their homes, and violations of females. It recommended laws to enable the governor to cope with the conditions. Brownlow got his laws. One authorized him to create a state militia. The other branded the Klan as an outlaw organization and imposed severe penalties for membership in it or association with its members, and provided penalties for officials who failed to take action against it.

The members of the assembly must have been aware that assembling a militia force would be difficult, for they authorized a committee of three, one from each grand division of the state, to lay before President Johnson an appeal for regular troops to restore order in Tennessee. Enforcement by local authorities in Middle and West Tennessee had failed. Not one offense in a long list of depredations had resulted in a conviction:

And so long as public opinion remains as it is, none will be, especially in the counties where the order [the Klan] is numerous. No person dare prosecute, for if he should his life will be endangered thereby. People are apprehensive, should they prosecute, that they would be murdered by the Klan. Indeed, they tell the people upon whom they inflict violence that if they should know any of them and disclose it, they will be killed. With this state of alarm and apprehension, no one will prosecute. Hence the civil authorities are powerless.

The committee suggested that federal troops in the rebellious counties would be more effective in restoring calm than state militia. The former would be better trained to deal with "riots or insurrections," and "they would have no local personal likes or dislikes to influence them to commit wrongs on peaceful citizens, nor be subject themselves, after discharge from service, to wrongs and outrages for having been in the State Military service." The committee carried its point. It wired the governor from Washington on September 12, 1868:

Mission accomplished. The President will sustain the civil authorities. Orders issued to department Commander [Thomas], to sustain and aid the civil authorities, and sufficient force will be furnished to accomplish such purpose.

Wm. H. Wisener

Thos. A. Hamilton

J. H. Agee

In accordance with the agreement a regiment was sent to Tennessee. It was distributed throughout the west and middle divisions where Klan activities had been boldest, and the state militia was not organized that year. Some historians hold the view that the state military service failed to attract members because of unpleasant experiences during the operation of the previous State Guard.[41]

The Radicals were determined to keep full control of the election, and the positioning of federal troops was credited with having helped the party vote. Yet, as these repressive measures were taken, the legislature and the governor offered a tiny ray of conciliation. The assembly members, in calling of the governor to suppress violence by organizing the State Guard, wrote into the joint resolution a stipulation: "If the peace and quiet of the State is maintained, and all the laws obeyed and enforced, said law will remain a dead letter on the Statute book, and not a man will be called out." The governor expressed the hope in his proclamation twice that it would not be necessary to call up troops for duty, and in a bow to white supremacists he pledged that black troops would be used in the field only as a last resort. Otherwise they would be kept in Nashville as reserves.[42]

Klan terrorism showed few signs of abating and actually may have been on the increase. The order was quite active at the polls in the effort to intimidate blacks from voting. The result was that, although the Radicals carried the State for General Grant and Schuyler Colfax of Indiana for President and Vice-President, the party lost strength in Middle and West Tennessee. Quiet was restored after the election, an indication that the Klan had achieved its purpose, despite the presence of federal troops in twenty-one counties.[43]

One of the most daring and grisly crimes of the Klan surfaced in February 1869. A detective, Seymour Barmore, who operated on the spectacular side, had been hired by the governor to infiltrate the Klan. The order worked in such secrecy that little was known of its internal affairs and organization. Barmore's first attempt was thwarted by the Klan. He was removed from a train by Klan members near Columbia and warned that if he persisted in trying to learn the secrets of the order he would die. Barmore was a man more given to audacity than discretion, and two nights later he headed for Pulaksi, on a freight train. Donning Klan regalia he got into a den meeting at Pulaski, caught a passenger train bound for Nashville, but again the order was tipped. The *Whig* of January 20, 1869, carried this terse bulletin:

Nashville, January 12—Detective Barmore, of this city, whilst returning from a business trip to Pulaski, was taken from a train on the Nashville and Decatur Railroad at 3 o'clock this morning by a band of Ku-Klux, some 25 in numbers, dressed in scarlet, with scarlet masks. Barmore made no resistance, and no one interfered in his behalf. What they did with him was not known. [44]

The newspaper uproar that followed was strident and biased. Each publication followed its political policy in its treatment of the story. The *Whig* saw in the abduction a design by the Klan to obtain the vote for the disfranchised and spit out this fury:

Raise a general [word blurred] , alarm the peaceful, law-abiding citizens, put men in fear of midnight raids, and arson and rapine. Lay it all to the injustice of withholding the ballot from the "ex rebels," and under this sort of pressure urge the passage of a universal franchise law as a sovereign panacea for all these terrors and ills. In other words, hug the venomous viper to your bosom to keep it quiet and to prevent it from stinging you to death. Turn the sheep over to the tender mercies of the wolves, *to pacify the wolves*.

The *Press and Herald*, assumed with no show of regret that Barmore had been hanged and offered this thought from "Ally Gator," its Nashville reporter:

The Kuklux [*sic.*] have captured a good detective, named Barmore, and is supposed to have hung [*sic.*] him.

Happy Barmore, to have been a martyr in the cause of loyalty, and to have been the means of pulling down the unchristian [*sic.*] and revolting sentiments in favor of enfranchising rebels.

A few days later the newspaper concluded:

The "missing detective" sensation seems to have played out at Nashville. It has served its purpose, however, as a pretext for Kuklux [*sic.*] legislation. It would be interesting to know how many members of the legislature were concerned in getting up the mysterious "disappearance of the 'dead beat.' "

On the morning of February 20, 1869, the body of Barmore was found floating in the Duck River, two miles from Columbia, a hideous example of illegal execution.

[The body] had evidently been weighted with a rock or other heavy weight which had slipped off, as there was a rope around his neck with a noose at the end of it. His arms were tied behind him with a linen handkerchief, and there was a single bullet-hole in his head. It was obvious that revenge rather than robbery had been the cause of his death. His two gold rings were still on the fingers of his left hand, and in his shirt front was the diamond-studded cross pin which he habitually wore. His wallet was in his pocket, his money undisturbed, and no list of Ku Klux members there when his body was found.

The *Press and Herald*, in reporting the finding of the body, at first questioned, "if, indeed, we can believe any report about him." In the same, however, it shifted ground somewhat:

Taking it for granted that this report is true and that Barmore was really kidnapped and murdered, as at first was reported, we most heartily unite with every lover of peace and justice and honor, in wishing that every participant in so revolting an assassination, may not only be detected, but brought to suffer the extreme penalties of the law. Barmore was, no doubt, a scoundrel himself, but he did not deserve the "deep damnation" of such a "taking off."[45]

The details of Barmore's death and identification of the individuals who acted for the Klan in the assassination remain secret to this day. Investigations produced nothing from the tight-lipped citizens. The abduction of the detective triggered Governor Brownlow into a final proclamation. On January 20, 1869, he called for the mustering of the State Guard. The call resulted in the organization of a force of 1,800 men. The governor dispatched them into nine Middle and West Tennessee counties where he had declared martial law. The need for these troops melted away, however. Soon after Brownlow resigned on February 25, 1869, to accept the Senate seat, General Forrest ordered the dissolution of the order. The objective which led to its creation had been achieved.[46] He might well have mentioned that its nemesis was leaving the state and the state government.

Brownlow's reasons for seeking the senate seat have never been made entirely clear. It was available to him, his for the asking. Perhaps he wanted to show old foes that he could get it, a display of defiance to them and their efforts to curb his political power. He loved power, and once elected he would be assured of a cozy, salaried post for six years, and one less draining on the little physical strength he retained. He knew his election would infuriate President Johnson, who would vacate his office the same day Brownlow took the Senate oath. Whatever the reason, it was compelling. It meant a final separation from what had been the great joy and satisfaction of his life, the *Whig*. His "Editorial Farewell," however, lacked the warmth of feeling that had flowed through the piece he had written when he turned the editorial chair over to his son and left to be governor. It was rather on the stiff and formal side for the Parson:

> The *Whig*, a journal I have edited for the last thirty years, now passes into other and more able and vigorous hands. As a member of the new company, owning the office, I shall feel a deep interest in the success of the enterprise, and will do all in my power to promote its success. In reviewing my long and eventful career as an editor, I have this to say, that had I my life to live over, I would pursue the same course I have pursued, only more so. If in past life I have been violent on some occasions, my apology is that like the Apostle Paul, on many occasions I have fought with "Beasts at Ephesus." In taking my leave of many of my readers, I will remind them that before they were born their parents were subscribers of mine. I have, however, the consolation to know that I have always taught both parents and children to hold fast to the forms of sound doctrine; and in defending them I have invariably uttered the words of truth and soberness. My friends, I wish every possible success in all the undertaking of life. Of my enemies, I have no favors to ask, but am willing to let by-gones be by-gones (*Whig*, January 6, 1869).

The *Press and Herald* gave the Parson this cynical salute, as an editor:

> How happy must that man be and in what sweet christian [Christian] fellowship must he have lived with his fellow man, who, upon laying aside his editorial armor and reviewing all the personal, official and political incidents of a long life spent in tumultuous strife with the "beasts at Ephesus" and "the world, the flesh and the devil," at large, can thus complacently and self-approvingly, withdraw from the scene of his conflicts! Happy, happy, thrice happy man!

Subtlety was cast aside for stinging bluntness as the *Press and Herald* rejoiced at the departure of Brownlow as governor:

> The retirement of Gov. Brownlow from all pretensions to the gubernatorial chair will mark a *post-bellum* epoch in the history of Tennessee. The abdication

of no hated monarch ever called forth a more heartfelt thanksgiving from the hearts of a long-suffering people than will swell from the very soul of Tennessee, when the assurance of the long prayed for riddance shall have been made doubly sure, by the departure of Senator Brownlow for the National Capital. The 25th day of February will be henceforth marked with a white stone in the Tennessee calendar . . . .

The feeling of the Tennesseean, today, is something akin to that of the jail-worn prisoner, who gladly dares and joyfully accepts all probable dangers, in lieu of his wasting confinement, or to drop all simile, it is in very truth the feeling of a long prostrate freeman, who feels the heavy foot of a tyrant withdrawn from his neck, and knows it can never be pressed again by a heavier one.[47]

The Parson had always been well supplied with bitter, wrathful, and articulate enemies. He probably liked it that way. It was fitting, the newspaper practices of that day being what they were, that he should receive this heavy smack, an accolade in reverse, from his Knoxville foe. It was truly a tribute to his ability to stimulate his enemies to the last.

CHAPTER XVII NOTES

[1] *Whig*, October 11, 1865; *Tennessee Senate Journal, First Adjourned Session, 1865*, pp. 4-26; hereafter referred to as *Senate Journal, First Adjourned Session, 1865*.

[2] *Whig*, September 27, 1865. Brownlow's first doubts about advantages of slavery, *ibid.*, April 30, 1845.

[3] For Brownlow's opinion of the black race, *ibid.*, October 31, 1840, January 11, 1843, September 13, November 29, 1848, October 17, 1857; *Tri-Weekly Whig*, February 1, 1859.

[4] *Whig*, October 11, 1865; *Senate Journal, First Adjourned Session, 1865*, pp. 4-26.

[5] White, *Messages*, V, pp. 478-479. White was severely criticized as lacking objectivity in his treatment of Brownlow. Enoch L. Mitchell, "Journal of Southern History," (Houston, May 1960) Southern Historical Association, V, 26, pp. 249-250. Alexander, *Political Reconstruction*, p. 99; *Whig*, October 18, 25, 11, 1865.

[6] Rodgers had represented Brownlow in the Patterson libel cases. Butler's circuit formerly was served by Judge D. T. Patterson, President Johnson's son-in-law and United States senator designate. For the appointments see *ibid.*, June 21, 1865, February 28, 1866.

[7] *Ibid.*, October 25, 1865; *Senate Journal, First Adjourned Session, 1865*, p. 70; *Whig*, December 13, 27, 1865; Alexander, *Political Reconstruction*,

pp. 100-101; Patton, *Unionism and Reconstruction*, pp. 128-129; Alexander, *Political Reconstruction*, p. 101; *House Journal, First Adjourned Session, 1865*, p. 295.

[8] *Whig*, February 28, March 7, 1866; Alexander, *Political Reconstruction*, pp. 105-108; Patton, *Unionism and Reconstruction*, pp. 115-116. The House took up the Franchise Bill, February 15, 1866, but was unable to transact business. *House Journal, First Adjourned Session, 1865-1866*, pp. 270-383; White, *Messages*, V, pp. 481-487.

[9] *Whig*, February 28, March 7, 1866.

[10] Johnson vetoed the Freedman's Bureau Bill, a Radical measure, in February 1866. White, *Messages*, V, p. 509.

[11] *Whig*, February 21, April 4, 1866. The speech was delivered in Knoxville on March 24, 1866.

[12] The *Whig* ran the letter in two issues, April 14, 1866. A handwritten copy of the letter is in the Rule Papers.

[13] *Whig*, March 14, 21, April 4, 11, 25, May 2, 9, 16, 1866; Alexander, *Political Reconstruction*, pp. 109-110; Patton, *Unionism and Reconstruction*, pp. 117-118; *Whig*, May 23, 1866.

[14] *Ibid.*, May 9, 16, 1866; Alexander, *T. A. R. Nelson*, p. 123.

[15] *Whig*, April 11, 1866; White, *Messages* V, pp. 450-451; Alexander, *Political Reconstruction*, pp. 108-109; White, *Messages*, V, p. 488, fn. 81; *House Journal, First Adjourned Session, 1865-1866*, pp. 424-425, 487; *Whig*, April 11, 18, 1866; See *House Journal, First Session, 1865*, p. 28, for Williams' affirmative vote in the first franchise bill.

[16] *Whig*, April 26, 1865; *House Journal, First Session, 1865*, pp. 38, 50, 65; White, *Messages*, V, pp. 427-428; *House Journal, First Adjourned Session, 1865-1866*, p. 426, *Whig*, May 2, 1866.

[17] *Ibid.*, April 13, May 23, 1866; Patton, *Unionism and Reconstruction*, p. 118; Alexander, *Political Reconstruction*, pp. 104-105; *Whig*, May 23, 1866.

[18] *Ibid.*, November 8, 1865, July 4, 1866; Brownlow to Temple, May 30, 1865. Temple Papers.

[19] See *Whig*, September 20, 1865 for Heiskell's defense. A number of meetings had been held in Knox County calling on Heiskell to resign. *Ibid.*, August 23, September 6, September 20, 1865. The Brownlow and Heiskell families apparently continued to remain on the best of personal terms. William Heiskell's son, Samuel, a prominent Democrat and Knoxville mayor for several terms, treated Brownlow with extreme deference in *Andrew Jackson and Early Tennessee History*, III, pp. 203-26, 227-272.

[20] *Whig*, November 8, 1865, June 13, May 16, 23, July 4, 11, 18, 1866, July 10, 24, 1867.

[21] *Ibid.*, February 14, 21, 28. The governor's appeal to East Tennessee loyalists appeared in *ibid.*, December 13, 1865. For a discussion of the Freedmen's Bureau see Patton, *Unionism and Reconstruction*, pp. 144-169.

[22] Alexander, *Political Reconstruction*, pp. 110-111; Patton, *Unionism and Reconstruction*, pp. 216-217; White *Messages*, V, pp. 508-510; Folmsbee et al., *Short History*, pp. 355-356; *Whig*, June 27, May 13, 30, 1866; Alexander, *Political Reconstruction*, p. 102; *Whig*, June 20, July 4, 1866.

July 4, 1866. "My Policy" was a term for Johnson's policy.

[23] *Ibid.*, July 18, 1866; White, *Messages*, V, p. 518; *Senate Journal, Extra Session, 1866*, pp. 23-24; Patton, *Unionisn and Reconstruction*, pp. 220-223; Alexander, *Political Reconstruction*, p. 111; White, *Messages*, V, pp. 519-524; *Whig*, July 18, 25, August 1, 22, 1866. The House was in a continual uproar from July 4, 1866, when it convened, to final action, July 18, 1866. *House Journal, Extra Session, 1866*, pp. 6-25; *Whig*, July 25, 1866. Johnson had called Forney a "dead duck." Patton, *Unionism and Reconstruction*, pp. 223-224.

[24] *Ibid.*, pp. 224-225; Alexander, *Political Reconstruction*, pp. 119-121; *Whig*, July 25, August 1, 22, 1866. Gordon Grainger was a Union general who had served in the East Tennessee area. For an extended discussion of the reported attempt to overthrow the Brownlow administration, see Alexander, *Political Reconstruction*, pp. 124-129.

[25] *Whig*, September 12, 19; Conklin, quoting the Chicago *Tribune* of September 12, 1866, p. 142.

[26] *Whig*, October 3, 17, 1866; Conklin, pp. 142-146.

[27] White, *Messages*, V, p. 530; Alexander, *Political Reconstruction*, p. 123; *Whig*, November 7, 14, 1866; White, *Messages*, V, pp. 531-532, 546; Alexander, *Political Reconstruction*, pp. 123-130; Patton, *Unionism and Reconstruction*, pp. 133-134; *Whig*, November 7, 1866, January 30, 1867, November 30, 1866. See also Alexander, *Political Reconstruction*, p. 147.

[28] *Whig*, April 4, August 22, 29, October 24, 1866; White, *Messages*, V, pp. 534-535. For a discussion of Brownlow's motives in asking for a state militia, see Alexander, *Political Reconstruction*, pp. 126-129.

[29] *Whig*, January 23, 30, 1867; White, *Messages*, V, p. 551. For a brief sketch of Case see *Whig*, April 12, 1865. The murder of Senator Case is not mentioned in Patton, *Unionism and Reconstruction*, or in Alexander, *Political Reconstruction*. The letter giving the name of the guerrilla was written to Representative J. W. Smith of Hardeman County, who did not reveal the name of his informant. *Whig*, January 30, 1867.

[30] *Whig*, March 6, April 3, 1867.

[31] *Ibid.*, February 27, March 13, 6, 20, 1867; Alexander, *Political Reconstruction*, p. 141.

[32] *Ibid.*, pp. 146-147; Patton, *Unionism and Reconstruction*, pp. 134-139; *Whig*, April 24, May 1, 8, June 5, 1867.

[33] *Ibid.*, January 9, 1867; Patton, *Unionism and Reconstruction*, p. 121. Baxter's attack and the Parson's counter-assaults, *Whig*, April 24, May 1, 8, 15, 22, 29, 1867, June 5, July 3, 10, 1867. For the Supreme Court opinion upholding the franchise law see *Whig*, March 27, 1867; Patton, *Unionism and Reconstruction*, pp. 120-123; White, *Messages*, V, pp. 540, 546; Gaut's role, *Whig*, July 3, 10, 1867; election returns, White, *Messages*, V, p. 506.

[34] Reports of the Parson's impending death, *Whig*, April 3, 1867; White, *Messages*, p. 563. Accounts of the Stanford case may be found in the *Whig*, January 30, April 24, May 22, 1867; White, *Messages*, V, author's note, p. 546; election returns, *House Journal, 1867-1868*, p. 25.

[35] *Whig*, August 21, July 30, August 7, 1867; Alexander, *Political Recon-struction*, pp. 153-156.

[36] Heiskell, *Andrew Jackson and Early Tennessee History*, III, preface.

[37] *Whig*, October 30, 16, 23, 1867; *Senate Journal, First Session, 1867*, pp. 23-24; *Whig*, October 30, 1867; *Senate Journal, First Session, 1867*, pp. 90-91; John Bell Brownlow to Temple, June 20, 1892. Temple Papers.

[38] Alexander, *Political Reconstruction*, pp. 176-182; Stanley Horn, *The In-visible Empire, The Story of the Ku Klux Klan*, enlarged edition (Cos Cob, Connecticut, 1969), pp. 9-15, 32-41. Hereafter referred to as *The Invisible Empire*. Folmsbee, *et al., Short History*, pp. 360-361.

[39] *Whig*, March 18, 25, April 1, 15, 22, 29, 1868; *Press and Herald*, June 18, March 22, 24, 29, April 22, 24, 29, 15, 25, July 2, 1868.

[40] For an extended account of the formation of the Klan and its activities in Tennessee, see *The Invisible Empire*, pp. 73-108. See also Folmsbee, *et al, Short History*, pp. 361-364; Alexander, *Political Reconstruction*, pp. 176-198; Patton, *Unionism and Reconstruction*, pp. 162-165, 170-200. For Brownlow's call for a special session, and the Whig's policy against the Klan, see *Whig*, March 11, 18, 25, April 15, 22, 29, May 13, 20, 27, June 10, 24, July 1, 29, August 12, 26, September 9, 16, 1868.

[41] *Senate Journal, Extra Session, 1868*, pp. 131-168; *House Journal, Extra Session, 1868*, pp. 185-222; *Acts of Tennessee, Extra Session, 1868*, Chap-ters 2 and 3, pp. 18-25; Alexander, *Political Reconstruction*, pp. 188-189; Patton, *Unionism and Reconstruction*, pp. 192-198; *Whig*, September 16, 1868; *Senate Journal Appendix, 1868-1869*, p. 10; Alexander, *Political Reconstruction*, pp. 188-199; Patton, *Unionism and Reconstruction*, pp. 198-199; Alexander, *Political Reconstruction*, p. 182.

[42] *Senate Journal, Extra Session, 1868*, pp. 138-168; *House Journal, Extra Session, 1868*, pp. 185-222; Patton, *Unionism and Reconstruction*, pp. 192-199; *Whig*, January 20, February 17, 1869.

[43] Patton, *Unionism and Reconstruction*, p. 142.

[44] *The Invisible Empire*, pp. 108-110; Alexander, *Political Reconstruction*, pp. 196-197; *Whig*, January 20, 1869.

[45] *Ibid., Press and Herald*, January 15, 17, 20, 24, 1869. Barmore's effects were attached to pay his debts. *Ibid.*, January 22, 1869; *The Invisible Empire*, pp. 111-112. See also excoriation of Barmore and a quasi-justifi-cation for the killing, by the Louisville *Courier-Journal. Ibid.*, p. 112.

[46] *The Invisible Empire*, pp. 112-113; Alexander, *Political Reconstruction*, pp. 187-198; Patton, *Unionism and Reconstruction*, pp. 199-200.

[47] *Press and Herald*, January 7, 1869.

"Yielding up the other cheek/Dropping humbly
on the knees; Closing lips when dared to speak/Will
not do in times like these."

Chapter No. 19

NEW FOES FROM OLD FRIENDS

Parson Brownlow's political course brought him a host of new and burning enemies. It also shattered some old and very close friendships. The oldest friend with whom he parted company was Frederick Steidinger Heiskell, one of Knoxville's early printers and newspaper publishers. Brownlow's first book, *Helps to the Study of Presbyterianism*, came out of Heiskell's shop. When the Parson moved to Knoxville, he borrowed money from Heiskell to bail himself out of a tight situation. The Knoxville printer also was most active in the affairs of the city. When the issue of secession arose he was a firm loyalist, although he was not as militant as some of the leaders.[1]

The Civil War found Heiskell a miserable old man, for loyal Unionist that he was, both of his sons went with the South. Carrick White joined the army, and Joseph B., a Rogersville lawyer, won a seat in the Confederate House from the First District. Union forces captured the congressman in upper East Tennessee late in the summer of 1864 and imprisoned him at Knoxville. The *Whig* credited him with having held a position of "respectability" prior to the war. But it accused him of having shown such hatred and ferocity against Unionists of East Tennessee during the war: "It is now time that the *halter* should be summoned to do its appropriate work; and no man in the ranks of the rebellion is a man more suitable to commence upon that than this same rebel congressman." The *Whig* made the grisly suggestion that if Joseph Heiskell was given his liberty, "He could not live

343

twenty-four hours, within the reach of the men he has abused, persecuted and outraged." The Union authorities concluded that they had insufficient grounds upon which to hold the congressman. He must have decided to go elsewhere than East Tennessee, for he next appeared in "the genial clime of Memphis," where he practiced law. [2]

Fred Heiskell became a Conservative. It would have been unthinkable for him to have turned Radical. He made a forlorn race for Congress in the summer of 1864 against a field of five Radicals that included Horace Maynard, who captured his old Second District seat. Heiskell received only 126 votes out of 2,500 cast in Knox County. Somewhere during the campaign, he picked up the title of major, at least the *Whig* gave him that handle. When the campaign ended the *Whig* accorded him more than a column of space in which he expressed his Conservative position, his opposition to the disfranchisement and election laws of the Radical administration, and his zeal to heal the wounds of war by restoring "the original order of things" with the exception of slavery. He was opposed to black equality. The *Whig* described Heiskell's statement as "a very foolish document to come from a sensible man." He lost, the newspaper said, because he had supported McClellan against Lincoln for President, a position unacceptable to the majority of East Tennessee Unionists. [3]

The *Whig* remained fairly tolerant of Heiskell until he accused the Parson of lying in a talk at the Knox County Courthouse. In the talk the governor charged, "As a class the newspapers of the South were disloyal and that hostility to the Government and Union men characterized the editorials of a majority of Southern journals." The *Whig* countered Heiskell's assertion by quoting abusive and hysterical language from a number of southern publications, but again treated the former publisher with considerable restraint. It referred to him rather mildly as "an old fossil." Restraint ended when a second newspaper, the *Commercial*, was started in Knoxville and opened its columns to Heiskell. It permitted him to attack the governor as having "never published a paper, political or religious, that could be introduced into a family without polluting it." The *Whig* recalled that Heiskell had visited Brownlow in the editor's home over a period of years, had expressed "great admiration for his newspaper, and had subscribed to it for many years. The *Whig* found that in his changed mood Heiskell

revels in slander as the chief element of the atmosphere on which he stands. He

is like the man . . . who was so fond of contradiction that he would throw up the window in the middle of the night and contradict the watchman who was calling the hour.

In a word, he is "the incarnation of malice, mendacity and cowardice" (*Whig*, May 2, 1866).

Young John Bell Brownlow was infuriated when Heiskell described him as a "squirt" and lunged at the old man [he was eighty years old] with this bit of background:

In August 1864, Joseph B. Heiskell [son of Frederick] was captured by the brigade to which we belonged. Joseph had been *particeps crimini* to the atrocious murder of several Union citizens, and through several counties had accompanied and encouraged a band of rebel bushwackers and thieves who *lacerated with whips the backs of the wives, sisters, and daughters of the Union soldiers.*

Because of these atrocious and inhuman acts it was with difficulty that Gen. Gillem could prevent the outraged Union soldiers of East Tennessee from taking the life of the 'worthy son of an illustrious sire.' In the presence of Heiskell's friends we publicly expressed the opinion that the '*woman whipper*' should be shot. Ever since then the father of the coward and brute has considered us a 'squirt'—Jo Heiskell was not shot, as he *should* have been, but was brought to this city and [in the presence of his illustrious 'parient'] [*sic.*] marched to the Knoxville jail, with *his hands tied behind him*. The father thought we exerted some influence to have this disposition made of his brutal son.[4]

Governor Brownlow must have decided John Bell was doing an inadequate job on Heiskell, for in an editorial bearing the Parson's unmistakable touch he bore down upon his old friend:

This old whisky-rotted, broken-down political hack has been for several months abusing and blackguarding the senior editor of the Knoxville *Whig*, through the columns of a dirty little daily, conducted by an insolent swindler, and a degraded little rebel sympathizer . . . .

The Parson listed five reasons for Heiskell's anger: 1) his failure to get a job under Brownlow as assistant special Treasury agent after the Union occupation, 2) the *Whig*'s account of Joe's arrest, 3) the father's ignominious race for Congress, 4) the removal of Joe's name from a charter submitted to the legislature for approval, and 5) the shelving of a bill prepared by Joseph "for the benefit of rebels." Then he summed up the elder Heiskell:

A case exemplifying more malice, more depravity, more scoundrelism, more contempt for generosity, more baseness, more blind devotion to a sinking cause and a disgraced band or leaders, and more profligacy, ingratitude and worthlessness has seldom or never been made public. A fugitive from the fold of truth, the walks of sobriety, and the abodes of patriotism, honor and integrity, the poor old apostate is held in utter contempt by the people who, until recently, have respected his grey hairs (*Whig*, June 13, 1866).

Feeble and palsied in body the Parson was, but he could still pile up the epithets with the vigor and variety of his earlier years.

Brownlow was at the peak of his political power, but he was having trouble getting his way in the courts, especially in litigation to punish rebels for injury done to Unionists. Early in 1865 he was awarded judgment of $25,000 against W. H. Sneed, John H. Crozier, and R. B. Reynolds, in Knox County Circuit Court. Reynolds was the Confederate commissioner who had issued the warrant for Brownlow's arrest in 1861. The editor charged that Sneed and Crozier met in the office of J. C. Ramsey, Confederate district attorney, and there conspired on how to get rid of him. The Parson said that they considered hanging him. Several other judgments were returned in favor of Unionists against influential Confederates accused of having persecuted to the point of property destruction and death. Among them was a judgment in favor of the heirs of Sam Pickens of Sevier County, a former state senator, who was marched away as an enemy of the Confederacy and died in prison. This judgment, against Sneed, Crozier, and Reynolds, was for $10,000. The Parson lost heavily as a result of being banished. Although he did recoup his fortunes extensively through his lectures and his book, he urged the filing of more suits against Confederates who were "a part and parcel of a general, wicked and most infernal conspiracy." In fact, he encouraged a deluge of litigation:

Other suits are on the docket, and others are to come. Let them be impoverished, and made bankrupt. Let them [the ex-Confederates] be made beggars, going from door to door for their bread. They brought on this rebellion—they caused all this suffering and trouble—let them now be made odious, and their estates be confiscated . . . .Now, let them feel the consequences of their wicked and rebellious conduct.

Among the Parson's losses in connection with the war was his failure to realize anything from the lawsuit against the trustees of the Bank of East Tennessee, which he had won in the State Supreme Court. The Parson had a personal stake in this lawsuit, which he prosecuted for himself and many other depositors who had lost in the bank's failure. Property of the bank was sold to satisfy judgments for $100,000, shortly before the war broke out, and funds were deposited in the Bank of Tennessee. Officials of the bank made away with the money during the war, and the Parson declined an offer of the Knox County clerk and master to accept Confederate money to satisfy the judgment. Nor did Brownlow realize any money, with the possible exception of some rents, from the properties of Sneed, Crozier, and Reynolds. When these properties were sold at court sale the Parson bid them in, but lost them later under United States Supreme Court rulings. The three Brownlow foes thus regained all their real estate. [5]

Sneed, Ramsey, and Crozier were old and established enemies of the Parson, both political and personal. Far more dreadful and emotionally draining was the break between Brownlow and two old friends and former Unionists, Connally F. Trigg and John Baxter. Both men had been welcomed effusively when they arrived in Knoxville to practice law. Trigg was the partner of O. P. Temple; and Baxter, a wealthy North Carolinian, signalled his arrival by the purchase of an "elegant residence" on Main Street. Baxter attained a practice rated by a contemporary as the largest in the state. Both lawyers went down the line ardently and vigorously for the Union in the hectic campaigns on separation in 1861. After the state voted for secession, Trigg fled to the North but Baxter remained in Knoxville. [6] The former came back to Tennessee in 1863 as a United States District Court judge. The Parson predicted that he would be a scourge to the rebels. The *Whig*, at the close of the Federal Court session, praised Judge Trigg for having "presided with great dignity and propriety. . . . It is a source of no little gratification to his numerous friends that he who, two years and a half ago, had to steal away from home like a thief in the night to avoid the murderers who were dogging him, came back with authority to vindicate the laws of the government which he then vainly sought to uphold and which effort constituted the crime that drove him into exile."

The legal philosophy of Judge Trigg, however, soon drove the *Whig* into indignation. The newspaper's first protest against the rather wholesale release of men indicted for treason was lodged against the amnesty proclamation "and the laws of Congress enacted in pursuance thereof." Most of those indicted were cleared of charges upon taking the amnesty oath. The *Whig* began to give personal coverage of the court and indicated a special interest in Eli Dickson or Dixon. He had made threats against one of the *Whig* editors and had vowed on the death of his son at Fort Donelson to kill "twelve Union men to pay for it." Dixon was freed upon taking the amnesty oath, was rearrested and reindicted for violation of his pledge, but Judge Trigg "lectured the jurors for their seeming disposition to persecute the man," and ordered his release.[7] This was the Parson's first printed criticism of the judge, and the newspaper seized upon it to point a moral:

A few days ago he [Dickson] undertook to act as a guide for about thirty rebel guerrillas crossing the Tennessee River into McMinn County . . . robbing and plundering innocent Union families—this old pet of the Federal Court piloting the raiders to the Union houses. A small party of Federal soldiers got after them, and overtook them as they approached old Eli's house—capturing eight of them—Dickson starting to run was halted, refusing to stop; the soldiers discharged their muskets, six balls taking effect and killing him instantly.

We suggest to those who entered into bonds for his loyalty and future good conduct, that they plead his death as a ground of forgiveness! . . . Old Eli went into the rebellion at the start and never got his right until a few days ago (*Whig*, February 1, 1865).

The feud between Brownlow and Trigg erupted into a conflict between the United States District Court and the Parson in his role as assistant special agent of the Treasury Department over a 500-acre farm in the Lyons Bend area of the Tennessee River, late in the winter of 1865. As Treasury agent Brownlow had seized the farm and leased it to Joseph Mullins on October 8, 1864. Three bachelor brothers—T. C. Lyon, a lawyer, Captain William Lyon of the Confederate army, and W. H. Lyon, owned the land. They were reported to be inside the Confederate lines. In January 1864 Judge Trigg ordered Mullins ousted and the property turned over to "a rebel lawyer, for the use of the rebel heirs of the Lyon family." Mullins sought to intervene and asked that the order be set aside and the suit transferred to Circuit Court. He protested that he had already sowed wheat on some of the land. Judge Trigg denied the application of Mullins and the United States marshal summoned a posse to remove the farmer. The Parson moved quickly and forcefully. He obtained troops from General Lewis Tilson, commanding at Knoxville, and they were stationed at the farm to protect the renter. The marshal and his deputies made no attempt to dislodge the soldiers.[8]

The outcome of the confrontation put the Parson in high spirits. He had been nominated for governor without opposition and he had defied, with the backing of the United States army, the order of a federal judge to overthrow a lease arrangement he had made. He loosed this hymn of triumph:

I will not play into the hands of *wealthy and influential rebels*, in violation of the laws of Congress, even though I incur the displeasure of the Federal court. I am willing to measure arms with the court, or in other words, to let the loyal people of East Tennessee decide upon our respective merits. I have never heard a more general complaint against any organization than is made by loyal men against the doings of this court. It has never, as Lawyers say, decided in favor of the Government when there was opposition made. It has not convicted any man of treason or of high misdemeanor, out of *twelve hundred indictments* and I believe never will. It admits a rebel Lawyer to practice in the court, indicted for treason; and it turns traitors loose upon the community who come in and take the amnesty oath, *after* they have been indicted for treason. . . . Its sessions are doing the Union cause no good and the best interests of the country would not suffer if it were to suspend its operations until the close of the war (*Whig*, March 1, 1865).

Trigg made a futile attempt in the following May to have the Parson, now governor, indicted for obstructing a United States District Court order, in the Mullins affair:

[He] delivered a charge to the grand jury in Knoxville, in which he directed them, in strong and dictatorial language, in a manner displaying a high state of excitement, to indict me for my action in the premises. It is probable . . . that the secret had got out that some such *stump speech* would be made from the Bench, for the rebel soldiers and citizens were in attendance, and they cheered lustily. The assault upon me, like the opinions and decisions of the Court generally, was popular with the rebels, and that class of Union men with whom his Honor drinks liquor and plays cards.

The governor was gratified, stating:

Much to the surprise and chagrin of the eminent patriot [Trigg], *whose every thought is as pure as an Angel's breath*,(!) he failed to bully the grand jury of his Court to find a bill against the editor of this paper.

Several days since the grand jury of the Federal Court was discharged, and the jurors *departed* . . . without making the presentment which Trigg's heart yearned for. . . . Some men have nobly served their country by dying on the battlefield. All men like Trigg would serve their country by dying anywhere (*Whig*, June 21, 1865).

The *Whig* was pleased with the grand jurors, but it had another reason to detest Trigg. The judge had held unconstitutional the Test Oath Act passed by Congress that required lawyers who had supported the Confederacy to swear that their adherence had not been voluntary before they could practice in Federal Court. This ruling, the newspaper complained, "admitted those lawyers to practice in his Court who not only *voluntarily* gave aid and comfort to the rebellion, but were original secessionists and *leaders* of the rebellion in East Tennessee." Trigg's opinion was ultimately upheld by the United States Supreme Court. The question had highly important legal aspects. One eminent attorney summed it up in this fashion:

The right of an attorney acquired by his admission to the bar, to appear for suitors and to argue cases is not a matter of indulgence, grace or favor revocable at the pleasure of the Court or the Legislature. Congress has the right to prescribe the qualifications for the office of attorney, but it has no right to inflict punishment for past conduct; such legislation is in conflict with the Constitutional provision prohibiting passage of bills of attainder.[9]

The hot wrath the *Whig* poured upon Judge Trigg for this ruling arose from personal, as well as political, reasons. John Bell Brownlow, who scribbled a number of highly derogatory statements about Trigg's moral habits on the margins of the *Whig* files, insisted, "Trigg literally owed his appointment absolutely to my father." The Brownlow son said he had a letter that Trigg had written to the Parson that implored the latter to see President Lincoln on the former's behalf, and stated that Military Governor Johnson would give him no assistance in seeking the appointment as federal judge. When the Parson made his plea on behalf of Trigg "he found there was already on the President's table a commission for Gen. John B. Rogers of Middle Tennessee as U.S. judge for Tenn. Had he been one day later it would have gone to the Senate. One of the first cases Lincoln ever had, one of the first fees, was given him by old Gen. Rogers in a land lawsuit."

The Brownlows were bitterly hacked when Trigg displayed a legal philosophy in complete opposition to their principle that all rebels were traitors. The United States Supreme Court decision that upheld Trigg in the test oath case vindicated him legally. The Brownlow view that he should have held the way those responsible for his appointment wanted him to scarcely conforms to ethics, legal or otherwise; but it appears true that Trigg, upon return from his northern refuge during the war, had altered his personal tastes for friends. Temple, who had extended to him a law partnership when he located in Knoxville, in later years wrote of him rather dourly:

Not many months passed after Judge Trigg ascended the bench before it became apparent that his sympathies and feelings were all on the side of those to whom he had been lately so hostile. This was the more striking when it was considered that he was not a fickle, emotional man, a man of hot impulses and bitter prejudices, but the very reverse. . . . And yet he changed, and never returned to his old life-long party affiliations. No one ever knew the reason. . . Possibly the subtle effect of social recognition and position, then as now, so strong in the State, silently and even unconsciously, touched his ambition, or his pride, and did its potent work. It is not ungrateful even to a judge to receive the flattering attention of the powerful and the rich, and to find the doors of elegant and hospitable homes at all times open to him.[10]

The "rebel lawyer" in whose favor Trigg decided the test oath case was John Baxter, the former militant Unionist. This circumstance added to the Brownlow wrath. Two old comrades of the Union cause in 1861 now stood in hostile and successful array against the Parson. One was a federal judge he had helped obtain his position and the other was a litigant granted a ruling that clashed with the governor's rigid conviction that all unrepentant rebels should be branded as traitors and remain stripped of some of their old privileges, in Baxter's case to practice law. In 1862, the same year he helped Trigg obtain his judgeship, the Parson had rated Baxter as a "moderate Secessionist." The lawyer had taken a Conservative course and fought Brownlow on the political front, although personal bitterness between the two men did not surface for two years.

Baxter brought the split into the open at the state convention of the Conservative Party at Nashville in April 1867. He loosed a tirade against the governor, and an element of his speech showed that he was furious because the Brownlow franchise law barred him from voting. The *Whig* then formally declared war. It ridiculed Baxter's appointment as chairman of his party's Central Executive Committee, and summed him up as a very bad man:

John Baxter, of Knox, has intrigued for the nomination for Governor for twelve months, and to hold him on to the party they had to make him *Chairman* of this Committee. But for this *promotion* he would have bolted, as twelve months is a long time for him to continue on one side of any question. He was once a candidate for the Rebel Congress in this District, and was shamefully defeated by a brother rebel. He, after that, shouldered his gun, and went with a company of rebels to Strawberry Plains to kill Union men! His next exploit was a proposition to Jeff Davis, through Senator Haynes, to furnish him with half a million of money to go North and *bribe* the Lincoln papers to espouse the rebel cause. And last, but not least, when Burnside came into Knoxville, he made a speech to him and his army, bidding them welcome, and rejoicing over their success.

A week later the *Whig* came down upon Baxter with a total of seven items on one page that denounced or reflected on Baxter. The short-lived *Commercial*, the Conservative newspaper, was enchanted at this spectacle. It revived the old story that the Parson had urged Baxter to make the race for the Confederate Congress, had himself decided to cast his lot with the South, and it added a new touch. It said that Trigg and Colonel John Williams had dissuaded the Parson from such a course. The *Whig* denied the story.[11]

Brownlow had announced that he was too feeble to campaign for reelection for governor. But he found the strength and fire to expand his capsuled denunciation of Baxter into an acrimonious catalog of the lawyer's characteristics and deeds and called his three-column production in the *Whig*

a plain, common sense *history* of a *North Carolina felon*, who is at present the *bell-weather* [*sic.*] of an East Tennessee flock of swindlers, liars and traitors, banded together for the two-fold purpose of swindling the Federal Government, and bolstering up their relatives and partners who were traitors during the war!

For two years past, upon the stump, on the streets, in the cars, and in the private circle, you have been blackguarding, slandering and villifying me, and at the same time meeting me, smiling, shaking hands, and enquiring after my health, in the most approved style of a hypocrite and an assassin—your corrupt nature and practice qualifying you for the one and your cowardice fitting you for the other. At the same time you have intentionally misrepresented every act of the Legislature, villified the officials of the State Government, and advised resistance to the laws by force, even to the shedding of blood (*Whig*, May 15, 1867).

Baxter admitted that his two-year campaign against the Brownlow policies was ineffective. The Parson decided to tell his readers why and listed fourteen particulars. He mixed fact, invective, and hyperbole in what may have been the most cutting attack made by the Brownlow pen. Some of it was new. Some of it consisted of old accounts refurbished with the Parson's highest skill in the use of the skinning knife. He charged the lawyer with having been forced to leave North Carolina because of abusive treatment of witnesses and jurors, unprofessional conduct with fellow members of the bar, "general swindling operations," and for having fought a duel, then a violation of state law. The sketch was in striking contrast with the puff the *Whig* had given Baxter when the latter arrived in Knoxville to practice law.

The Parson found it appropriate that Andrew Baxter, the lawyer's brother, had served a term in the Georgia penitentiary for horse stealing, and was "shot down like a dog," for barn burning in Polk County, Tennessee, because "He was the exact counterpart of yourself in . . . features, voice, manners and principles." In Tennessee, Baxter had tried to tyrannize young lawyers and to bully the older ones. This activity brought reproofs from the bench and created dislike for Baxter. In recent days he had accused the state judges, many of them appointed by Brownlow, as "corrupt and incompetent."

At the Greeneville Convention of 1861, the Parson charged, Baxter had "labored with might and main to defeat the Union Party and play into the hands of the rebel party. . . . And yet after that, falsely professing to be a Union man [he] shouldered your [his] gun, went into a rebel company as a private, and marched upon Strawberry Plains to aid in killing a portion of the Union members of the same Convention!" When Baxter ran for the Confederate Congress, he played a double role. Baxter pretended "in the private circle that [his] sole object was to serve the Union cause. Yet when electioneering with the Secessionists he claimed to be with the South, and to believe that the Confederacy was a fixed fact!" The lawyer's course while Knoxville was a part of the Confederacy drew the Parson's most stinging rhetoric. He charged:

[Baxter] sat upon the corners of the streets, like a vulture, awaiting with delight, the arrival and imprisonment of Union prisoners, that you might take their notes and mortgages on their farms for exorbitant fees, when you knew you could not render them any service, and that the rebel Court Martial refused to hear with respect anything you said. . . . You took a lein [*sic.*] upon Haun's little farm, and when he was hung [hanged] , you said on the street "damn him, he ought to hang." Within the last year I have seen your heartlessly written demand of his widow for your pay, or the sale of the land upon which you knew she had been ploughing bare footed with one horse, to raise bread for her fatherless children.

You wrote a letter to Haynes [Confederate Senator Landon C. Haynes, Baxter's law partner] at Richmond, offering to take a *bribe* from Jeff Davis, of half a million of money, to go North in the garb of a Union man and buy up the press, and get up a fire in the rear against the Federal Army. . . . Among my worst acts, after our forces took possession of East Tennessee, was to discourage the proposition to hang you!

Brownlow had personal as well as political reasons for distrusting Baxter. He had relied upon him as the family adviser while he was in jail. The lawyer, he said, had become

Offended at the Union men for not supporting you; [in the race for the Confederate Congress] you went to work actively and vindictively to destroy as many of them as you could. You caused the arrest and imprisonment of some, taking care to contrive the arrest of as many as you could who were able to pay you fees for defending them. Because I refused to vote for you, you denounced me as a bridge-burner, and was in part the cause of my having to lie out in the Smoky Mountains. Your main object was to drive me to sacrifice my printing establishment. Whilst I was in the mountains, you stated to a family in Knoxville that you had me in your power, and controlled a debt that I was not able to meet!

Whilst you had me in jail and after you had placed me in a condition to force me to let my office and fixtures go at half price, you started a rebel newspaper. . . .

When Gen. Burnside came into Knoxville in 1863, you thrust yourself forward to make a speech of welcome, rejoicing at the overthrow of the Confederacy, and with an effrontery that would make the Father of Lies ashamed, classed yourself with those who had been standing by the old flag.

The Parson accused Baxter of having tried unsuccessfully to obtain "a commission as a brigadier general in the rebel army," of joining in an effort to recruit troops for the Confederate forces, and of falsely taking credit for having obtained the editor's release to go North. Brownlow credited Joseph A. Mabry's influence at Richmond with having achieved this. He acknowledged that Baxter had returned the engine from his print shop, after the entry of federal troops, but attributed this to the laywer's having

felt mean because of the figure at which you got the establishment, and the circumstances under which I was forced to sell. Or you may have felt a little gratitude toward me for having discouraged the idea of arresting you for your *half million letter*, which was in the possession of the Provost Marshal General. It was seriously contemplating placing you in the military prison at Camp Chase, and had Maynard and myself said the word, it would have been done.[12]

Baxter's stinging charges of usurpation and corruption by the state administration, made in speeches and in a pamphlet, led the Brownlow forces to make vigorous replies. Secretary of State A. J. Fletcher delivered an extended and detailed defense at Cleveland on June 3, 1867. The Parson published in the *Whig* correspondence he had carried on with the New York banking house of Jay Cooke & Co., to justify himself against Baxter's charges. His own secretary, H. H. Thomas, who was a staff officer with Burnside when Federal troops entered Knoxville, recalled finding Baxter's letter to Haynes suggesting the half million dollar bribe, and the amazement of the rebels present when Baxter welcomed the Union army.[13]

Baxter was bold as well as brash. The Parson knew this from observing him in campaigns, and from a seven-page letter the lawyer had written him from Tazewell when he was running for the Confederate Congress in 1861. After speaking and going to a hotel, Confederate troops notified him

that he would have to leave the town in 20 minutes. He firmly told them he would not obey their orders. They went out, consulted, returned and made a rush upon him. The Landlord, his wife and daughters, planted themselves in the door, and forbid their entrance, but they rushed in and finding Baxter fortified in his room with a double-shotgun, and a Revolver, cocked and ready, and notifying them that he would kill the first man who presented a weapon at him—they desisted and he took the field, stayed all knight [sic.] and had gone on to his appointments.[14]

Baxter was indeed bold, but he also was an opportunist. He went from Unionist to Confederate. His enthusiasm for the South wilted when he was arrested as an enemy of the Confederacy in Memphis in 1862. Baxter blamed Governor Harris for his brief imprisonment, although Harris appears to have been responsible for his release. A Confederate general stationed at Knoxville early in the war doubted Baxter's loyalty to the South. Baxter was temperamental, argumentative and often given to extremes, qualities certain to bring hot replies from the old Parson, who relished articulate foes. His amazing political course, however, appeared to end with his appointment in 1877 by President Rutherford B. Hayes to the United States Sixth Circuit Court of Appeals. But on the bench he sometimes acted impulsively, "and was positive, often extreme; sometimes arbitrary; always combative." Temple, who tried to write in kindly fashion of every lawyer and judge, praised Baxter for many qualities but observed that his political shifts "showed a mental agility that is some-what remarkable."[15]

The *Whig* cast aside reserve when Knox County Circuit Court jurors found not guilty for the Parson's old Confederate foes who had been charged with murder in the hanging of three of the bridge burners of 1861. Three of the defendants—J. R. McCann, Reuben Roddy, and W. C. Kain—reportedly served on the Confederate court-martial which ordered the executions. The fourth was J. C. Ramsey, Confederate district attorney, whose connection with a military tribunal appears remote. The *Whig* was stung because "The rebel papers of the South have boasted of their acquittal by a Union jury," and it made lame efforts to explain the verdicts. One of them was:

... the zeal of the rebels to have the defendants acquitted, their anxiety to get on juries, and to get them to testify in their favor, together with the false reports of their papers and correspondents, and singular, are opening the eyes of loyal men to the wide-spread conspiracy of rebels in the South, and their purpose to browbeat the civil authorities, acquit guilty rebels, and convict and punish Union men.

When state charges of treason against Ramsey were dismissed a few months later upon payment of the costs, the *Whig* gave Ramsey the traditional newspaper shrug of contempt by putting his name last in a list of fourteen defendants cleared of such charges.[16]

A side effect of the trial of McCann, Roddy, Kain, and Ramsey was the revelation by the *Whig* that for two years the Parson had been reaching for the throat of the Rev. William B. Carter. The spectacle of the area's two great Union heroes at fierce odds opened at the East Tennessee Convention held at Knoxville in April 1864. It went almost unreported at the time. The only reference to it was a *Whig* item denying that the Parson had "handled severely" General S. P. Carter, brother of the Rev. W. B. Carter. The item also pointed out that the Parson had made "no allusion" to the general and had known him "only as a gentleman." The import of the item must have been understood by the men who were delegates to the convention, but to others of the *Whig*'s readers it must have been an enigma. The acquittal of the four former Confederates infuriated Brownlow to the point where he accused W. B. Carter of having brought on the hanging and persecution of Unionists, through the bridge burning. The result was that "the jails of East Tennessee, and the prisons of Mobile, Macon and Tuscaloosa were crowded with innocent Union men," and five citizens were hanged.

The Parson revealed that at the 1864 convention Carter engaged in a two-hour tirade against Lincoln, Secretary of War Edwin M. Stanton, "and the Republican Party generally." The Parson roared back that Carter had been furnished funds from private sources to finance his trip to Washington to "procure *relief* for the Union men." He left soon after the Greeneville Convention of 1861 "and through the influence of *Senator* Johnson, and with the sanction of Mr. Lincoln and General McClellan, obtained $22,600 with which to burn" the bridges. The Parson charged that Carter had not accounted for half of the amount and demanded that he make "a public statement as to his innocence or guilt." Brownlow waited two years "for his [Carter's] defense . . . and it is not forthcoming." It is quite possible that Carter was so bound by an oath taken before the bridge burning that he could not make a statement on the subject. Temple, who attempted to get detailed information on the plot and the participants, frequently ran into a stone wall. Most of the men who had engaged in the burning would not talk about it. Temple said he found that the government had given Carter only $2,500 for the project. But nowhere in Temple's two books on the times and the people does he mention the dispute between Brownlow and Carter.

The *Whig* finally brought out that the animosity went back to 1862 while Brownlow was in Boston on his lecture tour. Carter came to Knoxville and there denounced the Parson. The details of this attack are not available. After Brownlow became governor, the *Whig* related, Carter called the Parson "King Brownlow," and denied he had pocketed between $10,000 and $12,000 of the bridge burning funds. The *Whig* then tossed back a few more insults. It said Carter had "boarded" ten or twelve slaves at Knoxville, employed them to cut firewood, sold the fuel and kept the money; he had smuggled North $15,000 worth of tobacco and squandered some of the money given him for the bridge sabotage on the stock market. [17]

Among the friendships that were destroyed in the fires of Reconstruction politics was that of Brownlow and the brilliant, witty, but convivial John Fleming, lawyer, legislator, and editor. The two men had worked in harmony as Whigs, and later as members of the staunch Union band of 1861. Fleming was fond of the Parson, and the older man had a high regard for the younger man's leadership ability. On the eve of the secession-bent General Assembly of 1861 he wrote that Fleming "is a shrewd, long-headed man, and will have influence, and control the entire Union delegation from this end of the State. He is right and he is reliable." At the East Tennessee Convention of 1864 when the Unionists split into Radicals and Conservatives, Fleming went with the latter. He eventually turned Democrat as did Nelson. When the *Daily Free Press*, published by John M. Fleming & Co., appeared in Knoxville on June 29, 1867, Fleming wrote:

It may be expected by some that we will feel it in our duty to inaugurate our career by an indulgence in indiscriminate personal detraction of the Governor of this State. We think of doing no such thing. Throughout a period of some fifteen years or more our personal relations have been at times quite intimate and always of a friendly character. We have been indebted to him for many personal kindnesses in times past, and for the members of his family we have ever entertained a high regard. . . .

We expect, however, to do all in our power to aid in the legitimate overthrow of his State policy.

The *Whig* greeted the arrival of this friendly speaking competitor with a compliment:

Its editor is John M. Fleming, Esq. . . . Mr. Fleming is a lawyer of this city, and a fine writer. As a journalist, he has had several years experience, having been editor of the Knoxville *Register* in the days of Whiggery.

Judging from the tone of the first number of the *Free Press*, we anticipate—*personally*—friendly relations with our new neighbor.[18]

These pleasant exchanges seemed to indicate that the days of acrid and blistering volleys between competing editors were fading. J. Austin Sperry, whose issues of the *Register* just before and during the Civil War spewed hatred for the Parson, was gone. He had fled to Atlanta, just before the Union forces arrived in Knoxville. He had published his *Register* there briefly. He then issued his traveling newspaper from Bristol for a short time, until he was captured by the Federal army and jailed in Knoxville. Judge Trigg freed him. The judge said that there was no charge against him. The *Whig*, however, condemned him as "having edited and published, until Burnside came in, [one] of the most treasonable sheets that ever villified the Federal Government and persecuted Union men," and broadly hinted East Tennessee would not be a safe place for him. The *Daily Commercial*, which lived only a few months after appearing in December 1865, so offended John Bell Brownlow with its vituperation that he attempted to cane the editor, J. W. Patterson. A contrast was the exchange of warm personal expressions between John Bell Brownlow and M. J. Hughes, editor of the weekly *Messenger*, upon the sale of the latter to William J. Ramage. Ramage was editor of the *Daily Herald*, which was started on October 17, 1867. Young Brownlow and Hughes had fought each other vigorously on political grounds, yet they had enjoyed a cordial personal friendship.[19]

The sentiments expressed between the *Whig* and the *Free Press* were too idyllic to last. They did not. The heat of the campaign overthrew Fleming's good intentions, and he resorted to traditional abuse. He described the Radical Party as a "small minority of the most unprincipled ruffians within its borders," and the governor as "a foul-mouthed and abandoned wretch." The Parson took a personal hand in this new controversy. He promised the fullest exposure of his former friend, although "I have never written or said anything to the prejudice of Mr. Fleming."

The *Press* and the *Daily Herald*, started by Ramage late in 1867, were consolidated early in January 1868, with Fleming as editor and T. B. Kirby as associate editor. The needling of the Brownlows, the state administration, and the *Whig* increased. The *Press and Herald* took the line of white supremacy and played down the importance of the Ku Klux Klan, even to the point of suggesting that no such organization existed.[20]

The Brownlows exerted their political muscle to punish the *Press and Herald* and all Conservative and Democratic newspapers in the state. This happened after Judge Trigg in 1865 removed the court's legal advertising and placed it in the Chattanooga *Gazette*. This also left the *Whig* with unpaid bills for this service. The legislature enacted on February 17, 1868, a law that gave the governor authority to designate the newspapers in which legal advertisements could be placed, and declared void all such notices that appeared in newspapers not so approved. The *Whig* pointed this weapon directly at the judge and opposition newspapers, warning:

All the legal notices, such as Chancery sales and so forth, appearing in the *Press and Herald* of this city, are, by a late act of the General Assembly, made null and void, so far as the interests of the parties are concerned, as though no advertisement had been made.

The governor, under the law's authority, had designated other Radical newspapers throughout the state as official journals for such advertising. The *Whig* played upon the fears of litigants. It told its readers that the law "includes every notice required by law and every publication required by any court, from that of a justice of the peace to the Supreme Court," and "The title obtained to property acquired at a sale illegally advertised, when required by law to be advertised is, of course, worthless."[21]

The quarrel reached an odious state and hung there. The *Press and Herald* reported that the governor was dying. The *Whig* acknowledged "certain people" would consider his death a blessing. It then turned to speculation upon the demise of Fleming. It offered the view that many people, including quite a few to whom the *Press and Herald* editor owed money, would have looked upon his death "in infancy" as a boon. Fleming, who loved alcoholic beverages, selected this moment of controversy to pitch a spectacular drunk in a saloon. "He was drunk from head to foot, his feet were drunk and his legs were drunk and his Websterian brain was drunk," the *Whig* advised its readers, and the saloon keeper was perplexed on what to do with the prostrate form of Fleming when closing time came. He considered rolling Fleming into the street, "But he knew that the hogs would eat him before morning, in which case the hogs would die and Cox [the saloon keeper] feared an indictment under the statute against poisoning domestic animals." So he hired two black men to remove Fleming. They left him on the floor of his editorial room. Because Fleming was the voice of white supremacy, the *Whig* touched a final paragraph with political poison: "The colored people of Knoxville have been said to be ambitious to be in all things the equal of the white man. If John Fleming is to be considered the representative white man, they now desire to be excused from equality with him, or those like him."

The *Whig* was replying in kind, for Fleming had described the junior editor of his opposition as "Without ability, shrewdness or tact," and broadly suggested that when John Bell Brownlow killed a fellow student at Emory and Henry College in 1860 he had struck his victim from behind. The people of Tennessee, Fleming said, "tolerate them [the Brownlows] both as they tolerate horned frogs, calves with six legs, bearded women . . . or any other monstrosity, but the idea of taking any one of them as a guide in politics or religion, or paying any serious attention to them whatever is too supremely ridiculous to be thought of." Fleming struck a rather sharp blow when he printed a list of thirty-four "Brownlowisms," trite and hackneyed terms used by the *Whig* editors. The list included "high toned gentle-man," "God forsaken," "white livered," "hell deserving," and "un-mitigated scoundrel and liar."[22] Whether this justified criticism gained any attention in the midst of the roar of low-level epithets is unknown.

As the air was filled with torrents of abuse from the newspaper offices and hogs exercised liberty in the business sections of Knox-ville, hatred that stemmed from the Confederate occupation spilled blood upon a street. E. C. Camp, lawyer and former Union officer, killed H. M. Ashby near the Franklin House. Ashby was the former Confederate cavalry officer who had captured and driven through the streets of Knoxville almost 500 Union men and boys who had tried to escape to Kentucky. His treatment of these prisoners produced some of the most scathing of the Parson's prose. Ashby had come to make his home in the Knoxville area. His reasons for choosing to locate where he had stirred up so much hatred are difficult to under-stand. He had been cleared of a number of indictments against him that grew out of the war. Camp had assisted the state in the prosecu-tion of Ashby, and the latter, embittered, had assaulted and insulted Camp until they agreed to "settle it" by duelling. As the two men walked, side by side, to some point where they would not endanger the lives of others, Ashby was reported to have slapped Camp on the shoulder and flourished his revolver. Camp threw up Ashby's gun hand, drew his own weapon and shot Ashby three times, once after he had fallen. The authorities apparently decided it was a case of justifiable homicide in self defense and did not prosecute Camp.

The killing plunged the newspapers into an even more intense war of words. The *Whig* defended Camp, as was to have been expected. Fleming, the staunch Unionist of 1861, followed the ironical policy of printing tributes to Ashby as the "noble scion of a noble race," who was slain "by the cowardly bullet of an ignominious assassin." Camp was from Ohio, and the *Press and Herald* evaluated him as belonging "to that low order of shysters that frequent the police courts of Chicago and New York." Sentiment inside Knoxville ran in favor of Ashby, that of the county outside the city for Camp. So intense did the feeling run that the *Whig* saw a new war in the making by the old Confederates, and welcomed it: "Let the fight come and that speedily, and we will gut and clean out the infernal traitors and assassins who back Ashby."

The Parson himself threw into the inflammatory situation this blazing brand:

A portion of the rebel friends of the late Colonel Ashby are openly boasting that the fighting is not all over yet, and that they intend Camp shall bite the dust. Camp's cause is the cause of the Union men of Knox County, and if he shall fall, let the loyal men of the town and county fall with him. Let every loyal man in the town, white and colored, arm himself and be ready for the conflict. Let our friends in the country, when they come to town, come prepared to defend themselves. Let them act on the *defensive*, but mete out justice to their assailants, and to all who contribute to bring on a conflict.[23]

Somehow the county survived further bloodshed. Providence must have intervened.

The *Press and Herald* taunted John Bell Brownlow with cowardice. It claimed that a threat by Ashby had frightened the young editor into keeping his name out of the *Whig*. John retorted by referring to two items published during the eighteen months preceding the death of the former officer, in which "severe terms" were used. Fleming touched a sensitive spot in his competitor, for John had admitted two years earlier that he had submitted to the insults and denunciations of discharged rebel officers and soldiers on a train in Alabama, when outnumbered twenty to one. "A living Dog is Better than a Dead Lion," he had headlined his explanation.[24]

In the midst of this tempest of words the Rev. David Fleming, the father of John Fleming, and a Methodist minister for forty years, died. The Parson had known him for half a century and had lived near him as a boy in Wythe County, Virginia. The *Whig* paid him tribute as "essentially a good man—honest, upright and earnest as a minister, and remarkably successful in all the stations he filled, both as pastor and presiding elder. A man of one work, sharing the confidence of all who knew him, his record is marked by a singular purity and unselfish benevolence." The *Whig* had come to the preacher's defense in 1856 and 1857, when it appeared that he was being proscribed by Methodist Democrats because his son was a *Whig* and a Know Nothing leader.[25] The tribute was merited, but coming as it did, it cut two ways, depicting the father as a saint. The *Whig*, of course, had often gone to considerable extent to show the son was a sinner.

In the fall of 1867, the man most responsible for plunging Tennessee into the Confederacy, former Governor Isham G. Harris, a wanderer from his home land for six years, swallowed his pride and

wrote to an old friend, former Governor Neill S. Brown. Harris asked
Brown to intercede in his behalf for permission to return to his state
and his family at Paris. Harris hated President Johnson and rejected
the thought of an appeal to him. He asked his emissary to approach
the Parson. Brown did, and the governor, who had once penned a
malicious diatribe against Harris to accompany the legislature's offer
of a $5,000 reward for the capture of the fugitive, promised protec-
tion and immunity. The governor asked the legislature to withdraw
the reward offer. When Harris received word of the developments he
left Liverpool and went directly to Nashville. There, on a Sunday
morning in late November, Harris and Brown went quietly and un-
noticed to the capitol, where the governor slept and ate as well as
officiated. It was a moving scene. The Parson held out his arms to his
old political enemy whom he had denounced in the harshest terms,
and the spirit of the camp meeting led him to utter these lines from
an old hymn: "While the lamp holds out to burn, the vilest sinner
may return." Harris is said to have laughed, but if he did his laughter
must have lacked spontaneity. He had crossed an ocean and part of a
continent to obtain restoration of his citizenship. It was no time to
quibble.[26]

Brownlow's last years as governor saw the defection of Secretary
of State Andrew Jackson Fletcher. The secretary was one of the
Radicals' best campaigners, who often spoke for the ailing Parson,
and who took on with great skill, the task of blackening the character of John Baxter and resisting his assaults upon Brownlow policies.
Fletcher wanted to run for governor in 1867, and was embittered
when the Parson sought another term. The unhappy secretary, who
brought the split into the open in 1869, charged that Brownlow had
grasped so much power that it "destroyed the republican character
of the State government." He also dissented from Brownlow policies
on railroads, financing, "the use of the militia instead of county
police, the administration of the machinery of the franchise law, and
many other minor matters." He favored a more moderate policy on
the extension of the franchise, and he charged that the "excessively
severe policy of our party is about to produce its natural consequences. *It is about to explode for want of calibre.*" The *Press and
Herald* found Fletcher's views "notable and creditable." Brownlow
rejected Fletcher's claim that the break was entirely political. He
attributed it to the secretary's chagrin and disappointment at being
denied the opportunity to run for governor in 1867, and because

Brownlow had rejected patronage sought for some of Fletcher's relatives. It was a case of ingratitude the Parson said. He brought the secretary from exile to take the state post; "No sooner was he firm in his seat than he attempted to strike down the hand that had lifted him from obscurity to eminence and from utter penury to opulence."[27]

It was the last major piece of writing that the Parson produced for Brownlow's *Knoxville Whig*, for under a new arrangement the historic name long associated with the newspaper came down. It appeared under new direction as the *Weekly Knoxville Whig*.[28] The Parson had roared and fulminated in the newspaper since he had become its editor at Elizabethton in 1839. Now, thirty years later, he departed from the editorial chair in character and in style.

CHAPTER XVIII NOTES

[1] Rothrock, ed., *French Broad-Holston*, pp. 77, 115-116, 334, 422-424; W. G. Brownlow to F. S. Heiskell, September 18, 1849. Howard Papers. Temple, *East Tennessee and the Civil War*, pp. 182, 341; Humes, *The Loyal Mountaineers*, appendix, p. 352; *Whig*, April 27, June 1, 1861.

[2] *Ibid.*, June 13, 1861, August 31, 1864, October 18, 1865.

[3] *Ibid.*, August 1, September 6, 1865.

[4] *Ibid.*, April 11, 18, May 2, 16, 1866. Major General A. C. Gillem, who commanded troops in East Tennessee, was a graduate of the United States Military Academy, was a member of the 1865 convention and was elected to the Brownlow Legislature from Jackson County. *Whig*, November 16, 1864, January 11, April 26, 1865; Alexander, *Political Reconstruction*, pp. 25, 27, 105, 204.

[5] "The rebellion suspended and destroyed the editor's newspaper, the most valuable in the whole Southern Confederacy, bringing him an income of about $10,000. Besides this he recovered in a real estate lawsuit to the value of many thousands of dollars by the verdict of the Rebel Supreme Court of Tenn. The property was sold by order of the court just after he went North and the proceeds deposited by the Rebel clerk of Chancery Court with the Rebel officers of the Branch bank of Tenn. who speculated with the money during the war and [word illegible] the aforesaid clerk tendered the editor Confederate money after Burnside took E. T. when said trash was worthless. The editor was a heavy loser by the war." John Bell Brownlow marginal note. *Whig*, July 5, 1865. See also *ibid.*, March 15, 29, May 3, July 19, December 20, 27, 1865, November 28, 1866, December 25, 1867; "Diary of David Deaderick," typescript, pp. 47, 78-80. McClung Collection. Rothrock, ed., *French Broad-Holston*, pp. 327-328. See also *Whig*, December 25, 1867.

[6] Trigg was a native of Abingdon, Virginia, and had been known to Brownlow all his life. The Parson supported Trigg for Congress from a Virginia district in 1855 when the latter ran as the American Party candidate. The editor's zeal probably was stimulated because Trigg's opponent was Fayette McMullens, who had attacked Brownlow at a camp meeting in Sullivan County in 1842. *Ibid.*, March 24, May 5, 1855, February 2, May 9, 1856; Temple, *Notable Men*, pp. 202-212, 66-67; John Green, *Bench and Bar*, (Knoxville, 1947), pp. 33-35; Rule, ed., *Standard History*, pp. 482-483.

[7] *Whig*, November 11, 1863, June 25, December 7, November 30, 1864, February 1, 1865.

[8] *Ibid.*, March 1, May 31, June 21, 1865. Acreage of the Lyons farm is given in a list of tax sales, *ibid.*, May 3, 1865.

[9] *Ibid.*, June 21, 1865; Green, *Bench and Bar*, pp. 34-35.

[10] John Bell Brownlow to Temple, November 28, 1892. Temple Papers. For John Bell Brownlow's derogatory comments on Trigg see marginal notes, *Whig*, March 1, May 31, 1865. Temple, *Notable Men*, p. 211.

[11] Green, *Bench and Bar*, p. 34; *Whig*, April 24, May 1, 1867; Alexander, *Political Reconstruction*, pp. 147-148; *Whig*, May 8, 1867.

[12] *Ibid.*, May 15, 1867; Green, *Bench and Bar*, p. 58.

[13] *Whig*, May 22, 1867. Fletcher's speech was printed in a *Whig* supplement, June 22, 1867. See also Alexander, *Political Reconstruction*, p. 148.

[14] W. G. Brownlow to Robertson Topp, October 1, 1861. Robertson Topp Papers.

[15] Temple, *Notable Men*, p. 72; John Bell Brownlow to Temple, September 2, 1891. Temple Papers. *O.R.*, II, 1, Carroll to Benjamin, November 25, 1861, p. 903; Temple, *Notable Men*, pp. 71-73; Green, *Bench and Bar*, p. 60; Joshua W. Caldwell, *Sketches of the Bench and Bar of Tennessee* (Knoxville, 1890), p. 273; Temple, *Notable Men*, p. 73.

[16] *Whig*, June 27, July 4, 1866, February 27, 1867.

[17] *Ibid.*, July 4, 1866; Temple, *East Tennessee and the Civil War*, pp. 371-379; Temple, *Notable Men*, pp. 88-93; *Whig*, October 31, 1866.

[18] W. G. Brownlow to Robertson Topp, October 1, 1861. Robertson Topp Papers. Temple, *Notable Men*, pp. 120, 407; *Free Press*, June 29, 1867; *Whig*, July 3, 1867.

[19] *Ibid.*, April 30, October 19, 1864, January 11, July 19, December 20, 1865, May 2, 1866, November 20, 1867. See also *Register*, (published in Atlanta), October 7, 10, 23, 1863. Newspaper miscellany on microfilm. McClung Collection.

[20] *Whig*, September 4, 1867; *Press and Herald* (morning) January 7, February 1, 6, 20, March 24, 29, April 17, 27, 1868.

[21] *Whig*, September 6, 13, 1865, March 11, May 6, 20, July 1, 15, 1868. The Governor designated the favored newspapers and the list was confirmed by the Senate. *Ibid.*, March 11, 1868.

[22] *Whig*, June 17, July 8, 1868; *Press and Herald*, June 18, July 14, 1868.

[23] *Whig*, June 17, 1868, August 1, 1866; *Press and Herald*, June 18, July 11, 1868; *Whig*, July 22, 1868. The shooting must have taken place not very

far from the corner of Main Avenue and Walnut Street (then called Crook-
ed). Fleming was reported to have taken a stand at the Franklin House,
which stood near where the Knox County Courthouse is at this writing, a
point from which he could view the encounter. The shooting, however,
took place before the duellists arrived at the point where they were to
have fired at each other. *Whig*, July 15, 1868.

[24] *Ibid.*, July 22, 1868.
[25] *Ibid.*, September 9, 1868. For Brownlow's support of the Reverend Flem-
      ing see *ibid.*, November 26, 1865, March 3, 1857.
[26] Temple, *Notable Men*, pp. 335-339; John Bell Brownlow to Temple, July
      11, 1892. Temple Papers. Coulter, pp. 342-345.
[27] *Press and Herald*, January 13, 1869; *Whig*, January 20, 1869.
[28] Weekly *Knoxville Whig*, February 3, 1869.

Brownlow's Knoxville Whig

"Yielding up the other cheek/Dropping humbly   Chapter No. 18
on the knees; Closing lips when dared to speak/Will
not do in times like these."

THE *WHIG* DIES DEMOCRATIC

The outlook was bright and inviting as T. Haws & Co. published its first *Weekly Knoxville Whig* at 108 Gay Street on February 3, 1869. A daily was to be issued soon. Six influential citizens had raised $12,000 of capital to finance the undertaking. They were W. G. Brownlow, O. P. Temple, M. D. Bearden, Joseph A. Mabry, Tilghman Haws, General James A. Cooper, and William Rule. These men, with the exception of Mabry, were staunch and tried Radical Unionists.[1] Mabry could scarcely be classified as solid, but he was agile politically and financially. He managed to land on his feet through precarious times. He had been a rebel during the war, but he had emerged with wealth and was now operating in several business fields. He had been the Parson's friend when other Confederates plotted to get him killed. John Baxter found him

successfully performing the most wonderful political feat recorded in the annals of man. He is supporting three different and antagonistic characters at the same time, to wit: in all matters pertaining to local legislation he is a Conservative; in matters within the jurisdiction of the Governor he is a Senter Republican; and in all national affairs, such as getting payment for losses sustained by him when he was a rebel, he is a Radical without blemish and without guile.[2]

Brownlow was disassociating himself from the editorial department of the newspaper, but he would be sitting in the United States Senate at Washington. The *Whig* management had looked over the first title and decided that the *Knoxville Weekly Whig* sounded better and made the change with the second issue. Two experienced men remained in key positions on the *Whig*. Haws was business manager and Rule was local editor. Haws had been Brownlow's partner, and, in addition to running the business end, he had supervised the design and construction of the *Whig* Building on Gay Street. Rule had worked for the *Whig* before joining the Union army, and upon his return was made local editor. He displayed industry and talent in getting items principally for their newsworthiness, as contrasted to the Brownlow policy of evaluating stories chiefly for the political implications that could be extracted from them. Haws was to draw an annual salary of $2,000 and $800 yearly rental for the building, which he owned, and Rule was to be paid $800 a year. [3]

The management appointed the Rev. Thomas H. Pearne, D.D., an outsider from distant Oregon, general, political, and religious editor. Bishop D. W. Clark of the Northern Methodist Church imported Pearne to be the presiding elder of the Knoxville District of the Holston Conference, which had been reorganized with loyalist preachers and members of the denomination. Brownlow had been a leader in this reorganization. He had conferred with northern bishops before Pearne was selected. Perhaps Brownlow suggested him for the Parson had seen Pearne, as chairman of the Oregon delegation to the Union Party Convention of 1864, swing his group into support of Andrew Johnson for the nomination for Vice-President. Following the convention Pearne had stumped Oregon for the Lincoln-Johnson ticket. [4]

The Parson had fired some of his hottest tirades against ministers who supported the Confederacy, but he liked politically turned preachers if they were on his side. [5] He outlined his plans for dealing with the rebel Methodist preachers in the Holston Conference in a speech in McKendree Methodist Church in Nashville, in the fall of 1862, declaring:

The worst class of men, so help me God, on Southern soil, are the Methodist, Baptist, Presbyterian and Episcopalian preachers. . . . Last month the Methodist Church, of which I have been a member thirty-five years, held a Conference in Athens, which was presided over by a hoary-headed old man, Bishop John Early. With one sweeping resolution they expelled from the ministry all the Union preachers of the Holston Conference. . . . This old traitor, Bishop Early, also issued an order to the Presiding Elders to expel all loyal preachers within the Conference. I am going back, and intend to call a Conference of the local preachers, and we will expel the last devil of these rebel priests. We will put these seceders and rebels out and recover the church property which rightfully belongs to us, and not to the traitors. . . . These Parsons of the Methodist Publishing House employed me to write a book exposing that infernal scoundrel of the Baptist Church, Elder J. R. Graves. They denounced him for all that was vile and rascally, but now they are all standing shoulder to shoulder in stirring up rebellion. . . . I intend to expose their damnable hypocrisy, villainy, and falsehood to the gaze of the world. No man living but me can do it, for I know them better than anyone else. I intend to resurrect the *Knoxville Whig*, and pour hot shot into their rotten hulks (*Whig*, February 27, 1864).

Bishop Early, who was the brother of the Confederate General Jubal Early, had directed this harsh course of the Holston Conference, in the sessions of 1861, 1862, and 1863. Spencer Henry, a loyal Methodist preacher, wrote that in the 1862 conference, as a preacher was being examined as to which side he was on shouts rang out "Hang him, G-d d-n him." The *Whig* charged that Early "had a file of rebel soldiers stationed in the conference, with bayonets, and examined every preacher, one by one, as to his position upon the great issue, and notified them that anyone declaring for the Lincoln Government would be turned over to these soldiers"[6] Henry and the *Whig*, embittered though they were, were not off base, for R. N. Price, who was a chaplain in the Confederate army, and "a Southern man with Southern prejudices," but trying to be fair, termed the 1862 session "the conference of political dabbling." He found Early "aristocratic and haughty . . . a typical Southern fire eater." Early had rejected arbitrarily the chaplain's objection that the conference had no right to inquire into the "political opinions and the political actions," of ministers. The bishop ruled that "the conference had a right to arrest the character of any preachers who sympathized with the Union cause." The sensitive chaplain also was aghast at the reprisals taken against Southern sympathizers when federal troops occupied the area and the smothered hatreds accumulated by the Unionists under Confederate control, found release. He mourned that "Eternity alone" would reveal the suffering of these Southerners as occupation changed: "It was to them a reign of terror. Leading men were arrested and taken to Northern prisons, while hundreds of others preserved their liberty only by fleeing to other states."[7]

Reports of these reprisals may have led Pearne to deplore and regret "a disposition to interrupt and mob preachers of the Methodist Episcopal Church South." He cited some instances in McMinn County, of which Athens was the county seat, and he frowned upon the practice of riding these preachers on a rail. But he stoked the fires of dissension by adding:

> If preachers of the Methodist Church, South, with a record stained with
> disloyalty and bloody with rebellion, have the effrontery to preach in loyal
> communities where their deeds are well known, my counsel would be, *let* them
> do it . . . if loyal Methodists cannot sustain their cause by truth and free discus-
> sions, as against that of Southern Methodists in the field of argument and reason,
> it cannot be sustained at all" (*Whig*, December 20, 1865).

The North's victory put the Southern-supporting churches in a
position of misery and humiliation as they tried to re-establish their
loyalty to the old government and suppress the militancy they had
displayed for the South. The Presbytery of Union that met at Spring
Place Church, near Knoxville, in 1864, saw that the Confederates had
lost. It hastily backed away from a resolution adopted a year before
that it would not receive men unsympathetic to the South (*Whig*,
September 28, 1864). The Holston Methodist Conference, South,
that met at Marion, Virginia, a year later conceded that some of its
actions at the 1862, 1863, and 1864 sessions "might be so *construed*,
as to place us in an attitude of disloyalty to the Government under
which we now live." The conference urged members to be faithful to
the Union, and acknowledged that expelling ministers who adhered
to the North may have been "hasty," a lukewarm phrase that led the
Whig to snap:

> "*Was hasty*" was it? Nay, it was villainous, mean, cowardly and anti-christian [*sic.*]
> —a wicked and proscriptive conduct that would have disgraced a Mormon con-
> clave. . . . Why, reader, the conference at Athens was nothing more or less than a
> *Rebel Court Martial*. . . . Bishop Early . . . only wanted shoulder straps and a
> cocked hat to invest him with the dignity and authority of a Capt. Wirz. [8]
> [Captain Henry Wirz was the superintendent of the notorious Confederate pris-
> on at Andersonville, who was hanged for his cruel treatment of the inmates.]

The creation of the new Holston Conference by Brownlow and the
loyal preachers and members was by its nature divisive. The Parson
wanted no compromise and he wanted the conference to have an
articulate leader. Pearne filled that requirement. But he was an outsider in a region where strangers were met often with suspicion and
distrust, especially if they were as brash and imprudent as he was in
seeking to be introduced at the Holston Conference, South, that met
at Asheville, North Carolina, in the fall of 1866. He was rebuffed and
came away with the intelligence that northern ministers were rated as

"horse thieves" by their brethren of the South. The presiding elder's foes damned him as a "comparative stranger, cutting and hewing the character of ministers long known in a community."[9] Early in 1869 Fleming, a native East Tennesseean who understood and probably shared the prejudices of the area, bored into

our recently imported Brother Pearne who assumes to speak "on behalf of East Tennessee" . . . as though the ecclesiastical "capture" of a few dozen churches, gave him by right of religious conquest, the keeping of the social, moral and political tastes and interests of East Tennessee. He spreadeth himself entirely too grandly. He mistaketh his lattitude [*sic*]. He understandeth not the people.[10]

The new *Whig* editor was agile and busy. He was often in the newspapers. He took an active part in the opening of East Tennessee Wesleyan College at Athens. The college was under the control of the Holston Conference, North. This conference had purchased it after a Chancery Court sale. The southern conference had lost it during the war. He was an official of the Teacher's State Association which met in Knoxville on August 13, 1867. He moved dexterously from the religious to the political forum. He reported from Chicago that the General Conference of the Methodist Episcopal Church had admitted the loyal Holston Conference, and a week later from the same city he told of the nomination of General U. S. Grant for President by the Republican National Convention.[11] But, however well Pearne might write and however diligently he might labor, the unmistakable voice of the Parson was gone from the newspaper.

The *Whig* had been a "political journal" from its birth. It had thrived on political campaigns. Now, in the chaotic era that followed the Civil War, the vagarious winds of change carried it to destruction. As the Parson left for Washington to take his seat in the Senate he may have believed that he had left behind a state administration and a newspaper that would survive. The *Tri-Weekly Whig* had been discontinued after five months of publication, its death ignored by the weekly. It was mockingly mourned by the opposition,[12] but the new *Whig* management was soon out with a competitive morning daily (*Whig*, April 14, 1869).

Brownlow's trip to Washington in a special railroad car brought the expected displays of hostility. At Bristol, Virginia, a heckler shouted that he looked "like a d--d old turkey buzzard." A Lynchburg, Virginia, newspaper reported him traveling in Car No. 9 and recommended that "any decent man who passes over the road here-

after should avoid it as he would a leper." A student boarded the car
at Charlottesville and in an "act of bravado" brandished a revolver before the sleeping Parson. He was seized and left immediately. At the
capitol Brownlow was so weak that his arm was supported as he took
the oath. He found a boarding house one hundred yards from the
Senate chamber, walked to his post, and began to establish a record
of almost constant attendance. In that spring he assisted Representative Maynard in putting through Congress an appropriation of
$90,000 for a new Knoxville post office building. [13]

DeWitt C. Senter, state senate speaker, was now governor by the
line of succession. The thirty-six-year-old Grainger County farmer
and lawyer had served in the legislature at the beginning of the war
and after. He was imprisoned five months by the Confederacy.
Senter had been a slaveholder and a Whig, and he was the son of the
illustrious William T. Senter, an orator of ability, a delegate to the
Constitutional Convention of 1834 and a member of Congress from
the Second District for one term. Even the *Press and Herald* spoke of
him favorably, but took a shrewd look at the future and warned him
that to attempt a precipitate change in Brownlow policies would

require a steady brain and an iron nerve.

There is no man living on the American continent, nor, indeed, on any other
continent that could duplicate the administration of the retiring Governor. As it
never had a precedent, so it will stand in the future, without a parallel. Brownlow is *sui generis*, and Brownlowism is essentially and peculiarly a thing of his
creation and nuture. As with him it had its origin, so with him it must die. [14]

The Radicals soon split with something resembling obscene thun-
der, at the party's state convention held in Nashville on May 20 and
21. Reviewing it the *Press and Herald*, smugly commented that
"Nothing in the political history of Tennessee has ever been seen so
turbulent, vulgar, bitter or disgraceful." The forces of United States
Representative W. B. Stokes went into the convention with the advantage of Chairman A. M. Cate of the Republican State Central
Committee presiding. At the first step, the election of a temporary
chairman of the convention, Cate used that advantage by refusing to
recognize the nomination of Pearne by Judge L. C. Houk, a Senter
backer. Instead he recognized a Stokes supporter who nominated R.
R. Butler. Cate declared Butler elected temporary chairman. Houk
leaped upon a desk, assumed the role of a chairman, and declared
Pearne elected. Pearne and Butler attempted to take the chair but

Cate refused to budge, and

> The convention was soon turned into a bedlam fit only for lunatics. Champions of Senter and Stokes disputed together for the doubtful honor of making the most noise and confusion. Whiskey flowed freely, and drunken yells, curses, jeers and catcalls, furnished enjoyment only to the delighted and guffawing "Democrats in the galleries." Three hours of the afternoon session were wasted except for the excitement provided when D. M. Nelson, for Senter, slapped the face of Butler. Pistols were drawn. Joe Mabry, the ubiquitous politician from Knoxville, flourished a weapon. Police halted the brawl. Somehow the meeting was adjourned to the following day, May 21.

The Senter forces decided to take over the chair by strategy. When Cate arrived at the hall the next morning to assume his seat Pearne was in it, wearing the "placid air of a matronly hen on a nest." A strange agreement followed. A motion to adjourn *sine die* was made and Pearne and Cate each declared it passed. Each side then met separately, one group nominating Senter, the other Stokes. The congressman laid claim to the support of fifty-four county delegations and of forty thousand blacks.[15]

As Senter and Stokes opened the campaign, Pearne dutifully extolled his candidate as opposed to universal suffrage for the protection of "loyal men—white and colored—at whatever cost, the safety of the State by guarding against the enfranchisement of its enemies—unsubdued and unrepentant rebels." The editor probably was in the assembly of Senter partisans who heard him say that although "the time might arrive when the rebels could come up to the ballot box . . . that that day was a long way off." Certainly Pearne believed he was in accord with Senter, and he was, in effect, trying to warn Stokes against espousing universal suffrage, a step which it had been rumored he was about to take to win Conservative support. A switch came, but it was Senter who made it when he met Stokes in debate at Nashville on June 5. Senter came out firmly for universal suffrage.[16]

When Senter decided to reverse himself is not known. He may have done so in the heat of the confrontation with his opponent. The reversal placed Pearne in an almost intolerable position, but he loyally swallowed his chagrin, and turned about to follow his candidate. He denied reports that the *Whig* would switch to Stokes, and recalled other Radical reversals; an example was:

> On the subject of negro [*sic.*] suffrage and negro testimony when the transition

from utter and bitter hostility to warm and earnest support of it was remarkably speedy. Shall we conclude that the great Radical party of Tennessee were insincere in their hostility, or afterwards, in their early and warm support of it? Or, shall we conclude—can we avoid concluding—that if they were *honest* before, at the time of, and ever since notwithstanding the suddenness of the change? (*Whig*, June 23, 1869).

The *Whig* under Brownlow had made some unusual political shifts, but nothing as stunning as Senter's about-face. He had resorted to it purely as an expedient. Senator Brownlow backed Senter on the suffrage issue, but whether he was caught by surprise, had anticipated such a move, or was advised that it was coming he did not reveal; he had "never held an equivocal position on any great public question," and never would. At the time his administration had put through the law restricting the franchise, it "was an absolute necessity to prevent the State from being thrown into anarchy, and to protect the loyal people." The leaders of the rebellion should be denied voting privileges for life, but it was unjust to "keep a thousand men under disabilities, nine hundred of whom no longer require it." In any event, general enfranchisement would come gradually because the Radical Republicans had, in a recent statewide election, put their candidates into judicial posts for eight years. Constitutional revision would take at least two years. The third clause of the Fourteenth Amendment would keep rebels from taking over state offices. A recent decision of the State Supreme Court had restored the franchise to 20,000 former Confederates, and the Republican Party and President Grant were for universal suffrage (*Whig*, June 16, 1869).

Three weeks earlier, and before the juggling of the franchise issue, the senator had responded to a query made by several Senter delegates to the meeting at Nashville. Brownlow affirmed his support of the governor because Senter had stumped for the Parson in his campaigns, had backed his programs in the General Assembly, and had voted to send him to the Senate. The Parson did not mention that Senter had an interest in voting for him because Brownlow's election opened the way for the Grainger Countian to be governor, and therefore put him in a strategic spot to run for chief executive of the state (*Whig*, May 26, 1869).

The *Whig*'s stand for Senter opened a crack in the newspaper's organization. Local Editor Rule, a native of Knox County, a former Union soldier, and something of a Brownlow protege, refused to support Senter and resigned. Because Rule had roots deep in East

Tennessee soil, and had performed military service, his presence on the *Whig* staff may have partially offset the prejudice against Pearne as an outsider. Rule was for Stokes. This was understandable. Stokes also had served in the Union army and had risen to the rank of major general. The *Whig's* blatant switch also may have turned Rule's stomach, but he left the newspaper with quiet dignity and with the good wishes of the printers, who presented him with a gold-headed cane and assured him, "The readers of the *Whig* will miss his spicy paragraphs, and feel that his place is difficult worthily to fill." Rule had shown he was an excellent reporter. He loaded the third page of the newspaper with readable local items. His valedictory stated, "Without doing violence to my own feelings, I cannot remain longer connected with a journal, even as Local Editor, the political policy of which is directly opposite to my own views." He was "especially grieved to sever my connection with the employees of the *Whig* establishment, with whom my intercourse has ever been pleasant and agreeable." He did not mention Pearne. The general editor published a courteous note of farewell, but the two men could not have been bosom comrades. Thirty years later when the *Standard History of Knoxville, Tennessee*, edited by Rule, was published, it gave seven words to Pearne as an editor and none as a minister.[17]

Some of the *Whig* stockholders also wanted to switch to Stokes, and to fire Pearne. When they met at the Parson's residence, men holding seven of the twelve shares were reported to be for Stokes and five were for Senter. But the policy remained steadfast and Pearne continued as editor. The *Press and Herald* suggested that the Parson held the owners in line by revealing that he and Haws had not executed a conveyance of the partnership property to the stock company, but that they would do so, a hint with broad implications. Pearne, in a denial that policy would be changed, ignored the conveyance aspect. If such a conveyance was made it does not appear on the books of the Knox County register.[18]

In the campaign bedlam the Democratic *Press and Herald* was unable to remain neutral. The party, as did the Conservatives, nominated no candidate but stood at one side watching which way to jump, then fell in behind Senter. The *Press and Herald*, however, came out quickly for Senter because of his declaration in favor of universal suffrage, which was a major policy of the newspaper. At the same time Fleming caught the Parson with this swift, backhanded blow:

We do not pretend now, nor do we know that we will ever pretend, to solve the mystery that is now the puzzle of the politicians. We have no disposition now to quarrel with Senator Brownlow. It is enough for us to know . . . that he lends the weight of his name, and the power of his influence, to the undoing of the bonds that now fetter the thousands of disfranchised white men of his own State, in whose humiliation he has heretofore sought to perpetuate his power. [19]

The campaign was bitter and strident, but the outcome was never really in doubt. Senter won with a majority of 65,297 out of 173,369 cast. The black vote went to Stokes because of the disillusionment of the former slaves. They had not received the rewards that they had anticipated for keeping the Brownlow forces in the State House in 1867. Senter countered this, although it seems not to have been necessary, by removing between sixty and seventy county registration officials who did not go along with his policies. The new registrars, often Conservatives, threw open the registration to thousands of former rebels. The Conservatives also seized upon this development to run their partisans for the General Assembly, and they elected enough of their number to control it. They used this power to repeal Reconstruction laws and submitted to the electorate the question of holding a Constitutional Convention. It was approved five to one. [20]

Radicalism had been whipped and the Brownlow prestige damaged. John Bell Brownlow ran for floterial representative from Knox and Sevier counties and was beaten overwhelmingly. Editor Fleming who left his newspaper post to seek a seat as direct representative from Knox County, won. The Parson sold his share in the *Whig* to Mabry, some of the other shareholders sold or withdrew, and political ignominy descended upon the once proud and defiant newspaper. Mabry, whose shifts were the rule rather than the exception, made it Democratic, and placed in the editor's post one of the Parson's most hated foes, the Rev. C. W. Charlton. As Knoxville postmaster Charlton had opened Brownlow's mail and forwarded information to Governor Harris in 1861. [21] The *Press and Herald*, in noting these developments, praised the business and mechanical management of the old *Whig* by Haws, but added:

To the ungenerous fling of the dying Pearne that "had more money been expended on the paper," it "would have been more valuable." Mr. Haws might well retort that had there been less money and more decency and brains expended upon the editor, the cash accounts of the establishment would now present a more satisfactory showing.

From the beginning of his tenure as editor Pearne had been the target of Fleming's needle like jabs. In the spring of 1868 he observed:

We have never mentioned the "brother" except in a spirit of kindness to our readers. Now and then when Brother Pearne would leave this city in the guise of a wolf in sheep's clothing, to minister to the lambs of the flock we have notified the chickens on the route of the wolf, to roost higher, and the lambs to baa trebly and more piteously that the wolf might indeed be kept from their door.

This paragraph was the prelude to a nauseating tale which Fleming called "the Beaver Creek adventure" of Pearne. It reported that the *Whig* editor got drunk on a farmer's freshly distilled "korjil" [cordial], ate an enormous amount of boiled eggs and as a result suffered a most unpleasant and embarrassing reaction. When Mabry bought the *Whig* and Pearne was tossed out, Fleming mockingly sighed, "These be mournful times."

Of English extraction and northern and eastern education, Pearne spoke and exhibited speech and manners that must have grated upon most East Tennesseans. In turn his five years in what he called "reconstruction work," left him worn, ill, and unhappy. Senator Brownlow persuaded President Grant to appoint Pearne to a consulate at Kingston, Jamaica, in the British West Indies. In 1874 he returned to the Methodist ministry in the Cincinnati, Ohio Circuit and preached there for many years. In 1899 he wrote a book on his experiences during his sixty-one years in the pulpit and in public life. He told of perils and difficulties met during his five years in East Tennessee, but he wrote not a word of his feverish political and editorial experiences. [22] His memories of those days must not have been happy ones.

The conversion of the *Whig* to a Democratic policy and the appointment of Charlton must have caught the Parson by surprise and gored him deeply. In announcing the sale of his interest he claimed to have been given assurance

that it will be continued as a Republican journal advocating the principles and policy of the Republican Party and rendering a cordial support to President Grant and his administration. . . .

And further, it is pertinent for me to say, that so many in Tennessee who were at one time the most outspoken Union men, have proved untrue, and have turned back to the 'flesh pots of Egypt,' betraying the too generous friends who warmed them into life (*Whig*, September 15, 1869).

The Parson now was accused of having "perpetrated a fraud upon the people of East Tennessee" in telling them that the *Whig* would continue as a Republican newspaper, and of having known when he sold his interest to Mabry that Charlton would be the editor. The author of these charges was A. J. Ricks, a law partner of John Baxter. He held a grudge against Brownlow because the latter had barred him from getting the job of pension agent at Knoxville. The Parson got it instead for his son-in-law, Dr. David T. Boynton. Ricks earlier had accused the Brownlow administration of having plundered the state and sold the Republican Party to the Democrats.[23]

The Parson's defense led off with sharp criticism of Governor Senter's policy of making Conservatives in *many* counties the election registrars. Given this power these registrars enfranchised Conservatives and former Confederates to such an extent that Conservatives obtained a majority in the legislature. The Parson stormed:

When I retired from the office of Governor, I left to Senter the legacy of fifteen hundred State militia, armed and equipped and in the field. The so-called Conservatives raised the mad-dog cry of high taxes in sustaining a standing army.... Governor Senter was induced to disband them ... had I been Governor at the time I would have distributed these troops in the rebellious counties ... thereby securing a Republican legislature.

He offered no criticism of Mabry for having turned the *Whig* Democratic and installing Charlton as editor. Instead he noted:

The Gentleman to whom I sold my interest in the *Whig*, General Joseph A. Mabry, contributed liberally of means and efforts to the defeat of Andrew Johnson as a candidate for a seat in this body [the United States Senate], in his recent effort for election by the Tennessee Legislature.

A few weeks earlier Johnson had been defeated in his effort to win the vacant Senate seat. Johnson led in the balloting but his opposition then consolidated behind State Senator Henry Cooper of Davidson County and beat Johnson by four votes. The quotation from Brownlow clearly implies that by Mabry's efforts to deny Johnson the other seat in the United States Senate he atoned for turning the *Whig* Democratic and making Charlton editor. The Senate and the country were spared the spectacle of Johnson's and the Parson's snarling and spitting at each other in that august body. [24]

Whatever the arrangements were between Brownlow and Mabry on the sale of the *Whig* and the fight Mabry made against the former President who had come back to Tennessee in the hopes of returning to Washington in a Senate role, a note for $3,000 that Mabry gave Brownlow on November 23, 1869, remains in the hands of the Brownlow family, partially collected. Mabry pledged to pay "one day after date" [now known usually as a demand note] the $3,000 "for value received." The back of the instrument carries a notation from the Parson that on November 4, 1871, John Bell Brownlow collected $1,480 and turned it over to his father. [25]

So mixed were Knoxville politics, religion, and newspapers that H. H. Ingersoll, editor of the Greeneville *Union* described them as

almost beyond belief. The present editor of the *Whig* Rev. C. W. Charlton, is the same man who was connected with the old *Register* in war times, and who, Brownlow said in the *Whig*, less than two years ago, could never come back to Knoxville to live. It looks strange to see him now controlling the columns of Brownlow's Knoxville *Whig and Rebel Ventilator*, but such is the mutability of human affairs. Tomorrow he preaches at one Methodist church and Pearne his predecessor in the other. It is a matter of speculation who will have the largest congregation.

Looking at Knoxville from Louisville, Kentucky, George Prentice of the *Courier-Journal*, who had for many years exchanged insults with the Parson, offered this thought:

The *Whig* has never been a religious paper in the strict sense of the term, and yet it has always been edited by a minister of the Gospel, or by a man who claimed that title. It was first edited by Parson Brownlow, then by Parson Pearne, and now it is edited by Parson Charlton. Some decent infidel could make it a much more pious and useful paper than it has ever yet been [26].

Fresh uproars and complications followed. The instrument in the increased agitation was the Knoxville *Chronicle*, published by William Rule and Henry Tarwater. The two men saw the need for an East Tennessee newspaper to offset the two Democratic dailies in Knoxville and to encourage the disheartened Republican majority in the area. The *Chronicle* was published at "Brownlow's Old Stand." A weekly appeared on April 6, 1870, and the daily a month later. [27]

A series of letters started in the *Chronicle* by John Baxter led Joe Mabry to fire upon the lawyer on the morning of June 13, 1870, as

Baxter stood talking with other men in front of the Lamar House barber shop. Mabry spoke to Baxter and as the latter turned to him, Mabry fired a derringer. The bullet inflicted a flesh wound above the wrist of the right arm. Baxter attempted to draw his pistol but was unable to use his injured arm and retreated across the street. He first sought refuge behind a country wagon and then inside Cowan & McClung's store. Mabry, who had pursued the lawyer with a Navy pistol after having flung the derringer at his enemy, fired again, but missed. Sheriff V. F. Gossett arrested Mabry, took him before Squire Jourolmon, and the defendant made $1,000 bond. The grand jury, which had just gone into session, indicted Mabry and Charlton for malicious shooting. Charlton also made $1,000 bond. He was on the scene, his pistol drawn, but there was no report that he had fired it. Baxter's wound was not serious.

The adversaries had both been delegates to the Constitutional Convention of 1870. Thomas W. Humes, president of East Tennessee University, and T. A. R. Nelson prevailed on the men to "abstain from all acts of violence against each other, and to leave all matters of difference between them to public opinion and the final determination to the courts of law."[28] Honor was preserved and the shooting ended. The *Chronicle* continued to publish the remainder of Baxter's letters. There were ten in all. The brawl continued furiously in other forums.

Baxter's first letter in the *Chronicle* was a defense of the Exchange and Deposit Bank in handling the sale of $100,000 of state bonds for the Mineral Home Railroad Co., a firm that existed on paper only. Baxter owned the bank. A General Assembly committee had found the bonds illegal, but even so, Baxter said, the bank had acted only as the selling agent. It turned the proceeds over to the railroad company president. Baxter tried to get the legislature to investigate certain alleged frauds, and urged in particular that the legislators look into the operation of the Knoxville and Kentucky Railroad at Knoxville. Mabry was the receiver and both men were directors. The lawyer, in his broadsides, took in Mabry, Fleming, Charlton, Governor Senter, and unnamed "corruptionists," who "have followed me with such ruthless malice ever since I became a citizen of Knoxville." Two committees shrugged off the labor of investigating, a third accepted it, but Senter's cousin, Editor and Representative Fleming, "who when not drunk, was the controlling mind upon the committee," Baxter noted.

Old scandals were raked up by Baxter. Among them were the forged letters to Amos Lawrence of Massachusetts that bore the name of Andrew Johnson. Charlton had played a part in this plot. Baxter laid his brief arrest in Memphis during the Civil War to his implacable foes in Knoxville. Boring more deeply into Mabry's affairs, Baxter wrote that the legislative committee had found that Mabry had misapplied $217,905 of the Knoxville and Kentucky Railroad's funds. By Baxter's reckoning it was $570,377. He was bitter because the investigators had decided a lawsuit he had brought in Knox County to require an accounting from Mabry of the railroad management was a "private quarrel of no importance to the people of the State." Fleming had told a House committee at Nashville that Baxter had brought his charges against Mabry and others "to cover his corruption in the Mineral Home Railroad matters." He further stated that if investigating was to be done "let honorable men do it, and not such fellows as this."[29]

Baxter's trenchant letters led the *Chronicle*, Republican but not Radical, to explain that it was not identifying itself with the lawyer's course, but "We publish Mr. Baxter's letters because he is making war upon the corrupt leaders of his own party. . . . We know that corruption exists in the Democratic Party, and we are glad to have it exposed by one of the leaders of that party" (*Daily Chronicle*, June 12, 1870). The *Chronicle* did not accept Senter as a Republican, it offered him to the Democrats, and it carefully placed Mabry in the Democratic Party:

> Mr. Mabry was never a member of the Republican party. He at one time held intimate personal relationships with some of the party leaders, but his relations to the party . . . were temporary. He was a Republican, he said, in order that he might be of service to his friends, and for his own protection. . . . We do not intend that . . . the Republican party shall be held responsible for Mr. Mabry's sins. He is now, and in sentiment always was, a leading Democrat, and we propose that, as that party has the glory and the influence of the *Whig* and its publisher, it shall also have their record."[30]

The "glory and influence of the *Whig*" was sarcasm. Mabry sold it on August 20, 1879, to Rolfe Saunders, a former *Register* editor who had remained friendly with Brownlow in the 1853 fight for newspaper survival. Saunders took on I. S. Clark of Memphis as a partner and gave the newspaper the incongruous title of the *Whig and Register*. Mabry was so anxious to sell the property that he took the entire purchase price of $15,000 in five notes. Rule notarized the transaction.[31]

Early in 1871 Baxter was provoked into another broadside by statements of Senator Brownlow when the Senate passed a bill to compensate Malinda Harmon $4,696.70 for the loss of her Greene County Farm. The farm had been sold under court order to pay lawyers who represented her husband and son, Jacob and Henry Harmon, who were hanged at Knoxville for having participated in the 1861 bridge burnings. The Parson, as usual, said Baxter's services were of no value to his clients, and pictured him as greedily selling the widow's farm to collect his fee. The *Press and Herald* broke precedent. It praised Brownlow for helping

the widow and children of poor, crazed Harmon, who in a moment of agony signed away the homestead which had sheltered her. . . . From that day to this, the wretched woman has not know a moment of happiness, as every day she feared might be the last wherein her gray hairs, and her helpless children could find a home. Senator Brownlow may have committed many sins during his long lifetime, and who hath not, but his noble conduct in this matter will certainly cover a multitude of abuses.[32]

Fleming probably wrote the editorial; Baxter accused him of it. Baxter then revealed some surprising details. Harmon had retained Fleming and Montgomery Thornburgh, in addition to Baxter, to represent him in the criminal charges and in a lawsuit brought by the East Tennessee & Virginia Railroad seeking $100,000 in damages. Harmon put up $3,000 in notes secured by a trust deed on his Greene County farm. Baxter revealed the fact that Fleming was a partner in the law firm of Confederate Senator Landon C. Haynes and Baxter. This was a circumstance that Brownlow had never put in print, even during his most furious disputes with the younger editor and lawyer. Baxter said he had paid Haynes, Fleming and Thornburgh, $800, $200, and $1,000 respectively, for their interest in the fees. But instead of foreclosing directly, as he might have done, he had asked the Knox County Chancery Court to determine if the fees were reasonable. The court held they were proper and decreed the property should be foreclosed. Baxter bid it in for $4,650, but permitted the family to remain on the farm and use it. He anticipated that Congress would vote relief for Mrs. Harmon. He had moved cannily in asking the court's approval, for the chancellor who heard the suit was O. P. Temple, who was appointed to the post when the Parson was governor.

The lawyer charged Brownlow with malice and ingratitude. He accused the Parson of not having paid him so much as expenses for his trip to Richmond in which he made arrangements for Brownlow's passport to the North. Now Brownlow was accusing him unjustly. Fleming had pocketed his share of the Harmon fee nine years earlier and now, as editor of the *Press and Herald* used it, "to the perpetuation of Senator Brownlow's slander, to speak of the deed in trust, under which he has long since demanded and received his interest, as a 'mortgage to Jno. Baxter,' and the collection of money paid by me to him for the benefit of Harmon's family, as fraudulent and the robbery of a 'poor widow and orphans.' "

Baxter had just been warming up. He next sued six newspapers for $50,000 each, the *Whig and Register*, the *Press and Herald*, the Nashville *Banner*, the Nashville *Union and American*, the Athens *Post*, and the Sweetwater *Enterprise*. The *Whig and Register* had printed an attack on Baxter by State Senator John M. Clementson, chairman of a legislative committee investigating railroads, including the Knoxville and Kentucky. Baxter earlier had accused the senator of bribery and malfeasance in Ohio. The other newspapers had republished the article. When the trial of the *Whig and Register* was held in Knox County Circuit Court, the *Press and Herald* was most abusive of Baxter. It was stunned when a jury awarded the lawyer compensation of $27,500. The unsued *Chronicle* looking over the carnage, found the judgment "the heaviest verdict for libel in the State." Baxter's sensational victory led the remaining newspapers to settle by running retractions, assuming the costs of litigation, and paying the plaintiff from $500 to $2,000. The *Whig and Register* had failed to plead truth as its justification for publishing the Clementson statement. Instead it relied on a defense that the statement was part of the Chancery Court record in a suit by Baxter against Mabry. The trial brought out that the chancellor had refused to make the Clementson statement a part of the record and therefore was not privileged for publication. Clementson was not sued.[33]

The judgment crushed the *Whig and Register* and its owners, Saunders and Clark. They tried to appeal on a pauper's oath, and the newspaper was so reduced when the *Press and Herald* bought what was left of it, it did not consider either name of enough value to add it to its title.[34]

By coincidence the Daily *Chronicle* was one year old and growing lustily the day the *Whig and Register* was suspended. The two newspapers, once powerfully and ferociously at each other's throats, found rest together in what amounted to a pauper's grave, their names now valueless.[35]

The ashes of the *Whig* stirred with short life early in 1875. Senator Brownlow, his legislative record unimpressive except that he remained alive, completed his term. Andrew Johnson succeeded him, but lived only a few months. The Parson had found the *Chronicle* "too mild in its tone, and altogether too conciliatory, considering the party with which you have to deal, and how violent and hostile toward the loyal people that party is." He disliked the General Assembly's undoing of his programs so much that he predicted Congress would find it necessary to take over reconstruction. His extremism reached the point that

had I my way, I would reconstruct the Government of the United States so as to form a STRONG CENTRAL GOVERNMENT here in the District of Columbia and organize the states as so many colonial corporations as absolutely dependent upon and subject to the will of the central power at Washington as counties are to the States.

Thus I would wipe out and extirpate the whole theory and pretense of States Rights and State Sovereignty to which we are mainly indebted for the late rebellion.[36]

Rule promptly dissented with the Parson on this subject. The Democrats had tried to make it appear Brownlow's arbitrary position was that of the Republican Party. Rule's statement also threw further light upon his separation from Senter and Brownlow in 1869:

As soon as it was known who Governor Senter's supporters were we dicided [*sic.*] upon our position and steadfastly adhered to them. We charged then that Governor Senter was in league with the railroad corruptionists to restore the Democracy to power and for that reason refused to support him. His course since the election has confirmed all we ever charged against him, and we say now, as we said then, the Democracy are welcome to him and his railroad ring, and all they can make out of them.[37]

Rule's statement almost placed him in Baxter's corner. Certainly he was in opposition to Senator Brownlow on this and other issues. But he must have had a personal attachment to his former editor and to his basic political philosophy, because when the Parson's six-year term was up they combined again. Rule and A. J. Ricks, the latter having succeeded Tarwater, sold a half interest to Brownlow. A partnership of Brownlow, Rule, and Ricks took over the publication of the daily and weekly *Chronicle*. The name of the latter was expanded into the *Whig and Chronicle*. Brownlow was made principal editor and Rule managing editor. Ricks stepped out of the newspaper management and returned to the practice of law. As John Baxter's law partner in 1869, he had been furious at the senator for having barred him from the job of pension agent at Knoxville. Now he saw the Parson as "beyond question the best known and most experienced editor in the South," a statement which did not stretch the truth.[38]

Tennessee now presented an entirely different political face. Democrats controlled the statehouse, from governor to General Assembly. They were operating under a new state constitution and had elected six of the eight members of Congress from Tennessee.[39] Adversity may have played a part in bringing Brownlow and Rule together as the political power of the Republicans in the state dwindled. The combination of the Parson's prestige as an editor, feeble though he was in body, with the young, vigorous and respected Rule, made business sense. The *Whig and Chronicle* moved from the Parson's old location to Market Square. Brownlow said that the daily "has the largest circulation of any journal in East Tennessee, but the *Whig and Chronicle* will have as large a circulation as any newspaper in the State." The old editor pledged himself to make war on the Democrats and to expose corruption when found in his own party: "In a word I shall edit an Independent Journal. I shall endeavor to commend it to public support by showing that it deserves support." He stopped short of his old threat to treat his foes with personal "severity." He observed rather mildly that "it will not be my fault if my personal relations are not agreeable with my brethren of the press of all parties. In the discussion of public questions it is my purpose to treat all with courtesy who do not elect to be treated otherwise."[40] He must have noticed with some emotion a month later when the equipment of the old *Whig and Register* was sold under a Chancery Court order to satisfy judgments against Mabry and Saunders.[41]

The *Whig and Chronicle* and the *Chronicle* bore little resemblance to the old *Whig*. The weekly was an eight-page tabloid, the daily four pages with large body type. The news content was greater, especially in local, state, and national affairs. Much of it was received by wire. Rule, as mentioned, had specialized in getting local news. Editorializing still appeared in some news items, but it was gradually being

confined to the editorial page. Brownlow's writings were more philo-
sophical and more abundant with historical background. Outraged as
he was when the Democrats captured the lower house of Congress in
1875, he satisfied himself with heading an editorial on the subject:
"THE CONFEDERATE HOUSE OF REPRESENTATIVES."[42]
Tennessee's financial condition grew precarious and talk of repudiating the state debt arose. Brownlow blamed the Democratic administration which propelled Tennessee into the Confederacy,[43] and
sent a flaming message to the Republican State Convention in May
1876. He warned that the integrity of the state was at stake:

I have too long loved the fair name of Tennessee to be willing at this late date to
see it imperilled by lack of good faith. The noble old commonwealth whose
integrity was never doubted when repudiation lifted its brazen front in Penn-
sylvania, or when Jeff. Davis led Mississippi into the same putrid slough, from
the slime and stink of which that unfortunate State has never yet escaped,
cannot now be permitted to follow such unfortunate examples.

Complete repudiation never came, nor did Brownlow escape the conclusion of historians that his administrations were reckless spenders,
especially in issuing railroad bonds.[44]

Late in 1876 the signed editorials of Brownlow grew more infre-
quent, and on the night of April 28, 1877, after having paid workmen who had been making repairs on the home on East Cumberland
Avenue, he became ill and died at 2:05 a.m., on Sunday April 30.
The paralysis that had dogged his frame for years and had stripped
him of his proud and cherished ability to use his pen, struck his
abdomen. Rule wrote an obituary of more than five columns which
appeared in the *Chronicle* of May 1, 1877, and down from the masthead came the name of William G. Brownlow. In that position only
"Wm. Rule, Managing Editor," remained.

Rule laid aside his usual reserve and wrote a touching, emotional
piece on the man who had hired him in 1859 and started him off on
what would be a long and distinguished newspaper career. He extolled the Parson as a minister, editor, and public servant who was in
private life extraordinarily kind to his family, gentle to the ill and the
helpless, and generous to the impoverished. The old editor was
buried in Gray Cemetery,[45] where in 1854 he had joined with
Sexton Neddy Lavendar in laying to rest cholera epidemic victims.

The parson died with a reputation unblemished by any charge of
corruption. But in 1879 a legislative committee, investigating the

large amount of state bonds voted for the benefit of railroads after the war, turned up testimony that casts a shadow on his record. The Brownlow-Senter legislatures had voted so many bond issues, principally for the railroads, that in 1870 the total state debt exceeded $43,000,000, as compared with $25,277,000 when the Parson was elected. The state's railroads had been left in deplorable shape as the contending armies fought back and forth across Tennessee, and funds were required to restore them. The railroads in turn were held responsible to pay interest on these bonds and retire them. But large amounts of the bond money went into speculation for the benefit of railroad officials and owners, and to prime the legislative pump to keep the bond issues coming. The railroad lobbyists employed the usual devices to corrupt legislators—money, clothing, jewelry, liquor, and women. But as the minority report stated, these charges were general, and "There is indeed no proof . . . that would be sufficient, in a court of justice, to warrant the conviction of a single member of the Legislature." [46]

Testimony was produced that five bills of $1,000 denomination each were given to the Governor in July or August 1869 at his residence in Knoxville, and that at Brownlow's direction Joe Mabry placed them in Mrs. Brownlow's hands. Behind the presentation of the money lays a tale told by Mabry that strains credulity. Four Tennessee railroad officials and a New York banker had made almost $5,000 in bond speculation, and feeling the need of spiritual guidance:

Some of us consulted a celebrated New York Spiritualist, Mad. Mansfield, and she told us that bonds would go down and that there would be trouble in Tennessee and not to go to Nashville that we would be arrested, but that we could control "old scratch," meaning Governor Brownlow, with money. We seen [sic.] that the Legislature had been called. We had speculated in bonds on account of Governor Brownlow, and had made nearly $5,000. We then determined to make the governor a present of $5,000, furnishing out of our private means what we had failed of the $5,000 in our speculating for his benefit. I notified him the day before we would; Callaway and myself went up to present it; he was lying on a lounge, and he told us to give it to his wife and we did so, as before stated.

Q. Did Governor Brownlow know anything about these speculations in New York, for his benefit, or did you in any manner intimate to him that you had speculated for his benefit, or did he or his wife receive it purely as a present?

A. He never knew anything of these speculations, nor did I in any manner intimate to him anything about them, and it is my opinion that the $5,000 was received purely as a present.

Q. Was this present made in view of the advice of the spiritualist and was it made for the purpose of enabling you to control him?

A. We were advised by the spiritualist that we could control him and we entered into the speculation to make some money for him. We wanted to quiet him and we took this way of doing it.

The speculators were, in addition to Mabry, R. T. Wilson of New York, and Calvin McGhee, John R. Branner, and Thomas H. Callaway of East Tennessee. Mabry was the only one of the three who testified who mentioned the spiritualist, and he did not say who accompanied him. Wilson confirmed the decision to give the money to Brownlow, but he was silent on the medium and said he only knew of the delivery to the governor from Mabry having told him. McGhee, who was examined before Mabry told the story of the $5,000, mentioned it not at all in very guarded testimony, and was not recalled. Mrs. Brownlow told newsmen she had accepted the money and saw no harm in it because her husband had performed many services for the roads in his career.[47]

Rule accused the investigating committee of having been appointed "to discover a pretext for repudiation" of the state debt. This was an issue of utmost interest and was generally opposed by Republicans. He held, "The moral standard of the Legislature has sunk so low under the teachings of Gov. Marks inaugurated early in the years . . . that members appear to have lost all the faculty they ever did have for distinguishing between right and wrong, between honor and infamy."[48] When the Mabry testimony was printed [the *Chronicle* ran it in full], Rule bristled that the committee

not content . . . with blackening the character of the living by lugging into this investigation matters wholly irrelevant to the subject which they pretended to investigate; like ghouls and hyenas they have prowled among the graves of the dead for something to gratify their slanderous appetites. Fairly considered, there is nothing in the evidence of Joseph A. Mabry that would convict Gov. Brownlow of bribery or corruption, in the estimation of even an impartial stranger. But here, where he was best known, there is not a reasonable man of any party who would for one moment give credence to such a charge. In his long and eventful life . . . no one dared . . . to charge him with dishonesty or corruption.

No man ever approached William G. Brownlow with a bribe. No man who knew him ever dared to do it. He was above suspicion in this respect.

The *Chronicle* editor resorted to the theme expressed by Mrs. Brownlow that the money represented appreciation for her husband's constant support of the railroads as a medium of transportation:

Gov. Brownlow was regarded by the opposite party at the close of the war as an extreme man. He had had provocations to excite a spirit of revenge, and when he became Governor he had the power to take revenge had he thought proper to do so. The gentlemen who are said to have made his wife a present of five thousand dollars, at least a portion of them, were regarded as extreme men on the other side. The Governor showed no malicious disposition toward these men, but on the contrary received them in a spirit of friendship. He aided them in every possible way in their legitimate business enterprises. He actively and industriously used his influence to secure the release of railroad property in the State, in which they were largely interested, from the military authorities of the Government, and its restoration to the owners. . . . The property was released. They naturally felt grateful for his services. He was a poor man and had not been able to live upon his salary as Governor. They were all, then, regarded as wealthy. They desired to give some token of their appreciation . . . and could well afford to do it. They were his neighbors, and knew well that he could not be bribed. [49]

Rule's position received some support from a statement given to the Nashville *Daily American*. It was made by R. T. Wilson, one of the New York speculators, and a Loudon County native. He had opposed the Parson politically, but he considered him a man of the highest integrity and his personal friend, who "had been instrumental in procuring the prompt removal of my disabilities at the close of the war, for which I have always felt grateful." He understood that the $5,000 was to be given to a member of the Brownlow family. At the time of the speculation Wilson was a banker, but when the committee hearings were held he also was president of the East Tennessee, Virginia & Georgia, and of the Memphis and Charleston railroads. [50]

Wilson's statement was a tribute to the Parson, whether he helped to remove Wilson's disabilities as a Confederate supporter because he was a friend, or because he saw that Wilson could be useful in rebuilding the financial structure of the state. Perhaps both reasons played a part with Brownlow. It does show that Brownlow's personal friendships sometimes overrode his furious dislike of Confederates in general, and it also displays, assuming that he acted because he saw usefulness in Wilson in financial matters, his interest in the economic restoration of Tennessee.

In Knoxville the Democratic *Tribune*, which was opposed to repudiation of the state debt, decided that the committee had wandered far from its purpose of investigating the validity of this burden. Instead the committee had "closely devoted themselves to the search after assailable personal reputations, and that too by methods entirely indefensible. . . . Charges of the most calumnious character, without a syllable of legal testimony, have been greedily accepted at second hand. . . . Much of this so called 'evidence' is but the garbage of ten or twelve years ago, and has no relation whatever to the public debt of Tennessee." The *Tribune* was not taking up Brownlow's cause and it did not refer to the $5,000. It did protest the investigators digging up "All the old slanders and corruptions connected with the history of the State during the last few years," and of which the people were wearied.[51]

The presentation of the $5,000 could not be sustained as a high moral gesture with lofty motives. The acceptance remained a moral question. Senator J. W. Clapp, a Shelby County lawyer, wrote the minority report of the committee. He would have ignored the $5,000 had it not been mentioned in the majority findings, "for however reprehensible the transaction was, it had nothing to do with the passage of any law or the issuance of any bond, and is not, therefore, relevant to the matter being considered."[52] A puzzling aspect is Mabry's motive for telling the committee about making the gift. Brownlow had been his friend and benefactor and had helped Mabry in the period after the federal occupation of Knoxville to shed the disabilities of having been a Confederate. Yet he told on the Parson as he had on the men he said once plotted to destroy the *Whig* editor in 1861 and 1862. Mabry was an expert dodger on the witness stand, as his testimony showed. It is possible the committee had found some lever to pry the story from him, or offered him some inducement. But this does not appear in the record or in the reports.

A stripling publisher from Chattanooga, twenty-year-old Adolph S. Ochs, who had lived in Knoxville for several years, gave Brownlow a very high rating for integrity in this comparison with Mabry:

There are few of Governor Brownlow's enemies who will believe the story Jo Mabry told the Star Chamber Committee about him. Brownlow was a harsh man; a reliable hater; not particular to be politically consistent; eager to carry any point he set his head or heart on; endowed with a violent temper and a vindictive nature—those were some of the attributes the public saw. But he was never accused by his most earnest personal and political enemy of even winking at or overlooking corruption in his subordinates, much less of being guilty of receiving bribes. The story in this part, which Mabry got up for the delectation of the investigators, is probably out of whole cloth, and without foundation of any kind except in the muddled brain of its author.

We confess no admiration, personal or other, for the dead Governor and Senator. . . .

But we knew him and knew of him pretty thoroughly, from 1862 on up to the time of his death; and we freely say that a more hospitable and mild-mannered gentleman at his home was never met with by his peers; nor did ever a public man in Tennessee die with a cleaner record, for personal and official honor.

Mabry cannot harm Brownlow. He is too thoroughly known throughout the South. He left a photograph of himself, a moral and political picture, which will pass into history with all its lights and shades in strong relief. Detraction cannot hurt him nor praise help him.[53]

Young Ochs had been reared in Knoxville where his father, Julius Ochs, was in business. The editorial was written before the presentation of the gift had been verified. Yet it was a striking testimony to Brownlow's reputation for integrity.

The Parson left another enigma, the value of his estate. Technically it was small at his death, as Rule and Temple reported.[54] But beginning in 1870 he began to make gifts to his children, wife and a grandchild. The gifts consisted of real estate and interest bearing gold bonds of the United States that paid five percent and matured in twenty years. He deeded a house and lot at the northwest corner of Walnut Street and Clinch Avenue to his son, John Bell. He deeded a house and lot "near the Custom House" which stood at the southeast corner of Market Street and Clinch Avenue to Mrs. Daniel T. (Sue) Boynton; a house and lot on Cumberland Avenue, possibly No. 514, to Mrs. H. M. (Mary) Aiken. He gave to each of his three unmarried daughters—Fannie, Callie and Annie Brownlow—$5,000 in bonds, to his little granddaughter Lillie Sawyer, $1,000 in bonds, and to his wife, Eliza Ann, $5,000 in bonds. He stipulated that the proceeds from a $5,000 life insurance policy were to be invested in these bonds. The real estate, using the Parson's valuations, was worth $14,000 or more, and the bonds and insurance were valued at

$26,000. This did not include the Brownlow residence on Cumberland Avenue. The Parson's son, James P. Brownlow, was not mentioned, possibly because he had married the daughter of a rather wealthy Franklin resident, Dr. D. B. Cliffe. Dr. Boynton, the trustee under the "deed of gift" that bestowed the bonds, was given two strict directions: if he found that Fannie, Callie, Annie, or Lillie married a "drunkard, idler or gambler," the heirs were to receive the interest only, but if the husbands were found by the trustee to be otherwise, upon marriage, they were to receive the bonds. The administrator of the estate appraised the value of Brownlow's interest in the *Whig and Chronicle* Printing Co. at $3,500.[55] This suggests that the Parson's estate may have been worth close to $45,000. He left no will.

A letter written by Brownlow to Temple on March 19, 1877, a few weeks before the editor died, suggests at first glance that he was in dire need of money. But a closer examination indicates that he was chiding Temple for having let him have the note of an absconding preacher. It read:

> I understand that Preacher Howell, whose note you gave me, is fled the country. The note is in the hands of Logan.
>
> The premium on my life Ins. Policy will be due in a few days, and I would be glad if you could pay me some money to meet it—otherwise I cannot now see why I shall not be compelled to let it lapse. Please send me $175 to 200$ [*sic.*] —
>
> Resplly [*sic.*]
> Your friend
> W. G. Brownlow.

Temple made a notation on the back of the letter that three days later he "sent $200.00 as a *loan*. Wrote explaining matters."[56]

Confusing in Brownlow's "deed of gift" is the declaration that he had "given my daughter Mary M. Aiken, a certain house and lot on Cumberland Street [now Cumberland Avenue] for which I paid five thousand ($5,500) five hundred dollars," for no such deed is on record. However there is a deed from Thomas H. Calloway of Cleveland, the railroad official, to Mary B. Aiken, "free from debts and the control of her . . . husband," for Cumberland Avenue property valued as $2,400. The deed was dated November 24, 1869. Callaway had bought it at a Chancery Court sale for $2,300. Mabry had testified Callaway went with him to present the $5,000 in the late summer of 1869. Callaway was dead at the time of the investigation.[57]

Almost a century has elapsed since Brownlow died, and historians continue to give him low marks as a public official, although some revision of Reconstruction policies have appeared.[58] He was harsh and unsparing in his language. He employed excessive force and highly restrictive legislation to keep himself and his party in power and his enemies out. He permitted the railroad interests to lead the state into a precarious condition of indebtedness. He clung to office when he was so weak and palsied that he could stand for only a few moments. Some of his notable achievements, such as the bestowing of the franchise on the former slaves, were born of political expediency rather than from noble motivation. Brownlow did achieve the early restoration of the state to the Union. Tennessee was the first of the seceders to accomplish this. He set the courts and local governments to functioning. He urged the reopening of classroom doors that were closed throughout the war. The legislature was regrettably slow to move upon his recommendations.

The failures were written and the achievements recorded at a time when the furies of men and the devastation of lives and property remained livid and raw. Time had not wrought the healing effect of tolerance and compassion. Instead most men were in one or the other of two militant and muttering camps. Many of the victorious Unionists were determined to keep the political power which they had grasped by force of arms. The Confederates, smarting, crushed, and frustrated by battlefield defeat, wanted to regain the political voice that they had held in the old government, and from which they had sought to separate themselves by rifle, bayonet, and cannon.

In such a time it was inevitable that the Unionists should select the Parson for governor. He was nationally renowned and had been unyielding in his loyalty to the Union even when in jail and despairing of his life. The confinement in the jail at Knoxville probably shattered his once sturdy constitution. As an East Tennesseean he knew the suffering that the loyalists had endured under Confederate occupation, and he was highly articulate. This was a qualification that especially suited the men who had come back from service in blue uniforms, who were aware of their power, and were determined to hold it by restricting the vanquished rebels. If, as an historian has written, the Parson was the worst possible choice to restore peaceable order in Tennessee,[59] he was the only man considered for governor by the element in power. He was selected precisely because he possessed the characteristics that historians a century later deplored. If the Parson must be indicted for lack of moderation, then the same bill must lie against the men who put him in the governor's chair where his stringencies against the southern supporters and the hasty routes he took to power will bear comparison with the methods employed by Governor Isham G. Harris. The Civil War governor had whipped up sentiment for secession, had entered into a secret military league with the Confederacy, and had troops in training throughout the state before the electorate had approved separation. Brownlow rode into office on a reversal of this tide, and also by irregular methods. This development, it is true, imposed the will of a minority upon a majority, if it is assumed that the returning soldiers who had tried to sever themselves from the Union were entitled to lay down their rifles and pick up the ballot in one motion. This assumption was not acceptable to the victors. They were determined that the men who had fought against them must be deprived of the ballot, as a punitive measure, and restored, if ever, when they had demonstrated their integrity as citizens of the nation they had recently furiously and bitterly opposed. They had not come back into the Union voluntarily. They had returned because they were defeated. As a practical political matter it would have been folly for the men in power to hand to the former Confederates whether they had been in uniform, civil officials, ardent sympathizers, or guerillas, the weapon of the ballot. With their superior numbers in Tennessee, the former Confederates would have unseated the Unionists and put themselves back in the seats of power. In time this happened, but time eased emotions and produced less furious changes. The war had been fought upon the issue of secession, and the outcome in no way repealed the law of human nature which makes survival the great imperative. It is true that among the Unionists there were men who counselled moderation. This group formed the Conservative wing, but the Radicals saw to it that it did not gain an advantage.

Brownlow must have seen that the radicals could remain in power only as long as they denied the ballot to the old Confederates. He had been in politics too long not to have realized this. This realization must have prompted him to seek the security of the Senate seat. Time, or circumstances, did mellow Brownlow, for when Senter, as a political expedient came out for universal suffrage, the Parson supported him. He also offered a sound reason for the change. He believed that the majority of the men who had been deprived of the ballot had earned its return, regardless of a small number still undeserving.

The railroad officials clearly took advantage of the Parson's fascination for this form of transportation. Yet he was responsible for permitting their corruption of legislators and the swelling of the state debt. And by the acceptance of $5,000 from speculating railroaders, he left a shadow on an otherwise unblemished reputation for integrity. It was presented for no single purpose or set of purposes, achieved or to be achieved, as the minority report of the legislative investigating committee noted. It was not a medal of honor, and as Ochs pointed out, the hand that presented the money was not an unstained one. But such is Brownlow's reputation for rugged honesty that historians cautiously have avoided outright condemnation. They have preferred to assume that he was innocent of any evil purpose in taking the money. The odium in the transaction they have cast upon the donors.[60]

The qualities which Brownlow lacked and which would have made him a healing and uniting force as governor—objectivity, calmness, broadness of view and ability to compromise—were the ones that made him a successful editor. He learned at Elizabethton to pounce quickly and furiously upon his adversaries. It came easily and naturally to him. He saw that this policy brought him circulation, and readership was his goal. Therefore he intensified his efforts. Brownlow boasted that the *Whig* was one-sided, and he insisted upon and practiced, even flaunted his independence of views and of business operation. He would not permit the solicitation of advertising other than through the newspaper's columns and he made only a limited attempt, especially in his early experience, to go outside the office for news. Most of it had to be brought to his door.

The *Whig*'s success was built solely upon the Parson and his ability to bring to his writing novelty of approach and style that used exaggeration, caricature, hyperbole, sarcasm, and most intriguing of all, humor that flashed out at unexpected moments and which he even trained upon himself. It was almost impossible to predict how Brownlow would approach a subject or a situation, but once he tackled it the result would be diverting. He also was a natural roving reporter. The Parson revealed with the sharp point of his pen the many sides of the human creature, its follies and its nobilities, its glories and its degradations, its righteousness and its sins, its integrity and its hypocrisy. The human race fascinated him. He surely loved it. Brownlow was devoutly religious and at the same time he enjoyed hugely life upon this earth. Long faces and "sour godliness" he disliked, but "a flow of spirits" he relished. He was keenly awake to the importance of economic affairs, and while in Philadelphia he was impressed by the bustle of business, but his eye was also arrested by the sight of beautiful, exquisitely dressed women tripping along the walks. He found the mud in Memphis streets dismal, but the spectacle of the beaux and belles of the South dancing at the ball opening the Gayoso Hotel transported him. The fleshly charm of the sisters attending the Methodist General Conference at Nashville in 1854 took away his breath, in print. He was an extremist, but he was a rare creature of the breed, one with a sense of humor. Brownlow was a crusader, a chuckling, gouging knight in ring-streaked armor. He fought with laughing fury the dispiriting dragon of dullness. The Parson enlivened and repelled his readers but almost never left them bored. But the tribulations that fell upon him in 1861, the cession of his beloved Tennessee, the loss of his cherished newspaper, the indignities, scorns, and threats laid upon him because of his loyalty, his arrest and imprisonment, and the consequent shattering of his health, sapped him of his sense of humor. As governor his mind was almost as lacking of jest and quip as his body was of vitality. Once something of his old puckiness arose. He had been told that his enemies were denouncing him for seeking the United States Senate seat at a time when he appeared near death. The Parson smiled that "the Senate chamber is not a bad place from which to depart for heaven."[61]

However much Brownlow liked the power of the governor's chair and the Senate seat, newspapering was his great love, and the scene of his greatest accomplishments. He was editor, editor and publisher, publisher, but he preferred arrangements where he was entirely free to pursue independent editorial policies to the exclusion of all other newspaper cares. The Parson was not a successful business man in the field of management because he failed to give close attention to office detail. He trusted associates too fully, he endorsed too many notes, and he emptied his pockets too often for the impoverished. However, he did establish a cash-in-advance policy on subscriptions, a course forced upon him by the difficulty of collecting past due accounts. He was not an innovator in the business field. He set up no organization which produced a newspaper dynasty, but he was responsible for starting a line of succession that exists today in The *Knoxville Journal*, still a family-owned newspaper. Rule, who first worked under the Parson, then gave Brownlow a newspaper shelter for two years before he died, founded the *Journal*. He stayed at the helm of this newspaper until his death in 1928.

Brownlow's success was due entirely to his pen and his personality. As he died the style of newspapering was changing. It gave way to more reliance on news for news' sake, and was confining editorialization to a page of its own. As a human creature the Parson is frustrating to analysts, for he presented so many different, even conflicting sides of his nature that he defies categorization. Brilliant and bottle-loving Fleming, who knew Brownlow at close range for many years, threw up his hands at the task, and reached back into his legal training to come up with a Latin phrase, *sui generis*. Such he was. And in this singular and sparkling role he fought lustily, happily, and successfully that enervating bane of the human race—dullness.

CHAPTER XVIV NOTES

[1] *Whig*, January 6, 13, 1869; *Press and Herald*, January 2, 1869; Rule, Ed., *Standard History*, p. 325; Articles of Agreement on Whig organization, January 1, 1869, signed by Brownlow, Haws and Rule. Rule Papers.

[2] Knoxville, *Daily Chronicle*, June 4, 1870.

[3] *Whig*, January 6, 13, 1868; partnership agreement between Brownlow and Haws, *Knox County Deed Book A-1*. Rule was elected County Court clerk in the spring of 1866. *Whig*, March 7, 1866. He held this office in addition to reporting local news for the *Whig*. He added a miscellany of local events including real estate transfers, marriage licenses, disposition of court cases, visitors to the city, brawls, burglaries, building, street improvements and something entirely new, reports of baseball games. For examples see *Whig*, March 13, May 1, 15, 22, 1867; "Articles of Agreement." Rule Papers.

[4] *Ibid.*, *Whig*, October 18, 1865, May 28, July 23, 1864, October 18, 1865.

[5] *Ibid.*, November 11, 1863, February 20, 1864; *Parson Brownlow's Book*, pp. 135-136, 141-147, 177-179, 189-190.

[6] Coulter, p. 294; *Whig*, May 6, 1868, November 15, 1865.

[7] Price, *Holston Methodism*, IV, preface, v, vii, pp. 297, 299-304, 343-344, 285-286.

[8] *Whig*, October 4, November 15, 1865.

[9] *Ibid.*, October 24, 1866, November 20, 1867, December 19, 1866.

[10] *Press and Herald*, March 30, 1869.

[11] *Ibid.*, February 27, June 26, March 13, 1867, February 5, 1868, August 28, 1867, May 20, 27, 1868.

[12] *Press and Herald*, December 6, 1868.

[13] *Whig*, March 3, 10, April 7, 1869.

[14] Temple, *Notable Men*; *Whig*, April 12, 1865; *Press and Herald*, June 19, 1869. One of Senter's prison mates was Sevier County Senator Samuel Pickens, who died in Confederate confinement. Temple, *East Tennessee and the Civil War*, p. 404; *Press and Herald*, February 17, 1869.

[15] *Press and Herald*, May 22, 1869; J. A. Sharp, "The Downfall of the Radicals," East Tennessee Historical Society *Publications*, No. 5, pp. 112-114; Temple, *Notable Men*, p. 183; Folmsbee *et al.*, *Short History*; *Press and Herald*, May 21, 22, 23; *Whig*, May 26, June 2, 1869.

[16] *Ibid.*, May 26, 1869; *Press and Herald*, May 23, 1869; Alexander, *Political Reconstruction*, pp. 216-217; Sharp, "The Downfall of the Radicals in Tennessee," pp. 115-116.

[17] *Whig*, June 23, 1869; Rule, ed., *Standard History*, p. 325.

[18] *Press and Herald*, June 16, 17, 19, 1869; *Whig*, June 23, 1869.

[19] "The Downfall of the Radicals," p. 114-115; *Press and Herald*, June 11, 1869.

[20] Alexander, *Political Reconstruction*, pp. 217-219; "The Downfall of the Radicals," pp. 120-124; *Press and Herald*, August 7, 8, 1869; *Whig*, August 18, 1869.

[21] *Press and Herald*, August 7, 8, 1869; *Whig*, September 15, 1869; *Press and Herald*, September 15, 16, 19, 1869.

[22] *Ibid.*, September 17, 1869, May 1, 1868; Thomas Hall Pearne, *Sixty-one Years of Itinerant Christian Life in Church and State* (Cincinnati, New York, 1899), introduction, p. 11, pp. 311-313, 320, 327. A brother, William Pearne, was engaged in the Methodist ministry in West Tennessee during the reconstruction era. *Ibid.*, p. 320.

[23] *Whig*, August 11, April 28, 1869; *Press and Herald*, September 25, 1869.

[24] *Daily Press and Herald*, December 21, October 20, 21, 22, 23, 1869.

[25] The note is the property of Mr. and Mrs. George T. Fritts of Knoxville. Mrs. Fritts was Helen Brownlow, the great granddaughter of Parson Brownlow. Mr. Fritts manages the real estate firm founded in Knoxville by John Bell Brownlow under the name of J. B. and W. G. Brownlow. A copy of the note is in the McClung Collection, donated by Mr. and Mrs. Fritts.

[26] *Press and Herald*, October 2, 1869.

[27] Weekly *Chronicle*, April 6, 1870; Daily *Chronicle*, May 3, 1870.

[28] *Press and Herald*, June 14, 1870; Weekly *Chronicle*, June 15, 1870; *Knox County Circuit Court Minutes*, Book 19, pp. 754, 847. The Baxter letters appeared in the Daily *Chronicle* first on June 1, 1870, the last on June 22, 1870. The Mabry-Baxter agreement appeared in the Daily *Chronicle* June 28, 1870.

[29] Daily *Chronicle*, June 1, 4, 7, 10, 12, 17, 19, 21, 22, June 11, 1870.

[30] *Ibid.*, June 12, 28, 2, 1870.

[31] *Knox County Deed Book A1*, p. 364; Daily *Chronicle*, February 12, 1871.

[32] *Ibid.*, January 24, 1871; *Press and Herald*, January 25, 1871.

[33] *Ibid.*, January 6, February 11, 12, 1871; Daily *Chronicle*, February 12, 1871; *Knox County Circuit Court Minutes*, Book 20, pp. 624, 627, 634; *Press and Herald*, February 4, 5, 1873; Daily *Chronicle*, February 12, 1871.

[34] *Knox County Circuit Court Minutes*, Book 20, p. 220; *Press and Herald*, May 5, 1871.

[35] Daily *Chronicle*, May 6, 1871; *Press and Herald*, May 5, 1871.

[36] Weekly *Chronicle*, April 20, 1870; Daily *Chronicle*, May 3, 1870.

[37] *Ibid.*, June 28, 1870.

[38] *Ibid.*, February 21, 1875; *Press and Herald*, February 12, 1875, quoting Knoxville *Independent*.

[39] Folmsbee *et al., Short History*, pp. 377-378.

[40] Daily *Chronicle*, February 21, 1875.

[41] *Press and Herald*, February 26, March 11, 1875.

[42] *Whig and Chronicle*, January 19, 1876.

[43] *Ibid.*, February 2, 1876.

[44] *Ibid.*, May 24, 1876; Folmsbee *et al., Short History*, p. 380; Coulter, pp. 375-380; Alexander, *Political Reconstruction*, pp. 169-172.

[45] *Chronicle*, May 1, 1877; Rule, ed., *Standard History*, p. 326.

[46] Folmsbee *et al., Short History*, pp. 380-381; *Senate Journal Appendix, Forty-first General Assembly, The State Debt, Report of the Committee Appointed to Investigate it. Majority Report*, pp. 8, 15-17, *Minority Report*, pp. 29-30.

[47] *Ibid.*, testimony of Joseph A. Mabry, R. T. Wilson and Calvin M. McGhee, pp. 176-172, 94, 70-79; Folmsbee *et al., Short History*, p. 381.

[48] Daily *Chronicle*, February 7, 1879.

[49] *Ibid.*, March 6, 1879.

[50] Nashville Daily *American*, March 7, 1879; *Senate Journal Appendix, Forty-first General Assembly of Tennessee. The State Debt*, p. 86.

[51] Knoxville Daily *Tribune*, March 11, 12, 1879.

[52] *Tennessee Senate Journal Appendix, Forty-first General Assembly. The State Debt. Minority Report*, p. 31.

[53] Chattanooga Daily *Times*, March 7, 1879.

[54] Temple, *Notable Men*, p. 317.

[55] *Knox County Warranty Deed Book* P-3, p. 178, W. G. Brownlow to John B. Brownlow, improved lot, corner of Clinch Avenue and Walnut Street, September 13, 1876; *ibid.*, Book H-3, p. 168, William G. Brownlow to Sue C. Boynton *et al.*, deed of gift, November 11, 1870. See also corrected deed, *ibid.*, Book Q-3, March 24, 1877, *Knox County Estate Book*, No. 19, inventory of Brownlow estate assets, p. 72.

[56] Brownlow to Temple, March 9, 1877. Temple Papers.

[57] *Knox County Warranty Deed Book* G-3, p. 143, Thomas H. Callaway to Mary B. Aiken, *ibid.*, F-3, p. 359, Chancery Court to Callaway.

[58] Folmsbee *et al., Short History*, p. 372.

[59] Coulter, p. 362.

[60] *Ibid.*, p. 380; Folmsbee *et al., Short History*, p. 368.

[61] Temple, *Notable Men*, p. 340.

BIBLIOGRAPHY

Books

Alexander, Thomas B., *Political Reconstruction in Tennessee*. Nashville, 1950.

— — *Thomas A. R. Nelson of East Tennessee*. Nashville, 1956.

Archer, John Patton, *Western North Carolina. A History from 1790 to 1913*, Asheville, 1914.

d'Armand, Roscoe and Virginia, *Knox County Marriage Records. 1792-1900*. Knoxville, 1970.

Brownlow, William Gannaway, *Americanism Contrasted with Foreignism, and Bogus Democracy. In the Light of Reason, History and Scripture; in Which Certain Demagogues in Tennessee, and Elsewhere, Are Shown Up in Their True Colors*. Nashville, 1856.

— — *Baptism Examined*. Jonesboro, 1842.

— — *The Great Iron Wheel Examined; or, Its Falts Spokes Extracted, and, an Exhibition of Elder Graves, Its Builder*. In a Series of Chapters. Nashville, 1856.

— — *Helps to the Study of Presbyterianism, or an Unsophisticated Exposition of Calvinism, with Hopkinsian Modifications and Policy, with a View to a More Easy Interpretation of the Same. To Which is Added a Brief Account of the Life and Travels of the Author; Interspersed with Anecdotes*. Knoxville, 1834.

— — *The "Little Iron Wheel" Enlarged; or Elder Graves, Its Builder, Daguerrotyped, by Way of an Appendix. To Which Are Added Some Personal Explanations*. Nashville, 1857.

— — *A Political Register, Setting Forth the Principles of the Whig and Locofoco Parties in the United States. With the Life and Public Services of Henry Clay. Also an Appendix Personal to the Author; and a General Index*. Jonesboro, 1844.

— — *Sketches of the Rise, Progress and Decline of Seccession; with a Narrative of Personal Adventures among the Rebels.* (Title abbreviated by the binders to *Parson Brownlow's Book*). Philadelphia and Cincinnati, 1862.

— — Untitled work on temperance. Knoxville, 1850. No copies available.

Buckingham, James Silk, Ed., *The Slave States of America*, 2 vols. London, 1842.

Caldwell, Joshua W., *Sketches of the Bench and Bar of Tennessee.* Knoxville, 1890.

Carter, R. W., *History of the First Regiment of Tennessee Volunteer Cavalry in the Great War of the Rebellion, with the Armies of the Ohio under Generals Morgan, Rosecrans, Thomas, Stanley and Wilson, 1862-1865.* Knoxville, 1902.

Clemens, Samuel L., (Mark Twain), "Journalism in Tennessee," in *Editorial Wild Oats.* Freeport, N. Y., 1970.

Coulter, E. Merton, *William G. Brownlow, Fighting Parson of the Southern Appalachians.* Chapel Hill, 1937, Knoxville, 1971.

Davenport, F. Garvin, *Cultural Life in Nashville on the Eve of the Civil War.* Chapel Hill, 1941.

Folmsbee, Stanley J., Robert E. Corlew, and Enoch L. Mitchell, *Tennessee, A Short History.* Knoxville, 1969.

Fuess, Claude Moore, *Daniel Webster.* Boston, 1930.

Graf, Leroy P. and Ralph Haskins, eds., *The Papers of Andrew Johnson*, 4 vols. to date. Knoxville, 1967--.

Graves, J. R., *The Great Iron Wheel; or, Republicanism Backwards and Christianity Reversed. In a Series of Letters Addressed to J. Soule, Senior Bishop of the M. E. Church, South.* Nashville and New York, 1856.

— — *The Little Iron Wheel, a Declaration of Christian Rights and Articles, Showing the Despotism of Episcopal Methodism. By H. B. Bascom, D. D. Late Bishop of the M. E. Church, South. Notes of Application and Illustration.* Nashville, 1857.

Green, John, *Bench and Bar.* Knoxville, 1947.

Heiskell, Samuel, *Andrew Jackson and Early Tennessee History.* 3 vols. Nashville, 1920-1921.

Horn, Stanley J., *The Invisible Empire, the Story of the Ku Klux Klan, 1866-1871.* Cos Cob, Connecticut, 1969.

Humes, Thomas William, *The Loyal Mountaineers of Tennessee*, Knoxville, 1888.

Lacy, Eric Russell, *Vanquished Volunteers. East Tennessee Sectionalism from Statehood to Secession.* Johnson City, 1965.

Lloyd, Ralph Waldo, *Maryville College: A History of 150 Years, 1819-1969*, Maryville, 1969.

Merritt, Frank, *Early History of Carter County, 1760-1861.* Knoxville, 1950.

Miller, Charles A., *The Official and Political Manual of the State of Tennessee.* Nashville, 1890.

Moore, Frank, comp., *The Rebellion Record: a Diary of American Events, with Documents, Narratives, Illustrative Incidents, Poetry Etc.* 11 vols. New York, 1861-1868.

Oates, Stephen B., *To Purge This Land with Blood,* New York, 1970.

Parks, Joseph H., *John Bell of Tennessee.* Baton Rouge, 1950.

Parmet, Herbert S. and Marie B. Hecht, *Aaron Burr, Portrait of an Ambitious Man.* New York, 1967.

Patton, James W., *Unionism and Reconstruction in Tennessee, 1860-1869.* Gloucester, Massachusetts, 1966.

Pearne, Thomas Hall, *Sixty-One Years of Itinerant Christian Life in Church and State.* Cincinnati, 1899.

Price, Richard N., *Holston Methodism from its Origin to the Present Time.* 5 vols. Nashville, 1903-1914.

Prindle, Paul W., comp., *Ancestry of William Sperry Beinecke.* North Haven, Connecticut, 1974.

Reynolds, Major W. D., *Miss Martha* [sic.] *Brownlow, or, the Heroine of Tennessee.* Philadelphia, 1863. (The Philadelphia publisher also got out a German version under the title *Miss Maude* [sic.] *Brownlow oder Die Helden von Tennessee.*)

Ross, C. C., comp., *The Story of Rotherwood, from the Autobiography of Rev. Frederick A. Ross, D. D.* Knoxville, 1923.

Rothrock, Mary U., ed., *The French Broad-Holston Country.* Knoxville, 1940.

Rule, William, ed., *Standard History of Knoxville, Tennessee.* Chicago, 1900.

Seymour, Digby Gordon, *Divided Loyalties.* Knoxville, 1963.

Stern, Madeline B., *Purple Passage, The Life of Mrs. Frank Leslie.* Norman, Oklahoma, 1953.

Temple, Oliver Perry, *East Tennessee and the Civil War.* Cincinnati, 1899.

– – *Notable Men of Tennessee from 1833 to 1875 Their Times and Their Contemporaries.* New York, 1912.

Tennesseeans in the Civil War, A Military History of Confederate and Union Units Available with Rosters of Personnel, comp. Civil War Centennial Commission. Nashville, 1965.

White, Robert H., *Messages of the Governors of Tennessee.* 7 vols. Nashville, 1952-1972.

Williams Knoxville Directory, City Guide, and Business Mirror for 1859-1860. Knoxville, 1859.

Winton, Robert W., *Plebian and Patriot.* New York, 1928.

Newspapers

Nashville Daily *American,* 1879.

Daily *Press and Herald,* Knoxville, 1867-1876.

Daily *Southern Chronicle,* Knoxville, 1863.

Knoxville *Chronicle,* 1870-1879.

Knoxville *Press,* Knoxville, 1867.

Knoxville *Register,* Knoxville, 1841-1864.

Tennessee Sentinel, Jonesboro, 1841-1846.

Knoxville *Tribune,* Knoxville, 1879-1896.

Knoxville Weekly *Whig* and Daily *Chronicle,* 1875-1877.

Whig, Brownlow's newspaper appeared under the following titles:

Tennessee Whig, with some inside pages headed Elizabethton *Whig,* Elizabethton, May 16, 1839, through May 14, 1840.

Whig (Sometimes with inside pages headed The Jonesborough Tennessee *Whig*), Jonesboro, May 20, 1840, through May 11, 1842.

Jonesborough *Whig and Independent Journal,* Jonesboro, May 18, 1842, through April 19, 1849.

Brownlow's Knoxville Whig and Independent Journal, Knoxville, May 19, 1849, through April 7, 1855.

Brownlow's Knoxville Whig, Knoxville, April 14, 1855, through July 27, 1861.

Brownlow's Weekly Whig, Knoxville, August 3, 1861, until suspended, October 26, 1861.

Tri-Weekly Whig, Knoxville, January 4, 1859, through August 3, 1861. (A *Tri-Weekly Whig,* was issued for five weeks in 1868.)

Brownlow's Knoxville Whig and Rebel Ventilator, Knoxville, November 11, 1863, through February 21, 1866.

Brownlow's Knoxville Whig, Knoxville, February 28, 1866, until Brownlow relinquished complete control of the newspaper, January 1, 1869. (A few issues of the weekly *Whig* and of the tri-weekly are in loose, miscellaneous newspaper files in the McClung Collection. The main files of the newspapers are on microfilm in the McClung Collection and at the University of Tennessee.)

Periodicals and Compilations

Bellamy, James W., "The Political Career of Landon Carter Haynes," East Tennessee Historical Society *PUBL.,* No. 28, Knoxville, 1956.

Burt, Jesse, ed., "Editor Eastman Writes James K. Polk," ETHS *PUBL.,* No. 39, Knoxville, 1867.

Calvinistic Magazine, Abingdon, 1846-1856.

Conklin, Royal Forrest, "The Public Speaking Career of William Gannaway (Parson) Brownlow," dissertation, University of Ohio, 1967.

Creekmore, Pollyanna, ed., "Tennessee Marriage Records, Carter County, 1796-1850." McClung Collection. Knoxville, 1958.

Crouch, Barry A., "The Merchant and the Senator: An Attempt to Save East Tennessee for the Union," ETHS *PUBL.,* No. 46, Knoxville, 1974.

Fink, Paul M., "The Early Press of Jonesboro," ETHS *PUBL.*, No. 10, Knoxville, 1938.

Gray Cemetary Record Book, 1851-1867. Knoxville, University of Tennessee Special Collections.

Haley, Nancy Marlene, "Cry Aloud and Spare Not; The Formative Years of Brownlow's *Whig*, 1839-1841," thesis. University of Tennessee, August, 1966.

Jonesborough Monthly Review, Jonesboro, 1847-1849.

Jonesborough Quarterly Review, Jonesboro, 1847.

McClary, Ben Harris, ed., "The Sale of Brownlow's *Whig*: An Article of Agreement between William Augustus Kinsloe and William G. Brownlow," ETHS *PUBL.*, No. 35, Knoxville, 1963.

McMilan, Faye E., "A Biographical Sketch of Joseph Anderson (1757-1837)." ETHS *PUBL.*, No. 2, Knoxville, 1980

Mitchell, Enoch L., *The Journal of Southern History*, V. xxvi, No. 2, May, 1960. Houston.

Sharp, J. A., "The Downfall of the Radicals," ETHS *PUBL.*, No. 5, Knoxville, 1933.

Turner, Ruth Osborne, "The Public Career of William Montgomery Churchwell," thesis, University of Tennessee, 1954.

Turnley, Mrs. Mattie, "Survivor of a John Brown Family Raid." *Tennessee Historical Magazine*, V. 7, No. 3. Nashville, (dated October, 1921, issued August, 1923).

Manuscripts

Arnell, Samuel Mayes, unpublished typescript, "The Southern Unionist." University of Tennessee Special Collections.

Crabb, Landon, letter to "My Dear Mother," property of author.

Deaderick, David, diary. McClung Collection.

Howard, Mrs. J. T., Papers. Sherrod Library, East Tennessee State University, Johnson City.

Kennerly, W. R., memorandum of conversation with John Bell Brownlow and letter of John Bell Brownlow to A. T. Patterson. Presented by Sam Young. University of Tennessee Special Collections.

Nelson, T. A. R., Papers. McClung Collection.

Pendleton, Gaines Strother, "Genealogical Tables," University of Tennessee Special Collections.

Polk-Yeatman Papers. Tennessee State Library and Archives. Nashville.

Rule, William, Papers. McClung Collection.

Temple, Oliver Perry, Papers. University of Tennessee Special Collections.

Government Publications and Records

Acts of Tennessee, General Assembly, 1842, 1851-1852, 1861, 1865-1869.

Biographical Directory of the American Congress. Washington, 1961.

House Journal, Tennessee General Assembly, 1865-1866. Nashville, (This session has no number but is referred to as the Brownlow legislature.)

House Journal, Thirty-Fourth General Assembly, 1861-1862, comp., Tennessee Historical Commission. Nashville, 1957.

Knox County Circuit Court Minutes, Nos. 19, 20.

Knox County Deed Book, A-1.

Knox County Estate Book, No. 19.

Knox County Warranty Deed Books, H-3, Q-3, G-3, F-3.

Senate Journal, Forty-First General Assembly, 1865-1869.

Senate Journal Appendix, Forty-First General Assembly.

Sixth Census of the United States, Washington, 1840.

The War of the Rebellion: A Compilation of the Official Records of the Union and Confederate Armies, 130 vols. Washington, 1880-1901.

INDEX

This book was designed by Spencer Qualls. The type-
face is Journal Roman, similar to the types in use in
Parson Brownlow s time, and was set in type by Ad-
Tech of Fairfax, Inc. The paper is Mead Publishers
Smooth White.

ABOUT THE AUTHOR

STEVE HUMPHREY attended Washburn College in Topeka, Kansas from 1920 until 1924 earning a B.A. in English. For over forty years he worked in the journalism field for publications such as *The Nebraska State Journal, The Arkansas Gazette,* and the *Memphis Press-Scimitar.* In 1944 he became a professor at the University of Tennessee, and left in 1947 to finish out his career at the *Knoxville Journal.* Humphrey retired in 1969 and passed away on December 2, 1990, in Tallahassee, Florida.

CPSIA information can be obtained
at www.ICGtesting.com
Printed in the USA
BVHW03s1826020718
520623BV00001B/37/P

9 781469 638225